First World War
and Army of Occupation
War Diary
France, Belgium and Germany

12 DIVISION
Headquarters, Branches and Services
Commander Royal Artillery
1 January 1918 - 31 May 1919

WO95/1833

The Naval & Military Press Ltd
www.nmarchive.com
Published in association with The National Archives

Published by

The Naval & Military Press Ltd

Unit 10 Ridgewood Industrial Park,

Uckfield, East Sussex,

TN22 5QE England

Tel: +44 (0) 1825 749494

www.naval-military-press.com

www.nmarchive.com

This diary has been reprinted in facsimile from the original. Any imperfections are inevitably reproduced and the quality may fall short of modern type and cartographic standards.

Contents

Document type	Place/Title	Date From	Date To
Heading	12th Division C.R.A. Jan 1918-May 1919		
Heading	12th Div. Arty. C.R.A. 12th Division. January 1918 May 19		
Heading	War Diary Headquarters, 12th Divisional Artillery, January, 1918. (Vol. XXXII).		
War Diary	Aire Merville Ref. Sheet 36 & 36th 1/40,000	01/01/1918	14/01/1918
War Diary	Croix Du Bac	15/01/1918	16/01/1918
War Diary	Ref. Sheet 36 36A 1/40000 Croix Du Bac	17/01/1918	31/01/1918
Miscellaneous	12th Divisional Artillery-Location Statement.	17/01/1918	17/01/1918
Heading	12th Div. Arty. C.R.A. 12th Division February 1918		
Heading	War Diary Headquarters, 12th Divisional Artillery, February, 1918		
War Diary	Ref Sheet 36 1/40,000 Croix Du Bac	01/02/1918	28/02/1918
Heading	12th Divisional Artillery. War Diary C.R.A. 12th Division March 1918 Appendices attached:- Artillery Orders.		
War Diary	Ref Sheet 36 1/40,000 Croix Du Bac	01/03/1918	08/03/1918
War Diary	Ref Sheet 36 1/40000	08/03/1918	10/03/1918
War Diary	Ref Sheet 36 1/40000 Croix Du Bac	10/03/1918	21/03/1918
War Diary	Les Lauriers (Sheet) 36 1/40000 B6A	22/03/1918	22/03/1918
War Diary	Hazebrouck 5th 1/100,000	23/03/1918	23/03/1918
War Diary	Lens Amiens 1/100,000	24/03/1918	24/03/1918
War Diary	Albert 1/40000	25/03/1918	25/03/1918
War Diary	Senlis	25/03/1918	28/03/1918
War Diary	Toutencourt	29/03/1918	31/03/1918
Operation(al) Order(s)	12th Divisional Artillery Order No.84	07/03/1918	07/03/1918
Miscellaneous	To all recipients of 12th D.A. Order No.84 and 64th A.F.A. Bde. (for B/64). Reference 12th Divisional Artillery Order No.84 dated 7th March.	07/03/1918	07/03/1918
Operation(al) Order(s)	12th Divisional Artillery Order No.85.	07/03/1918	07/03/1918
Miscellaneous	To all recipients of 12th D.A. Order No.85. Reference 12th D.A. Order No.85 dated 7th March 1918. Zero hour will be 5 p.m. on March 8th.	07/03/1918	07/03/1918
Operation(al) Order(s)	12th Divisional Artillery Order No.86.	07/03/1918	07/03/1918
Miscellaneous	To all recipients of 12th D.A. Order No.86. Reference 12th Divisional Artillery Order No. 86.	07/03/1918	07/03/1918
Miscellaneous	Reference 12th D.A. Order No.86. Amendment No.3 to R.A. 499.	08/03/1918	08/03/1918
Miscellaneous	To all recipients of 12th D.A. Order No.86. Reference-12th B.A. Order No. 86 dated 7.3.18.	08/03/1918	08/03/1918
Miscellaneous	Amendment No.4 to R.A. 499. Reference Amendment No. 3 to R.A. 499 dated 8.3.18.	08/03/1918	08/03/1918
Miscellaneous	Reference 12th D.A. Order No.86. Amendment No.3 to R.A. 499.	08/03/1918	08/03/1918
Miscellaneous	To all recipients of 12th D.A. Order No.86. Reference 12th Divisional Artillery Order No. 86.	07/03/1918	07/03/1918
Miscellaneous	Reference R.A. 499 dated 6th March, 1918 X. Day Is March 7th. Y. Day Is March 8th. Z. Day Is March 9th.	07/03/1918	07/03/1918
Miscellaneous	Addenda No.1 to R.A. 499 dated 6th March, 1918.	06/03/1918	06/03/1918
Miscellaneous	Amendment No.1 to 12th D.A. R.A. 499.		

Miscellaneous	The attached Tables form part of Operation Order which will be issued shortly.	06/03/1918	06/03/1918
Miscellaneous	Amended Table IV.		
Miscellaneous	12th Divisional Artillery. Raid On Z Day. 4.5 Inch Howitzer Tasks-Amended.		
Miscellaneous	12th Divisional Artillery. Raid On Z. Day. Heavy Artillery Tasks-Amended.		
Miscellaneous	12th Divisional Artillery. Raid On Z. Day. 18 Pr. Tasks.		
Miscellaneous	12th Divisional Artillery. Raid On Z. Day. 4.5 Inch Howitzer Tasks.		
Miscellaneous	12th Divisional Artillery. Raid On Z. Day. Heavy Artillery Tasks.		
Operation(al) Order(s)	12th Divisional Artillery Order No.91.	17/03/1918	17/03/1918
Miscellaneous	Reference 12th D.A. Order No.92.	18/03/1918	18/03/1918
Miscellaneous	Amendment No.1 to 12th Divisional Artillery Order No.92.	18/03/1918	18/03/1918
Operation(al) Order(s)	12th Divisional Artillery Order No.92.	17/03/1918	17/03/1918
Miscellaneous	Ref. Maps-Fleurbaix Bois Grenier Aubers Radinghem 1/10,000. Table I. 18 Pr. Tasks.		
Miscellaneous	Ref. Maps-Fleurbaix Bois Grenier Aubers Radinghem 1/10,000. Table II. 4.5 Inch Howitzer Tasks.		
Miscellaneous	Ref. Maps-Fleurbaix Bois Grenier Aubers Radinghem 1/10,000. Table III. Heavy Artillery Tasks.		
Miscellaneous	Copies to all recipients of 12th D.A. Order No.93. Reference 12th Divisional Artillery Order No. 93 dated 19th March, 1918.	20/03/1918	20/03/1918
Heading	War Diary C.R.A. 12th Division April 1918		
War Diary	Ref Amiens 1.100,000 And 57 D.S.E, 1.20,000	02/04/1918	03/04/1918
War Diary	Warloy	03/04/1918	11/04/1918
War Diary	Contay	12/04/1918	22/04/1918
War Diary	Raincheval	23/04/1918	25/04/1918
War Diary	Raincheval 57d 1/40000	27/04/1918	27/04/1918
Operation(al) Order(s)	12th Divisional Artillery Order No.99.	21/04/1918	21/04/1918
Miscellaneous	Amendment No.1 to 12th Divisional Arty. Order No.99.	22/04/1918	22/04/1918
Miscellaneous	12th Divisional Artillery. Reference 38th Divn. Order No.17.	22/04/1918	22/04/1918
Operation(al) Order(s)	12th Divisional Artillery Order No.101.	24/04/1918	24/04/1918
Heading	12th Div. Arty C.R.A. 12th Division. May 1918.		
Heading	War Diary Headquarters, 12th Divisional Artillery, May, 1918 (Vol. XXXVI).		
War Diary	Raincheval 57d 1/40,000	01/05/1918	24/05/1918
War Diary	Raincheval	24/05/1918	27/05/1918
War Diary	Beauquesne	27/05/1918	30/05/1918
Operation(al) Order(s)	12th Divisional Artillery Order No.102.	01/05/1918	01/05/1918
Miscellaneous	12th Division (G). Vth Corps R.A. Vth Corps H.A. 37th Infantry Bde. 63rd Brigade R.F.A.	14/05/1918	14/05/1918
Map			
Miscellaneous	V Corps Heavy Artillery Instructions No.76.	13/05/1918	13/05/1918
Miscellaneous	Centre Group Artillery Order No.1.	15/05/1918	15/05/1918
Miscellaneous	Table A. Creeping Barrage.		
Miscellaneous	Table B. Standing Barrage.		
Miscellaneous	Table C.		
Miscellaneous	Headquarters, 315th Brigade R.F.A. 29th Brigade R.F.A.	16/05/1918	16/05/1918
Miscellaneous	Addendum No.1 to 37th Infantry Brigade Order No.194 dated 15th May, 1918.	18/05/1918	18/05/1918

Operation(al) Order(s)	37th Infantry Brigade Order No.194.	15/05/1918	15/05/1918
Miscellaneous	Reference Centre Group Artillery Order-Raid	16/05/1918	16/05/1918
Miscellaneous	Warning Order.	21/05/1918	21/05/1918
Miscellaneous	63rd (R.N.) Divisional Artillery Operation Order No.183. To Accompany Appendix 1.	22/05/1918	22/05/1918
Miscellaneous	18 Pdrs On Left Infantry Brigade Front.		
Miscellaneous	4.5" Hows. On Right Infantry Brigade Front.		
Miscellaneous	12th Division No.G.X. 1466	22/05/1918	22/05/1918
Miscellaneous	12th Division No.G.X.1504	23/05/1918	23/05/1918
Miscellaneous	Administrative Instructions issued in conjunction with 36th Infantry Brigade Order No.289.	23/05/1918	23/05/1918
Miscellaneous	Amendment No.1 to Administrative Instructions issued in conjunction with 56th Infantry Brigade Order No.289.	23/05/1918	23/05/1918
Miscellaneous	Amendment and Addenda to V Corps H.A. Instructions No.81 dated 23/5/18	24/05/1918	24/05/1918
Miscellaneous	V Corps Heavy Artillery Instructions No.81. Reference Sheet 57d. S.E. 1/20,000	23/05/1918	23/05/1918
Operation(al) Order(s)	36th Infantry Brigade Order No.289.	23/05/1918	23/05/1918
Miscellaneous	Addendum No. 1 to 12th Divisional Artillery Order No. 106.	23/05/1918	23/05/1918
Miscellaneous	Reference 12th Divisional Artillery Order No.106	24/05/1918	24/05/1918
Operation(al) Order(s)	12th Divisional Artillery Order No.106.	22/05/1918	22/05/1918
Miscellaneous	Heavy Artillery.		
Miscellaneous	Issued with 12th D.A. Order No.106		
Map			
Miscellaneous	Counter Battery Instructions. Reference V Corps H.A., S.G. 11/46 of 23/5/18.	24/05/1918	24/05/1918
Miscellaneous	Table "A" Zero Programme	24/05/1918	24/05/1918
Miscellaneous	4.5" Hows. on Right Infantry Brigade Front.	24/05/1918	24/05/1918
Miscellaneous	63rd (R.N.) Divisional Artillery. Amendment No.2 to Operation Order No.183, Appendix 1.	24/05/1918	24/05/1918
Miscellaneous	To all recipients of 63rd (R.N.) Divisional Artillery Operation Order No.183.	24/05/1918	24/05/1918
Miscellaneous	Reference 12th Divisional Artillery Order No.106	24/05/1918	24/05/1918
Miscellaneous	Issued with 12th D.A. Order No.106.		
Miscellaneous	Reference this Office Operation Order No.183 of Yesterdays date.	24/05/1918	24/05/1918
Miscellaneous	A Form Messages And Signals.		
Miscellaneous	12th Division No.G.X. 1542	24/05/1918	24/05/1918
Heading	12th Div. Arty. C.R.A. 12th Division, June 1918.		
Heading	War Diary Headquarters, 12th Divisional Artillery June 1918 (Vol XXXVII)		
War Diary	Beauquesne 57D 1/40,000	01/06/1918	17/06/1918
War Diary	Toutencourt	18/06/1918	30/06/1918
Miscellaneous	V Corps. G.S. 435.	14/06/1918	14/06/1918
Miscellaneous	V Corps GS. 435.	16/06/1918	16/06/1918
Miscellaneous	Vth Corps Artillery Instruction No.158	16/06/1918	16/06/1918
Miscellaneous	Table "A" Vth Corps Artillery Instruction No. 158 Action Of Field Artillery from Zero to Zero plus 50 minutes.		
Miscellaneous	Table "C" of Vth Corps Artillery Instruction No. 158. Period Zero plus 3 hours 50 mins. to Zero plus 3 hours 55 minutes.		
Miscellaneous	35 D.A. 10/186. 17th June 1918.	17/06/1918	17/06/1918

Operation(al) Order(s)	12th Division Order No.258., dated 17th June, 1918. Addendum No. 1.	17/06/1918	17/06/1918
Operation(al) Order(s)	12th Division Order No.258.	17/06/1918	17/06/1918
Miscellaneous	12th Division No. G.X. 2248	17/06/1918	17/06/1918
Miscellaneous	Time Table-issued with 12th Division Order No.258, dated 17/6/18.	17/06/1918	17/06/1918
Miscellaneous	C Form. Messages And Signals.		
Operation(al) Order(s)	38th Divisional Artillery Operation Order No. 64.	18/06/1918	18/06/1918
Miscellaneous	Table "A"		
Miscellaneous	To Brigade Major 12 Div. Arty. Ref. 12 DA Order No.107	18/06/1918	18/06/1918
Miscellaneous	Addenda No.1 to V Corps H.A. Instructions No.107 (S.G.11/91.)	19/06/1918	19/06/1918
Miscellaneous	V Corps Heavy Artillery Instructions No.107.	18/06/1918	18/06/1918
Miscellaneous	Table "A" Heavy Artillery action from Zero minus 2 Hours to Zero minus 5 minutes.		
Miscellaneous	Table "B" Heavy Artillery action from Zero to Zero plus 50 minutes.		
Miscellaneous	Reference R.A. V Corps Instructions No.158 of 16/6/18 and V Corps Heavy Artillery Instructions No. 107 for a Chinese attack on Aveluy Wood.	18/06/1918	18/06/1918
Operation(al) Order(s)	37th Infantry Brigade Order No.201	18/06/1918	18/06/1918
Miscellaneous	12th Battalion Machine Gun Corps. Operation Order No.23.	18/06/1918	18/06/1918
Operation(al) Order(s)	12th Divisional Artillery Order No.107.	18/06/1918	18/06/1918
Miscellaneous	Table A Issued With 12th D.A. Order No.107.		
Miscellaneous	Table B Issued With 12th D.A. Order No.107		
Miscellaneous	Amendment No.1 to 12th Divisional Artillery Order No.107.	18/06/1918	18/06/1918
Miscellaneous	Addendum No.1 to 12th Divisional Artillery Order No.107.	18/06/1918	18/06/1918
Miscellaneous	References Vth Corps Artillery Instruction No.158 dated 16th June 1918	18/06/1918	18/06/1918
Miscellaneous	Appendix 'Z' to C.B.S. 77 of 18/6/18	19/06/1918	19/06/1918
Miscellaneous	Amendment No.2 to 12th Divisional Artillery Order No.107.	19/06/1918	19/06/1918
Miscellaneous	12th Division No.G.X. 2303	19/06/1918	19/06/1918
Miscellaneous	12th Division No.G.X. 2302	19/06/1918	19/06/1918
Heading	Raid 20/21 June by 38th Div		
Miscellaneous	Vth Corps Artillery Instruction No.162	18/06/1918	18/06/1918
Miscellaneous	12th Division No.G.X. 2308	19/06/1918	19/06/1918
Miscellaneous	12th Division No.G.X. 2334	20/06/1918	20/06/1918
Miscellaneous	Amendment No.1 to 12th Divisional Artillery Order No.108.	19/06/1918	19/06/1918
Operation(al) Order(s)	12th Divisional Artillery Order No. 108.	19/06/1918	19/06/1918
Miscellaneous	R.A. 38th. Div. No. G.S. 1936/14.	20/06/1918	20/06/1918
Miscellaneous	Addendum No.1 to 38th D.A.O.O. No. 63.	19/06/1918	19/06/1918
Operation(al) Order(s)	38th Divisional Artillery Operation Order No.63.	17/06/1918	17/06/1918
Miscellaneous	Appendix 1		
Miscellaneous	Counter Battery Instructions.	20/06/1918	20/06/1918
Miscellaneous	V Corps Heavy Artillery Instructions No.109	19/06/1918	19/06/1918
Miscellaneous	Table "A" Action of V Corps Heavy Artillery from Zero to Zero plus 30 minutes.		
Map	38th D.A. Map A		
Heading	38th Raid War Diary		
Miscellaneous	12th Division No. G.X. 2431.	22/06/1918	22/06/1918

Miscellaneous	12th Division No.G.X. 2413	22/06/1918	22/06/1918
Miscellaneous	12th Division No.G.X. 2430	22/06/1918	22/06/1918
Miscellaneous	12th Division No.G.X. 2464	24/06/1918	24/06/1918
Miscellaneous	Warning Order.	24/06/1918	24/06/1918
Miscellaneous			
Miscellaneous	37th Infantry Brigade Operation In W.15 Instructions No.1	25/06/1918	25/06/1918
Miscellaneous	37th Infantry Brigade Operation In W.15 Instructions No.2		
Miscellaneous	Operation W.15.d.-Memo. No. 3.	25/06/1918	25/06/1918
Miscellaneous	Addendum No.2 to 12th Division Order No. 261 dated 28th June, 1918.	29/06/1918	29/06/1918
Miscellaneous	Addendum No.1 to 12th Division Order No. 261 dated 28th June, 1918.	28/06/1918	28/06/1918
Operation(al) Order(s)	12th Division Order No. 261.	28/06/1918	28/06/1918
Miscellaneous	12th Division No.G.X. 2619.	29/06/1918	29/06/1918
Operation(al) Order(s)	Addendum No.1 to 12th Divisional Artillery Order No. 110.	29/06/1918	29/06/1918
Operation(al) Order(s)	12th Divisional Artillery Order No. 110.	28/06/1918	28/06/1918
Miscellaneous	Issued with 12th Divl. Artillery Order No. 110. 18 pr. Tasks.		
Miscellaneous	Issued with 12th Divl. Artillery Order No. 110 4.5 inch How. Tasks.		
Miscellaneous	Issued with 12th Divl. Artillery Order No. 110 6 inch Newton T. Ms.		
Miscellaneous	Issued with Divn Order No.110 Table A 18 Creeping Barrage		
Operation(al) Order(s)	18th Divisional Artillery Operation Order No. 133.	27/06/1918	27/06/1918
Miscellaneous	Reference 18th D.A. O.O. No.133	29/06/1918	29/06/1918
Miscellaneous	18th D.A. O.O. No. 133. 18-pdr. Tasks.		
Miscellaneous	18th D.A. O.O. No. 133 4.5" How. Tasks.		
Miscellaneous	18th D.A. O.O. No. 133. Heavy Artillery Tasks.		
Miscellaneous	18th D.A. O.O. No. 133. Counter Preparation On Morning And Evening Of 1st July.		
Map	Map 'A'		
Operation(al) Order(s)	37th Infantry Brigade Order No. 204.	28/06/1918	28/06/1918
Miscellaneous	Table of Attacking Formations and Assembly Positions To Accompany 37th Infantry Brigade Order No. 204.	28/06/1918	28/06/1918
Miscellaneous	37th Inf. Bde. No. G.O. 794.	29/06/1918	29/06/1918
Miscellaneous	Addendum and Amendment No.1 to 37th Inf. Bde. Order No. 204	29/06/1918	29/06/1918
Miscellaneous	Time Table of Barrages.		
Miscellaneous	37th Infantry Brigade No. O.O. 785	27/06/1918	27/06/1918
Miscellaneous	Addendum and Amendment No.2 to 37th Inf. Bde. Order No. 204.	29/06/1918	29/06/1918
Miscellaneous	Addendum and Amendment No.3 to 37th Inf. Bde. Order No. 204	30/06/1918	30/06/1918
Map			
Operation(al) Order(s)	38th. Divisional Artillery Operation Order No. 66.	29/05/1918	29/05/1918
Miscellaneous	Table "X"		
Miscellaneous	Issued with 38th D.A. O.O. No. 66 18th Creeping Barrage.		
Operation(al) Order(s)	38th Divisional Artillery Operation Order No 65.	29/06/1918	29/06/1918
Operation(al) Order(s)	17th Divisional Artillery Order No. 204.	29/06/1918	29/06/1918
Miscellaneous	V Corps Heavy Artillery Instructions No. 125.	29/06/1918	29/06/1918

Miscellaneous	Table "A". Action of V Corps H.A. From Zero until ordered to 'Cease Fire'.		
Miscellaneous	Counter Battery Instructions.	29/06/1918	29/06/1918
Miscellaneous	Amendment No. 2. to Vth Corps Arty. Instn. No. 168 dated 29th June 1918.	29/06/1918	29/06/1918
Miscellaneous	38th Division. 63rd Division.	28/06/1918	28/06/1918
Miscellaneous	38th Division. 63rd Division.	27/06/1918	27/06/1918
Miscellaneous	Vth Corps Artillery Instruction No. 168	29/06/1918	29/06/1918
Miscellaneous	12th Division No. G.X. 2632	29/06/1918	29/06/1918
Miscellaneous	Reference Division Order No. 261, Para 7 (c).	30/06/1918	30/06/1918
Miscellaneous	Reference 12th Division Order No. 261.	30/06/1918	30/06/1918
Miscellaneous	12th Divisional Artillery Daily Summary. (From 6 am. 30th June to 6 am. 1st July 1918).	01/07/1918	01/07/1918
Map	Part Of Sheet 57d S.E. Scale 1.10000		
Map			
Heading	12th Div. Arty. C.R.A. 12th Division July 1918.		
Heading	War Diary Headquarters, 12th Divisional Artillery, July 1918. Vol XXXIII		
War Diary	Toutencourt Sheet 57d S.E. 1.20000	01/07/1918	12/07/1918
War Diary	Rubempre Sheet 57d SE	12/07/1918	13/07/1918
War Diary	Loeuilly (Rit Sheet Amiens 17)	13/07/1918	21/07/1918
War Diary	Guyencourt Ref Sheet F.P.D Moreuil	22/07/1918	24/07/1918
War Diary	Loeuilly Rit Sheet Amiens 17	25/07/1918	31/07/1918
Heading	12th Div. Arty. C.R.A. 12th Division. August 1918.		
War Diary	Cagny Ref 62D 1/40000	01/08/1918	06/08/1918
War Diary	B5a80	07/08/1918	08/08/1918
War Diary	Barcelcave V11 d 80	09/08/1918	11/08/1918
War Diary	E23c22	12/08/1918	25/08/1918
War Diary	D26c83	25/08/1918	26/08/1918
War Diary	J3b15	27/08/1918	28/08/1918
War Diary	Hidden Wood	29/08/1918	29/08/1918
Heading	12th Divisional Artillery C.R.A. 12th Division, August, 1918.		
Heading	War Diary Headquarters, 12th Divisional Artillery, August, 1918. Vol. XXXIV		
War Diary	Cagny Reference 62 1/40000	01/08/1918	05/08/1918
War Diary	Cagny	05/08/1918	06/08/1918
War Diary	N35a80	07/08/1918	08/08/1918
War Diary	Marcelcave	08/08/1918	08/08/1918
War Diary	V11d80	09/08/1918	14/08/1918
War Diary	E23c22	15/08/1918	17/08/1918
War Diary	E22c22	18/08/1918	25/08/1918
War Diary	D26b83	26/08/1918	26/08/1918
War Diary	J3b15	27/08/1918	29/08/1918
War Diary	Hidden Wood F10 Central	30/08/1918	30/08/1918
War Diary	Hidden Wood	31/08/1918	31/08/1918
Heading	Appendix I War Diary H.Q. R.A. 12th Division August 1918		
Operation(al) Order(s)	12th Divisional Artillery Warning Order No. 1.	29/07/1918	29/07/1918
Operation(al) Order(s)	12th Divisional Artillery Warning Order No. 2.	04/08/1918	04/08/1918
Operation(al) Order(s)	12th Divisional Artillery Order No. 114.	31/07/1918	31/07/1918
Miscellaneous	H.Q. Right Group. H.Q. Left Group. H.Q. 8th Canadian Army Bde. 4th Aust. Division (C) 2nd Australian D.A. for information.	02/08/1918	02/08/1918
Operation(al) Order(s)	12th Divisional Artillery Order No. 115.	04/08/1918	04/08/1918
Operation(al) Order(s)	12th Divisional Artillery Order No. 116.	04/08/1918	04/08/1918

Miscellaneous	Headquarters 12th Division Infantry	16/08/1918	16/08/1918
Miscellaneous	Reference R.A. 883 dated 18th August, 1918 Para. 3	16/08/1918	16/08/1918
Miscellaneous	In Contimuntion of No. R.A. 883 dated 16th August 1918	16/08/1918	16/08/1918
Heading	12th Div. Arty. C.R.A. 12th Division September 1918		
Heading	War Diary Headquarters, 12th Divisional Artillery. September 1918. Vol XL		
War Diary	F10 Central	01/09/1918	06/09/1918
War Diary	U29a38	06/09/1918	16/09/1918
War Diary	D16co9	17/09/1918	30/09/1918
Miscellaneous	A Form Messages And Signals		
Miscellaneous	A Form Messages And Signals.		
Operation(al) Order(s)	12th Divisional Artillery Order No. 120.	15/09/1918	15/09/1918
Miscellaneous	12th Divisional Artillery Instructions No. 1 issued with 12th D.A. Order No. 120	14/09/1918	14/09/1918
Operation(al) Order(s)	12th Divisional Artillery Order No. 121.	16/09/1918	16/09/1918
Map			
Miscellaneous	Amendment No.1 to 12th Divisional Artillery Instructions issued with 12th Divisional Artillery Order No. 121.	16/09/1918	16/09/1918
Miscellaneous	12th Divisional Artillery Instructions No. 1 Issued with 12th Divl. Artillery Order No. 121.	16/09/1918	16/09/1918
Miscellaneous	Appendix "A" Issued With 12th D.A. Instructions No.1		
Miscellaneous	Appendix "B". 4.5" Howitzer Tasks. Issued with 12th Divl. Artillery Insts. No.1		
Miscellaneous	83rd Brigade R.F.A.	16/09/1918	16/09/1918
Diagram etc	Tracing B 4.5 How Tasks		
Miscellaneous	12th Divisional Artillery Instructions No.2	16/09/1918	16/09/1918
Miscellaneous	12th Divisional Artillery Instructions No.3-issued with 12th Divisional Artillery Order No.121		
Miscellaneous	62nd Brigade. R.F.A. 63rd Brigade R.F.A. 106th R.F.A. Brigade. 112th Brigade R.F.A. 231st Brigade R.F.A.	17/09/1918	17/09/1918
Miscellaneous	62-Founder Table for 139th D.B. B.O.A.		
Operation(al) Order(s)	12th Divisional Artillery Order No.122.	10/09/1918	10/09/1918
Miscellaneous	Appendix "A" Issued With 12th Divisional Artillery Order No.122		
Operation(al) Order(s)	12th Divisional Artillery Order No.123	23/09/1918	23/09/1918
Miscellaneous	Addendum No.1 to 12th Divisional Artillery Order No.123	23/09/1918	23/09/1918
Miscellaneous	Addendum No.2 to 12th Divisional Artillery Order No.123	24/09/1918	24/09/1918
Operation(al) Order(s)	12th Divisional Artillery Order No.124	24/09/1918	24/09/1918
Operation(al) Order(s)	12th Divisional Artillery Order No.125	25/09/1918	25/09/1918
Map	12th Div. Barrage Map		
Operation(al) Order(s)	12th Divisional Artillery Order 126	25/09/1918	25/09/1918
Miscellaneous	Amendment No.1 to 12th D.A. Order No.126 and Instructions.	26/09/1918	26/09/1918
Miscellaneous	2nd Amendment to 12th Divisional Artillery Order No.126 and Instructions.	26/09/1918	26/09/1918
Miscellaneous	12th Divisional Artillery Instructions No.1 issued with 12th D.A. Order No.126		
Miscellaneous	12th Divisional Artillery Instructions No.2 issued with 12th D.A. Order No.126		
Miscellaneous	12th Divisional Artillery Instructions No.3 issued with 12th D.A. Order No.126		

Miscellaneous	12th Divisional Artillery Instructions No.4 issued with 12th D.A. Order No.126		
Miscellaneous	12th Divisional Artillery Instructions No.5 issued with 12th D.A. Order No.126	26/09/1918	26/09/1918
Miscellaneous	12th Divisional Artillery Instructions No. 6		
Diagram etc	Tracing A		
Operation(al) Order(s)	12th Divisional Artillery Order No.127	28/09/1918	28/09/1918
Miscellaneous	Amendment No.1 to 12th D.A. Order No.127 and Instructions.	28/09/1918	28/09/1918
Miscellaneous	12th Divisional Artillery Instructions No.1 issued with 12th D.A. Order No.127		
Miscellaneous	12th Divisional Artillery Instructions No.2 issued with 12th D.A. Order No.127		
Miscellaneous	12th Divisional Artillery Instructions No.3	28/09/1918	28/09/1918
Miscellaneous	A Form Messages And Signals.		
Heading	12th Div. Arty. C.R.A. 12th Division. October 1918.		
Heading	War Diary Headquarters, 12th Divisional Artillery, October, 1918. Vol XLI		
War Diary	D16c19	01/10/1918	13/10/1918
War Diary	M35b06	13/10/1918	18/10/1918
War Diary	Raimbeaucourt	18/10/1918	22/10/1918
War Diary	Orchies	22/10/1918	23/10/1918
War Diary	Sameon	23/10/1918	31/10/1918
Operation(al) Order(s)	12th Divisional Artillery Order No.128	11/10/1918	11/10/1918
Miscellaneous	Table A. Issued with 12th Divisional Artillery Order No. 128		
Miscellaneous	Table B. Issued with 12th Divisional Artillery Order No. 128		
Heading	12th Div. Arty. C.R.A., 12th Division, November 1918.		
Heading	War Diary Headquarters, 12th Divisional Artillery, November, 1918. Vol XLII		
War Diary	Sameon	01/11/1918	03/11/1918
War Diary	Prais Marais	03/11/1918	11/11/1918
War Diary	Sameon	11/11/1918	11/11/1918
War Diary	Leewarde	27/11/1918	27/11/1918
Heading	12th Div. Arty. C.R.A. 12th Division December 1918		
Heading	War Diary Headquarters, 12th Divisional Artillery, December, 1918. Vol XLIII		
War Diary	Lewarde	01/12/1918	31/12/1918
Heading	War Diary Headquarters, 12th Divisional Artillery, January, 1919. Vol XLIV		
War Diary		01/01/1919	31/01/1919
Heading	War Diary of the Headquarters 12th Divisional Artillery February-1919. Volume XLV		
War Diary	Lewarde	01/02/1919	28/02/1919
Heading	War Diary of the Headquarters 12th Divisional Artillery. From:- 1st March to 31st March. 1919 Volume-XLVI.		
War Diary	Lewarde	01/03/1919	31/03/1919
Heading	War Diary of the Headquarters, R.A.-12th Divl. Artillery. for the Month Of April 1919. Volume XLVII		
War Diary	Lewarde	01/04/1919	07/04/1919
War Diary	Auberchicourt	07/04/1919	30/04/1919
Heading	War Diary of the 12th Div. Artillery Headquarters for month of May 1919 Volume XLVII		
War Diary	Auberchicourt	01/05/1919	31/05/1919

12TH DIVISION

C. R. A.

JAN 1918-MAY 1919

12th Div. Arty.

C. R. A.

12th DIVISION,

JANUARY 1918.

May '19

CONFIDENTIAL.

WAR DIARY

Headquarters, 12th Divisional Artillery,

January, 1918.

(Vol. XXXII).

WO 32

Instructions regarding War Diaries and Intelligence Summaries are contained in F. S. Regs., Part II. and the Staff Manual respectively. Title pages will be prepared in manuscript.

WAR DIARY
~~or~~
~~INTELLIGENCE SUMMARY~~.
(Erase heading not required.)

January 1918 VOL. XXXII — H.Q. 12th Div. Arty

Army Form C. 2118.

Sheet I

Place	Date	Hour	Summary of Events and Information	Remarks and references to Appendices
AIRE	~~8~~		~~HQ 12 D.A. moved to MERVILLE~~	
MERVILLE	1.		Major NOEL R.L. CHANCE M.C. R.F.A. joined from acting B.M. 3rd Div. and was posted Brigade Major R.A. 12 Div. vice Capt (acting Major) C.A. CLOWES M.C. A.F.A. who returned to ANZAC CORPS.	
Ref: Sheets 36 + 36A 1/40000	2.		Brig. Gen. H.M. THOMAS C.M.G. was awarded D.S.O. in New Years Honours List.	
	8.		Headquarters moved from AIRE to MERVILLE, the batteries remaining in the HAVERSKERQUE area.	
	9.		C.R.A. inspected the Bdes. in "skeleton order".	
	10.		C.R.A. inspected D.A.C. + T.M. All officers were lectured to by G.O.C. R.A. XV Corps. The Divisional Commander inspected the Artillery and presented medal ribbons.	
			1 N.C.O. 4 Sappers instructed each Bde in rapid wiring. 1 Officer 1 O.R. per battery started a course of Lewis gun.	
	11.		Capt (acting Major) RONEY-DOUGAL C.N. R.F.A. was attached to H.Q. to learn duties of Brigade Major.	
	12.		Guns and Howitzers of the Divisional started calibration under Lt Col. WYNNE D.S.O. at the 1st Army Calibration Range (St HILAIRE).	
			Major (temp Lt Col) R.G. THOMSON C.M.G. D.S.O. R.F.A. joined the Divisional + was posted to command the 63 Bde. vice Lt Col. R.C. CORTES D.S.O. (to England).	
	13.		7 guns & Hows were calibrated on the range.	
	14.		7 guns were calibrated on the range.	
CROIX DU BAC	15.		10 guns were calibrated. C.R.A. took over from C.R.A. 38 Div. at CROIX DU BAC.	
	16		1 section each Battery relieved one section of 38 Div. A.F.S.	

A5834 Wt. W4973/M687 750,000 8/16 D. D. & L. Ltd. Forms/C.2118/13.

Army Form C. 2118.

Instructions regarding War Diaries and Intelligence Summaries are contained in F. S. Regs., Part II. and the Staff Manual respectively. Title pages will be prepared in manuscript.

WAR DIARY
or
INTELLIGENCE SUMMARY.
(*Erase heading not required.*)

January 1918 Vol XXXII — H.Q. 12 Div Arty — Sheet II

Place	Date	Hour	Summary of Events and Information	Remarks and references to Appendices
Ref: Sheet 36 – 36a 1/40000 CROIX DU BAC	17		Remaining sections relieved 38 Div Arty. Front now covered about 8000yds N8d 05 80 – 120d be. Field Artillery divided into two groups (Lt Col WYNNE DSO Right group (62 Bde RFA and 10 Btys) and Lt Col THOMSON CMG DSO Left group (63 Bde RFA and 97th Bty). (Location statement attached) Policy to be pursued, to inflict as much loss on enemy as possible without calling for vindictive retaliation on his part. There is much work to be done in the area, communications are bad gunpits unsound and no shell proof command posts. Personnel mostly living in houses. The positions have been occupied for a long time & must be well known to the enemy.	
	18		C.R.A. reconnoitred positions for batteries, according to Defence Scheme for Reenforcement of Portuguese Corps front	
	19		Major N.R.L. CHANCE M.C. RFA, went on leave. Captain (a/Major) C.N. RONEY-DOUGAL RFA took over duties of acting Brigade Major. C.R.A. continued reconnaissance. BOIS GRENIER slightly shelled with 15cm. Registration & calibration proceeding	
	20		C.R.A. finished reconnaissance. BOIS GRENIER again slightly shelled. Registration & calibration continued by all batteries of the Division. A few shells into wagon lines	
	21		Two shells of a hostile battery firing at a Heavy Battery in rear fell short & hit 10th Bty HQ. 1 officer Capt HART and three men wounded.	

A5834 Wt. W4973/M687 750,000 8/16 D. D. & L. Ltd. Forms/C.2118/13.

Instructions regarding War Diaries and Intelligence Summaries are contained in F. S. Regs., Part II. and the Staff Manual respectively. Title pages will be prepared in manuscript.

Vol XXXII

WAR DIARY
or
INTELLIGENCE SUMMARY.
(*Erase heading not required.*)

HQ 12th Div Arty

Army Form C. 2118.

Sheet III

Place	Date	Hour	Summary of Events and Information	Remarks and references to Appendices
Ref. Sheet 36 36A 1/40,000 CROIX DU BAC	~~22~~ 31		The attitude of the enemy has been uniformly quiet, with very little Artillery activity. The time of all units of 12th Divisional Artillery has been fully occupied in repairing the positions they took over, and reconnoitring fresh ones. After the reorganisation now in progress, each battery will have three positions – known as Normal Battery Position, Alternative Position (for use in case of the Normal Battery Position being subjected to heavy shelling) and the Main Battle Position. There is much work to be done but in spite of material being scarce, owing to Thaw precautions and Floods, much progress has already been made. Preparations were made to assist a raid organised by the 57th Division on our left. Raid due at 8.45 and all preparations complete to create a diversion on the extreme left of our Divisional Front. Operations however were indefinitely postponed at 8 pm.	

C. V. Roney-Dougal
Major RFA
for Brigade Major,
12th Divisional Artillery.

A5834 Wt. W4973/M687 750,000 8/16 D. D. & L. Ltd. Forms/C.2118/13.

S E C R E T.

12th DIVISIONAL ARTILLERY - LOCATION STATEMENT.

12th D.A. H.Q. Br. Gen. H.M. THOMAS, C.M.G., D.S.O. G 6 c 9 4

RIGHT GROUP. Commanded by Lt.Col. H.E.S. WYNNE, D.S.O.
H.Q. at H 31 a 75 75.

	Guns.	Co-ordinates	Normal O.P.	Wagon Lines.
A/62.	2	H 27 d 22 70		
	1	H 27 b 25 10	N 5 a 95 60	G 27 b 8 5
	2	H 27 a 92 50	CONVENT	
B/62 (Silent)	5	G 30 c 54 75	N 8 a 60 80 KILDARE	G 21 b 4 1
C/62	3	H 31 c 18 84	-do-	G 21 d 7 1
	2	H 25 d 40 00		
10th B'ty.(Silent)	5	H 16 c 40 10	N 5 a 95 60	H 1 d 4 2
D/62 (How.)	2	H 31 b 70 30		
	1	H 33 a 30 30	N 4 a 90 05	G 27 d 3 7
(Silent)	2	H 21 a 40 60	THE MILL.	

LEFT GROUP. Commanded by Lt.Col. R.G. THOMSON, D.S.O.
H.Q. at H 21 c 90 95.

	Guns.	Co-ordinates	Normal O.P.	Wagon Lines.
A/63 (Silent)	6	H 16 central	I 25 a 05 80 MOAT FARM	G 6 a 1 8
B/63	1	H 18 b 10 15		
	2	H 24 a 92 75	-do-	G 8 c 4 3
	2	H 24 b 20 95		
C/63	3	H 28 a 20 10	H 35 c 50 10	G 26 d 8 1
	2	H 28 a 85 30	DAVID'S HOUSE	
	1	H 28 a 60 60		
97th B'ty.	2	H 22 b 10 60	-do-	H 7 b 1 9
(Silent)	3	H 16 d 40 00		
D/63 (Silent)	2	H 16 b 30 40		
(How.)	1	H 24 a 10 10	I 25 a 05 80	H 7 a 2 3
	1	H 24 c 10 90		
	1	H 24 c 15 15		

C/332. At Wagon Lines	G 19 b 6 6
12th D.A.C. H.Q.	G 25 d 3 8
No.1 Sec:	G 20 d 9 9
2 "	G 20 d 0 1
3 "	G 26 d 8 0
147th Brigade H.Q.	G 16 d 3 7
B.A.C.	G 15 c 1 2
H.Q., T.M. Batteries.	H 9 c ~~4~~ 2 ~~7~~ 3

[illegible] Major
for Br. General,
C.R.A., 12th Division.

17th Jany., 1918.

12th Div. Arty.

C. R. A.

12th DIVISION,

FEBRUARY 1918

C O N F I D E N T I A L.

Vol 33

W A R   D I A R Y

Headquarters, 12th Divisional Artillery,

February, 1918.

(Vol.XXXIII)

Instructions regarding War Diaries and Intelligence Summaries are contained in F. S. Regs., Part II. and the Staff Manual respectively. Title pages will be prepared in manuscript.

Army Form C. 2118.

WAR DIARY
or
~~INTELLIGENCE SUMMARY.~~
(Erase heading not required.)

February 1918
Vol. XXXIII

HQ. 12th Div. Artillery   Sheet I

Place	Date	Hour	Summary of Events and Information	Remarks and references to Appendices
Ref Sheets 36 ~~36a~~ 1/40,000.	1st	8.30 p.m	The raid organised by the 57th Division on our left and originally intended for the night of Jany 31st, was successfully conducted. The Left Group of the 12th Divisional Artillery carried a diversion on the Left of the Divisional Front, and from ZERO to ZERO plus 10 minutes put a box barrage on INCOMPLETE TRENCH I26 c and d, where wire had previously been cut by our T.M's. No casualties sustained, and four prisoners brought back.	
CROIX DU BAC.	2nd		Major N.R.L Chance, M.C, on returning from leave resumed the duties of Brigade Major. About ~~dusk~~ 4.30 pm. both Infantry brigades in the line reported unusual hostile movement and Trench Mortar activity. No action however materialized.	
	3rd		Enemy raided PENSHAN POST I 32 a 2.8, obtaining a few prisoners. No S.O.S. signal was given, nor was the Left Group informed till about half an hour after the raid when the Infantry reported "Situation Normal".	
	5th	2 am	The Right Group "stood by" from ZERO (2 a.m) to support a raid by the Right Infantry Brigade (9th ESSEX REGT) on Enemy post at N 15 b 13.98. Three Germans known to have been killed, four prisoners taken and 1 M.G. captured. We suffered no casualties and no Artillery support was called for.	
	10th		D/63 were fairly heavily shelled with 5.9s + had to clear, but no damage was done.	
	11th		A/62 position S of FLEURBAIX was intermittently shelled throughout the day: this resulted in 2 guns being slightly damaged.	
	15		Lt S.T.D. WALLACE of C/63 was awarded the V.C. for his gallantry at CAMBRAI. The Divisional Artillery have up to date received 1 V.C. 5 D.S.O.s (2 D.S.O.) M.C. 4 MC. 6 DCM. 16 M.M. for this battle (bar M.M.)	

A5834 Wt. W4973/M687 750,000 8/16 D. D. & L. Ltd. Forms/C.2118/13.

Army Form C. 2118.

WAR DIARY
or
INTELLIGENCE SUMMARY.
(Erase heading not required.)

Instructions regarding War Diaries and Intelligence Summaries are contained in F. S. Regs., Part II. and the Staff Manual respectively. Title pages will be prepared in manuscript.

Feb. 1918
Vol. XXXIII

HQ. 12 Div. Arty   Sheet II

Place	Date	Hour	Summary of Events and Information	Remarks and references to Appendices
	16		D/62 was shelled by a 5.9 and 4.2 Bty. About 160 rounds fell round the position. No casualties & no damage done. 1 Section per Battery of 64 Bde relieved 147 Bde. R.F.A.	
	17.		Remaining sections 64 (Army) Bde relieved remaining sections 147 (Army) Bde. A/64 relieved 97th Bty in the left group and C/64 relieved 10th Bty in Right group. Col. BARTON assumed command of Right group.	
	18.		Capt (acting Major) BLEWETT D.S.O. joined the Division & took command of C/63.	
	19.		Decided to move C/62 to position further back at H 19 c 5.7.	
	20.		C.R.A. held conference with group Commanders reference proposed raid by a Battalion of 35th Inf Bde. Conference with 38th Div. Arty and Corps H.A. in afternoon. D.T.M.O. started to cut wire all along the front.	
	21.		Visited 4th Squadron R.F.C. so that the C.R.A. could see the latest photos and confer with Squadron Intelligence Officer ref: raid. Visited Portuguese 2nd Div R.A. Wire cutting continues - little retaliation.	
	22.		M.G. R.A. 1st Army visited Left group. G.O.C. R.A. G.H.Q. visited C.R.A. during the afternoon.	
	24.		Sent out "warning orders" to groups ref: raid so that they could ... Lt Col. WYNNE D.S.O. returned from leave and took over the command of the Right group. The C.R.A. assumed command of the Division, the Divisional Commander having gone on leave.	
	25.		C.R.A. attended rehearsal by 7th Norfolk Battalion who will carry out the raid. Since wire cutting commenced it has continued each day covered by the R.F.A. groups. Enemy reply has been very feeble.	
	26.		C.R.A. had conference with group Commanders on Raid; also with Corps Commander & G.O.C. 35th Inf. Bde. Wind cutting ...	
	27.		Rehearsal of Raid. Group & Batteries Commanders attended. Corps Commander present.	
	28.		Raid postponed as the Inf. Commander did not think the gaps in the wire large enough for the size of the Raiding Party.	(wire cutting)

A5834 Wt. W4973/M687 750,000 8/16 D. D. & L. Ltd. Forms/C.2118/13.

[signature] Brigade Major,
12th ... Artillery

12th Divisional Artillery.

WAR DIARY

C. R. A.

12th DIVISION.

MARCH 1918

Appendices attached :- Artillery Orders.

Army Form C. 2118.

Instructions regarding War Diaries and Intelligence Summaries are contained in F. S. Regs., Part II. and the Staff Manual respectively. Title pages will be prepared in manuscript.

WAR DIARY
or
~~INTELLIGENCE SUMMARY~~.
(Erase heading not required.)

March 1918. Vol. XXXIV H.Q. 12 Div. Arty. Sheet I

Place	Date	Hour	Summary of Events and Information	Remarks and references to Appendices
Ref Sheet 36 1/40.000	1.	9 a.m.	6" Newtons continued wire cutting with covering fire by Left Group R.F.A.	
CROIX DU BAC			Hostile artillery very quiet during the day	
			G.O.C.-in-C visited 12 Div. H.Q.	
			Bde Major to England on 14 days Senior officers course Shoeburyness	
		7.10 p.m.	Enemy shelled the area from Davids House ( ) to ELBOW FARM with gas shell Grp. [illegible] Groups retaliated + H.A. fired on active hostile batteries. Hostile raid expected tonight [illegible]	
		9.10 p.m.	Hostile fire ceased exactly after 2 hours duration.	
		10 p.m.	Left Bde (35th Inf Bde) raided enemy's line at INDEX Tr. covered by guns of Left Groups no retaliation, no M.G. fire, no coloured lights seen. Raiding party entered enemy's trench at O1a1065 – O1a2275. One prisoner taken of the 2nd Battn 371 I.R. 10 Ersatz Div who state they had relieved a Bavarian Division about 14 days ago	
	2.	6.10 a.m.	Fairly heavy firing heard to the South where enemy raided the right of 2nd Portuguese Div. on our right and took some prisoners	
			Very quiet on whole front throughout the day	
		11.50 p.m.	38th Div. on our left raided enemy trenches at I16b60 – I17a03 and captured 1 prisoner	
	3.		Very quiet day nothing reported	
		11.40 p.m.	Heavy bombardment N of Armentieres, all quiet on Div. front.	
	4.		A quiet day but E.A. active and 15 planes crossed our lines at different times. At 12.45 p.m. Hostile 10.5 cm active from N17c08, all active batteries turned on and silenced it.	

A5834 Wt. W4973/M687 750,000 8/16 D. D. & L. Ltd. Forms/C.2118/13.

Army Form C. 2118.

Instructions regarding War Diaries and Intelligence Summaries are contained in F. S. Regs., Part II. and the Staff Manual respectively. Title pages will be prepared in manuscript.

March 1918

Vol XXXIV

WAR DIARY
or
~~INTELLIGENCE SUMMARY.~~
(Erase heading not required.)

H.Q 12 Div. Arty

Sheet II

Place	Date	Hour	Summary of Events and Information	Remarks and references to Appendices
Ref Sheet 36 1/40000	5			
Croix du Bac.	6.	11.30 a.m.	Much movement reported by II Port. Div. Arty	
		12 noon	Sound rangers report 4.2" gun active in I33 b0225. Left Group fire 20 rds. 4.5 How on same.	
		9.10 pm	Enemy shelled Fleurbaix with gas shell + trench mortared our trenches in left ~~station~~ sector. Hostile fire ceased at 10 p.m.	
	7.	3.45	Hostile Trench Mortars again bombarded Peter Post at I32c95 - now fairly active	
			Left Group opened fire on S.O.S. lines	
		5.15	Heavy hostile Bombardment on right of 2nd Port. Div. where hostile raid took place.	
			Enemy aircraft very active	
		1.30 pm	Enemy shelled H15 near Left Group H.Q. Counter batteries informed + fire neutralized	
		3.10 pm	Heavy bombardment about Fauquissart Sector 2nd Port. Div	
			Heavy Artillery bombarded enemy trenches in and about I31c where a raid is proposed for morning of 9th. Enemy retaliated on N5 central fairly heavily with 10.5 cm Hows.	
		6.35	Hostile fire ceased	
	8.	4.30 am	The 7th Bn. Royal Sussex 36 Inf Bde. raided enemy trenches in N35a + b under cover of artillery barrage by Right Group and supported by 8 6" Hows of XV Corps HA as per O.O. 84 attached. Enemy barrage not heavy and came down at zero +5. 7 prisoners obtained of 10th Ersatz Div.	O.O. 84.
		5.05	Situation normal.	

A5834 Wt. W4973/M687 750,000 8/16 D. D. & L. Ltd. Forms/C.2118/13.

Instructions regarding War Diaries and Intelligence Summaries are contained in F. S. Regs., Part II. and the Staff Manual respectively. Title pages will be prepared in manuscript.

March 1918
Vol XXXIV

WAR DIARY
or
~~INTELLIGENCE SUMMARY~~.
(Erase heading not required.)

H.Q. 12 Div. Arty

Sheet III

Army Form C. 2118.

Place	Date	Hour	Summary of Events and Information	Remarks and references to Appendices
Ref. Sheet 36 1/40000	8		Hostile artillery active throughout the day in N10a, H35d and Croix Blanche	
		5 p.m.	Enemy shelled our C.T. Cellar Farm Avenue with 77 mm	
		5.00	Left Group + XV Corps HA bombarded enemy's trenches in I26d for 15 mins. There was practically no retaliation. Two red rockets were sent up but no action followed	O.O. 85.
	9.	5.31 a.m.	The 6th Bn. R.W. Kent Reg raided enemy's trenches in O1a + I31d in the ~~Right Bde sect~~ Left Bde sector supported by Field + Heavy Artillery barrage as per O.O. 86 attached. 9 prisoners obtained many enemy killed. Enemy barrage was very weak + raiding party returned at 5.51 a.m. 1 M.G. Captured. Prisoners were of 267 R.I.R. Throughout the day enemy artillery fire increased N5a. PINNEYS Avenue, Croix Blanche being shelled in the morning with 4.2 + 5.9's. Our trenches were again continuously shelled during the afternoon especially N5a + N6b. Towards the evening all roads in vicinity of battery positions were shelled intermittently with 5.9's 4.2's + 7.7 cms	O.O. 86
		11 pm.	Time advanced 1 hour to Summer Time	
	10		Two deserters to Portuguese report enemy will commence a heavy bombardment on morning of 10th	
		4.45 am	Heavy hostile barrage Right + Left of 12th Div. front: confirmed later as attempted raid on Portuguese + on Division on our left.	
		10 am	Col Cotter (286 Bde RFA) reported with B/286 C/286 + D/286 batteries to reinforce our right + went into action under O.C. Right Group in G28B, G35a + G29D.	

A5834 Wt. W4973/M687 750,000 8/16 D. D. & L. Ltd. Forms/C.2118/13.

Army Form C. 2118.

WAR DIARY
or
~~INTELLIGENCE SUMMARY.~~
(Erase heading not required.)

Instructions regarding War Diaries and Intelligence Summaries are contained in F. S. Regs., Part II. and the Staff Manual respectively. Title pages will be prepared in manuscript.

March 1918
Vol XXXIV

H.Q. 12 Div. Arty

Sheet IV

Place	Date	Hour	Summary of Events and Information	Remarks and references to Appendices
Ref Sheet 36 1/40000	10	.	Hostile fire increased throughout the day. La Gorgue Station, Steenwerck St shelled by 24 cm H.V. guns	
Croix du Bac		12 noon	Lt Col. Lloyd Comdg 12th A.F. Art Bde reported & ordered to stand by at Bailleul to be ready to reinforce at 6 hours notice. Position reconnoitred to reinforce left Group	
	11	5 a.m.	Heavy bombardment heard. S.O.S. S.R. given in Left Group. Percy & Baltic ? Posts raided by enemy who left behind 1 dead & 1 wounded man & 1 M.G. (369 R.I.R.) 2 of our men missing. 38th Div. also raided but successfully driven off. Hostile fire on trenches & back areas again much above normal throughout the day.	
	12	6.00 a.m	Heavy bombardment about junction of Portuguese with 12 DIV. Right Group opened fire on S.O.S. lines. 2nd Portuguese Div. raided at several points along whole front. Right of 12 Div not raided. 2nd Port. Div. taken 5 prisoners. Hostile fire again very active throughout the day.	
		10.58	S.O.S. call on right of 12 Div front & at junction with 2nd Portuguese. Very heavy hostile barrage with 5.9's & T.M's	
		11.46	Fire died down. Enemy attempted raid ~~on~~ about Cellar Farm Avenue but driven off leaving 3 dead	

Instructions regarding War Diaries and Intelligence Summaries are contained in F. S. Regs., Part II. and the Staff Manual respectively. Title pages will be prepared in manuscript.

March 1918

Vol XXXIV

Army Form C. 2118.

WAR DIARY
or
~~INTELLIGENCE~~ ~~SUMMARY~~.

(*Erase heading not required.*)

H.Q. 12 Div. Arty

Sheet V

Place	Date	Hour	Summary of Events and Information	Remarks and references to Appendices
Sheet 36 1/40000 Croix du Bac	12th		Hostile fire still very active on our trenches in N8a + on roads + back area. We retaliated on tender spots in enemy support line + on C.T.s During the evening and after dusk roads + back areas were shelled with bursts of fire Harassing fire maintained during the night on communications within 800 yds of front line	
	13th		Estaire shelled in neighbourhood of bridge + road junction at L30c.	
	14th		Harrassing fire carried out during the night on all communications within 800 yds. Wet day, hostile fire during the morning below normal. At 11 a.m. N8a+b and N9c+d were shelled steadily with 77, 10.5 + 15 cm heavily. Enemy appeared to be wire cutting. This ceased at 1.40 p.m but recommenced again at 3 p.m and continued very heavily all the afternoon. At dusk FLEURBAIX, BAC ST MAUR and back areas were shelled	
	15th		From 9 p.m to 11 p.m. all enemy's lines of communication within 2000 yds of front line were harassed by all active batteries in conjunction with H.A. From 5.30 to 6.15 a.m Counter preparation was fired by all active batteries Much T.M. activity on Portugese Front. Portugese report wire has been cut along whole of their front + enemy has cut gaps in his own wire.	
	16th		At 10.07 p.m. 38th. Div. on our left raided enemy's front-line about I11a. + obtained 12 prisoners + one M.G. with only slight casualties. Hostile fire much quieter on our trenches, some shelling of back areas	

A5834 Wt. W4973/M687 750,000 8/16 D. D. & L. Ltd. Forms/C.2118/13.

Instructions regarding War Diaries and Intelligence Summaries are contained in F. S. Regs., Part II. and the Staff Manual respectively. Title pages will be prepared in manuscript.

March 1918
Vol XXXIV

WAR DIARY
or
~~INTELLIGENCE SUMMARY~~.
(Erase heading not required.)

H.Q 12 Div Arty

Army Form C. 2118.

Sheet VI

Place	Date	Hour	Summary of Events and Information	Remarks and references to Appendices
Sheet 36 1/40000	16th		Quiet night except for some harassing fire about H26c+d and Erquinghem	
Croix du Bac			No harassing fire carried out by our artillery	
		4.30 a.m.	Orders received that all Field guns + 4.5 How to undertake counter battery work within 3000 yds of enemy front line.	
	17th	9.30.	Heavy shell fire heard on Portugese front, ceased at 9.40. Enemy fire 10 rds with 4.2 H.V. gun into Croix du Bac between 5 am + 6.a.m no damage. Many hostile Observation Balloons up along the whole front + enemy aircraft very active. Left Group assisted by H.A. cut wire about I32a + c. Heavy shelling of back areas throughout the day. C/63 position in H22c heavily shelled with 5.9's + 7.2's two guns damaged. B/63 was also shelled. Several forward hostile batteries were engaged by Right Group	
	18th		Hostile shelling below normal. At 8.30 p.m we raided enemy trenches in N10b. No enemy were encountered. At 11.10 p m a second raid covered by all batteries of Right + Left Groups supported by H.A was carried out on INCREASE + INCONSISTENT trenches. Raiding party encountered an enemy raid in No man's Land. In the fight we took 2 prisoners. During the night several efforts were made to raid our trenches in all four attempts which failed. Orders for relief of 12th Div. Arty by 57th Div. Arty received. Bde Major 57 Div Arty	O.O No 91. O.O No 92
	19th		called to arrange details of the relief. Orders for relief issued	O.O No 93
		11 p.m.	Some hostile shelling + T.M. activity on Left Batt Left Bde. We retaliated on enemy trenches + H.A engaged hostile T.M.S 12 midnight hostile activity ceased. Quiet night with some shelling of ~~[illegible]~~ Bac St. Maur Road by enemy 4.2 H.V. guns.	
	20th		Bde Major returned from Overseas Senior Officers Course	
	21st		57th Div RA. relieved one section per Bty 63rd Bde covering the LAVENTIE SWITCH.	

A5834 Wt. W4973/M687 750,000 8/16 D. D. & L. Ltd. Forms/C.2118/13.

Instructions regarding War Diaries and Intelligence Summaries are contained in F. S. Regs., Part II. and the Staff Manual respectively. Title pages will be prepared in manuscript.

March 1918
Vol XXXIV

WAR DIARY
or
INTELLIGENCE SUMMARY.
(Erase heading not required.)

HQ 12 Div Arty Sheet VII

Army Form C. 2118.

Place	Date	Hour	Summary of Events and Information	Remarks and references to Appendices
LES LAURIERS (Sheet) 36A 1/40000	22		Remaining Sections relieved by 57 Div. Arty. 62 Bde moved to billets round DOULIEU and the D.A.C. to HAVERSKERQUE area. Relief complete at 11 pm. 63 Bde remain under command of 57 Div.	
HAZEBROUCK 5A 1/100.000	23.		Orders came in during afternoon that Artillery was to concentrate tonight in HAVERSKERQUE area: 63rd Bde are pulling out under orders from 57 D.A. & came under our orders on arrival in billets.	
LENS / AMIENS 1/100.000	24		Artillery marched to AMES area. H.Q. to LEBEUVRE. Inf. went by bus to BAISIEUX area.	
ALBERT 1/40.000	25		Artillery marched to VILLERS CARTEL – CANDAS area. C.R.A. & B.M. went on to Div. H.Q. at SENLIS. Inf. went into action E of ALBERT & retired by order during the night to hold line W of River ANCRE from ALBERT (inclusive) to HAMEL (inclusive) 17 D.A. covering 35 Inf Bde. 47 D.A. 36 Inf Bde & 63 DA covering 37 Inf Bde. 1800 yd front for 1 Div.	
SENLIS.	26		35 Inf Bde on right covered by two Bdes RA. 34 & 41. 36 Inf Bde in centre covered by 34 DA Bde 37 Inf Bde on the left covered by 63 DA. Enemy attacked ALBERT all night & succeeded in crossing the river ANCRE, by day light he had been pushed back & we held the railway west of river. On the left a few isolated patrols penetrated AVELUY WOOD & were easily dealt with. Corps on right (7th) & left (4th) both bent back slightly.	
~~[illegible]~~	27		Enemy pressed his attacks against ALBERT with varying success. 17 Div. took over the line from ALBERT to AVELUY at midday, the 35th Inf Bde remaining in until they could be relieved. 12 D.A. marched to ORVILLE on 26th under Col. WYNNE DSO & concentrated W of ACHEUX by 12 noon 27th. Bde. Commanders & Bty commanders rode forward & reconnoitred positions to cover 37 Inf Bde ~~[illegible]~~ & to relieve 63 D.A. Relief carried out without incident. Artillery defence reorganised so that Right group consisted of 78th & 34th Bdes. Centre group of 48 & 77 Bdes. Left group 62 & 63 Bdes.	
	28.		36 Inf Bde, which were covered by 48th 77th Bdes were strongly attacked, but held their ground. 2nd Div. Arty took over the Command of the front at 4.30 pm. 12 D.A. H.Q. returning to TOUTENCOURT. 62nd & 63rd Bdes remained in the line under 2nd D.A.	

Army Form C. 2118.

WAR DIARY
or
~~INTELLIGENCE SUMMARY.~~
(Erase heading not required.)

Instructions regarding War Diaries and Intelligence Summaries are contained in F. S. Regs., Part II. and the Staff Manual respectively. Title pages will be prepared in manuscript.

March 1918
Vol XXXIV

H.Q. 12 Div Arty   Sheet VIII

Place	Date	Hour	Summary of Events and Information	Remarks and references to Appendices
TOUTENCOURT	29		During the action 25-28 while 12 Div. were holding the line, the policy of the senior Colonel commanding the group of artillery covering the Inf Bde living with the Inf. Bde was ordered to be adopted. This was done, but the Inf Brigade HQ were in all cases in front of the gun line, & it was found that communication between Div Arty HQ and the Group Commanders was so uncertain that important orders often took too long to deliver to be of any use. Group Commanders also complained that they were continually losing touch with their batteries.	
			The C.R.A. reconnoitred positions for 9 Bde R.F.A. to cover a line MILLENCOURT - WEST of BOUZENCOURT - East of ENGLEBELMER.	
	30.31.		No change.	

Noel [signature] Major
B.M. 12 D.A.

A5834 Wt. W4973/M687 750,000 8/16 D. D. & L. Ltd. Forms/C.2118/13.

S E C R E T.

12th Divisional Artillery Order No. 84.

Ref. Maps - FLEURBAIX)
BOIS GRENIER) 1/10,000. 7th March, 1918.
RADINGHEM)
AUBERS)

1. The 7th Bn. Royal Sussex Regt., 36th Infantry Brigade, will carry out a Raid on March 8th. for the purpos of obtaining identifications and information of the enemy's intentions.

2. The objective will be enemy's posts on and supporting NECKLACE Trench and its junction with NAVAL Trench and the road N 9 d 35 10 and as far South as the road running through N 15 a to N 15 b 45 80.

3. Strength of Raiding Party will be about one Company.

4. Right of the Raiding Party will be directed on the enemy's post at N 9 c 9 1. The left will be directed along the RUE DELVAS and will form blocks where necessary 50 yards East.

5. The Operation will be covered by Field and Heavy Artillery as laid down in Table I, pages 1, 2 and 3 of 12th D.A. R.A. 499 dated 6th March and as detailed in 62nd Brigade R.F.A. G.S./206 dated 5th March. There will be no bombardment before Zero.
There will be no signal for a withdrawal. Not later than Zero plus 20 mins. the Raiding Party will begin to withdraw. The Artillery Barrage will continue from Zero to Zero plus 30 mins, and from Zero plus 30 mins. to Zero plus 35 mins. will gradually die down.

6. The 2nd Portuguese Artillery have arranged to co-operate by firing on trench N 15 c 65 95 to N 15 b 05 25 from Zero to Zero plus 30 minutes.

7. 12th Divisional Artillery will synchronise watches with 2nd Portuguese Artillery between 11 a.m. and 12 Noon and 6 p.m. and 7 p.m. to-day.
62nd Brigade R.F.A. will arrange to synchronise watches with 36th Infantry Brigade between 11 a.m. and 12 Noon and 6 p.m. and 7 p.m. to-day.

8. Zero hour will be notified later.

Please acknowledge.

Alfred Fox
Captain,
for Brigade Major, 12th D. A.

To all recipients of 12th D.A. - R.A. 499.

S E C R E T.

R.A. 499/6.

To all recipients of 12th D.A.
Order No. 84 and 64th A.F.A. Bde. (for B/64).

Reference 12th Divisional Artillery Order No. 84 dated 7th March.

Zero Hour will be 4.30 a.m. March 8th.

Please acknowledge.

Alfred [signature]
Captain,
7th March 1918. for Brigade Major 12th D.A.

S E C R E T.

12th Divisional Artillery Order No. 85.

Ref. maps FLEURBAIX.)
BOIS GRENIER)
AUBERS)
RADINGHEM)

7th March, 1918.

1. The enemy's trenches in I 26 b and d will be bombarded on 8th March by Field guns, Howitzers and Heavy Artillery as laid down in Table III of R.A. 499 dated 6th March 1918.

2. Watches will be synchronised from H.Q. 12th Divisional Artillery.

3. Zero hour will be notified later.

Please acknowledge.

Captain,
for Brigade Major, 12th D.A.

To all recipients of 12th D.A. - R.A. 499.

HEADQUARTERS
12th DIVISIONAL ARTILLERY

S E C R E T.   R.A. 499/7.

To all recipients of 12th D.A. Order No. 85.

Reference 12th D.A. Order No. 85 dated 7th March 1918.

Zero hour will be 5 p.m. on March 8th.

Watches will be synchronised by an officer from 12th Divisional Artillery H.Q. between 10 a.m. and 11 a.m. and 1 p.m. and 2 p.m. tomorrow March 8th., who will take correct time to XV Corps H.A. and Left Group.

Please acknowledge.

Alfred M Fox

Captain,
for Brigade Major, 12th D.A.

7th March, 1918.

S E C R E T.

12th Divisional Artillery Order No. 86.

Ref. Maps - FLEURBAIX) BOIS GRENIER) AUBERS) RADINGHEM) 1/10,000.

7th March, 1918.

1. The Left Infantry Brigade (37th Infantry Brigade) will carry out a Raid at an early date (Z.Day) with a view to obtaining as many prisoners and as much information as possible of enemy's intentions.

2. The object will be enemy's front and support trenches between INDEX STREET (inclusive) and the road in I 31 c leading to LE BRIDOUX (exclusive).

3. Two Companies will be employed.

4. In addition to wire cutting by Heavy Artillery, 18 Pounders and Trench Mortars along whole Divisional front, two bombardments will take place as follows -

(a) On March 7th. by XV Corps H.A. as per Table II of 12th D.A. No. R.A. 499 of March 6th.

(b) On March 8th. by XV Corps H.A. and Field Artillery of Left Group as per Table III of R.A. 499 dated 6th March. Zero hour will be notified later.

5. The Raid will be carried out by daylight under barrages of Heavy and Field Artillery and Smoke as detailed in Table IV. amended of 12th D.A. - R.A. 499/4 dated 7th March.
38th Divisional Artillery will assist with 3 - 18 pr. batteries.

6. The Officer Commanding Left Group will arrange with Officer Commanding Right Group, 38th Divisional Artillery, for use of O.Ps. previous to Z. Day.

7. B/64 Battery will move 2 guns into N 3 a and 2 guns near LE CROMBALOT, which will come under the orders of Officer Commanding Right Group for this Operation.

8. The O.C. Left Group will detail an officer to act as Liaison Officer with the O.C. Raid.

9. Lt. Col. THOMSON, C.M.G., D.S.O. will give the order to stop fire under instructions from G.O.C. 37th Infantry Brigade. He will first inform Right Group H.Q., then H.Q. 12th D.A., who will pass the order to XV Corps H.A. and 38th D.A.

10. Z. Day, Zero hour and arrangements for synchronisation will be notified later.

Acknowledge please.

[signature]
Captain,
for Brigade Major, 12th D.A.

To all recipients of R.A. 499 and
64th A.F.A. Bde. (for B/64).

S E C R E T.   R.A. 499/8.

To all recipients of 12th D.A. Order No. 86.

Reference 12th Divisional Artillery Order No. 86.

Para. 1, line 1. For "36th Infantry Brigade" Read "37th Infantry Brigade".

[signature]
Captain,
7th March 1918.   for Brigade Major, 12th D. A.

S E C R E T.

Reference 12th D. A. Order No. 86.

R.A. 499/10.

AMENDMENT No. 3 to R.A. 499.

1. Reference Amended Table IV. 18 pr. Tasks -

(a) Phase II. For "Zero plus 5 mins. to Zero plus 7 mins".
Read "Zero plus 5 mins. to Zero plus 9 mins".

Phase III. For "Zero plus 7 mins. onwards".
Read "Zero plus 9 mins. onwards"

(b) At Zero plus 24 mins. all 18 prs. on the line O 1 a 4500 - O 1 b 6080 will fire one round of Smoke shell as a signal for withdrawal to the Infantry.
Left Group Commander will arrange that his smoke screen is so placed as to conceal this signal from enemy O.P's.

(c) Left Group Commander will arrange that the batteries firing between O 1 a 6597 - I 31 d 2530 open fire on the front line and not 50 yards short as given in Remarks column, and these batteries will not lift 25 yards at Zero plus 1 and Zero plus 2 minutes.

2. Reference R.A. 499, Table IV. 4.5" How. Tasks - Amended.

All 4.5 in. Howitzers firing on the line O 1 a 4500 - O 1 b 6080 will at Zero plus 4 minutes raise M.P.I. 50 yards.

Please acknowledge.

[signature]
Captain,
for Brigade Major, 12th D.A.

8th March, 1918.

To all recipients of 12th D.A. Order No. 86 and R.A. 499.

S E C R E T.

R.A. 499/12.

To all recipients of 12th D.A. Order No. 86.

Reference - 12th D.A. Order No. 86 dated 7.3.18.
R.A. 499. Amended Table IV. Amendment No. 1.
,, Addenda No. 1.
,, Amendment No. 3.
,, Amendment No. 4.

Zero Hour will be 5.30 a.m. March 9th.

Watches will be synchronised as follows -
XV Corps H.A. By an officer from 12th Division (G).
38th D. A.)
Right Group) By an officer from 12th D. A.
Left Group)

between 12 Noon and 1 p.m. and again between 6 p.m. and 7 p.m. to-day.

O.C. Left Group 12th D.A. will give the time to O.C. Right Group, 38th D. A.

Please acknowledge.

[signature]
Captain,
for Brigade Major, 12th D.A.

8th March, 1918.

S E C R E T.

.A. 499/12.

To all recipients of 12th D.A. Order No. 86.

Reference - 12th D.A. Order No. 86 dated 7.3.18.
R.A. 499. Amended Table IV. Amendment No. 1.
,, Addenda No. 1.
,, Amendment No. 3.
,, Amendment No. 4.

Zero Hour will be 5.30 a.m. March 9th.

Watches will be synchronised as follows -

XV Corps H.A.	By an officer from 12th Division (G).
38th D. A.)	
Right Group)	By an officer from 12th D. A.
Left Group)	

between 12 Noon and 1 p.m. and again between 6 p.m. and 7 p.m. to-day.

O.C. Left Group 12th D.A. will give the time to O.C. Right Group, 38th D. A.

Please acknowledge.

Captain,
for Brigade Major, 12th D.A.

8th March, 1918.

S E C R E T.   R.A. 499/11.

AMENDMENT No. 4 to R.A. 499.

Reference Amendment No. 3 to R.A. 499 dated 8.3.18.

Para. 1, sub-para. (b) Reading "At Zero plus 24 mins. all 18 prs. on the line O 1 a 4500 - .... this signal from enemy O.P's.",

is cancelled.

Please acknowledge.

Captain,

8th March, 1918.   for Brigade Major, 12th D.A.

SECRET.

Reference 12th D. A. Order No. 86.

HEADQUARTERS
R.A. 499/10.
12th DIVISIONAL ARTILLERY

AMENDMENT No. 3 to R.A. 499.

1. Reference Amended Table IV. 18 pr. Tasks :-

(a) Phase II. For "Zero plus 5 mins. to Zero plus 7 mins".
Read "Zero plus 5 mins. to Zero plus 9 mins".

Phase III. For "Zero plus 7 mins. onwards".
Read "Zero plus 9 mins. onwards"

(b) ~~At Zero plus 24 mins. all 18 prs. on the line O 1 a 4500 - O 1 b 6080 will fire one round of Smoke shell as a signal for withdrawal to the Infantry.
Left Group Commander will arrange that his smoke screen is so placed as to conceal this signal from enemy O.P's.~~

(c) Left Group Commander will arrange that the batteries firing between O 1 a 6597 - I 31 d 2530 open fire on the front line and not 50 yards short as given in Remarks column, and these batteries will not lift 25 yards at Zero plus 1 and Zero plus 2 minutes.

2. Reference R.A. 499, Table IV. 4.5" How. Tasks - Amended.

All 4.5 in. Howitzers firing on the line O 1 a 4500 - O 1 b 6080 will at Zero plus 4 minutes raise M.P.I. 50 yards.

Please acknowledge.

8th March, 1918.

for Brigade Major, 12th D.A.
Captain,

To all recipients of 12th D.A. Order No. 86 and R.A. 499.

S E C R E T.   R.A. 499/8.

To all recipients of 12th D.A. Order No. 86.

Reference 12th Divisional Artillery Order No. 86.

Para. 1, line 1. For "36th Infantry Brigade" Read "37th Infantry Brigade".

Captain,

7th March 1918.   for Brigade Major, 12th D. A.

S E C R E T.

HEADQUARTERS
R.A. 499/4.
12th DIVISIONAL ARTILLERY

Reference R.A. 499 dated 6th March, 1918.

X. Day is March 7th.

Y. Day is March 8th.

Z. Day is March 9th.

Please acknowledge.

Captain,

7th March, 1918. for Brigade Major, 12th D.A.

To all recipients of R.A. 499.

2 copies to be QOTA Bde

S E C R E T.

ADDENDA No.1 to R.A. 499 dated 6th March, 1918.

1. Raid on Z. Day. Table IV.

Rates of fire.

18 prs.	Phase I.	4 rounds per gun per min.	
	II.	4 ,,	,,
	III.	2 ,,	,,
4.5" Hows.	Phase I.	3 ,,	,,
	II.	2 ,,	,,

Ammunition.

18 prs.	Phase I.	All shrapnel.
	II.	All shrapnel.
	III.	H.E. non-delay.

2. One 18 pr. battery Left Group will fire Smoke in Phases I, II and III. Rate of fire and objective will be ordered by Group Commander.

3. 1 Section of Battery of 38th Divisional Artillery firing on I 32 a will fire Smoke unless wind is N.E.

4. Reference Table III - Bombardment on Y. Day. All 18 pr. batteries will fire 1 round of Smoke per gun per minute from Zero to Zero plus 5 minutes.

S E C R E T.

Amendment No. 1 to 12th D.A. O.O. 499.

Table I.	The following amendments will be made -	
	Phase II.	Zero plus 4 mins. to Zero plus 6 mins.
	Phase III.	Zero plus 6 mins. to Zero plus 8 mins.
	Phase IV.	Zero plus 8 mins. to Zero plus 30 mins.

Table IV. 18 pr. Tasks - Page 1 is cancelled in all Phases and attached amended Table IV. is substituted.

4.5" How. Tasks - Cancel page 2 and substitute attached amended 4.5 in. How. Tasks.

Heavy Artillery Tasks - Cancel page 3 and substitute attached amended Heavy Artillery Tasks.

HEADQUARTERS
R.A. 499.
12th DIVISIONAL ARTILLERY

S E C R E T.

The attached Tables form part of Operation Orders which will be issued shortly.

They refer to a series of Minor Operations which will take place in the near future.

A.M. Fox

Captain,
6th March, 1918. for Brigade Major, 12th D.A.

Copies to -

Right Group (7)
Left Group (7)
D. T. M. O.
and to R.A. XV Corps
12th Divn. (G)
38th D.A.
2nd Port: D.A.
H.A. XV Corps
36th Inf. Bde.
37th Inf. Bde.

Amended Table IV. 18 Pr. Tasks. SECRET. TABLE IV.

Phase	Time From	Time To	Unit	No. of guns	Target	Remarks
I	Zero	Zero plus 5 mins.	Right Group	24	N 6 b 90 50 - O 1 a 65 97	Begin 50 yds. short of trench, lift 25 yds. after 1 min. and another 25 at Zero plus 2.
			do.	B/64 (2) (2)	O 1 b 53 73 - O 2 a 15 73) NEAR AVENUE N6d8665-O1c0040)	From Zero onwards thro' Phases II & III.
			Left Group do.	13 6	O 1 a 65 97 - I 31 d 25 30 Firing Smoke as directed	
			38th D. A.	6) 9 3)	I 31 d 25 30 - I 31 d 55 50	
			do.	3	I 32 c 06 80 - I 32 c 14 94	
			do.	~~6~~ 4	I 32 a 45 10 - I 32 a 50 32	Zero onwards thro' Phases II & III, one Section firing Smoke.
II	Zero plus 5 mins.	Zero plus 9 mins.	Right Group do.	24 B/64 (2) (2)	N6b9055-O1a0560-O1a2535-O1a8570 O 1 b 53 73 - O 2 a 15 73 NEAR AVENUE N6d8665-O1c0040	As in Phase I.
			Left Group	18	O 1 a 8570 - I 31 d 4505 - I 31 d 2530.	
			do.	6	Firing Smoke as directed.	
			38th D. A.	6) 9 3)	I 31 d 25 30 - I 31 d 55 50	
			do.	3	I 32 c 0680 - I 32 c 1494	
			do.	6	I 32 a 4510 - I 32 a 5032	One Section to fire Smoke.

Amended Table IV. **SECRET.** TABLE IV. contd.

18 Pr Tanks.

Phase	Time From	Time To	Unit	No. of guns	Target	Remarks
III	Zero plus 9 mins.	Onwards	Right Group	24	O 1 a 0560 - O 1 a 4500 - O 1 b 0540	
			do.	B/64 (2)	As in Phases I and II.	
				(2)	do. do. do.	
			Left Group	18	O 1 b 0540 - O 1 b 6080 - I 31 d 4505	
			do.	6	Firing Smoke as directed.	
			38th D. A.	12	I 31 d 4505 - I 31 d 2530 - I 31 d 4345	
			do.	8	I 32 a 4510 - I 32 a 5032	One Section to fire Smoke if wind suitable.

Maps - FLEURBAIX)
BOIS GRENIER)
AUBERS) 1/10,000.
RADINGHEM)

SECRET. TABLE IV. contd.

12TH DIVISIONAL ARTILLERY.

Raid on 2. Day.

4.5 inch Howitzer Tasks - Amended.

Unit	Zero to Zero plus 4 mins.		Zero plus 4 mins. onwards.		Remarks.
	Hows.	Targets.	Hows.	Targets.	
Right Group	1	N 6 c 65 50	1	N 6 c 65 50	
	2	O 1 a 45 50	1	N 6 b 95 54	
	2	O 1 a 75 70	2	O 1 a 20 23	
	2 (a)	O 1 a 82 82	2	O 1 a 45 00	
	2	O 1 a 94 78	2	O 1 a 82 27	
			1	O 1 b 00 40	
Left Group	2	O 1 b 09 90	2	O 1 b 22 62	Raise M.P.I. 50 yds. at Zero plus 4.
	2	I 31 d 55 50	2	O 1 b 40 70	Raise M.P.I. 50 yds. at Zero plus 4.
	2	I 32 d 05 60	1	I 32 d 05 60	
	1 (a)	I 31 d 25 16	2	I 32 c 15 90	
	2	O 1 b 40 98	2	I 31 d 55 50	

(a) After two minutes lift to Phase II.

Maps - FLEURBAIX)
BOIS GRENIER)
RADINGHEM) 1/10,000.
AUBERS)

SECRET. **TABLE IV. contd.**

12TH DIVISIONAL ARTILLERY.

Raid on Z. Day.

Heavy Artillery Tasks - Amended.

Zero to Zero plus 1 minute	Zero plus 1 min. to Zero plus 2 mins.	Zero plus 2 mins. onwards.
1 How. N 6 c 6050 from Zero onwards.) " N 6 d 0360 " ") " O 7 b 6595 " ") " (b) O 1 b 4035 " ") " O 2 a 1275 " ") " I 32 c 1540 " ") " I 32 c 4075 " ") " I 32 a 7034 " ")	8 Hows. as detailed for Phase I.	8 Hows. as detailed for Phases I and II.
Remainder on Support Trench O 1 a 38 40 - O 1 b 10 80	Remainder on line joining O 1 a 38 40 - O 1 b 10 80	Remainder N 6 d 5080 N 6 b 8500 (not 106 fuse) O 1 c 1515 O 7 b 4036 O 2 a 0047 O 2 a 3867 (HOUSSEM FARM) I 32 c 2095 I 32 a 4525 I 31 d 5255 (not 106 fuse) 1 How. N12a8264 & N12b1090) Trench Mortars 1 How. N 12 b 4535.) and O.Ps. 1 How. I 32 b 7018)

(b) At Zero plus two minutes lift to O 2 d 1270.

Maps - FLEURBAIX.
BOIS GRENIER. } 1/10,000.
AUBERS.
RADINGHEM

SECRET. TABLE IV.

12TH DIVISIONAL ARTILLERY.

Raid on Z. Day.

18 Pr. T a s k s.

Phase	Time From	Time To	Unit	No. of guns	Target	Remarks
I	Zero	Zero plus 3 mins.	Right Group	24	N 6 b 90 55 - O 1 a 65 97	
			do.	2.B/64.	O 1 b 53 73 - O 2 a 15 73	Zero onwards thro' Phases II and III.
			Left Group	24	O 1 a 65 97 - I 31 d 40 45	
			38th D.A.	3	I 31 d 50 46 - I 31 d 53 55	
			do.	3	I 32 c 06 80 - I 32 c 14 94	
			do.	6	I 32 a 45 10 - I 32 a 50 32	Zero onwards thro' Phases II and III; one Section to fire Smoke.
II.	Zero plus 3 mins.	Zero plus mins.	Right Group	6	N 6 b 90 55 - O 1 a 2275	
			do.	6	O 1 a 22 75 - O 1 a 40 45	
			do.	12	O 1 a 40 45 - O 1 a 93 77	
			do.	2	As in Phase I.	
			Left Group	12	O 1 a 93 77 - I 31 d 42 06	
			do.	6	I 31 d 42 06 - I 31 d 25 30	
			do.		Firing Smoke as directed.	
			38th D.A.	6	I 31 d 25 30 - I 31 d 43 45	
			do.	6	Same as Phase I.	As Phase I.
III.	Zero plus mins.	Onwards.	Right Group	12	O 1 a 22 75 - O 1 a 58 10	
			do.	12	O 1 a 58 10 - O 1 b 10 42	
			do.	2	As Phase I and II.	
			Left Group	12	O 1 b 10 42 - O 1 b 60 84	
			do.	12	I 31 d 25 30 - I 31 d 42 06	
			38th D. A.	6	I 31 d 42 12 - O 1 b 60 84	
			do.	6	Same as Phase I and II.	

Amendment follows to phase II + III

Maps - FLEURBAIX)
BOIS GRENIER) 1/10,000.
AUBERS)
RADINGHEM)

SECRET. TABLE IV. contd.

12TH DIVISIONAL ARTILLERY.

Raid on Z. Day.

Z. Day =

Zero Hour =

4.5 inch Howitzer Tasks.

Unit	Phase I. Zero to Zero plus		Phase II. Zero plus to Zero plus		Phade III. Zero plus to Zero plus		Remarks
	Hows.	Targets	Hows.	Targets	Hows.	Targets	
Right Group	1	N 6 c 65 50	2	N 6 b 95 54	2	Same as Phase II.	
	2	O 1 a 45 50	2	O 1 a 20 23	2	do. do.	
	2	O 1 a 75 70	2	O 1 a 45 00	2	do. do.	
	2	O 1 a 82 82	2	O 1 a 82 27	2	do. do.	
	2	O 1 a 94 78	1	O 1 b 00 40	1	do. do.	
Left Group	2	O 1 b 08 90	2	O 1 b 22 62	2	Raise M.P.I. 50 yds.	
	1	I 31 d 05 25	2	O 1 b 40 70	2	Same as Phase II	
	2	I 31 d 15 10	1	I 31 d 40 00	1	do. do.	
	2(a)	I 31 d 25 15	2	I 31 d 30 20	2	do. do.	
	2	O 1 b 40 98	2	I 31 d 30 36	2	do. do.	

(a) After one minute lift to I 31 d 55 55.

Maps - FLEURBAIX)
BOIS GRENIER) 1/10,000
RADINGHEM)
AUBERS)

SECRET. **TABLE IV. contd.**

12TH DIVISIONAL ARTILLERY.

Raid on Z. Day.

Heavy Artillery Tasks.

Zero to Zero plus 1 minute	Zero plus 1 min. to Zero plus 2 mins.	Zero plus 2 mins. onwards.
1 How. N 6 c 6050 from Zero onwards.) " N 6 d 0560 " ") " O 7 b 6535 " ") " O 1 b 4035 " ") " O 1 b 7570 " ") " I 32 c 1540 " ") " I 32 c 4075 " ") " I 32 a 7034 " ") Remainder on Support Trench O 1 a 38 40 - O 1 b 15 98	8 hows. as detailed for Phase I. Remainder on line joining O 1 a 38 40 - O 1 b 15 98	) 8 Hows. as detailed for Phases I and II. Remainder N 6 d 5080 N 6 b 8500 (not 106 fuse) O 1 c 1515 O 7 b 4030 O 2 a 0047 O 2 a 3867 O 2 a 1572 I 32 c 2095 I 32 a 4525 (searching inwards) I 31 d 5255 (not 106 fuse) 1 How. N12a8264. N12b1090.) Trench Mortars 1 How. N12b4535. I32b7018) and O.Ps.

S E C R E T.

12th Divisional Artillery Order No. 91.

Ref. Trench Map 36 S.W.2. 1/10,000.

17th March, 1918.

Right Group.
Left Group.

1. The 7th Bn. Suffolk Regt. will carry out a silent raid, strength one Company, to enter enemy's trenches between N 10 d 4 9 and N 10 b 80 35 and to penetrate as far as the support line, inclusive.

The Right of the Raiding Party will investigate supposed gas projector emplacements in rear of support trench N 10 d 45 65 to N 10 d 55 70.

2. There will be no bombardment or barrage, but the Right Group R.F.A. will arrange to fire on the interior of the moat at N 11 a 1 0 with H.E. during the raid.

Right Group will also stand by to fire to each flank of the Raiding Party and on NEGATIVE DRIVE and NED LANE if called upon to do so.

Details to be arranged between G.O.C. 35th Infantry Brigade and O.C. Right Group.

3. Zero Hour will be 8.30 p.m. March 18th., 1918, and watches will be synchronised at 35th Infantry Brigade H.Q. by Right Group.

Please acknowledge.

Alpress(?) [signature]
Captain,
for Brigade Major, 12th D.A.

Copies to -
12th Divn. (G).
R.A., XV Corps.
H.A., XV Corps.
38th D.A.
2nd Port. D.A.
35th Inf. Bde.

S E C R E T.

R.A. 516/3.

Reference 12th D. A. Order No. 92.

1. Zero Hour will be 11.10 p.m. March 18th.

2. Please acknowledge.

Captain,

18th March, 1918. for Brigade Major, 12th D. A.

To all recipients of 12th D.A. Order No. 92.

SECRET.

Amendment No. 1 to 12th Divisional Artillery Order No. 92.

1. Para. 2. First line. For "INCANDESCENT" read "INCONSISTENT".

2. Reference para. 9. Watches will be synchronised again at 3 p.m. as well as at 12 Noon.

3. Table I, 18 pr. Tasks. Rates of fire -
Flank barrages of Left Group will fire at rate of 3 rounds per gun per minute during Phase III and not 2 rounds per gun per minute as given.

Please acknowledge.

Alfred Fry

Captain,

18th March, 1918. for Brigade Major, 12th D.A.

To all recipients of 12th D.A. Order No. 92.

S E C R E T.

12th Divisional Artillery Order No. 92.

Ref. Maps - FLEURBAIX.)
BOIS GRENIER) 1/10,000.
AUBERS)
RADINGHEM)

17th March, 1918.

1. The 6th Bn. The Queens will carry out a raid on 18th March, 1918, to obtain identifications and inflict losses on the enemy.

2. The objective will be INCREASE and INCANDESCENT Trenches from I 32 c 10 87 to I 32 a 40 00.

3. Strength of Raiding Party will be 2 Officers, 6 N.C.Os. and 66 men.

4. The raid will be supported by Artillery barrages commencing at Zero as per attached Tables I, II and III showing 18 pr., 4.5 inch Howitzer and Heavy Artillery Tasks.

5. The 38th Divisional Artillery are assisting with one 18 pr. and one 4.5 inch Howitzer battery.

6. At Zero plus 35 minutes fire will gradually die down.

7. O.C. Left Group will detail an officer to act as Liaison Officer with O.C. Raid.

8. Zero hour will be notified later.

9. Watches will be synchronised as follows -
O.C. Right Group and O.C. Left Group will send an officer with watch to 37th Infantry Brigade H.Q. at 12 Noon on 18th.
O.C. Left Group will send an officer to synchronise watches with O.C. Right Group, 38th D.A.
H.Q., 12th D.A. will give time to XV Corps H.A.

Please acknowledge.

[signature]
Captain,
for Brigade Major, 12th D.A.

Copies to -
Right Group (7)
Left Group (7)
64th Brigade.
286th Brigade.
D. T. M. O.
and to 12th Divn. (G)
R.A., XV Corps.
H.A., XV Corps (3)
38th D.A. (4)
2nd Port. D.A.
37th Inf. Bde.

S E C R E T.

E. Operations.

Ref. Maps - FLEURBAIX / BOIS GRENIER / AUBERS / RADINGHEM } 1/10,000.

TABLE I. 18 pr. Tasks.

Phase	Time: From	Time: To	Unit	No. of guns	Tasks	Remarks.
I	Zero	Zero plus 5 mins.	Right Group	12	I 31 d 6050 - I 32 c 0075	Rates of fire - Phase I & II. 4 rounds per gun per minute. Phase III. 2 rounds per gun per minute. Flank barrages Left Group 3 rds. p.g.p.m. Ammunition - Phase I & II. Shrapnel Phade III. H.E. Non-delay. Flank barrages Shrapnel through Phases I, II and III.
			Left Group	24	I 32 c 0075 - I 32 c 2595 - I 32 c 3092(enfl:) - I 32 a 4608	
			38th D. A.	6	I 32 a 4608 - I 32 a 5030	
II	Zero plus 5 mins.	Zero plus 6 mins.	Left Group	6 6	I 31 d 8360 - I 32 c 1030. Flank barrage I 32 a 4520 - I 32 c 8090 -do-	
			Right Group	12	I 32 c 0535 - I 32 c 3565. Support trench	
			Left Group	12	I 32 c 3565 - I 32 a 7000. Support trench	
			38th D. A.	6	I 32 a 4520 - I 32 a 6253	
III.	Zero plus 6 mins.	Onwards	Same as Phase II, but Left Group on Support trench I 32 c 3565 - I 32 a 7000 will raise M.P.I. 50 yds. until Zero plus 30. At Zero plus 30 mins. lower M.P.I. 50 yds. From Zero plus 6 mins. onwards 2 guns of all 18 pr. batteries, except 2 Batteries of Left Group on flank barrages, will search forward by lifts of 50 yards to a distance of 300 yards and drop back to original line of Phase III, and will continue to repeat this process until fire dies down.			

All Batteries will open fire 50 yards short of front line and lift by 25 yards at Zero plus 1 min. and Zero plus 2 mins. so as to bring them on to the front trench at Zero plus 2 minutes.

S E C R E T.　　Ref. Maps - FLEURBAIX) BOIS GRENIER) AUBERS) RADINGHEM) 1/10,000.

E. Operations.

TABLE II. 4.5 inch Howitzer Tasks.

Unit	Zero to Zero plus 4 mins.		Zero plus 4 - onwards		Remarks
	Hows.	Targets	Hows.	Targets	
Right Group	1 1 1 1 2	I 32 c 15 45 I 32 c 40 75 I 31 d 05 25) I 31 d 55 55) I 31 d 30 18)	1 1 Zero onwards	I 31 d 65 55 I 31 d 80 30	Rates of fire - Zero to Zero plus 6 mins - 2 rounds per How. per minute. Zero plus 6 onwards - 1 round per How. per minute. Ammunition. BX. (a) Sweeping up and down front line. between these points
Left Group	6	Support trench I 32 c 35 65 to I 32 a 75 08	1 2 3	I 32 c 00 15 I 32 a 80 15 I32c6065-I32c8055	
38th D. A.	1(a) 1(a) 1(a) 1 1 1	I 32 a 90 95) I 32 a 90 85) I 32 a 68 63) I 32 a 62 53) I 32 b 10 55) I 32 b 13 08)	Zero onwards		

SECRET.

E. Operations.

Ref. Maps - FLEURBAIX)
BOIS GRENIER)
AUBERS) 1/10,000.
RADINGHEM)

TABLE III. Heavy Artillery Tasks.

	Zero onwards		
	Hows.	Tasks	
	1	O 1 b 42 95	
	1	O 2 a 36 75 (HOUSSAIN FARM)	
	2	On Trench I 32 c 50 04 to I 32 c 93 43	
	1	I 32 d 05 60 (LA MOTTE HOUSSAIN)	
	1	To be allotted by XV Corps H.A.	
	1	I 33 c 75 52	
	1	I 26 c 90 00	
	1	I 26 d 26 18	
	1	I 27 c 12 08	

Copies to all recipients of 12th D.A. Order No. 93.

R.A. 526/1.

Reference 12th Divisional Artillery Order No. 93 dated 19th March, 1918.

1. Units of the 12th Divisional Artillery will march by road from G 16 a 2 1 - G 9 c 3 9 - G 19 b 6 8 - L 11 d 5 2 - L 11 c 3 8 - NEUF BERQUIN,

The 62nd Brigade will march straight to their Wagon Lines from L 11 c 3 8 and the D.A. Column will march through the North end of MERVILLE and LE SART.

2. The 57th Divisional Artillery will march via ESTAIRES

[signature] Major,
Brigade Major, 12th D. A.

20th March, 1918.

WAR
DIARY

C: R. A.

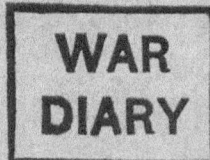

12th DIVISION

APRIL 1 9 1 8

Army Form C. 2118.

Instructions regarding War Diaries and Intelligence Summaries are contained in F. S. Regs., Part II. and the Staff Manual respectively. Title pages will be prepared in manuscript.

April 1918

Vol: XXXV

WAR DIARY
or
INTELLIGENCE SUMMARY.
(Erase heading not required.)

H.Q. 12th Divl Artillery

Sheet I.

Place	Date	Hour	Summary of Events and Information	Remarks and references to Appendices
Ref: AMIENS 1.100.000 and 57 D.S.E 1.20.000 WARLOY.	2.		Visited 17 D.A. at CONTAY reference taking over front from AMIENS – ALBERT road E3 central to W15 a.5.6. covered by 78th 79th + 34th Bdes.	
	3.		12 Div. took over above front and command passed at 7.30 am. Quiet day. 78th Bde. moved some battery positions which were too cramped. All 3 Bdes. moved their HQ out of SENLIS. A concentration of all How: in Corps which could be brought to bear was directed on houses in W27d 4pm to 4.10pm.	
	4		At 1.22 pm. Right Inf Bde (35th) reported enemy attacking. All S.O.S. opened. All quiet by 1.59 pm. Apparently enemy attack 1 Coy R. B[illegible] in two waves and were repulsed. At 5.40pm report came in from prisoner captured by 4th Australian Div. on our right that enemy meant to attack. Ordered bursts of fire on likely assembly places. Stopped firing at 6.40pm. At 11.35pm. 5th Corps RA rang up to say an attack was expected on 4 Aust. Div. tomorrow early. Extra vigilance + night firing required. 62 + 63 Bdes. who have been covering 2nd Div. were relieved by 63 D.A. The 62 Bde relieved 1 section per Bty of the 34 Bde, 63 Bde withdrawn to W.L.	
	5.		5.15 am 34th Bde O.P. reported barrage north AVELUY wood. All quiet on our Div. front. 5.45 am. 4th Australian Div reported concentrations of enemy from ALBERT southwards. Counter preparation ordered by all groups. 7. am S.O.S. went up on 35 Inf Bde (R. Bde) front. All Batteries heavily shelled with 5.9 and gas. 8 am hostile fire died down a bit. 9. am. Enemy put heavy barrage on front + support trenches on whole Div. front + on batteries. 10.30 am. Australians were attacked twice. Each attack repulsed. 35 Inf. Bde. attacked. Attack repulsed. Wires were continually cut by enemy shelling and once by ~~[illegible]~~ our own Tanks. Enemy shelled WARLOY with 4.2 H.V. gun. One direct hit on Div Art HQ	

Instructions regarding War Diaries and Intelligence Summaries are contained in F. S. Regs., Part II. and the Staff Manual respectively. Title pages will be prepared in manuscript.

April 1918
Vol XXXV

WAR DIARY
or
~~INTELLIGENCE SUMMARY~~.
(Erase heading not required.)

H.Q. 12th Div. Artillery.

Army Form C. 2118.

Sheet II

Place	Date	Hour	Summary of Events and Information	Remarks and references to Appendices
WARLOY	5 (Cont)		1.57 pm. 36th Inf Bde were attacked: slightly driven back in W.21.c. Wire again cut. Fighting and shelling went on whole day until 8.30 pm. when things quieted down. Counter attack by 36 Inf. Bde to restore ground in W.21.c failed: though Artillery barrage as requested was put down by 79 Bde. 1 section 63 Bde. relieved 1 section 78 Bde remaining sections 62 Bde relieved remaining sections 34 Bde. Col WYNNE D.S.O. now commands 62 + 78 Bdes who cover 35 Inf Bde. and Col WARREN commands 79 Bde covering 36 Inf Bde assisted by Machine Guns. As result of days fighting Australians slightly withdrew their left flank + right of 35 Inf Bde was withdrawn to conform. 36 Inf Bde line intact with exception of 300 yds just in W.21.c. Our casualties for the day in 34. 78. 79 + 62 Bdes were 2 major killed 1 major wounded 6 subalterns wounded 2 OR. killed 54 O.R. wounded 1 signaller Div Arty H.Q. killed.	
	6.		Night was quiet. Harrassing fire on all approaches was carried out by both groups. 5.20 am. 78 Bde F.O.O. reported S.O.S. went up on his front. Guns opened but it proved a false alarm. 5.5 pm. Germans reported to have rushed Quarry in W.27.c. At 6.3 pm. Germans were holding ALBERT-AMIENS road in E3a in force and giving our right Battalion a bad time. Turned Heavies on to them while the Div. Art. pinned them down. 6.42 pm. S.O.S. went up along the whole Corps front + Aust. Div. on our right but no infantry action seems to have materialized. All quiet at 7.15 pm. Remaining sections 63 Bde relieved 78 Bde and Artillery now grouped so that 63rd Bde cover Rt Inf Bde 79 Bde cover Lt Inf. Bde + 62 Bde support both Bdes.	

A5834 Wt. W4973/M687 750,000 8/16 D. D. & L. Ltd. Forms/C.2118/13.

Army Form C. 2118.

WAR DIARY
or
INTELLIGENCE SUMMARY.
(Erase heading not required.)

Instructions regarding War Diaries and Intelligence Summaries are contained in F. S. Regs., Part II. and the Staff Manual respectively. Title pages will be prepared in manuscript.

April 1918
Vol. ~~XXXV~~

H.Q. 12 Div. Art[y]

Sheet III

Place	Date	Hour	Summary of Events and Information	Remarks and references to Appendices
WARLOY		7	A quiet night. Vigorous harassing fire carried out by groups and Counter Preparation at 5 am. assisted by Corps H.A. groups fired 80 rounds per gun during the night.	
		8.	Quiet day on the whole. A barrage was put down on our front system of the Left Bde. at 7.30 pm but all was quiet 7.50 pm. No infantry attack. ~~The~~ Germans used gas shell on SENLIS in the early morning	
		9.	Quiet night. 6.30 am Enemy ~~heat~~ gas shelled round SENLIS probably because our planes undoubtedly saw the 35 Inf. Div relieving the 47th Div. We carried out harassing fire and at 10.~~30~~ am. and 10.30 am. the Divisional Artillery in conjunction with the H.A. gas ~~[illegible]~~ shelled ALBERT and AVELUY. Throughout the morning Enemy shelled SENLIS with 8". & continued in the afternoon.	
		10.	D/63 gassed area southern half W16d. at 4.30 am 5 am & 5.30 am. Heavy firing at dawn on the Australian front but all quiet on ours. A quiet day.	
		11.	Vigorous night firing by all Bdes. 250 A per Bty 4.5 How gassed ALBERT in cooperation with H.A. at 5 am.	
CONTAY.		12	Vigorous Night firing. 300 A per Bty gassed area W16D. 34th A.F. Bde. relieved 79th Bde. R.F.A. & cover the Left Inf. Bde. 38 Div. relieved the 12 Div. Command passed at 8 am. C.R.A. 12 Div. remained in line to command Artillery covering the 38 Div. as the C.R.A. 38 Div. was with his artillery in the First Army. H.Q. closed at WARLOY and opened at CONTAY. 2nd Aust. Div. relieved [illegible] Div. on our Right.	
		13.	Usual Night harassing fire on roads. Gassed area W22d.	
		15.	48 Army Bde. R.F.A. (Lt Col. BUTCHART DSO) came under our orders and went into action as a Silent Bde at V10 ~~[illegible]~~ & ready to cover our left & the 35 Div. right if called upon. A quiet day	

(A7092). Wt. W12839/M1293. 750,000. 1/17. D. D. & L., Ltd. Forms/C.2118/14.

Instructions regarding War Diaries and Intelligence Summaries are contained in F. S. Regs., Part II. and the Staff Manual respectively. Title pages will be prepared in manuscript.

WAR DIARY
or
INTELLIGENCE SUMMARY.
(Erase heading not required.)

Army Form C. 2118.

April 1918
Vol. XXXV

H.Q. 12 Div Art'y

Sheet V

Place	Date	Hour	Summary of Events and Information	Remarks and references to Appendices
	16	3.25pm	Virgin on ALBERT church was knocked down by 8".	
	17-21		The front has been quiet. No C.O.s. has gone up.	
	22.		At 7.30pm. covered an attack made by 38 Div. on high ground in W 21 a. (See Order No 99) 35th Div also attacked on our left. 38th Div. partly successful & took 61 prisoners & 3 machine guns. 35th Div failed. To cover our front we had 34. 48. 282 Army Bdes. 62 & 63 Bde. 157 Bde of the 35 Div and 1 section 77 Bde. The 2nd Aust. DA cooperated on the right of the attack. Both V & Aust. Corps HA cooperated. Communications - both telephone & visual were excellent throughout; our O.P.s were the channel through which nearly all the information during the battle was sent. The Liaison Officer with advanced Inf Bde. also sent valuable information.	
RAINCHEVAL	23		63 Div. Art'y H.Q. took over from us at 10 am. to act for the 38th Div. whose Div Art'y is still up North. We joined our Div. at RAINCHEVAL preparatory to taking over from the N.Z. on 25th. 63 Bde. were relieved by 282 Bde. 62 Bde. were relieved by 48th Bde & became a Labour Bde. 63 Bde came into the wagon lines & became Corps Mobile Reserve.	
	24.		CRA. reconnoitred new front from Q 17 d 0 0 - Q 4 a 8.4.	
	25.		6 am. took over 93 Bde (Lt Col STILLWELL) 232 Bde (Lt Col OSBORNE) and 315 Bde (Lt Col HIGGINBOTHAM) all Army Bdes. to cover new front now held by 12 Div. Formed these Bdes into two groups (see Order No 101)	

(A7092). Wt. W12839/M1293. 750,000. 1/17. D. D. & L., Ltd. Forms/C.2118/14.

Army Form C. 2118.

WAR DIARY
or
INTELLIGENCE SUMMARY.
(Erase heading not required.)

Instructions regarding War Diaries and Intelligence Summaries are contained in F. S. Regs., Part II. and the Staff Manual respectively. Title pages will be prepared in manuscript.

April 1918
Vol. XXXV

HQ. 12 Div. Art. Sheet VI.

Place	Date	Hour	Summary of Events and Information	Remarks and references to Appendices
RAINCHEVAL 57D 1/40000	27		62 Bde pulled out into their Wagon Lines and came into Corps. Mobile Reserve.	

Noel Chance
Major
BM 12 Div. A.T.

1/5/18

(A7092). Wt. W12839/M1293. 750,000. 1/17. D. D. & L., Ltd. Forms/C.2118/14.

S E C R E T.

12th Divisional Artillery Order No. 99.

34th Army Bde., R.F.A.
48th Army Bde., R.F.A.
62nd Brigade, R.F.A.
63rd Brigade, R.F.A.
282nd Army Bde, R.F.A.
D. T. M. O.
Liaison Officer
and to 38th Divn. (G).)
17th, 35th & 2nd Aust. D.A.)
R.A. V Corps. H.A. V Corps.) for information.
157th Brigade, R.F.A.)
113th, 114th, 115th Inf. Bdes.)

38th Dm G.O.

Ref. Sheet 57D S.E. 1/20,000. 21st April, 1918.

1. On the evening of the 22nd instant the 38th and 35th Divisions will capture and consolidate the line W 21 b central - 16 a 0 0 - 10 c 0 7 - 4 c 8 0 - 4 b 1 3.

The Dividing line between the Divisions is a line drawn East and West through W 10 c 0 7.

2. The attack on that part of the objective allotted to the 38th Division will be carried out by G.O.C. 113th Brigade.

3. The 19th D.L.I. (35th Division) have been ordered to capture and consolidate the line W 10 c 0 7 - W 9 b 9 3 and will come under the orders of G.O.C. 113th Brigade from Zero until this line is captured.

4. In support of this Operation the Artillery will fire a Creeping and Protective barrage.

5. The Creeping Barrage will open as shewn on the accompanying tracing at Zero hour. The 34th Army Brigade R.F.A. at Zero plus 4 minutes will creep forward at the rate of 100 yards every 3 minutes, the remaining Brigades joining in and moving forward at Zero plus 10 minutes. At Zero plus 16 minutes the whole barrage will pause for 6 minutes until Zero plus 22 minutes when it will again creep forward at the rate of 100 yards every 3 minutes until it reaches the Protective Barrage line (marked red in tracing) where it will stand until Zero plus 50 minutes.

6. At Zero plus 50 minutes all 18 prs. will creep forward by 100 yards lifts every 3 minutes to the Railway where they will stop for 30 minutes, after which they will jump back to the Protective Barrage line until Zero plus 2 hours 30 minutes.

If during the period they are creeping forward to the Railway, the S.O.S. signal goes up they will at once jump back to the Protective Barrage line.

7. The following 18 prs. will enfilade roads and trenches as under, lifting in all cases with the frontal barrage -

(a)	6 - 18 prs.	282nd Bde.	Trench W 15 c 8 0 to D 8 2.
(b)	2 - 18 prs.	17th D.A.	Sunken Rd. W 15 d 7 5 to W 22 a 1 9.
(c)	2 - 18 prs.	48th Bde.	W 15 a 65 50 to W 15 d 7 5
(d)	2 - 18 prs.	A/63.	W 9 c 8 1 to W 9 d 9 5
(e)	2 - 18 prs.	35th D.A.	W 15 b 9 3 to W 16 c 0 5
(f)	2 - 18 prs.	48th Bde.	W 15 b 9 3 to W 16 b 3 3

They

They will cease fire when the barrage reaches the end of their enfilade and stand by ready to engage any suitable targets.

8. 4.5 inch Howitzers will form a creeping barrage 150 yards to the East of the 18 pr. barrage, with the exception of the 34th Army Brigade, R.F.A., but from Zero to Zero plus 8 minutes 4 Howitzers of the 48th Army Brigade R.F.A. will fire on hollow at W 9 d 25 00, after which they will join the Howitzer creeping barrage.

9. From Zero plus 16 minutes to Zero plus 22 minutes during the 18 pr. pause the 4.5 inch Howitzers will fire on the final objective.

10. 4.5 inch Howitzers of 34th Army Brigade will form a smoke screen from W 16 b 8 0 to W 10 d 9 2 from Zero to Zero plus 1 hour and while the 18 pr. barrage creeps from the Protective Barrage Line to the Railway if the wind is not in the East. If the wind is in the East they will conform to the other Howitzer Barrage.

11. When the Howitzer Barrage reaches the Protective Barrage line the Howitzers will lift on to the following targets until Zero plus 2 hours 30 minutes -

48th Army Bde. R.F.A.	Sunken road W 16 a 95 25 to B 2 3.
34th Army Bde. R.F.A.	After Zero plus 1 hour Bank W 16 c 85 25 to 16 a 85 25.
62nd Brigade R.F.A.	Bank W 16 c 85 25 to 16 a 85 25
63rd Brigade R.F.A.	BRICKWORKS W 22 a 45 45.

12. Two 6 inch Newton T.M. will fire on hollow at W 9 d 25 00 from Zero until Zero plus 8 minutes after which they will conform with the 4.5 inch Howitzer barrage up to the limits of their range when they will cease fire.

13. The Heavy Artillery are co-operating with a 6 inch Howitzer creeping barrage 150 yards to the East of the 4.5 inch Howitzer barrage and by bombarding selected points and hostile batteries.

14. The 2nd Australian D.A. are putting down a barrage to the South of the Divisional Barrage in accordance with V Corps Artillery Instruction No. 132.

15. The 35th D.A. are forming a Creeping Barrage opening on the line W 9 d 0 7 to W 9 b 0 5 at Zero and conforming as to lifts with the 12th Divisional Artillery barrage until it reaches the line running due North and South through W 9 b 90 50 whence it jumps straight to the Protective Barrage.

16. The G.O.C. Infantry Brigade is clearing the trenches in W 21 central.

17. O.C. 34th Army Brigade R.F.A. will detail a Liaison Officer to report to-day to O.C. 16th Royal Welsh Fusiliers who is in the last house in HARLOY on the BAIZIEUX Road. This officer will remain with O.C., R.W. Fusiliers throughout the operation and will arrange to have a telephone laid from his H.Q. in the line to SENLIS MILL and so maintain communication with O.C. 34th Army Brigade. R.F.A. He should take all the necessary signallers with him.

18.

18. Rates of fire -

Zero to Zero plus 35 mins. and during the creep forward from the Protective Barrage line to the Railway -

18 prs. 3 rounds per gun per minute.
4.5" Hows. 3 rounds per how. per 2 minutes.

Zero plus 35 mins. to Zero plus 50 mins.

18 prs. 2 rounds per gun per minute.
4.5" Hows. 1 round per how. per minute

Zero plus 50 mins. to Zero plus 1 hr. 30 mins.

18 prs. 1 round per gun per minute.
4.5" Hows. 1 round per how. per 2 minutes.

Zero plus 1 hr. 30 mins. to Zero plus 2 hours 30 mins.

18 prs. and 4.5" Hows. - 1 round per gun per 2 minutes.

19. 18 prs. will fire shrapnel with the corrector set to allow 50% burst on graze in Creeping Barrages and half shrapnel half H.E. in the Protective Barrage.

4.5 inch Howitzers will use 106 Fuse except where the line of fire forms an angle of 25 degs. or more with due East and West line, in which case they will use 101 Fuse. They will not use 106 Fuse North of PIONEER Road or WEST of ALBERT - HAMEL road in W 10 after Zero plus 12 minutes.

20. Orders as to synchronisation of watches and Zero hour will be issued later.

Please Acknowledge.

Noel Chance
Major,
Brigade Major, 12th D. A.

Issued at 3 p.m.

S E C R E T.

AMENDMENT No. 1 to 12th DIVISIONAL ARTY. ORDER No. 99.

1. Delete para. 6 and substitute -

"At Zero plus 50 minutes all 18 prs. will creep forward by 100 yards lifts every 2 minutes as far as the Railway when they will form a protective barrage 200 yards East of the Railway until Zero plus 1 hour 30 minutes.

This barrage will then drop back in irregular jumps to the original Protective Barrage.

Batteries which, owing to range, cannot fire A., will fire AX. with 106 Fuse during this phase.

If during the period they are creeping forward to the Railway, the S.O.S. signal goes up they will at once jump back to the Protective Barrage line".

2. Para. 8. Add -

"D/282 will fire on W 16 c 0 0 from Zero until Zero plus 18 minutes".

3. Rates of fire as laid down in para. 18 will be amended as follows -

Zero plus 50 mins. to Zero plus 1 hr. 30 mins.

18 prs.	3 rounds per gun per minute.
4.5" Hows.	3 rounds per how. per 2 minutes.

Zero plus 1 hr. 30 mins. to Zero plus 2 hr. 30 mins.

18 prs. and 4.5" Hows. 1 round per gun per minute.

Noel Chance
Major,
Brigade Major, 12th D. A.

22nd April, 1918.

Copies to all recipients of
12th D. A. Order No. 99.

S E C R E T. 38th Dn. S.S. 125/5. R.A. 12th Divn. 616/1.

12th Divisional Artillery.

x x x

Reference 38th Divn. Order No. 17.

1. Zero hour will be 7.30 p.m.

2. V Corps Signal time will be telephoned from Divisional Headquarters to 113th Brigade Headquarters, 104th Brigade H.Q. and 38th Battalion M.G.C. at 12 Noon and 3 p.m. C.R.A., 12th Division will instruct Artillery Brigade Commanders or their representatives to report at H.Q., 113th Brigade at V 15 a 5 8 at these hours for the purpose of synchronising watches. Watches of Commanders of Heavy Artillery are being synchronised direct from Corps Headquarters.

3. A Contact patrol will be over our lines at 5.30 a.m. and in response to a Klaxon Horn or the firing of Very Lights from the aeroplane our troops will signify their position by waving helmets or (if ordered by 113th Brigade) by lighting flares.

4. A counter-attack aeroplane will be over the objective at Zero plus 30 and again at 5.30 a.m. 23rd instant.

This plane will communicate by wireless with the Artillery and will indicate the position of any hostile troops forming for counter-attack by dropping smoke bombs over that position.

5. 104th Inf. Brigade will be under the orders of G.O.C., 38th Division from Zero till 8 a.m. 23rd instant.

19th D.L.I. will be under the orders of Brigadier General Commanding 113th Brigade from Zero till 8 a.m. 23rd instant and not as stated in para. 3 of 38th Division Order No. 171.

Issued at 6.30 a.m. 22. 4. 1918.

sd. J.E. Mumby, Lt. Colonel, G.S., 38th Division.

2.

To all recipients of 12th D.A. Order No. 99.

Reference above. Please send officers as in para. 2 and arrange that an officer takes this watch after synchronisation to each Battery.

Please acknowledge by wire.

22nd April, 1918.

Noel Chance Major,
Brigade Major, 12th D.A.

S E C R E T.

12th Divisional Artillery Order No. 101.

93rd)
232nd) Army Brigades, R.F.A.
315th)
and to 12th Divn. (G) and (Q).)
V Corps R.A. V Corps H.A.)
17th and New Zealand D.As.) for information.
35th. 36, 37th Inf. Bdes.)
12th Divn. Signals. 15 Squad. R.A.F.)

Ref. 57D. 1/40,000. 24th April, 1918.

1. The 12th Division is relieving the New Zealand Division on the front between the Grid Line South of Q 13, 14, 15, 16, 17 and a line through Q 1 and 2 central - Q 2 b 70 15 - Q 3 a 80 35 - Q 4 a 8 4.

2. The front will be held by two Brigades in the line and one Brigade in reserve. The Dividing Line between Brigades will be the Grid line through Q 8 c 0 6 - Q 8 d 0 6.
The 36th Inf. Bde. (H.Q. - Q 13 b 1 8) will be on the Right.
35th .. .. (H.Q. - P 12 b 9 8) .. .. .. Left
37th .. . (H.Q. - ACHEUX) .. .. in Reserve.
Divisional H.Q. and Divisional Artillery H.Q. are at RAINCHEVAL.

3. The Field Artillery covering the front will be the 93rd, 232nd and 315th Army Brigades, R.F.A. who will be divided into two Groups.
RIGHT GROUP. Covering Right Infantry Brigade, commanded by Lt. Col. W.D. STILLWELL, D.S.O. (H.Q. - P 17 c 8 2) consisting of 93rd Brigade and C/315 and D/315.
LEFT GROUP. Covering Left Infantry Brigade, commanded by Lt. Col. L.G.GISBORNE, C.M.G. (H.Q. - P 17 a 8 3) consisting of 232nd Brigade and A/315 and B/315.

4. Group Commanders will be relieved from time to time. For the present O.C. 315th Brigade will be at the Brigade Wagon Lines.

5. Group Commanders will arrange the details of their S.O.S. lines in consultation with the G.O.C. Infantry Brigade concerned, arranging to overlap the S.O.S. lines of Groups on either flank by at least 50 yards. Map co-ordinates will be forwarded to Divisional Artillery H.Q. by last D.R. 25th instant and any subsequent alteration will be communicated immediately. The M.P.I. of 18 prs. will be as near as possible 200 yards in front of our front line.

6. Rates of fire for S.O.S. will be -
18 prs. 3 rounds per gun per min. for 10 minutes,
then 2 .. .. 5 minutes.
4.5" Hows. 2 rounds per how. per min. for 5 minutes,
then 1 .. .. 10 minutes.
They will then cease fire unless the S.O.S. Signal or order is repeated.

7. Each Group will detail one officer (a Major or Captain) to be Liaison Officer at the H.Q. of the Infantry Brigade which they are covering. He will visit Group H.Q. each day and keep in touch with the dispositions of all the Artillery on the Divisional front.
Group Commanders are responsible that the Infantry are informed beforehand of any shoots or bombardments which have been ordered.

8. If gas shell is ordered to be fired, Battery Commanders are

responsible that it is not fired if the wind is unsuitable or dangerous. Attention is directed to S.S. 134 "Instructions on the use of Lethal and Lachrymatory Shell - March 1918".

9. Each Group will man with an Officer's Party the necessary number of O.Ps. by day or night so that the whole of their Group front is kept under observation. Those Group O.Ps. will be supplied with S.O.S. rockets or grenades, and will repeat all S.O.S. signals on their Group front. S.O.S. signals will be confirmed by telephone or by runner, if the line has been broken.

10. When the enemy is seen massing in his front trenches or when an intense barrage is put down on our front system Groups will order the following Bombardment -

All 18 prs. will open on their S.O.S. lines for 5 minutes. They will then creep forward 100 yards a minute for 5 minutes, then jump back to their S.O.S. lines for 2 minutes.

4.5 inch Howitzers will fire on S.O.S. targets throughout.

Rates of fire - 18 prs. 2 rounds per gun per minute.
4.5"Hows. 1 round per howitzer per minute.

11. Normally, ordered bombardments will take the form of "CRASHES" when all guns and howitzers which can be brought to bear will fire for 2 minutes at rate of 2 rounds per gun or howitzer per minute.

12. During the night Groups will arrange vigorous harassing fire on all roads and communications on their fronts to the limits of range with occasional "CRASHES" on H.Q., likely places of assembly or ration points.

One 18 pr. per Brigade will be run forward to different sites each night under arrangements which have been carefully thought out beforehand. This gun will fire 100 rounds during the night. Subaltern officers should be detailed by Group Headquarters to carry out this operation.

13. By day all firing should be by visual observation and the earliest opportunity must be taken to check S.O.S. lines from our front system.

14. The Heavy Artillery covering the Divisional front will be the 35th Heavy Group - Lt. Col. MITCHELL, D.S.O. and the 93rd Heavy Group - Lt. Col. MOULTRIE, D.S.O.

15. The command of the Artillery covering the front passes to B.G., C.R.A., 12th Division at 6 a.m. 25th instant, after which the hour arrangements detailed above will come into force.

PLEASE ACKNOWLEDGE.

Noel Chance
Major,
Brigade Major, 12th D. A.

C. R. A.

12th DIVISION,

MAY 1918.

CONFIDENTIAL.

W A R   D I A R Y

Headquarters, 12th Divisional Artillery,

May, 1918.

(Vol. XXXVI).

Army Form C. 2118.

WAR DIARY
or
INTELLIGENCE SUMMARY.
(*Erase heading not required.*)

Instructions regarding War Diaries and Intelligence Summaries are contained in F. S. Regs., Part II. and the Staff Manual respectively. Title pages will be prepared in manuscript.

May 1918 Vol XXXVI

H.Q. 12 Div Arty

Sheet 1

Place	Date	Hour	Summary of Events and Information	Remarks and references to Appendices
RAINCHEVAL	1.		The Divisional front is to be held by 3 Inf Bdes in the line permanently. (See D.A.O.102) H.Q. 315 Bde. (Lt Col HIGGINBOTHAM D.S.O.) went into action to command his brigade covering the centre subsector.	
57D 1/40,000	3.		The 62 Bde. went into action as a 'silent' Bde to cover the Divisional front: in addition to the 3 Bdes. now in the line. Enemy put down a creeping barrage of all natures of guns for 6 minutes.	
	4.		New S.O.S. lines as ordered by the Corps came into force at 5 pm. 1 Section per Battery 63rd Bde R.F.A. relieved 1 section 315 Army Bde. R.F.A.	
	5.		Remainder of 63rd Bde. relieved 315 Army Bde. R.F.A who on relief joined the 17th Div. Arty.	
	14		62 Bde. moved into new positions and relieved the 232 Bde. covering the Left Inf Bde. The 232 Army Bde became a 'silent' Bde.	
	16.		37th Inf Bde. carried out a raid at 9.20pm. Raid went according to programme and was over in 35 minutes. Took 3 prisoners: identification normal.	
	18.		63rd (Naval) Division on our right carried out a raid with 2 Coys and took 4 prisoners and 4 machine guns. 93rd Army Bde. R.F.A + D/63 assisted.	
	20.		Div. Front now held by 2 Inf. Bdes in the line and 1 in Reserve. Artillery therefore divided into 2 groups. Right group under Lt Col. THOMPSON C.M.G. D.S.O. consists of 63rd Bde (less B+C batteries) and A.B.C 93rd Army Bde. Left group under Lt Col LORNNE D.S.O. consists of 62nd Bde + B+C 63rd Bde. with 232 Bde. 'silent'.	
	24		The Div. raided Enemy trenches in Q17 and Q18 (see orders attached) in conjunction with 63 (Naval) Div on our right. Strength of Div raiding party 1 Batt. (36 Inf Bde) The terrain of the raid was difficult being on a steep down slope. Zero was 11.15pm and cease fire went at 2 am. (25th inst). The	

(A7092). Wt. W12839/M1293. 750,000. 1/17. D. D. & L., Ltd. Forms/C.2118/14.

Army Form C. 2118.

Instructions regarding War Diaries and Intelligence Summaries are contained in F. S. Regs., Part II. and the Staff Manual respectively. Title pages will be prepared in manuscript.

May 1918
Vol XXXVI

WAR DIARY
or
INTELLIGENCE SUMMARY.
(Erase heading not required.)

H.Q. 12 Div. Arty.

Sheet 2.

Place	Date	Hour	Summary of Events and Information	Remarks and references to Appendices
RAINCHEVAL	24		two divisions captured 1 officer 31 O.R. and 12 machine guns. Infantry expressed their satisfaction in the Artillery support and the Army Commander sent a message of congratulation to the divisions.	
	25		1 section 78th + 79th Bde (17th Div Arty) relieved 1 section 93rd and 232nd Army Bdes.	
	26		Remaining sections of 17 Div Arty relieved the 93rd and 232 Army Bdes who moved to HARPONVILLE and came into Corps Mobile Reserve.	
BEAUQUESNE	27.		17 Div. took over command of the sector at 4. am and Division H.Q. moved to VALVION and the Div. Arty H.Q to BEAUQUESNE.	
	30.		The Div. came into GHQ. reserve ready to move at six hours notice.	
			Throughout the month the enemy Artillery have been active, causing much annoyance by employing our system of "crashes" put down anywhere without any apparent method or target. Gas shells have been freely used. Altogether a trying month for the Artillery but there have been few casualties. The sector cannot be called a 'noisy' sector but it is certainly far from quiet or pleasant.	

(A7092). Wt. W12839/M1293. 75,000. 1/17. D. D. & L., Ltd. Forms/C.2118/14.

31. 5. 18

[signature]
Major
B.M. 12th D.A.

1

S E C R E T.

12th Divisional Artillery Order No. 102.

93rd, 232nd, 315th Brigades, R.F.A.
D. T. M. O.
and to 12th Divn. (G); 12th Divn (Q).)
12th Divn. Signals.)
D.M.G.C.) for information
V Corps R.A., V Corps H.A.) (without map).
17th & New Zealand D.As.)
35th, 36th, 37th Inf. Bdes.)
15 Squadron, R.A.F.)

93 Bde R.F.A.

1st May, 1918.

1. The Divisional front will be held in future by three Brigades permanently in the line, with -

36th Infantry Brigade	holding	Right Sub-Sector.
37th	..	Centre ..
35th	..	Left ..

2. Inter-Brigade Boundaries are shown on the attached tracing.

3. The Field Artillery covering the Division remains the same but will be sub-divided tonight 1/2nd. so that -

93rd Army Brigade R.F.A.	covers the	36th Infantry Brigade.
315th	..	37th .. ..
232nd	..	35th .. ..

4. Officers Commanding Brigades will, as soon as accommodation is available, live at the Headquarters of the G.Os.C.Infantry Brigades whom they are covering.

5. Officer Commanding 315th Army Brigade R.F.A. will take over the command of his Brigade as soon as the Inter-Brigade reliefs of the Infantry are complete.

6. Location statements and S.O.S. lines will be forwarded to this office by last D.R. tonight.

7. As the 93rd Army Brigade R.F.A. has no Howitzer battery the zones covered by the two Howitzer batteries will remain as they are now.
O.C. 93rd Brigade will maintain a line to D/315 and will have the call on 1 Section.

8. Completion of reliefs tonight will be notified to this office by wiring the Code word "HUNT".

Please acknowledge.

Noel Chance
Major,
Brigade Major, 12th D. A.

S E C R E T.

R.A. 706.

12th Division (G).
Vth Corps R.A.
Vth Corps H.A.
37th Infantry Bde.
63rd Brigade R.F.A.

14th May, 1918.

1. Herewith map showing Artillery support for raid which the 37th Infantry Brigade are going to carry out.

2. Blue ink represents 18 prs. which will form a creeping barrage and standing box barrage.
(a) The box barrage from Zero to Zero plus 7 minutes will be formed by the "Silent" Batteries of the Brigades. After Zero plus 7 minutes the Silent Batteries "cease fire" and until STOP it will be formed by the Active Batteries.

(b) From Zero to Zero plus 7 minutes the Active Batteries will form a creeping barrage with lifts as shown on the map.

3. Green ink represents 4.5 inch Howitzers which will fire on the points shown on the map from Zero until STOP with the exception of -

1 How.	at	Q 10 b 97 72	which lifts to	Q 11 a 6 8
1 ..	..	Q 10 b 95 85	.. .. ..	Q 11 a 25 95
1 ..	..	Q 4 d 90 00	.. .. ..	Q 4 d 95 20

at Zero plus 5 minutes.

4. Brown ink represents 6 inch Hows. which fire on M.G. emplacements and strong points selected by B.G. C.R.A. in consultation with B.G., C.H.A. from Zero until 'STOP'.

5. Details as to rates of fire and tasks are being issued by O.C. 63rd Brigade R.F.A. to all concerned. He will also give the order to 'STOP' to all Brigades and to the O.C. 93rd Brigade R.G.A. who will pass it on to the Heavy Batteries concerned.

Please acknowledge.

Sgd. H.W. Thomas.
Brig-General,
C.R.A., 12th Division.

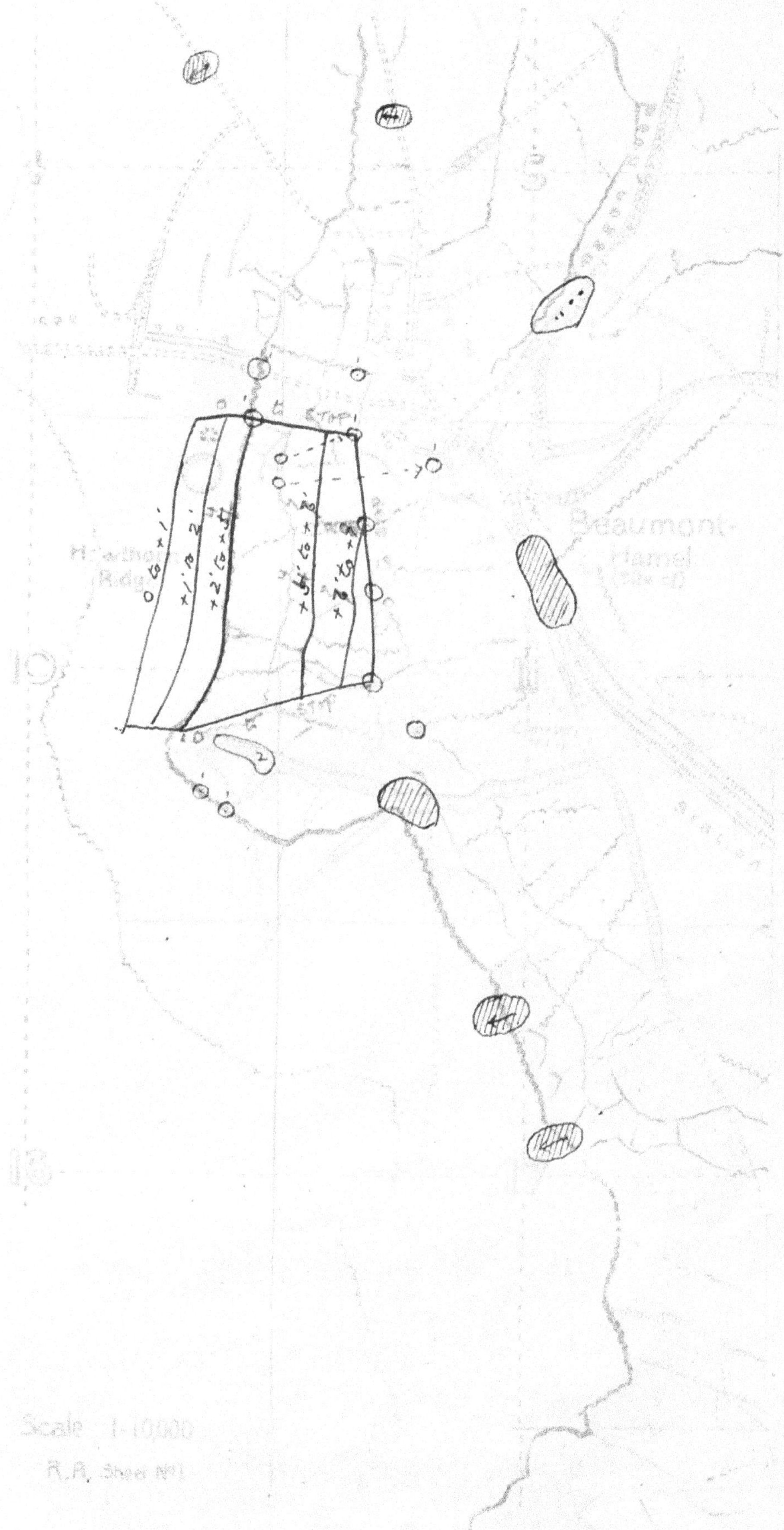

Blue · 18 pdrs
Green · 4.5 Hows
Brown 6" Hows

SECRET.

H.A. V Corps.
S.G. 11/38.

V CORPS HEAVY ARTILLERY INSTRUCTIONS NO. 76.

1. On 16th inst. at a time to be notified later, the 37th Infantry Brigade will raid the enemy's trenches at about Q.10.b.8.3. working up North to the Crater Q.10.b.7.8.

2. The H.A. will support the raid as under :-

From Zero until ordered to stop.

```
67th.S.B.              (a) Area Q.5.d.20.65.- Q.5.d.4.0.- Q.5.d.2.3.- Q.5.d.4.6.
251st.S.B.(2 Hows)(b) M.G. Q.5.a.45.20.
170th.S.B.)            (c) Gas Q.11.a.95.55.- Q.11.b.22.(Dug-outs)
139th.S.B.)                Actual M.P.Is will be detailed later, according to
                           the direction of the wind.
231st.S.B.(2 Hows)(d) M.G. Q.17.a.90.65.
237th.S.B.(2 Hows)(e) M.G.    Q.17.b.15.15.
232nd.S.B.(2 Hows)(f) M.G. Q.4.b.70.35.
237th.S.B.(2 Hows)(g) Ravine  Q.11.c.6.5.
112nd.S.B.(2 Hows)(h) Area Q.5.c.85.05.- Q.5.c.95.05.- Q.11.a.90.85.- Q
                           Q.11.a.80.85.
232nd.S.B.(2 Hows)(i) Trench Q.11.b.10.45.- Q.11.b.4.7.
274th.S.B.(2 Hows)(j) Trench Junction Q.11.b.25.55. Area round.
```

3. **Rates of Fire**

6" Hows. 2rounds per How. per 3 Minutes.
8" Hows. 1 round per How. per 2 Minutes.

4. GAS Concentration vide subpara (c) above.:-

Zero to Zero plus 6 minutes. 7 rounds per How.
Zero plus 15 minutes to Zero plus 20 minutes. 6 rounds per How.

5. The operation will probably last about 30 minutes, Batteries will continue to fire until the order " Stop " is sent from this office.

6. Batteries should if possible datum on the morning of the 16th May.

7. Watches will be synchronised from this office at 3-30 p.m. and 6-30 p.m. on the 16th May.

8. Zero hour will be notified later.

9. Brigades to acknowledge.

P. Raleigh
Major., R.A.

15/5/18. Brigade Major., V Corps Heavy Artillery.

Issued to :- 34th Bde.R.G.A., 35th Bde.R.G.A., 62nd Bde.R.G.A., 93rd Bde.R.G.A., 78th

R.A., V Corps.
C.B.S.O. V Corps.
12th.Div.Arty.

17th Bde.R.G.A.)
58th Bde.R.G.A.) For information.
Ammn.Officer H.A.)

S E C R E T.   Copy No.

Centre Group Artillery Order No. 1.

Ref. Map 57D S.E. 1/20,000.   15th May, 1918.

1. The 37th Infantry Brigade will carry out a Raid on the evening of 16th May 1918, with the object of securing identities and information and inflicting loss upon the enemy.

2. The Raiding Party will consist of 3 Officers and 100 other ranks of the 6th Battalion The Buffs.

3. The enemy's trenches will be entered about Zero plus 5 minutes between Q 10 b 75 30 and Q 10 b 75 70 and cleared between these points.

A party will push forward to about Q 10 b 90 70 and block the trench there, a second party will enter the Crater Q 10 b 70 80 to capture or destroy any garrison or material.

The Raiding Party is expected to return about Zero plus 30 minutes.

4. The Artillery covering the Raid will be -

18 prs.	9 Batteries	(54 guns)	Tasks as in Tables A and B.
4.5" Hows.	2 ,,	(12 hows)	,, ,, Table A.
6" Hows.	5 ,,	(20 hows)	,, ,, Table C.
8" Hows.	1 ,,	(4 hows)	,, ,, Table 3.

These will take part in the Barrage as follows -

(a) Creeping barrage Zero to Zero plus 7 mins. 4 Batteries 18prs.
(b) Box barrage ,, ,, ,, 5 ,, ,,
(c) Protective barrage Zero plus 7 mins. until ordered to STOP - 6 Batteries 18 prs.
(d) 4.5" Hows. and Corps H.A. from Zero until ordered to STOP on points and tactical areas.
Rates of fire are given in Tables A, B and C.

5. Fire will continue until the order "Stop firing" is sent by O.C. 63rd Brigade R.F.A. This order will be sent when it is known that the Raiding Party has returned.

After receiving the order to "STOP", simultaneous bursts of fire from each R.F.A. Brigade (excluding Silent 18 pr. Batteries and 4.5" How. Batteries) will be fired on the line of the Rear barrage at the following intervals of time from a "CRASH ZERO" which will be notified

7 minutes after "CRASH ZERO"
11 ,, ,, ,,
18 ,, ,, ,,
21 ,, ,, ,,

Each burst of fire will consist of 2 rounds gun fire.

6. 2nd Lieut. F. Hatfield Smith, C/63, will be Liaison Officer with O.C. Raid. He will use the following Code words -
"Objective gained" - "CHERRY".
"Raiding Party all back - "BRANDY".

7. Synchronisation of watches will be -
(a) 37th Infantry Bde. and 63rd Bde. R.F.A. 4.30 p.m. 16/5/18 at 37th Infantry Bde. H.Q.
(b) 63rd Brigade and 93rd Army Bde. R.F.A., 62nd Bde. R.F.A., 93rd Brigade R.G.A. 5.30 p.m. at 63rd Bde. H.Q. P 11 b 4 7.

8. Zero

8. Zero hour will be notified later.

9. Please acknowledge.

Lt. Colonel,
Commanding 63rd Brigade, R.F.A.

Copies to -

1 - 5	62nd Bde. R.F.A.	
6 - 10	93rd Bde. R.F.A.	
11 - 13	93rd Bde. R.G.A.	
15.	A/63	
16.	B/63	
17.	C/63	
18.	D/63	
19.	37th Inf. Bde.	)
20.	6th Bn. The Buffs.	) for information.
21.	12th D.A.	)
22.	File	
23.	Spare	

SECRET

TABLE A.

CREEPING BARRAGE.

18 prs.

Phase	Time	Unit	Task	No. of guns	Rate of Fire	Remarks
I	Zero to Zero plus 1 min.	Right Bde.	Q 10 d 40 30 to Q 10 b 50 05	6	3 rds. P.G.P.M.	
		Centre Bde.	A/63. Q 10 b 50 05 to Q 10 b 55 40	6	,,	
			C/63. Q 10 b 55 40 to Q 10 b 60 75	6	,,	
		Left Bde.	Q 10 b 60 75 to Q 4 d 70 00	6	,,	
II	Zero plus 1 to Zero plus 2 mins.	Right Bde.	Q 10 d 50 80 to Q 10 b 63 05	6	,,	
		Centre Bde.	A/63. Q 10 b 63 05 to Q 10 b 67 40	6	,,	
			C/63. Q 10 b 67 40 to Q 10 b 70 75	6	,,	
		Left Bde.	Q 10 b 70 75 to Q 4 d 80 00	6	,,	
III	Zero plus 2 to Zero plus 5 mins.	Right Bde.	Q 10 d 60 80 to Q 10 b 75 05	6	,,	From Zero plus $4\frac{1}{2}$ to Zero plus 5 mins. the rate of fire will be increased to 5 rds. P.G.P.M. as an indication to the Raiding Party that the Barrage is about to lift off the enemy front line
		Centre Bde.	A/63. Q 10 b 75 05 to Q 10 b 80 40	6	,,	
			C/63. Q 10 b 80 40 to Q 10 b 80 70	6	,,	
		Left Bde.	Q 10 b 80 70 to Q 4 d 90 00	6	,,	
IV	Zero plus 5 to Zero plus 6 mins.	Right Bde.	Q 11 c 10 90 to Q 11 a 12 17	6	,,	
		Centre Bde.	A/63. Q 11 a 12 17 to Q 11 a 15 42	6	,,	
			C/63. Q 11 a 15 42 to Q 11 a 20 70	6	,,	
		Left Bde.	Q 11 a 20 70 to Q 11 a 20 95	6	,,	
V	Zero plus 6 to Zero plus 7 mins.	Right Bde.	Q 11 c 22 91 to Q 11 a 27 20	6	2 rds. P.G.P.M.	
		Centre Bde.	A/63. Q 11 a 27 20 to Q 11 a 30 42	6	,,	
			C/63. Q 11 a 30 42 to Q 11 a 32 70	6	,,	
		Left Bde.	Q 11 a 32 70 to Q 11 a 27 95	6	,,	
VI	Zero plus 7 to order to STOP.	Right Bde.	Q 11 c 37 95 to Q 11 a 37 20	6	1 rd. P.G.P.M.	Fire will continue until the order to Stop Firing is sent from 63rd Bde. RFA H.Q.
		Centre Bde.	A/63. Q 11 a 37 20 to Q 11 a 35 45	6	,,	
			C/63. Q 11 a 35 45 to Q 11 a 32 70	6	,,	
		Left Bde.	Q 11 a 32 70 to Q 11 a 27 95	6	,,	

4.5" Hows.

T A B L E A. - contd.

Phase	Time	Unit	T a s k	No. of guns	Rate of Fire	Remarks
Phases I, II and III.	Zero to Zero plus 5 mins.	Centre Bde.	D/63. (A) M.G. Q 10 d 82 42	1 How.	2 rds. P.H.P.M.	
			(B) M.G. Q 10 d 70 52	1 How.		
			(C) 'Y' Ravine Q 11 c 00 65 to Q 10 b 70 70	2 Hows.		
			(D) Trench junction Q 11 c 57 80	1 How.		
			(E) Trench junction Q 11 c 37 95	1 How.		
		Left Bde.	D/62. (F) Trench junction Q 11 a 37 32	1 How.		
			(G) ,, ,, Q 11 a 32 60	1 How.		
			(H) ,, ,, Q 5 c 30 20	1 How.		
			(I) ,, ,, Q 11 a 00 75	1 How.		
			(J) ,, ,, Q 11 a 00 85	1 How.		
			(K) T.M. Q 5 c 30 15	1 How.		
Phases IV, V and VI.	Zero plus 5 to order to STOP.	D/62 & D/63.	A, B, C, D, E, F, G, H and K as in Phases I, II and III.	9 Hows.	1 rd. P.H.P.M.	
			(I) lift to Q 11 a 60 80	1 How.		
			(J) lift to Q 11 a 25 95	1 How.		

18 Prs.

TABLE B.

STANDING BARRAGE.

Phase	Time	Unit	Task	No. of guns	Rate of Fire	Remarks
Phases I to V.	Zero to Zero plus 7 mins.	Right Bde.	Flank barrage from Q 10 d 60 80 to Q 11 c 37 97.	6	2 rds. P.G.P.M.	Rear barrage will be formed by the 'Silent' Bty. in each Brigade
		,,	Rear Barrage from Q 11 c 37 97 to Q 11 a 37 32	6		
		Centre Bde.	B/63. Rear Barrage Q 11 a 37 32 to Q 11 a 32 65.	6		
		Left Bde.	Flank Barrage Q 4 d 90 00 to Q 11 a 27 95	6		
		,,	Rear Barrage Q 11 a 32 65 to Q 11 a 27 95	6		
Phase VI.	Zero plus 7 mins. onwards	Right, Centre and Left Brigades.	Flank Barrage as in Phases I to V until order to STOP is given. Silent Batteries on Rear Barrage stop firing at Zero plus 7 mins.	12	2 rds. P.G.P.M.	

T A B L E   C.

From Zoro until "STOP".	2 - 6	inch How:	will bombard	M.G.	Q 4 b 70 38
	2 - 6	,,	,,	M.G.	Q 5 a 45 18
	4 - 8	,,	,,	Aroa	Q 5 d 25 55
	2 - 6	,,	,,	Quarry	Q 11 a 90 90
	2 - 6	,,	,,	Tronch	Q 11 b 30 62
	2 - 6	,,	,,	,,	Q 11 b 30 30
	4 - 6	,,	,,	Dugouts	Q 11 b 00 45 (Gas shell)
	2 - 6	,,	,,	Y. Ravine	Q 11 c 50 50
	2 - 6	,,	,,	M.G.	Q 17 a 90 63
	2 - 6	,,	,,	M.G.	Q 17 b 15 15

H.Q.,
63RD (ROYAL NAVAL)
DIVL. ARTILLERY.
No. S.T. 374/14
Date 16.5.18

S E CR E T

Headquarters,
315th Brigade R.F.A.
79th Brigade R.F.A.

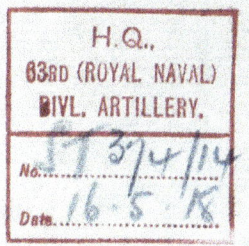

The Division on our Left are carrying out a minor operation to-night (probably about 9.30 pm.), Object, examination and destruction of enemy Post in Q.10.b.8.9.

To distract the attention of the hostile guns, flank artilleries are asked to put down a barrage some distance right and left of the objective.

315th Brigade R.F.A. will therefore be prepared to carry out the following tasks:-

	Task	Rate.	Amm.
(a)			
ZERO + 10 min. to ZERO + 15 "	Put down barrage on enemy lines from Q.23.b.40.80. to Q.17.d.40.70.	3.r.p.g.p.m. 2.r.p.h.p.m.	A BX
(b)			
ZERO + 15 " to ZERO + 20 "	Lift 100 yds. a minute for 5 minutes.	2.r.p.g.p.m. 1.r.p.h.p.m.	A BX
(c)			
ZERO + 20 " tp ZERO + 25 "	Bombard from Q.24.a.40.80 to Q.18.c.40.70.	3.r.p.g.p.m. 2.r.p.h.p.m.	AX BNC *

* If weather is favourable.

Howitzers of 79th Brigade R.F.A. will co-operate in Task (c).

Only active guns and howitzers will take part.

ZERO is the time at which the operation commences.

ACKNOWLEDGE.

G.C. Walford

Major R.A.
Brigade Major,
63rd (R.N.) Divisional Artillery.

16th May 1918.

Copies to :-

12th Div. Arty.
63rd (R.N.) Division.
76th Brigade R.F.A.
78th Brigade R.G.A.
17th D.A.C.
R.A. Vth Corps.

U R G E N T.

S E C R E T.

Copy No ..11...

ADDENDUM NO.1 to
37TH INFANTRY BRIGADE ORDER NO.194
dated 15th May, 1918.

Reference para.1.

ZERO hour will be 9.20 p.m., 16th instant.

ACKNOWLEDGE.

Captain,
a/Brigade Major,
37th Infantry Brigade.

16/5/1918.

Issued at 11 a.m. to all recipients of 37th Inf.Bde.Order No.194

SECRET

S E C R E T

Copy No. 11.

37TH INFANTRY BRIGADE
ORDER NO. 194.

Ref:- 1:20,000 57D. S.E.

15th May, 1918

1. The 6th Battn. "The Buffs" will carry out a raid on night 16th/17th May, 1918, with a view to obtaining identifications and inflicting loss upon the enemy.
Zero hour will be notified later.

2. The strength of the Raiding Party will be 4 Officers, 100 O.R. organised into 4 Groups.

3. Objectives.
Enemy Front Line trench, Q.10.b.75.30 to Q.10.b.75.70., and the Crater at Q.10.b.75.80.

4. Plan of Attack.
Party will form up in "No Man's Land" close in front of our wire, moving forward at Zero.
Enemy's trenches will be entered between Q.10.b.75.30 and Q.10.b.75.70 and cleared between these points, blocks being established on approaches from the South and East. ("C" and "D" Groups).
"B" Group will push forward to about Q.10.b.90.70 to deny enemy approach from the N.E., i.e., Q.10.b.95.85 and vicinity, which show signs of enemy occupation.
"A" Group, covered on East and N.E. by "B" Group, will enter Crater from the S.E. and capture or destroy the garrison or material.
Posts will be established in "No Man's Land" to secure line of withdrawal, which will commence at Zero plus 25 minutes, or on completion of task.

5. Artillery.
As per programme attached - Appx.I.
The relative position of the Infantry and the M.P.I. of the Barrage from Zero to Zero plus 5 minutes, when assault is launched, is shown on Appx.II.
The final lift at Zero plus 5, will be advertised by intensive barrage from Zero plus 4½ mins. to Zero plus 5 minutes.

6. Machine Guns.
As per programme attached - Appx.III.

7. Light Trench Mortars.
As per programme attached - Appx.IV.

NOTE:- Appendices I,II,III and IV attached to copies for 6th Buffs and 12th Division "G", only.

8.All badges........

P.T.O.

8. All badges or papers likely to afford an identification will be removed from the Raiding Party and left behind.

9. Prisoners will be escorted to Brigade H.Q. without delay.

10. Medical Officer, 6th Buffs will make the necessary Medical arrangements in conjunction with O.C., 37th Field Ambulance.

11. Officers Commanding 6th Buffs, 12th Bn.M.G.Corps, 37th T.M. Battery and 35th T.M.Battery will send a watch to Brigade H.Q. at noon on 16th instant to be synchronized.

12. ACKNOWLEDGE.

Norman Smithers
Captain,
a/Brigade Major,
37th Infantry Brigade.

Issued at . p.m.

Distribution:-

Copy No.1 6th Queen's
2 6th Buffs
3 6th R.W.Kent Regt.
4 37th T.M.Battery
5 35th T.M.Battery.
6 Centre Group, R.F.A.
7 D.M.G.C.
8 "D" Coy., 12th Bn., M.G.Corps.
9 12th Division "G".
10 C.R.E.
11 C.R.A.
12 D.T.M.O.
13 35th Inf.Bde.
14 36th Inf.Bde.
15 87th Field Coy., R.E.
16 37th Field Ambulance.
17 Staff Captain.
18 War Diary.
19 File.

War Diary

H.Q.
63RD BRIGADE
R.F.A.
No. 1/1.
Date

REFERENCE CENTRE GROUP ARTILLERY ORDER - RAID.

SECRET.

1. Demonstrations will be made as follows at Zero plus 10 minutes to Zero plus 25 minutes by flank Divisions :-

   (a) 63rd Divl.Arty. Concentrations and Creeping Barrage on trenches in Q.17.b. ~~and c~~.

   (b) New Zealand Artillery will fire from Zero plus 10 minutes to Zero plus 25 minutes; concentrations and Creeping Barrage ont trenches in K.5.a.

2. The following proportions of ammunition will be fired by Batteries during the Raid.

   18-pdrs. Creeping Barrage, 100% Shrapnel.
   Flank Barrage. 100% Shrapnel.
   Rear and Protective Barrage - 50% Shrapnel, 50% H.E.

   4.5" Hows.H.E.- 50% Delay fuzes, 50% Non-delay fuzes.

3. A.B.C & D/63rd Brigade will each send an Officer with a watch to 63rd Brigade Headquarters at X 6 p.m.tonight for synchronisation.

4. ZERO HOUR will be at 9.20 p.m.tonight, 16th May, 1918.

5. Please acknowledge.

Caldwell
Captain.

16th May, 1918.

~~Adjutant~~, 63rd Brigade R.F.A.
for O.C.

Copies to:-
62nd Brigade R.F.A.
93rd Brigade A.F.A.
93rd Brigade R.G.A.
A/63rd Brigade R.F.A.
B/63rd Brigade R.F.A.
C/63rd Brigade R.F.A.
D/63rd Brigade R.F.A.
37th Infantry Brigade.
6th Battn." The Buffs "
✓12th DIV.ARTY.
F.O.O.
File.

S E C R E T.

HEADQUARTERS
R.A. 723.

Right Group.
Left Group.
232nd Army Bde. R.F.A.
and to 93rd Army Bde. R.F.A. - for information.

Ref. Sheet 57D, SE, 1/20,000. 21st May, 1918.

Warning Order.

1. The raids proposed for the 23rd May will not take place.
Instead two raids on a large scale will be undertaken on night 24/25th in conjunction with a series of similar raids to be carried out by the 63rd Division.

2. (a) The 36th Infantry Brigade will raid area about Q 17 central and S.E. as far as Q 18 c 5 3.
(b) The 35th Infantry Brigade will raid area just South of Crater in Q 10 b and as far E. as the line Q 11 a 4 2 - Q 11 a 4 7.

3. To support (a) 232nd Brigade will make all necessary arrangements to move 2 - 18 pr. batteries forward, one battery to position vacated by B/63 at Q 1 c 45 20 and one battery to a position about Q 13 a.
D/232 will move to the new Howitzer position which the Brigade is now preparing in Q 13 d. Actual moves will not take place until further orders but ammunition to the amount of 120 A: 40 AX per gun and 100 BX per How. will be dumped at the positions forthwith.

4. On completion of the raids all batteries and guns which have been moved will return to their present positions.

5. The relief of the 93rd and 232nd Army Brigades have been postponed 72 hours. Details will be issued later.

Major,
Brigade Major, 12th D. A.

SECRET.

63rd (R.N.) DIVISIONAL ARTILLERY
OPERATION ORDER No. 183.
To accompany Appendix 1.
....

H.Q., R.A., 63rd Divn.
22nd MAY 1918.

1. On the night 24/25th May 1918 an operation consisting of simultaneous raids will take place on the whole Divisional front NORTH of AVELUY WOOD, and on a part of the 12th Divisional front.

2. The limit of advance will be the River ANCRE.

3. Raiding troops will be out for two and a half hours.

4. The 63rd (R.N.) Divisional Artillery will cover these operations with creeping and standing barrages co-ordinated with that of the 12th D.A. on the left, and prolonged by the 35th D.A. on the Right.
Silent guns will take part.

5. Brigade Commanders will please ensure that the nature and extent of hostile artillery reply is recorded and reported to these Headquarters.

6. Sufficient ammunition must be dumped beforehand so that the normal amount per gun in on the positions after these operations are over.

7. Gas shell will be fired into THIEPVAL WOOD East of the N. & S. grid-line through Q.30.central if conditions are favourable.

8. The nature of the Corps Heavy Artillery programme (issued separately by H.Q., 5th Corps H.A.) is shown on attached map. *

9. C.B.S.O. has been asked to prepare a programme in the event of counter-battery work being required.

10. Arrangements will be made by Div. Arty. Signal Officer for watches to be sychronised on the 24th May 1918.
Zero hour will be notified later.

11. No mention of these operations is to be made on the telephone.

12. ACKNOWLEDGE.

J. C. Walford
Major R.A.,
Brigade Major,
63rd (R.N.) Divisional Artillery.

Copies of Maps only to *
Copies to :-
* R.A., V Corps.
H.A. V Corps.
* 63rd (R.N.) Division.
12th D.A.
35th D.A.
C.B.S.O.
63rd (R.N.) Dn. M.G.Bn.
78th Bde R.G.A.
* 315th A. Bde R.F.A.
* 317th Bde R.F.A.
* 223rd Bde R.F.A.
63rd (R.N.) D.A.C.
D.T.M.O., 63rd Divn.
Heavy T.M. Bty.
O.i/c Sigs, D.A.
Staff Captain.
Rec. Officer.
War Diary.
File.

TABLE 'A'.

18 pdrs on LEFT INFANTRY BRIGADE FRONT.

UNIT.	TIME.	TASK.	RATE.	REMARKS.
1 Bty, 223rd Bde.	Zero to Z.+ 4.	223rd Bde (1 Bty) from Q.23.d.5.0. (30) to Q.23.d.30.60.	3 r.p.g.p.m.	
3 Btys, 315th Bde.	- do -	315th Bde from Q.23.d.05.60 to Q.23.a.90.75.	"	
	Z + 4 to Z +28.	(Lift 100 yards per 3 mins. to Protective Barrage (223rd Bde (1 Bty) from Q.24.c.90.00 to Q.24.c.80.50. (315th Bde from Q.24.c.80.50 to Q.24.a.00.55. (70)	2 r.p.g.p.m.	
		On arrival at line of Protective Barrage 18 pdrs search and sweep the slopes in Q.24.d.	1 r.p.g.p.m.	
12th D.A.	Zero to Z.+ 4. Zero + 4 to +19. Z.+19 onwards.	Opens on line Q.23.b.90.75 Northwards. Lifts 100 yards every 3 mins. Barrage swings to line of Railway pivoting on Q.24.a.15.55. Finally forms protective barrage covering the line of Railway, Right Boundary joining 63rd Final Protective Barrage at Q.24.a.55.45.		

18 pdrs on CENTRE INFANTRY BRIGADE FRONT.

UNIT.	TIME.	TASK.	RATE.	REMARKS.
223rd Bde less 1 Battery.	Zero to Z.+ 16.	1 - 18 pdr Bty less 1 gun on crossings River ANCRE in Q.29. and Q.30. 1 gun on passage Q.30.a.00.08 (00) to Q.30.c.25.95. 1 - 18 pdr Bty less 2 guns search & sweep THIEPVAL WOOD in Q.30.b. & d. 2 guns on passage running E. from Q.29.d.90.25.	) Zero to Z. + 4 - 3 r.p.g.p.m.) Z. + 4 to Z. + 16) 2 r.p.g.p.m.	
	Zero + 16 onwards.	All the above lift on to THIEPVAL WOOD and search and sweep.	1 r.p.g.p.m.	

18 pdrs on RIGHT INFANTRY BRIGADE FRONT.

UNIT.	TIME.	TASK.	RATE.	REMARKS.
35th D.A. (3-18pdr Btys).	Zero to Z + 4.	From Q.35.c.30.50. to Q.35.d.20.70.	(Zero to + 4 - 3 r.p.g.p.m. (Z + 4 to +14- 2 r.p.g.p.m. (Z +14 to +34- 1 r.p.g.p.m.	
317th Bde. (3-18 pdr Btys).	Zero to Z + 4.	From Q.35.d.20.70 to Q.35.d.50.90. to Q.35.b.40.95.	2 r.p.g.p.m.	
35th D.A.	Z.+ 4 to + 34.	Swing & lift from Q.35.c.60.50 to Q.35.d.60.50. — to Q.36.c.0.8	1 r.p.g.p.m.	

Contd/.

TABLE 'A' (Contd). 18 pdrs on RIGHT INFANTRY BRIGADE FRONT.

UNIT.	TIME.	TASK	RATE.	REMARKS.
317th Bde.	Zero + 4 to Z.+ 34.	Lift from Q.35.d.60.50 to Q.35.d.99.80 to Q.35.b.99.95.	1 r.p.g.p.m.	
35th D.A.	Z + 34 onwards.	Q.35.c.60.50 to Q.36.c.60.50. to Q 36 c 65.75	1 r.p.g.p.m. - Zero +33 to Z.+ 45. ½ r.p.g.p.m. - Z + 45 onwards.	Flank Barrage. Final Protective Barrage.
317th Bde.	Z + 34 to Z.+ 46.	Lifts 100 yards per 5 mins to Protective barrage from Q.36.c.~~60.50~~ 65.75 to Q.36 central to Q.36.a.99.90.	Fire in bursts.	

1 Brigade 35th D.A. opens at Zero on line from Q.35.c.60.50 Southwards corresponding to their S.O.S. lines, and searches and sweeps EASTWARDS to the line of the Railway in bursts. Expenditure averaging 1 r.p.g.p.m.

TABLE 'B'. 4.5" HOWS. on RIGHT INFANTRY BRIGADE FRONT.

UNIT.	TIME.	TASK	RATE.	REMARKS.
Right Bde Howitzers.	From Zero onwards.	Bombard steep banks from Q.36.c.65.70 to Q.36.cont. to Q.36.a.65.99.	Z + 3 to Z + 34 1 r.p.h.p.m. Z + 34 onwards. ½ r.p.h.p.m.	NOT to fire gas.
		4.5" Hows. on CENTRE INFANTRY BRIGADE FRONT.		
Centre Bde Howitzers.	Zero onwards.	Search and sweep THIEPVAL WOOD in Q.30.b.	Z to Z + 30 1 r.p.h.p.m. Z + 30 onwards ½ r.p.h.p.m.	Gas shell if wind is favourable.
		4.5" Hows. on LEFT INFANTRY BRIGADE FRONT.		
Left Bde Howitzers.	Lifts off at + 4.	(a) 1 How on Q.23.d.45.55. (b) 1 How. on Q.23.b.40.20. (c) 1 How. on Q.23.b.35.45.	2 r.p.h.p.m.	
	Lifts off at + 6	(d) 1 How on Q.23.d.75.30.		
	Lifts off at + 10.	(e) 1 How. on Q.23.b.95.60. (f) 1 How. on Q.23.b.95.60.		See Map.
	Lifts off at + 10.	Hows. (a), (b) & (c) along Railway Q.23.d. & Q.24.a.		
	Lifts off at + 10.	Hows. (e) and (f) on Q.24.a.20.50. How. (d) lifts on to slopes in Q.24.d. and searches and sweeps.		
	Zero + 10.	(a), (b) & (c) Hows. lift on to slopes in Q.24.c & d, search and sweep.		See map.
	Zero + 10	(e) & (f) Hows. lift on to slopes in Q.24.b., search and sweep.	1 r.p.h.p.m.	

Table 'C' contd/

TABLE 'C'.

6" NEWTON TRENCH MORTARS on RIGHT INFANTRY BDE FRONT.

	TIME.	TASK.	RATE.	REMARKS.
1 mortar (a)	Z to Z + 2.	On strong Point Q.35.d.35.70.	8 r.p.m.p.m.	
1 mortar (b)	Z to Z + 2.	On Q.35.d.30.99.	"	
1 mortar (c)	Z to Z + 2.	On Q.35.b.41.20.	"	
Mortars (b)& (c)	Z + 2 to + 34.	MILL Q.36.c.15.70.	4 r.p.m.p.m.	
Mortar (a)	Z + 2 onwards.	Switches to Railway Line Q.35.d.30.20.	In bursts.	
Mortars (b)& (c)	Z + 34 "	Q.35.d.50.30.		
		6" NEWTON TRENCH MORTARS on CENTRE INFANTRY BDE FRONT.		
6 mortars	Z to Z + 4.	Bombard QUARRY in Q.29.b.	8 r.p.m.p.m.	
	Z + 4 to + 16	2 mortars Railway Line Q.29.d.80.30.	4 r.p.m.p.m.	
		2 mortars Q.30.c.60.30.	"	
		2 mortars Q.30.a.10.35.	"	
		Those 6 mortars cease firing at Zero + 16.		
		6" NEWTON MORTAR on LEFT INFANTRY BRIGADE FRONT.		
1 mortar.	Zero to Z + 16.	Bombards Q.23.b.90.60.	8 r.p.m.p.m.	
		This mortar ceases fire at Zero + 16.		

SECRET.

12th Division No. G.X. 1466

35th Inf. Bde.
36th Inf. Bde.
37th Inf. Bde.
C.R.A.
C.R.E.
12th Bn. M.G.C.
63rd Division.
N.Z. Division.
17th Division.
V Corps.

---

1. The 36th Infantry Brigade will carry out a raid on the night 24th/25th May - Strength 1 Battalion - Objective the Area Q.17.a.5.1 - Q.18.c.5.2: Q.23.a.4.7 - Q.24.a.1.5. The object of the raid will be to kill and capture Germans and to secure identifications, to destroy dugouts and emplacements and capture Machine Guns and Mortars.

2. The Raid will be carried out simultaneously with a number of similar raids by the 63rd Division: the 188th Inf. Bde. raiding on our right in the direction of HAMEL.

3. The Raid will be supported by Artillery and Machine Gun barrages, details of which will be worked out by the C.R.A. and O.C. 12th Bn. M.G.C. respectively in consultation with the Brigadier, 36th Infantry Brigade.
The 17th Division is supplying one M.G.Coy. to assist in the operation.

4. The hour of Zero will be notified later by B.A.B. Code No. 4.

W.R. Pinwill

Lieut.Colonel,
General Staff,
12th Division.

22nd May, 1918.

1

S E C R E T.

12th Division No. G.X. 1504.

35th Inf. Bde.
36th Inf. Bde.
37th Inf. Bde.
C.R.A.
C.R.E.
12th Bn. M.G.C.
63rd Division.
N.Z. Division.
17th Division.
V Corps.

In continuation of 12th Division No. G.X. 1466 dated 22nd May.

1. As many prisoners as possible will be brought in

Special arrangements will be made by the 36th Inf. Bde. for the collection of documents, maps, paybooks, etc. from enemy dead. Dugouts will be carefully searched before being destroyed.

2. Synchronization of Watches:

(a) A General Staff Officer from Divisional Headquarters will synchronize watches as under :-

H.Q. 12th Divnl. Artillery.	3.15 p.m.	24th May.
H.Q. 36th Inf. Bde. H.Q. 12th Bn. M.G.Corps.	4 p.m.	do.
H.Q. 35th Inf. Bde. H.Q. 37th Inf. Bde.	4.45 p.m.	do.

(b) The C.R.A. will arrange for the synchronization of watches of Field and Heavy Artillery concerned.

(c) The O.C. 12th Bn. M.G. Corps will arrange similarly for all M.G. Coys. taking part.

HMS

[signature]

Lieut.Colonel,
General Staff,
12th Division.

23rd May, 1918.

SECRET

Copy No. 10

ADMINISTRATIVE INSTRUCTIONS issued in conjunction with 36th Infantry Brigade Order No.289.

23rd May 1918.

1. Medical arrangements will be made direct between O.C. 5th Bn.R.Berkshire Regt. and O.C.37th Fd.Ambulance.
5th R.Berkshire R.gt. will be responsible for clearing the area forward of the front line system.
In order to facilitate this O.Cs. 9th R.Fusiliers and 7th R.Sussex Regt. will each allot 8 stretcher bearers to 5th R.Berkshire R.gt. Arrangements to be made by O.Cs. concerned.

2. All prisoners will be taken under escort of 5th R.Berkshire R.gt. to Battn. H.Q. Q.13.c.2.2. where 10 guides will be provided from the Company of 7th R.Sussex R.gt. in the Purple Line to guide parties of prisoners to Advanced Brigade H.Q. P.12.b.8.8. where they will be ~~xxxx~~ taken over by A.P.M.
These guides must reconnoitre the shortest route from Battn.H.Q. Q.13.c.2.2. to Advanced Brigade H.Q.
A N.C.O. should be placed in charge of guides and see ~~xxx~~ that the first prisoners are despatched with all possible speed.

W.K.Hardy Captain.
Staff Captain.
36th Infantry Brigade.

DISTRIBUTION.

As for 36th Infantry Brigade Order No.289.

S E C R E T.
Copy No. 16

Amendment No.1. to Administrative Instructions issued in conjunction with 36th Infantry Brigade Order No.289.

23rd May 1918.

Reference paragraph 2.

The A.P.M. will take over the escort of prisoners at the A.D.S.,BEAUSSART, not at Advanced Brigade Headquarters as stated therein.

Escorts will take all prisoners to Advanced Brigade Headquarters before proceeding to BEAUSSART.

[illegible] Captain.
Staff Captain.
36th Infantry Brigade.

DISTRIBUTION.
As for 36th Infantry Brigade Order No.289.

H.A.,V Corps.
S.G. 11/48.

Amendments and Addenda to V Corps H.A. Instructions No.31 dated 23/5/1918.

Para 3.(a) Delete task of 36th.S.B. and substitute :-
36th.S.B. 2 Hows. Trench R.19.a.50.65. to R.13.d.0.3.
2 Hows. Area Q.30.c.7.8. to Q.30.c.6.3. to Q.30.d.1.3. to Q.30.central.

Para 3.(b) Delete and substitute :-

(b) From Zero until ordered to Cease Firing. Form a Protective Barrage :-
278th.S.B. Q.36.b.0.2. to Q.30.d.7.1.
112th.S.B. R.25.c.0.0. to R.25.central to R.25.a.8.4.
224th.S.B. Area Q.24.central to Q.24.c.85.50. to Q.24.d.1.3. to Q.24.b.4.0.
274th.S.B. Trench R.19.c.10.60. to R.19.a.70.15.
170th.S.B. R.19.a.00.00. to Q.24.b.60.50. to Q.18.d.80.00.
232nd.S.B. (2 Hows.) Q.18.d.80.00. to R.13.a.50.00.

Para 3.(c) Delete and substitute :-

(c) From Zero until ordered to Cease Firing. Engage Targets as follows:-

215th.S.B. Q.12.d.60.25. (Area.)
251st.S.B. (2 Hows.) R.13.a.35.65. (Mill.)
251st.S.B. (2 Hows.) Trench Q.17.b.8.3. to Q.18.a.35.00.
215th.S.B. (2 Hows.) Q.17.b.70.25. (Dug-outs.)
267th.S.B. (2 Hows.) Trench & Road Q.18.b.1.8. to Q.18.b.3.7.
267th.S.B. (2 Hows.) Q.24.b.70.15. to Q.24.d.50.80.
267th.S.B. (2 Hows.) Q.18.central. (Block Road.)
159th.S.B. (2 Hows.) Trench Q.12.d.4.0. to Q.12.d.9.0.

Para 3 (e) Delete and substitute :-

(e) Zero to Zero plus 15 minutes.
251st.S.B. (2 Hows.) Bombard Trench Q.18.c.3.7. to Q.18.c.5.6.
At Zero plus 15 minutes. Block Road Q.18.central.

Para 3.(f) Delete and substitute :-

(f) Zero to Zero plus 15 minutes.
232nd.S.B. (2 Hows.) Bombard Road Q.18.c.40.15. to Q.18.central.
(2 Hows.) Bombard Mound. Q.18.c.70.15. to Q.24.a.75.90.
At Zero plus 15 minutes, these 4 Hows. lift and join Section of Battery in Q.18. and R.13.

Para 3.(h). Delete.
This Section is now available for Counter Battery work from Zero onwards.

Para 3.(i) Delete and substitute :-

(i) Zero to Zero plus 20 minutes.
36th.S.B. Bombard Road Q.36.c.55.45. to Q.36.c.10.00.
At Zero plus 20 minutes. Lift to Eastern edge of Village & continue firing until ordered to stop.

Para 8. Zero hour will be at 11-15 p.m. on May 24th.

Add Para 10. 106 Fuzes will not be used by Sections of 36th.S.B. in Q.30. & Q.36. 224th.S.B. Sect.251st.S.B. on Trench Q.17.b. after Zero plus 15 minutes.

Brigades to acknowledge.

C Raleigh
Major R.A.
Brigade Major,V Corps Heavy Artillery.

24th.May.1918.

Issued to all recipients of H.A.,V Corps S.G.11/46.

S E C R E T.

H.A.,V Corps.
S.G. 11/46.

V CORPS HEAVY ARTILLERY INSTRUCTIONS No. 81.

Reference Sheet 57D. S.E. 1/20,000

1. The 12th. and 63rd.Divisions are carrying out a combined raid on the night 24th./25th.May.1918.

2. The raid of the 63rd.Division will be carried out on the whole Divisional Front North of AVELUY WOOD and will be pushed through as far as the Railway,at least.

The 12th.Divisional raid will be carried out against the Area Q.17.a.5.1. - Q.18.c.5.2. - Q.23.a.4.7. - Q.24.a.1.5. and will be pushed through as far as Railway Road.

3. The action of the Heavy Artillery will be as under :-

(a) From Zero until ordered to Cease Firing. Bombard Trenches :-

108th.S.B.	Trenches	Q.36.a.95.35. to Q.30.c.70.45.	63
87th.S.B.	..	Q.30.c.70.45. to Q.30.b.35.55.	
248th.S.B.	..	Q.30.b.35.55. to Q.24.central.	
51st.S.B.(P.34.a.)	..	Q.24.central. to Q.24.b.60.50.	X
36th.S.B.(4)	..	R.19.a. and R.13.c.	

(b) From Zero until ordered to Cease Firing. Form a Protective Barrage :-

278th.S.B.	Q.36.central. to R.25.c.00.00.	
** 112th.S.B.	R.25.c.00.00. to R.25.central.	**)Search Area West for 500)yards in irregular jumps
** 324th.S.B.	R.25.central. to R.19.d.00.40.	)during the operations.
274th.S.B.	R.19.d.00.40. to R.19.a.00.00.	X
170th.S.B.	R.19.a.00.00. to Q.24.b.60.50. to Q.18.d.80.00.	X
232nd.S.B. (4 Hows.)	Q.18.d.80.00. to R.13.a.50.00.	X

(c) From Zero until ordered to Cease Firing. Engage Targets as follows :-

215th.S.B.	Q.12.d.60.25. (Area).	65.07 Trench
231st.S.B.	(2 Hows.) R.13.a.35.65. (Mill.).	
231st.S.B.	(2 Hows.) Q.17.b.25.55. (M.Gs.).	W.O
215th.S.B.	(2 Hows.) Q.17.b.70.25. (Dug-outs.).	
267th.S.B.	(2 Hows.) Q.17.b.35.65. to 75.50. (Trench.)	WO.
237th.S.B.	(2 Hows.) Search & Sweep STATION Road about Q.12.c.1.0.	W
237th.S.B.	(2 Hows.) Q.18.central. (Block Road.)	X
159th.S.B.	(2 Hows.) Q.12.c.00.60. to Q.12.d.00.00.	X ?

(d) From Zero until ordered to Cease Firing. 60-Pdrs. will Search and Sweep Roads,with Shrapnel,as under :-

93rd.Bde.R.G.A.	Two 60-Pdr.guns.	HILL Road. Q.24.d.	
	One 60-Pdr.gun.	Q.24.a.6.0. to Q.24.b.3.2.	X
62nd.Bde.R.G.A.	Two 60-Pdr.guns.	On Miraumont Road Q.18.b.	X

(e) Zero to Zero plus 15 minutes.
231st.S.B. (2 Hows.) Bombard Trench Q.18.c.3.7. to Q.18.c.5.6. X
Zero plus 15 minutes. Cease firing and become available for Counter Battery work.

(f) Zero to Zero plus 15 minutes.
232nd.S.B. (2 Hows.) Bombard Road and Dug-outs Q.18.c.40.15.
At Zero plus 15 minutes. Lift to Mound Q.18.d.10.10. + Q.24.a.70.80
At Zero plus 30 minutes. Lift and join remainder of Battery.

P.T.O.

3.(Contd.)

(g) Zero to Zero plus 20 minutes.
142nd.S.B. Bombard Trench Q.36.c.55.25.to Q.36.a.95.35.
At Zero plus 20 minutes,until ordered to stop. Bombard from Q.36.central to Q.33.d.00.00.

(h) Zero to Zero plus 20 minutes.
56th.S.B. (2Hows.) Bombard MILL. Q.36.c.05.60.
At Zero plus 20 minutes. Cease firing and become available for Counter Battery work.

(i) Zero to Zero plus 20 minutes.
35th.S.B. (2 Hows.) Bombard Road through AUTHUILLE Village W.6.a. and Q.36.c.
At Zero plus 20 minutes. Lift to Eastern edge of Village & continue firing until ordered to stop.

4. Rates of fire.

Zero to Zero plus 15 minutes.	60-Pdrs. & 6" Hows.	2 rounds per piece per 3 minutes.
	8" Hows.	1 round per piece per 2 minutes.
Zero plus 15 mins. to Zero plus 45 mins.	8" Hows.	1 round per piece per 3 minutes.
	60-Pdrs. & 6" Hows.	1 round per piece per 2 minutes.
Zero plus 45 mins. until ordered to stop.	8" Hows.	1 round per piece per 4 minutes.
	60-Pdrs.and 6" Hows.	1 round per piece per 3 minutes.

5. The C.B.,S.O.,V Corps is issuing Counter Battery instructions for the rest of the Heavy Artillery available.

6. Watches will be synchronised at 3-45 p.m. to-morrow 24th.May,at H.A.,H.Qrs. Brigades will send representatives.

7. The operation will probably last about 2 hours.

8. Zero hour will be notified later.

9. Brigades to acknowledge.

P. Rawleigh
Major R.A.
Brigade Major,V Corps Heavy Artillery.

23rd.May.1918.

Issued to :- 17th.34th.35th.58th.62nd.78th.93rd.Brigades R.G.A.

Copies for information to)
C.B.,S.O.,V Corps.
12th.Divn.Arty.
35th.Divn.Arty.
Staff Captain H.A.
R.A.,V Corps.
63rd.Divn.Arty.
Signal Officer H.A.
Ammn.Officer H.A.

S E C R E T. Copy No. 10

36th Infantry Brigade Order No. 289.

23rd MAY 1918.

REF:- Sheet 57d. S.E. 1/20,000. Ed. 5b. (Local).

1. The 5th Bn. Royal Berkshire Regt. will carry out a raid on the night 24th/25th May with a view to inflicting casualties on the enemy and to secure identifications, by means of prisoners and documents, to destroy dug-outs and emplacements, and capture Machine Guns and Mortars.

2. The raid will be carried out simultaneously with a number of similar raids, by the 63rd Division, the ANSON Battalion raiding on our immediate right in the direction of HAMEL.

3. The boundaries of the area to be raided are as under :-

Western boundary :- Present British Front Line from Q.23.a.30.80 to Q.17.a.5.1.

Southern boundary:- Q.23.a.3.8. - Q.23.b.15.90. and along the Trench, inclusive, through Q.23.b.5.7. and Q.23.b.70.65 to the point where HILL ROAD cuts the Railway at Q.24.a. 15.55.

Northern Boundary:- Q.17.a.5.1. - Q.17.a.7.0. - thence along Trench inclusive, through Q.17.d.05.85 Q.18.c.0.4. - Railway at Q.18.c.45.05.

Eastern boundary :- Railway (inclusive) from Q.24.a.15.55 - Q.18.c.45.05.

4. The raid will be made under cover of an Artillery, Machine Gun and Trench Mortar barrage, details of which will be communicated to all concerned.

5. The duration of the raid will be the time necessary for the attainment of the objects stated in paragraph 1.

6. 5th Bn. Royal Berkshire Regt. will establish liaison posts with ANSON Battalion at the following points :-

In British front line ...	Q.23.a.3.8.
On Road at	Q.23.b.15.90.
Trench junction ...	Q.23.b.5.7.
Trench junction. ...	Q.23.b.70.65.
Junction of HILL ROAD and HAMEL - BEAUCOURT Road...	Q.24.a.1.5.

7. Officer Commanding 5th Bn. Royal Berkshire Regt. will arrange with Officer Commanding ANSON Battalion to co-ordinate the withdrawal of their troops.

Liaison posts will withdraw together.

8. Officer Commanding 5th Bn. Royal Berkshire Regt. will be responsible for the defence of the British front line from ZERO minus one hour to ZERO hour, between the limits mentioned in paragraph 3.

9. Officer Commanding No. 3 Section 12th Divisional Signal Coy. will be responsible for communication between Advanced Brigade Headquarters, and Battle Headquarters of 5th Bn. Royal Berkshire Regt.

10. Prisoners of War, and captured documents will be sent without delay to Advanced Brigade Headquarters. All captured material will be sent to Brigade Headquarters, ACHEUX.

11. 37th Field Ambulance will evacuate wounded.

12. Advanced Brigade Headquarters will be opened at P.12.b.8.8. (37th Infantry Brigade Headquarters) at ZERO minus one hour.

13. ZERO hour will be notified later to all concerned.

14. A C K N O W L E D G E.

P. G. J. Gusterbrock
Captain,
Brigade Major,
36th Infantry Brigade.

Issued through Signals at 7 a.m.

** DISTRIBUTION **.

py No. 1. 9th Royal Fusiliers.
2. 7th Royal Sussex Rgt.
3. 5th Royal Berkshire Rgt.
4. 36th Trench Mortar Bty.
5. 12th Division.
6. do.
7. 35th Infantry Brigade.
8. 37th Infantry Brigade.
9. 188th Infantry Brigade.
10. C.R.A.
11. C.R.E.
12. D.M.G.O.
13. A.D.M.S.
14. A.P.M.

No. 15. No. 3 Coy. 12th Div. Train.
16. Staff Captain,
17. No. 3 Sec. 12th Div. Sig Co.
18. War Diary.
19. do.
20. Office file.
21. 37th Field Ambulance.
22. Bde. Transport Officer

S E C R E T.

Addendum No. 1 to

12th Divisional Artillery Order No. 106.,

23rd May, 1918.

Para. 4. - Rates of Fire -

18 prs. Batteries employed on the CREEPING BARRAGE will quicken their rate of fire to 3 rounds per gun per minute from Zero plus 22 to Zero plus 32 minutes.

Please acknowledge.

Major,
Brigade Major 12th D. A.

To all recipients of 12th D.A. Order No. 106.

S E C R E T.   O. 106/2.

Reference 12th Divisional Artillery Order No. 106 -

1. The attached revised Table 'A' should be substituted for the Table issued with the Order, which should be destroyed.

2. LEFT GROUP will fire on Q 17 a 85 80 from Zero onwards with 2 - 18 pr. guns in addition to the 1 Howitzer.

Please acknowledge.

[signature]

Major,
Brigade Major 12th D. A.

24th May, 1918.

Copies to all recipients of 12th D.A. Order No. 106.

SECRET.

12th Divisional Artillery Order No. 106.

RIGHT GROUP 7
LEFT GROUP /2
93rd) Army Bde.
232nd) R.F.A.
and to 12th Dn. (G); Signals; D.M.G.C.) for information.
35th, 36th, 37th Inf. Bdes.)
V Corps R.A., V Corps H.A.)
63rd (Naval) Div.Arty., N.Z. Divl.Arty)

Ref. - Sheet 57D, S.E., 1/20,000. 22nd May, 1918.

1. The 36th Infantry Brigade are carrying out a raid on the night 24/25th May - strength 1 Battalion. Objective: the area -
Q 17 a 5 1 - Q 18 c 5 2 - Q 23 a 4 7 - Q 24 a 1 5

2. Simultaneously the 63rd (Naval) Division is carrying out similar raids.

3. To support the raid the RIGHT GROUP, (which will be augmented for the raid by 2 - 18 pr. batteries and 1 - 4.5" Howitzer battery from the 232nd Army Brigade R.F.A.) will put down a Creeping Barrage and the LEFT GROUP will put down a Flank Standing Barrage (see Map attached).

The action of the 4.5 inch Howitzer batteries and the Heavy Artillery are shewn on Tables A. and B. attached.

4. Rates of Fire -

18 Prs.	Zero to Zero plus 15 minutes	3 rounds P.G.P.M.
	Zero plus 15 to Zero plus 37 mins.	2 .. ..
	Zero plus 37 to Zero plus 60 mins.	1 .. ..
	Zero plus 60 minutes onwards.	½ .. ..
4.5" How.	Zero to Zero plus 37 minutes	1 .. P.H.P.M.
	Zero plus 37 to Zero plus 60 mins.	½ .. ..
	Zero plus 1 hour onwards.	1 .. P.H. per 3 minutes.

All necessary ammunition for the raid will be dumped at the guns before Zero Hour.

The raid will probably take 2 hours.

5. Lt Colonel STILLWELL, D.S.O. will be the Artillery Officer in Liaison with G.O.C., 36th Infantry Brigade and he will be in direct communication with each Group, the Left Group 63rd (Naval) Division and with the Heavy Artillery, the latter through Divisional Artillery H.Q.

O.C. RIGHT GROUP will detail a lisison officer to accompany O.C. Raiding Party.

6. Orders as to synchronisation of watches and Zero Hour will be notified later.

7. Please acknowledge.

Noel Chance [signature]
Major,
Brigade Major, 12th Divisional Artillery.

HEAVY ARTILLERY.

Table "B"

The Heavy Artillery will bombard the following targets from Zero onwards -

Work in Q 12 d 70 10 and any known M.G. emplacements in Q 12 c

Stop on Road and Railway Q 18 central to Q 18 d 35 70

Dug-outs Q 18 c 40 15 ~~from~~ to Zero plus ~~18.~~ 16

ST. PIERRE DIVION Road - R 13 c 68 82 - work
R 13 c 20 50 - possible M.G.
Q 18 d 90 07
Q 24 b 55 55
Q 24 b 30 15

Trenches on hight ground in R 13 and 19.

4.5 inch Howitzers. Issued with 12th D.A. Order No. 106.

TABLE "A"
(Ref. Map 1/20,000.)

Phase	From	To	Unit	No. of Hows.	Target.	Remarks
I	Zero	Zero plus 2 minutes	RIGHT GROUP	3	Q 17 d 07 90	
				2	Q 17 d 45 70 (A)	
				2	Q 17 d 40 50 (B)	
				1	Q 17 d 36 45 (C)	
				4	Q 17 d 15 00	
			LEFT GROUP	3	Q 18 b 00 15 - Q 17 b 75 45	SMOKE (if wind favourable)
				1	Q 17 a 85 80	
				2	Q 17 b 25 10	101 Fuse throughout
II	Zero plus 2 mins.	Zero plus 7 mins.	RIGHT GROUP	2	Target (A) - Phase I	
				2	,, (B) - ,, I	
				1	,, (C) - ,, I	
				2	Q 17 d 30 37 (D)	
				2	Q 17 d 30 15 (E)	
				5	Q 23 b 5 7	
			LEFT GROUP	6	Same as Phase I	
III	Zero plus 7 mins.	Zero plus 10 mins.	RIGHT GROUP	2	Target (D) - Phase II	
				2	,, (E) - ,, II	
				5	Q 24 a 15 45 - 20 72	
				1	Q 18 c 35 64 - Q 18 c 60 60 (F)	
				2	Q 18 c 38 05 - Q 18 c 5 5 (G)	
				2	Q 24 a 30 90 - Q 18 c 35 00 (H)	
			LEFT GROUP	6	Same as Phase I	
IV	Zero plus 10 mins.	Zero plus 25 mins.	RIGHT GROUP	2	Target (F) - Phase III	
				2	,, (G) - ,, III	
				6	,, (H) - ,, III	101 Fuse after Zero plus 22 mins.
				2	Road Q 18 c 65 55	
			LEFT GROUP	6	Same as Phase I	

TABLE "A".

Sheet 2.

Phase	From	To	Unit	No.of Hows.	Target	Remarks
V	Zero plus 25 mins.	STOP	RIGHT GROUP	2 6 4	Target (F) - Phase III Search ST.PIERRE DIVION Road Q 24 b 25 15 to Q 18 d 95 40 On Left Flank Barrage Line - (see Map).	101 Fuse
			LEFT GROUP	6	Same as Phase I.	

6 B'tys Right Group
Z to Z + 4
Z + 4 to Z + 10
Z + 10 to Z + 16
Z + 16 to Z + 22
Z + 22 to Z + 28
Z + 28 to Z + 31
+22 to +25
+25 to +28
+28 to 31
+31 to +37
3 B'tys Right Group Z + 37 onwards
3 B'tys Left Group Z onwards
3 B'tys Right Group
Protective Barrage
Z + 37 onwards

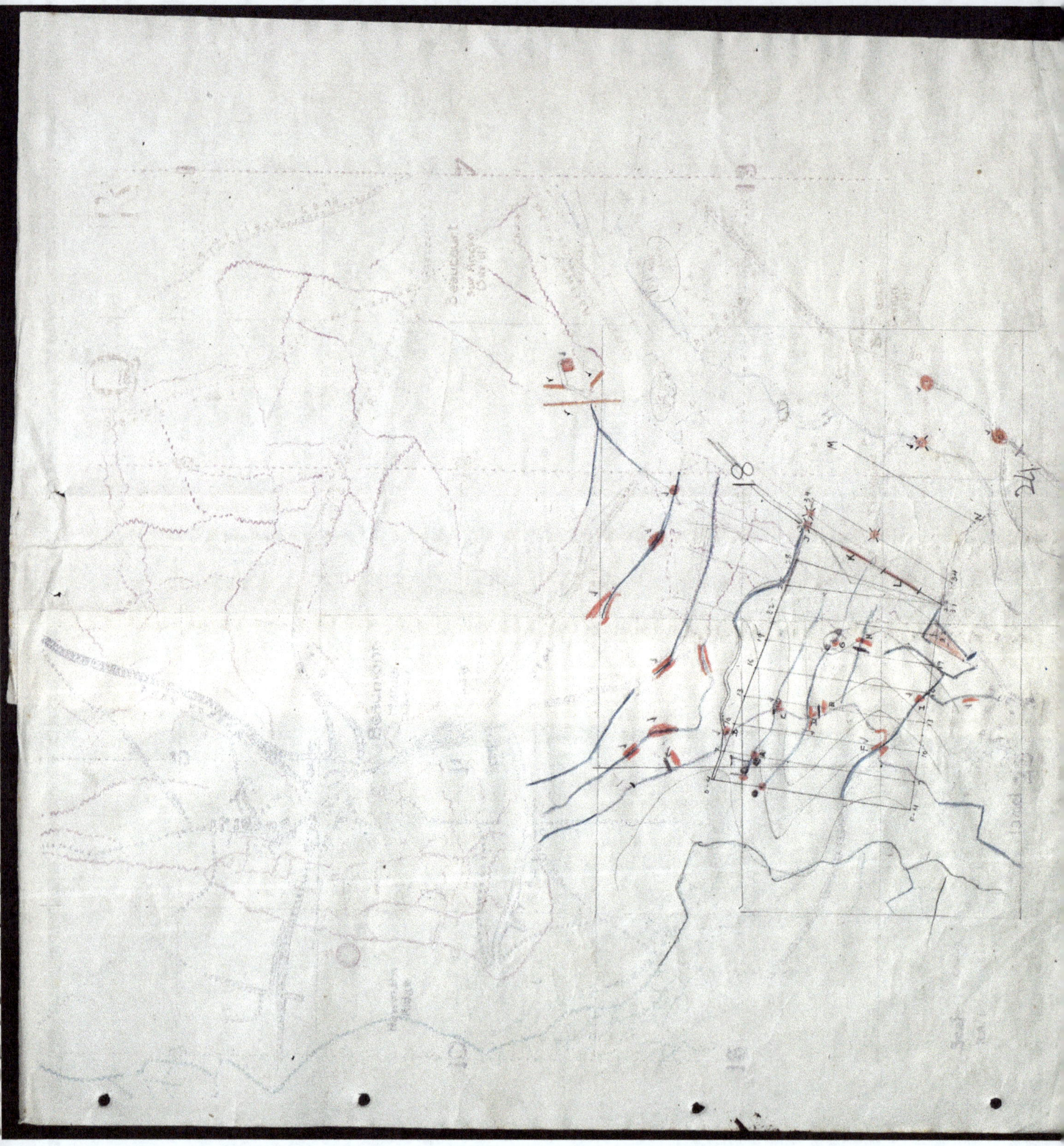

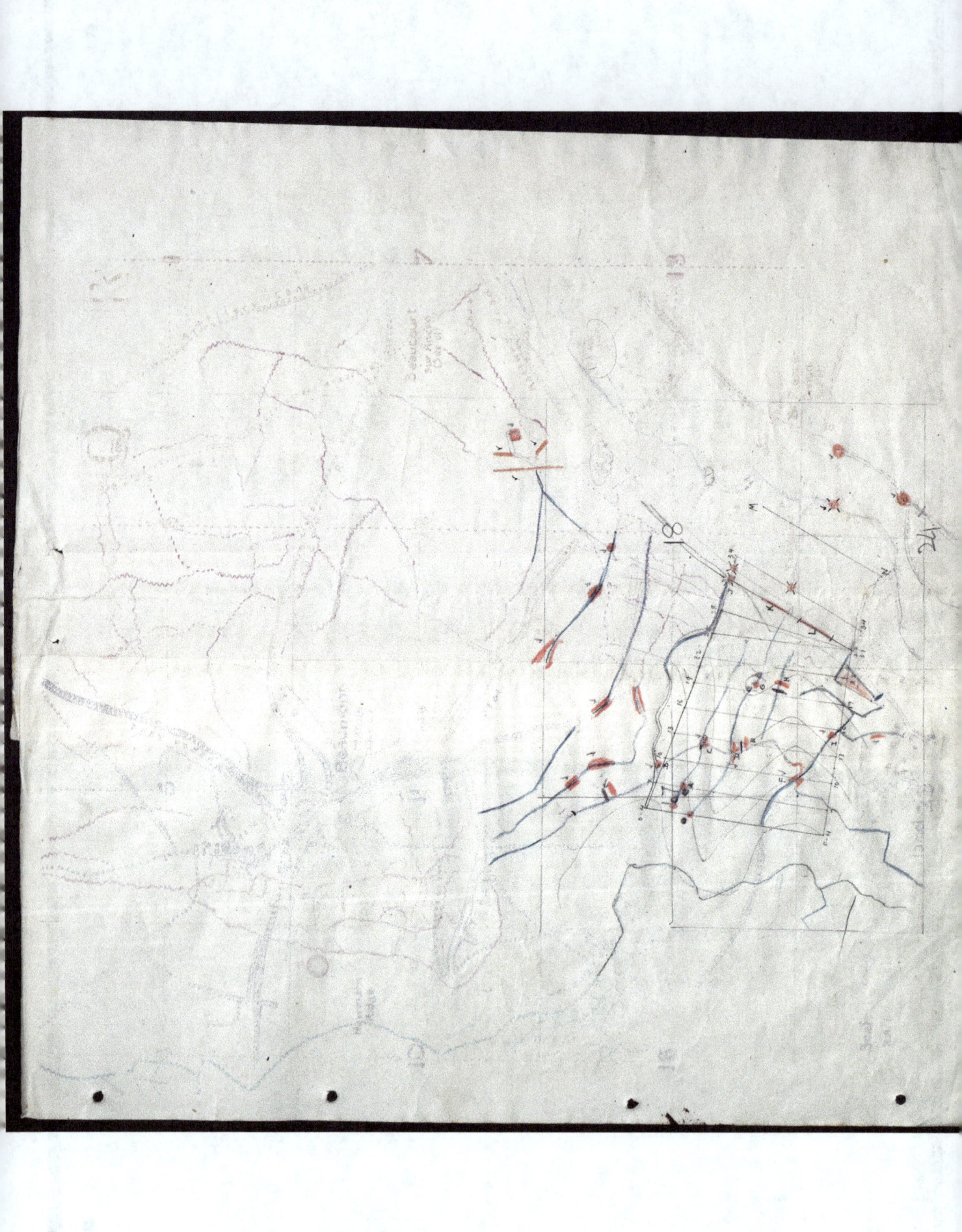

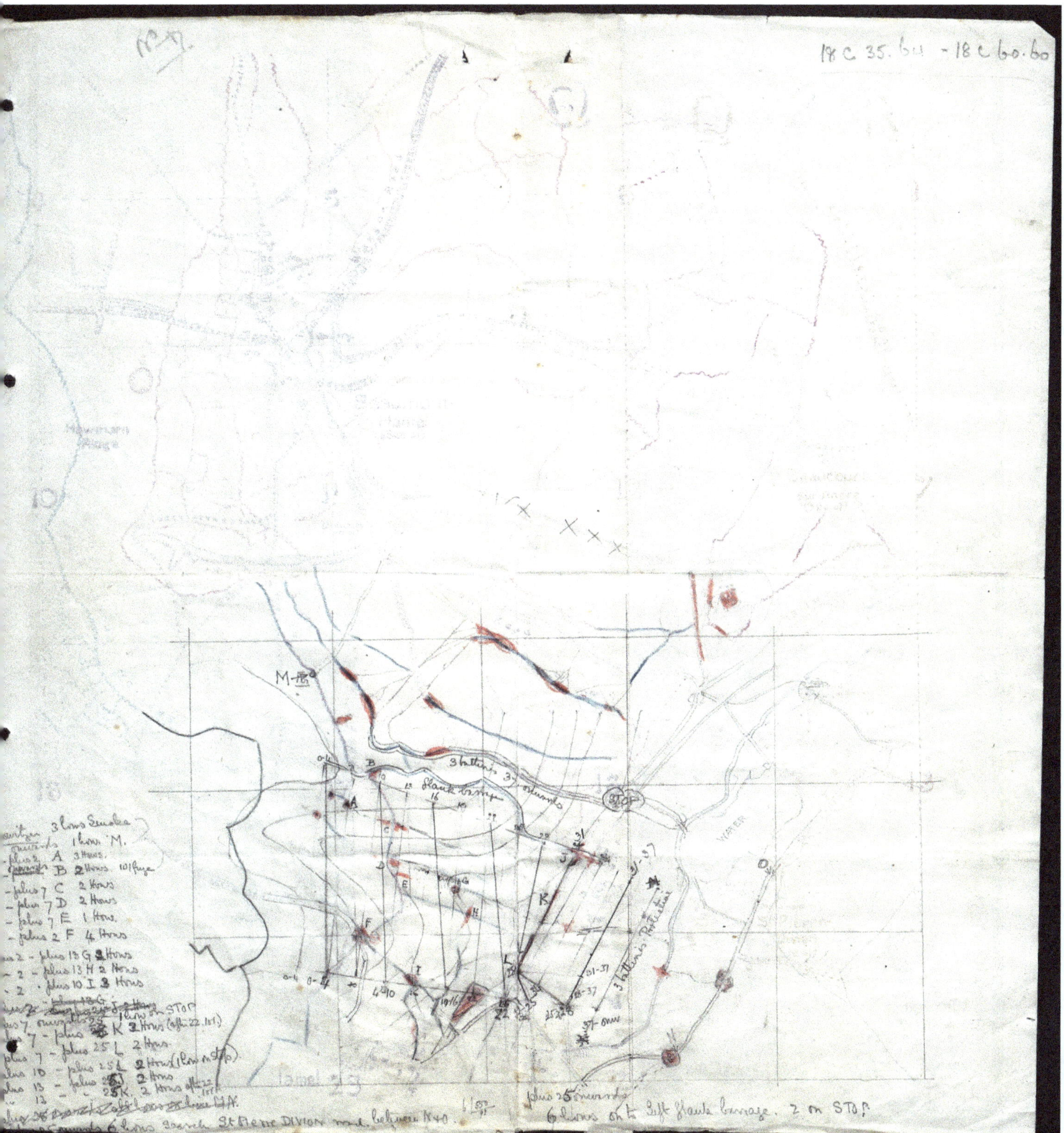

18 C 35. 64 - 18 C 60. 60
M
A
B
C
D
E
F
G
H
I
J
K
L
STOP
WATER
3 batteries 37 onwards
flank barrage
3 batteries Protection
3 hrs Smoke
1 how M.
plus 2 A 3 Hows.
B 2 Hows. 101 fuze
plus 7 C 2 Hows
plus 7 D 2 Hows
plus 7 E 1 How.
plus 2 F 4 Hows
plus 13 G 2 Hows
plus 13 H 2 Hows
plus 10 I 3 Hows
1 how on STOP
K 2 Hows (after 22.101)
plus 25 L 2 Hows
plus 25 L 2 Hows (1 how on STOP)
plus 25 J 2 Hows
25 K. 2 Hows after 22 101
St Pierre DIVION road, between K & O.
plus 25 onwards
6 hows on to left flank barrage. 2 on STOP

S E C R E T.   C.B.S. 69.

COUNTER BATTERY INSTRUCTIONS.

Roforonco V Corps H.A., S.G. 11/46 of 23/5/18.

Countor Battery arrangements for the operations therein referred to will be as undor:-

1. The following Artillery of the V Corps H.A. will be available.

35th.H.A.Brigade.

111th. Heavy Battery.
145th. Heavy Battery.

93rd.H.A.Brigade.

35th. Heavy Battery.)
2/1 Lowland H.Bty.) Less 3 Guns.
231st. Siege Battery:- 2 Hows. after zero plus 15 minutes.
124th. Siege Battery.

62nd.H.A.Brigade.

122nd. Heavy Battery)
126th. Heavy Battery) Less 2 Guns.
67th. Siege Battery.
76th. Siege Battery.

78th.H.A.Brigade.

139th. Siege Battery 2 Hows.

17th.H.A.Brigade.

135th. Heavy Battery.
2/1 Lancs. H.Battery.
51st. Siege Battery (less 1 Section)
56th. Siege Battery (less 2 Hows until zero plus 20 minutes)
13th. Siege Battery.

58th.H.A.Brigade.

6" Guns and 12" Hows.

2. Certain guns will carry out a zero programme as detailed in Table 'A' attached.
The remainder will stand by to engage targets as required, in accordance with information received of hostile shelling.

3. All Brigades will keep this office, quickly and accurately informed of the state of hostile shelling.

4. O.C., 18 Observation Group will do likewise.

5. IIIrd and IVth. Corps have been asked to assist in C.B. work on our flanks.

6. H.A.Brigades and 18 Observation Group please acknowledge by wire.

F. Nasmyth [signature]
Lt. Col. R.A.
24/5/18.   Counter Battery Staff Officer V Corps.

Issued to:-17th.,34th., 35th., 62nd., 78th., 93rd., and 58th Brigades.
18 Observation Group F.S.C.   18 Balloon Co.
15th Squadron R.A.F.   R.A., V Corps.
V Corps H.A.   C.B.S.O. III Corps.
C.B.S.O. IV Corps.   12th. Div. Arty.
35th. Div. Arty.   63rd. Div. Arty.

S E C R E T. APPENDIX TO C.B.S. 69.

TABLE "A"

ZERO PROGRAMME

35th.Brigade. R.G.A.

60-pdrs. R.1.d.15.15., , R.8.d.70.30. R W 6.

R W 4, R.8.c.90.60. to d.00.50.

93rd.Brigade. R.G.A.

60-pdrs. R.14.c.90.80. to R.14.b.10.10., R Y 1,

R Y 2, R W 3.

231 Siege Battery (as soon as available)
Gas Valley R.14.d.30.60. to R.20.a.80.90.

62nd.Brigade.R.G.A.

60-pdrs. R Y 5, R Y 8, R.32.b.80.70. and 1 gun R.27.a.20.20.

67th. Siege Battery. R.13.c.60.65. to 90.70. and R Y 7.

78th.Brigade.R.G.A.

139th. Siege Battery. X.3.b.20.20. to 30.45.

17th.Brigade. R.G.A.

60-pdrs. (4 Guns) Road X.3.a.40.00. to 80.60., X W 7,

R.26.d.50.20., R.26.b.80.20., X.13.c.90.90. to 90.60.

51st. Siege Battery. W X 1., X W 6.

56th. Siege Battery. X.8.c.00.10. to 20.20.

13th. Siege Battery. W X 2.

Rates of fire, bursts average normal rate pending information.

6" Hows. if conditions are suitable will use gas shell as far as possible.

24/5/18.

TABLE 'B' 4.5" HOWS. on RIGHT INFANTRY BRIGADE FRONT.

U N I T.	T I M E.	T A S K.	R A T E.	REMARKS.
Right Bde Howitzers.	From Zoro onwards.	Bonbard stoop banks from Q.36.c.65.70 to Q.36.cent. to Q.36.a.65.99.	Z + 3 to Z + 34 1 r.p.h.p.m. Z + 34 onwards. ½ r.p.h.p.m.	NOT to fire gas.
		4.5" HOWS. on CENTRE INFANTRY BRIGADE FRONT.		
Contro Bde Howitzors.	Zero to Z + 4.	6 Hows. on Railway from Q.29.b.~~30.50~~ 60.80 to Q.23.d.70.~~00~~ 40	Z to Z + 30 1 r.p.h.p.m.	Gas shell if wind is favourable.
	Z + 4 onwards.	Lift on to THIEPVAL WOOD in Q.30.b., search and swoop.	Z + 30 onwards ½ r.p.h.p.m.	
		4.5" HOWS. on LEFT INFANTRY BRIGADE FRONT.		
Loft Bde. Howitzors.	Z to Z + 4.	(a) 1 How. on Q.23.d.45.55. (b) 1 How. on Q.23.b.40.20. (c) 1 How. on Q.23.b.35.45.	2 r.p.h.p.m.	
	Z to Z + 6	(d) 1 How. on Q.23.d.75.30.		
	Z to Z + 10.	(e) 1 How. on Q.23.b.95.60. (f) 1 How. on Q.23.b.95.60.		
	Z + 4 to + 10.	Hows. (a), (b) & (c) along Railway ~~and~~ in Q.24.a.		See map.
	Z + 6 ~~to + 10~~.	How. (d) lifts on to slopes in Q.24.d. searches and swoeps.	½ r.p.h.p.m.	
	Z + 4 to + 10.	Hows. (e) and (f) on Q.24.a.20.50.		
	Z + 10.	(a), (b) & (c) Hows. lift on to slopes in Q.24.c & d. search and swoop.		See map.
	Z + 10.	(e) & (f) Hows. lift on to slopos in Q.24.b., search and swoop.	1 r.p.h.p.m.	

Table 'C' /

SECRET.

63rd (R.N.) Divisional Artillery. S.T. 328/15.

AMENDMENT No. 2. to OPERATION ORDER No. 183, Appendix 1.

24th MAY 1918.

(1) In Table 'A' cancel times and tasks for 12th Divisional Artillery. These have been issued separately to those concerned by 12th Divisional Artillery.

(2) Add :-

O.C., 315th Army Brigade R.F.A. will arrange to have a 50 yard overlap with 12th D.A. on his Northern Boundary from Zero onwards.

J. C. [signature]

Major R.A.
Brigade Major,
63rd (R.N.) Divisional Artillery.

Copies to all recipients of
Operation Order No. 183.

24th May 1918.

To all recipients of 63rd (R.N.) Divisional Artillery Operation Order No. 183.

****

Headquarters, 63rd (R.N.) Divisional Artillery will open at P.27.b.30.30. tonight at 10-0 p.m.

J. C. A. [signature]
Major, R.F.A.
Brigade Major,
63rd (R.N.) Divisional Artillery.

S E C R E T.

O. 106/2.

Reference 12th Divisional Artillery Order No. 106 -

1. The attached revised Table 'A' should be substituted for the Table issued with the Order, which should be destroyed.

2. LEFT GROUP will fire on Q 17 a 85 80 from Zero onwards with 2 - 18 pr. guns in addition to the 1 Howitzer.

Please acknowledge.

24th May, 1918.

Major,
Brigade Major 12th D. A.

Copies to all recipients of 12th D.A. Order No. 106.

4.5 inch Howitzers.

Issued with 12th D.A. Order No. 106.

TABLE "A"
(Ref. Map 1/20,000.)

Phase	From	To	Unit	No. of Hows.	Target	Remarks
I	Zero	Zero plus 2 minutes	RIGHT GROUP	3 2 2 1 4	Q 17 d 07 90 Q 17 d 45 70 (A) Q 17 d 40 50 (B) Q 17 d 36 45 (C) Q 17 d 15 90	
			LEFT GROUP	3 1 2	Q 18 b 00 15 - Q 17 b 75 45 Q 17 a 85 80 Q 17 b 25 10	SMOKE (if wind favourable) 101 Fuse throughout
II	Zero plus 2 mins.	Zero plus 7 mins.	RIGHT GROUP	2 2 1 2 2 3	Target (A) - Phase I ,, (B) - ,, I ,, (C) - ,, I Q 17 d 80 37 (D) Q 17 d 90 15 (E) Q 23 b 5 7	
			LEFT GROUP	6	Same as Phase I	
III	Zero plus 7 mins.	Zero plus 10 mins.	RIGHT GROUP	2 2 3 1 2 2	Target (D) - Phase II ,, (E) - ,, II Q 24 a 15 45 - 20 72 Q 18 c 35 64 - Q 18 c 60 60 (F) Q 18 c 38 05 - Q 18 c 5 5 (G) Q 24 a 30 90 - Q 18 c 35 00 (H)	
			LEFT GROUP	6	Same as Phase I	
IV	Zero plus 10 mins.	Zero plus 25 mins.	RIGHT GROUP	2 2 6 2	Target (F) - Phase III ,, (G) - ,, III ,, (H) - ,, III Road Q 18 c 65 55	101 Fuse after Zero plus 22 mins.
			LEFT GROUP	6	Same as Phase I	

TABLE "A".

Sheet 2.

Phase	From	To	Unit	No. of Hows.	Target	Remarks
V	Zero plus 25 mins.	STOP	RIGHT GROUP	2 6 4	Target (F) - Phase III Search ST.PIERRE DIVION Road Q 24 b 25 15 to Q 18 d 95 40 On Left Flank Barrage Line - (see Map).	101 Fuse
			LEFT GROUP	6	Same as Phase I.	

<u>S E C R E T.</u>

63rd(R.N.) Divn. G.232/2.
63rd D.A. No. B.T. 333/16.

Reference this Office Operation Order No. 183 of yesterdays date.

ZERO HOUR will be 11.15 p.m. 24th May 1918.

Please acknowledge by wire.

Major R.A.,
Brigade Major,
63rd (R.N.) Divisional Artillery.

24th MAY 1918.

"A" Form.

MESSAGES AND SIGNALS.

Army Form C.2121 (In pads of 100).

No. of Message ....

Prefix .... Code .... m. | Words | Charge

Office of Origin and Service Instructions.

Sent

At .... m.

To ....

By ....

This message is on a/c of: .... Service.

(Signature of "Franking Officer.")

Recd. at .... m.

Date 24.V.18

From ....

By ....

ARMY TELEGRAPHS 24.V.18 L

TO ~~TITAN~~ CRA
~~TRIGGER~~ ~~D.M.G. Batt~~
~~TEXAN~~

Sender's Number.	Day of Month.	In reply to Number.	AAA
* G 32	24th		

GGG	453	460	188.	818	023
015	812	005	024		

Raid will take place Hour zero is 11-15 pm

~~#~~. May. 24th.

From TINO G

Place

Time 12.50pm

The above may be forwarded as now corrected.

(Z) Sd J H Andrew Lt for C.G.

Censor. Signature of Addressor or person authorised to telegraph in his name.

* This line should be erased if not required.

W 2186 -M509. H. W. & V., Ld. 6/16.

S E C R E T.

12th Division No. G.X. 1542

C.R.A.
35th Inf. Bde.
36th Inf. Bde.
37th Inf. Bde.
12th Bn. M.G.C.

Reference 12th Division No. G.X. 1466 dated 22nd May, para. 4. and in confirmation of B.A.B. Code Message:

Zero hour will be 11.15 p.m. May 24th.

Acknowledge by wire.

W. H. Pennell [signature]

Lieut.Colonel,
General Staff,
12th Division.

24th May, 1918.

Copies to :- V Corps.
N.Z. Division.
63rd Division.
17th Division.
C.R.E.

12th Div. Arty.

C. R. A.

12th DIVISION,

J U N E 1 9 1 8.

CONFIDENTIAL.

WAR DIARY

Headquarters, 12th Divisional Artillery,

June, 1918.

(Vol. XXXVII)

Instructions regarding War Diaries and Intelligence Summaries are contained in F. S. Regs., Part II. and the Staff Manual respectively. Title pages will be prepared in manuscript.

June 1918
Vol XXXVII

WAR DIARY
or
INTELLIGENCE SUMMARY.
(Erase heading not required.)

H.Q. 12 Div Arty. Sheet 1

Army Form C. 2118.

Place	Date	Hour	Summary of Events and Information	Remarks and references to Appendices
BEAUQUESNE	1		One section per Battery was relieved in the line by 17 D.A.	
57D 1/40.000	2.		Remaining sections were relieved by 17 D.A. and Brigades concentrated in RAINCHEVAL area at 2 hours notice.	
	4.		Div. were transferred to 22nd Corps in G.H.Q. reserve at 6 hours notice to move.	
	4–15		Batteries trained for open warfare & showed great improvement. Much more progress could have been made if the training ground had been more suitable. All greatly benefitted by being out of the line for a bit.	
	15.		One section per Battery relieved batteries of 35 D.A. in AVELUY sector and the Div. was transferred to the V Corps.	
	16/17		Remaining sections & Bde H.Q. relieved remainder of the 35 D.A. H.Q. RA moved to TOUTENCOURT	
TOUTENCOURT	18		12 Div. took over command of the AVELUY sector at 3.15 am.	
	19.		Brig Gen H.M. THOMAS C.M.G. D.S.O. proceeded to England on leave & Lt Col. H.S. WYNNE D.S.O. took over the command	
	20.		Div. Arty cooperated in Division attack on AVELUY WOOD. Enemy retaliation was small in comparison to the amount of shell we fired. A certain amount of gas shell was fired from 5 am to 7 am round our battery areas. Zero hour was 2 am.	
	21.		The Div Arty cooperated in a raid by the 28th Div (on our right). Zero hour 2.5 am. Result of raid was capture of 3 M.G. the enemy having vacated his trenches.	
	25.		One section per battery 93rd Army Bde R.F.A relieved one section per Battery 315 Army Bde. R.F.A.	
	26.		Remainder of 93rd Army Bde R.F.A relieved 315 Army Bde. R.F.A.	

Army Form C. 2118.

WAR DIARY
or
INTELLIGENCE SUMMARY.
(Erase heading not required.)

Instructions regarding War Diaries and Intelligence Summaries are contained in F. S. Regs., Part II. and the Staff Manual respectively. Title pages will be prepared in manuscript.

June 1918
Vol. XXXVII

H.Q. 12 Div. Arty. Sheet II

Place	Date	Hour	Summary of Events and Information	Remarks and references to Appendices
TOUTENCOURT	29.		315 Army Bde. came into the line under the orders of O.C. 63 Bde. R.F.A. in order to support a minor operation –	
	30.		The Div. carried out a minor operation on Order No 110. They captured 21 prisoners + 2 m.g. & consolidated on the line W15 d 8.0 northwards along enemy support line to W15 d 8.7 to W15 d 5.9 to W15 d 3.7 to W15 c 8.4. Two strong points at W15 d 8.7 and W15 d 5.9 are already wired & two C.Ts dug across no-mans land. One S.O.S. went up at 2.10 am on 1/7/18 but quieted down at 2.25 am. Counter preparation was fired at 3.15 am for 15 minutes.	

1.7.18

M. L. Chance [signature]
Major.
Bm, 12 Div Arty

(A7092). Wt. W12839/M1293. 750,000. 1/17. D. D. & L., Ltd. Forms/C.2118/14.

S E C R E T.
V CORPS.
G.S. 435.
14th JUNE, 1918.

THIRD ARMY.

1. The following outline plan is put forward for a "simulated" attack on that portion of AVELUY WOOD held by the enemy.

2. (a) The attack to take place on the night 19th/20th June.
(b) The imaginary Infantry attack to be made under cover of Creeping Artillery and Machine gun barrages, combined with a very heavy Trench Mortar fire.
(c) The imaginary Infantry objective will be roughly the line of No. 5. ride.
(d) Gas shell will be fired on all approaches.
(e) Counter-battery work will be intense from Zero onwards and Heavy Artillery will fire on all roads and tracks.
(f) Smoke will be used on the flanks if the wind suits.
(g) Suggested hour of Zero about 2 a.m.
(h) A very heavy Artillery and Trench Mortar bombardment will be put down on the Wood from Zero minus 2 hours to Zero minus 5 minutes.
(i) The Creeping barrage will remain on the front line for 3 minutes and lift back 50 yards every 2 minutes to the line of Ride 5. and then lift to the line of the Protective barrage (About Ride No. 7.) where it will remain until Zero plus 40 minutes at which time it will lift back direct on to enemy front line where it will remain until Zero plus 50 minutes at which hour all fire will cease.
Trench Mortars and 18-pdrs will form the creeping barrage. 4.5" Hows will enfilade selected trenches, 6" and Heavy Hows. will form a barrage 150 yards ahead of the creeping barrage and for the last 10 minutes will fire irregularly over whole area of Wood.
(j) There will be no fire on communications between Zero plus 50 minutes and Zero plus 3 hours 50 minutes unless movement is seen.
At Zero plus 3 hours 50 minutes whole area will be bombarded for 5 minutes.
(k) By arrangement with Third Army all available long range guns will shell known enemy Headquarters.

3. Third Army will arrange for the following if possible :-
(a) On Z - 1 Day.
(i) Concentration of Balloons.
(ii) Movement of troops.
(in this connection the relief of 35th Division by 12th Division will provide movement in the Corps Area).
(iii) Night bombing of known Headquarters.

(b) On Z Day.
(i) Low flying aeroplanes with bombs and Lewis guns.
(ii) Long Distance Aeroplane reconnaissance.

4. The following additional measures will be taken to give the impression of an impending attack :-
(a) Deliberate registration will be carried out during the three preceding days by single guns placed for preference in new or unoccupied positions.
(b) Dummy messages bearing on the operation will be sent by wireless which will be very active.
(c) All telephonic communications will be suspended for about 18 hours previous to Zero.
Previous to this, arrangements will be made for several "indiscreet" conversations over the telephone.

Lieutenant-General,
Commanding V Corps.

VERY SECRET.

V Corps
GS. 435.
14th June, 1918.

12th Division.
17th Division.
35th Division.
58th Division.
63rd Division.

Herewith for your information copy of outline plan of Chinese Attack on AVELUY WOOD, submitted to Third Army.

Orders for this attack will be issued later.

Right and Centre Divisions in the line will complete the installation of Trench Mortars and the dumping of the necessary ammunition as already arranged, by the night of June 19th.

(Sgd) J.M.R. HARRISON, Lt.Col.
for B.G., G.S.,
V Corps.

Copy to :-
G.O.C., R A.
Q.

(2). 12th Division No. G.X. 2169.

C.R.A.
C.R.E.
35th Inf. Bde.
36th Inf. Bde.
37th Inf. Bde.
12th Bn. M.G.C.

For information.

Lieut.Colonel,
General Staff,
12th Division.

16th June, 1918.

COPY No. 2

SECRET

VTH CORPS ARTILLERY INSTRUCTION NO.158

16th JUNE 1918

1. On a date and at an hour to be notified later, a Chinese attack will be made on the Southern portion of AVELUY wood, accompanied by a heavy bombardment of the Northern portion of the Wood.

2. The attack will be preceded by a preliminary bombardment which will be carried out by Corps Heavy Artillery, 4.5" Howrs. of Field Artillery of Right and Centre Divisions.
All Heavy Trench Mortars available, and Medium T.M.Batteries of Right and Centre Divisions will take part.
This Bombardment will begin at ZERO minus 2 hours and continue till ZERO minus five minutes; and will include :-

(a) the portion of AVELUY WOOD that lies SOUTH and EAST of our present front line, and

(b) the trenches in Q.35.b, W.10.b. and d.

Programmes will be drawn up in consultation between Divisions and B.G.,C.H.A.
During this preliminary bombardment, Counter Battery Work will be carried out actively on hostile batteries that are reported to be firing.

3. From ZERO minus five minutes to ZERO, all guns will be silent.

4. For the period from ZERO to ZERO plus 50 minutes, the action of the Field Artillery of Right and Centre Divisions, and of Corps H.A. is shewn on TABLES "A" and "B" attached.
During this period the C.B.S.O. will carry out such Counter Batty. work as is possible. B.G.,C.H.A. will arrange to allot any available batteries to the C.B.S.O.,for this purpose.

5. From ZERO plus 50 minutes to ZERO plus three hours and 50 mins. all fire will cease, with the following exceptions :-

(i) Counter Battery work on hostile batteries that are active, will be vigorous: gas will be freely used.

(ii) Any movement observed in hostile lines will be engaged.

6. From ZERO plus three hours and 50 mins to ZERO plus three hours and 55 minutes, artillery action will be as laid down in table "C"

7. RATES OF FIRE

(a) From ZERO minus two hours to ZERO minus 5 minutes :-

6" and 4.5" Howrs.	One round a gun every two minutes
Heavy Howrs.	One round a gun every four minutes
6" Trench Mortars	As arranged by Divisions.

(b)......./

7.
(b) From ZERO onwards :-

	Zero to zero plus 35 mins.	Zero plus 35 mins. to zero plus 50 mins.	Zero plus 3 hrs. 50 mins. to zero plus 3 hrs 55 mins.
18 pdrs.	3 rds.per gun per minute.	3 rds.per gun per two minutes.	3 rds.per gun per minute.
4.5" Howrs.	3 rds. per gun per two minutes	3 rds.per gun per four minutes.	2 rds.per gun per minute.
6" Howr. & 60 pdrs.	1 rd. per gun per minute.	1 rd. per gun per two minutes.	1 rd. per gun per minute.
Heavy Howrs.	1 rd. per gun per two minutes.	1 rd. per gun per four minutes.	1 rd. per gun per two minutes.

Trench Mortars ----as ordered by Divisions-----------------

8. No firing will take place from batteries in silent areas.

9. The B.G.,C.H.A. will arrange with the Right and Centre Divisions as to the clearing of any of our trenches that may be necessary for the preliminary bombardment and for the period from ZERO to ZERO plus 50 minutes.

10. Adjustments of Artillery for the purposes of this operation will take place as shown below :-

(a) 18 pdrs., 4.5" Howrs., 6" Howrs., and 60 pdr Sections or Batteries in silent areas will be moved forward to take part, and will be registered.

(b) The three 6" Howr. batteries of 34th Bde.R.G.A., and the two 60 pdr batteries of 17th Bde.R.G.A. will be brought into the line and registered.

(c) Six 6" Medium Trench Mortars of 35th Division, will be lent to each of the Right and Centre Divisions to re-inforce. These Trench Mortars will be manned by the reserve personnel of the T.M.Batteries of the Right and Centre Divisions, and will be mounted in the alternative positions which have been prepared.

11. Registration of active batteries and sections on the area of attack will be commenced forthwith.

12. Synchronisation of watches will be carried out under arrangements to be notified later.

13. Div.Artys. and C.H.A. to acknowledge.

Lieut.Colonel
For B.G.,G.S.,Vth Corps

Issued at 7-30 p.m.

Copy.No.1 12th Div.	9.63rd Div.	17.15 Squadron R.A.F.
2.12th D.A.	10.63rd D.A.	18.18 Balloon Coy.R.A.F.
3.17th Div.	11.Vth Corps H.A.	19.III Corps
4.17th D.A.	12.C.B.S.O.,V Corps	20.R.A.III Corps
5.35th Div.	13.Vth Corps"G"	21.IV Corps
6.35th D.A.	14.S.C.R.A.,V Corps	22.R.A.IV Corps
7.38th Div.	15.Amm.Off.V Corps	23.R.A.Third Army
8.38th D.A.	16.M.G.O.,V Corps	24.A.D.Sigs.Vth Corps

TABLE "A" Vth CORPS ARTILLERY INSTRUCTION No.158

Action of FIELD ARTILLERY from ZERO to ZERO plus 50 minutes.

TIME	NATURE	ACTION	REMARKS
		(a) RIGHT DIVISION	
ZERO to ZERO plus 3 mins.	All 18 pdrs. & 6" T.Ms.	Open a barrage on Western edge of AVELUY WOOD from W.10.a.4.6. to W.4.a.3.0.	
ZERO plus 3 mins. to ZERO plus 35 mins.	-do-	Creep Eastwards for 800 yards in 16 lifts	Rate of lift will be 50 yards every two minutes.
ZERO plus 35 mins.to ZERO plus 40 mins.	-do-	Form a protective barrage on RIDE 7	
ZERO plus 40 mins to ZERO plus 50 mins.	-do-	Return to Western edge of Wood from W.10.a.4.6. to W.4.a.3.0.	
ZERO to ZERO plus 35 mins.	4.5" Howrs.	Engage hostile trenches in W.4.a & c, lifting Eastwards with the 18 pdr. barrage, to which they will conform.	
ZERO plus 35 mins to ZERO plus 40 mins.	-do-	Form a protective barrage on RIDE 7.	
ZERO plus 40 mins. to ZERO plus 50 mins.	-do-	Return to hostile trenches in W.4.a.& c	

NOTE :- 18 pdrs will use H.E. (50% 106 FUZE and 50% 101 FUZE without delay)

TIME	NATURE	ACTION	REMARKS
		(b) CENTRE DIVISION	
ZERO to ZERO plus 50 mins.	All 18 pdrs. 4.5" Howrs. & Medium T.Ms.	Engage hostile trenches North of RIDE "E" (- including trenches round the huts in Q.35.b. as far North as Q.35.b.4.6.)	18 pdrs.fire H.E.(25% 106 FUZE and 75% 101 FUZE without delay)

P.T.O.

TABLE B ARTILLERY INSTRUCTION No.158

Action of CORPS HEAVY ARTILLERY from ZERO to ZERO plus 50 mins.

	TIME	ACTION	REMARKS
(a)	Zero to zero plus 5 mins	Form a barrage 150 yards East of 18 pdr. barrage formed by Right Divisional Artillery	
(b)	zero plus 5 mins. to zero plus 35 mins.	Creep back to line or railway in six lifts.	Rate of lift will be 150 yds. every 5 minutes.
(c)	Zero plus 35 mins to zero plus 40 mins.	For a protective barrage along the line of the Railway.	
(d)	Zero plus 40 mins. to zero plus 50 mins.	Bombard the area of the Wood, East of the opening barrage line of Field Artillery.	
(e)	Zero to zero plus 50 mins.	BOMBARD :- (i) Area about Q.35.b.central, Q.35.b.5.0., Q.35.d.5.8., W.5.a.5.8. (ii) Trenches and sunken road in W.10.b.& d. (iii) AVELUY CHATEAU.	
(f)	--do--	Engage all communications within 1000 yards of the ANCRE between the AVELUY-OVILLERS road and THIEPVAL AVENUE.	
(g)	--do--	Search and sweep the ridges South of AVELUY Wood in W.10.a.& b with 60 pdr. shrapnel.	3 guns to be employed
(h)b	--do--	Search and sweep PIONEER VALLEY with 60 pdr. shrapnel.	3 guns to be employed.

TABLE "C" of Vth CORPS ARTILLERY INSTRUCTION NO.158.

PERIOD. ZERO plus 3 hours 50 mins. to ZERO plus 3 hours 55 minutes.

ACTION OF ARTILLERY :- RIGHT AND CENTRE DIVISIONS and CORPS HEAVY ARTILLERY

NATURE	ACTION	REMARKS
(a) 18 pdrs.	Mask each footbridge over the ANCRE	One Section of 18 pdrs to each bridge.
(b) 4.5" Howrs. & C.H.A.	Heavily bombard all AVELUY WOOD within safety limits.	Our infantry will have returned to our front line.
(c) Corps Heavy Artillery	Engage all approaches within 1,000 yards of the ANCRE, between the AVELUY - OVILLERS road and THIEPVAL AVENUE.	

SECRET.

Office Copy

SECRET.

35 D.A. 10/186.
17th June 1918.

62nd Bde R.F.A.
63rd Bde R.F.A.
315th Army Bde R.F.A.

In continuation of Warning Order 35 D.A. 10/182.

1. Reference para. 6., the 62nd Bde will move 1 section of each Battery in the silent positions up into temporary positions tonight, and the remainder tomorrow night.

Registration will be carried out from these temporary positions on 18th and 19th June.

2. Reference para. 4., Bdes and T.Ms. must begin taking up ammunition at once.

3. D/62 and D/315 will remain in their present positions until the conclusion of the operation. The order with regard to moving 3 guns of D/62 back to their silent position and 3 guns of D/315 to position in V.6.a. (35 D.A. 10/179 of 16th June) will therefore be held in abeyance until the conclusion of the operation.

4. (a) The table of tasks will be issued later by 12th D.A.

(b) The 18-pr creeping barrage will open on the line W.10.a.4.6. to W.4.a.3.0.

4.5" Hows, will engage hostile trenches in W.4.a. and c and lift eastward in conjunction with the 18-pr creeping barrage.

(c) The order of Bdes. on this line will be:-

63rd on right.
315th on left.
62nd. 2 Batteries to right (probably A and D).
2 Batteries to left (probably C and B).

sgd. P.S.ABRAHAM. Lt R.A.
for Major R.A.
Bde-Major 35th Div. Arty.

Copy to 35th Division.

S E C R E T.

12th Division No.G.X.2257.

12th Division Order No. 258., dated 17th June, 1918.

ADDENDUM No. 1.

---

1. The operation will be carried out on the 20th June, 1918. ZERO hour will be at 2 a.m.

2.(a) para 2(a) Substitute
The 35th, 36th and 37th L.T.M.Batteries (less Mortars of the 36th T.M.Battery which cannot safely be moved from their Battle position) will act as follows :-
(1) 0.00 to 0.05. Bombard trenches in West edge of Wood in W.4.c.
(2) 0.00 to 0.08. Bombard trenches North of W.4.central.
(3) 0.40 to 0.50. As in (a) and (b)
(4) 3.50 to 3.55. As in (a) and (b)
Ammunition as necessary, up to 200 rounds per mortar.

(b) para 2(b) Substitute.
The 37th Inf. Bde. will allot positions and targets to the three L.T.M.Batteries referred to in para 2(a) as amended above.

(c) para 2(c) Substitute.
Under arrangements being made by the Corps Machine Gun Officer, two M.G.Companies, 12th Bn. M.G.C. will fire a creeping barrage in conjunction with the Field Artillery barrage at 0.00 (ZERO).
On the F.A.barrage becoming protective, the guns will concentrate their fire on selected localities until 0.50. when they will cease fire.
At + 3.50, the guns will open fire on Ride 5 and the spur in W.10.a. and b. and will search back to the railway - fire lasting 5 minutes.

3. Synchronisation of Watches - An Officer of the Divisional Staff will synchronise watches on the 19th June, as under.

3.15 p.m.	At Divisional H.Q.,"G" Office.	12th Div.Artillery.
4. 0 p.m.	At H.Q. 37th Inf. Bde.	All Bdes. and 12th Bn. M.G.C.

4. A C K N O W L E D G E.

W. R. Pinwill
Lieut-Colonel,
General Staff,
12th Division.

17th June, 1918.

To all recipients of 12th Div.Order No.258.

Ref.Sheet 57.D. 1:40,000.

SECRET.

Copy No.....2.....

12th Division Order No. 258. 17th June,1918.

1.(a) On a date and at an hour to be notified later, a Chinese attack will be made by the Right and Centre Divisions on the Southern portion of AVELUY WOOD accompanied by a heavy bombardment of the Northern portion of the wood.

(b) Time Table of Artillery Bombardments will be forwarded shortly.

2. The 12th Division will co-operate in the above scheme as follows.

(a) The 35th and 36th L.T.M.Batteries will engage hostile T.M. emplacements and other suitable targets in W.4.c. and W.10.a. firing from the vicinity of HEATHCOTES BANK (W.3.d.)

(b) The 37th L.T.M.Battery will engage hostile T.M.emplacements in W.4.d., firing from positions selected in W.4.a. and W.3.b.

(c) The L.T.M.Batteries will act in conjunction with the 18 prs. Time Table will be drawn up by the Brigadier 37th Inf. Bde. in consultation with Artillery Brigades concerned. Rounds 200 per L.T.M.

(d) At Zero plus 0.50., the 37th Inf. Bde. will send out fighting patrols to search selected portions of the area bombarded and obtain identifications and information as to results. They will return by Zero plus 3.40 (vide serial No. 5 of Table).

3. Front Line trenches will be cleared as necessary (except for sentries and a proportion of Lewis Guns) and all Troops will be kept under cover as far as possible during the operation,

4. The following preparations will be taken in hand forthwith.

(a) All L.T.M.Batteries will reconnoitre and select positions & will prepare the necessary emplacements, under the supervision of 37th Inf. Bde.

(b) 35th Inf. Bde. will arrange for the necessary ammunition to be dumped, 36th and 37th Inf. Bdes. providing guides as necessary and giving all possible assistance.

The following dumps of T.M.Ammunition exist in the forward area and may be drawn on: but permanent T.M.positions are not to be reduced below the normal amount of ammunition kept in them for current use and S.O.S.

W.3.d.7.3.(HEATHCOTES BANK)	1600	rounds.
W.9.a.2.8.	600	"
W.8.b.9.2.(1 gun in position)	800	"
W.9.c.4.7.	1200	"
W.9.c.1.1.(2 guns in position)	1400	"
W.15.c.1.2.	400	"
W.14.b.8.4.(2 guns in position)	500	"
W.15.d.1.1.	400	"
W.15.c.5.2.(1 gun in position)	400	"

(c) These preparations will be completed by midnight 19/20th June so as to admit of the operation being carried out on the morning of the 20th June if required,

5. ACKNOWLEDGE.

Issued at..1.30.p m.

G. R. Pinnie (signature)

Lieut-Colonel,
General Staff,
12th Division.

P.T.O.

Copies to :-

1. "Q".
2. C.R.A.
3. C.R.E.
4. 35th Inf. Bde.
5. 36th Inf. Bde.
6. 37th Inf. Bde.
7. 5th Northamptonshire Regt.
8. 12th Bn. M.G.C.
9. 12th Div. Signal Coy., R.E.
10. A.D.M.S.
11. Div. Gas Officer.
12. V Corps.
13. 38th Division.
14. 18th Division.

15 -21. G.S. and Records.

SECRET.

12th Division No. G.X.2248.

"Q".
C.R.A.
C.R.E.
35th Inf. Bde.
36th Inf. Bde.
37th Inf. Bde.
5th Northamptonshire Regt.
12th Bn. M.G.C.
12th Div. Signal Coy., R.E.
A.D.M.S.
Div. Gas Officer.
V Corps.
38th Division.
18th Division.

Herewith, (overleaf) Time Table of Artillery Bombardment for attachment to 12th Division Order No. 258.

Lieut-Colonel,
General Staff,
12th Division.

17th June, 1918.

P.T.O.

TIME TABLE - issued with 12th Division Order No.258, dated 17/6/18.

Column Serial No.	1. From Zero.	2. To Zero.	3. Artillery & T.Ms. engaged.	4. Action.
1.	-2.00 (hours)	-0.05.	Corps Heavy Artillery. All available Heavy T.Ms. 4.5 How. Batteries of Right & Centre Divisions. Medium (6") T.M. batteries of Right & Centre Divisions.	Preliminary bombardment of the portion of AVELUY WOOD lying South and East of our present front line: and the trenches in Q.35.b., W.10.b. and d. Counter-battery work on active hostile batteries.
2.	-0.05.	0.00 (Zero)	All guns and T.Ms. silent.	
3.	0.00	+0.50	Corps Heavy Artillery. Field Artillery, Right and Centre Divisions.	Creeping and protective barrages, bombardment of wood, AVELUY Chateau & communications etc. Right Division - Barrage W. end of AVELUY wood from W.10.a.4.6. to W.4.a.3.0.; creep Eastwards for 800 yards and stand on Ride 7: 4.5 Hows. engage Hostile trenches in W.4.a. and c., lifting E. with 18-pr. barrage. Barrages creep back to starting points Zero +0.40 - +0.50. Centre Division - Engage hostile trenches N. of Ride E., including trenches round the huts in Q.35.b. and far N. as Q.35.b.4.6.
4.	+0.50.	+3.50	All guns & T.Ms. silent except	(a) Counterbattery work on active hostile batteries. (b) Observed movement in hostile lines will be engaged.
5.	+3.50.	+3.55.	Corps Heavy Artillery. Do. & 4.5. Hows. 18-prs.	Engage approaches between the AVELUY-OVILLERS Road and THIEPVAL AVENUE. Bombard AVELUY WOOD within safety limits. Mask footbridges over the ANCRE.

Army Form C. 2123
(In books of 100.)

"C" FORM.

MESSAGES AND SIGNALS.

No. of Message........

Prefix......Code......Words......	Received.	Sent, or sent out.	Office Stamp.
£ s. d	From......	At......m.	TELEGRAPHS 17.VIII.18
Charges to Collect	By......	To......	
Service Instructions		By......	

Handed in at...... Office......m. Received......m.

TO 12 Div Arty

*Sender's Number.	Day of Month.	In reply to Number.	AAA
B.C. 61	17	—	

Following wire received from 5 Corps begins aaa No ax will 106 fuz available aaa ends

for information

A.C.

FROM 35 Div Arty

PLACE & TIME

* This line should be erased if not required.

(3866.) Wt. W528/M1970. 100,000 Pads. 5/17. H. W. & V., Ld. (E. 1213.)

SECRET.

Copy No....10....

18.6.1918.

38th.DIVISIONAL ARTILLERY OPERATION ORDER No.64.

Ref. 57D. S.E. 1/20,000.
38th.D.A. Map "A" 1/10,000 (issued with O.O.63).

1. (a) On night 19/20 a "Chinese" attack will be made on the Southern portion of AVELUY WOOD, accompanied by a heavy bombardment of the Northern portion of the Wood.
(b) There is to be no Infantry action.

2. The table below shows the general scheme of the bombardment.

TIME.	ARTILLERY TAKING PART.	TASKS.
(a) Zero - 2 hrs to - 5 mins.	C.H.A. 4.5" How.Btys. Right and Centre Divisions. All available H.T.M's. M.T.M's Right and Centre Divisions.	(1) The portion of AVELUY WOOD lying S. and E. of our front line (2) Trenches in Q.35.b.,W.10.b. and d. (3) C.-B. work.
(b) -5mins. to Zero.	All guns silent.	
(c) Zero to + 50 mins.	As in (a) plus all 18-pdrs.	(1) Creeping and Standing barrages on S.portion of WOOD. (2) Bombardment of N. portion of WOOD. (3) Harassing fire on back areas.
(d) + 59 to + 3 hrs.50 mins.	All guns silent except for :-	(1) C-B.work on active batteries. (2) Any movement seen to be engaged.
(e) + 3 hrs.50 mins. to + 3 hrs.55 mins.	As in (c) (less T.M's.)	(1) ANCRE Crossings. (2) AVELUY WOOD. (3) Approaches within 1000 yards of R. ANCRE.

3. Details of tasks for 38th.D.A. are given in Table "A" attached.

4. Registration on the area to be bombarded will start forthwith.

5. Six 6" T.M's of 35th.D.A. are being lent to 38th.D.A. for the operations. They will be brought into action on Right Group front in emplacements now being prepared, and manned by reserve personnel of 38th.T.M.B's.

6. For the preliminary bombardment and up till zero+50 our front line is to be cleared from Q.34.d.5.0. - Q.29.c.8.0.

7/Arrangements/

7. Arrangements for synchronization of watches and zero hour will be notified later.

8. ACKNOWLEDGE.

J. E. Marston [signature]

Major R.A.

Brigade Major 38th.Divisional Artillery.

Issued at 10 a.m.

Copy No.1 to Right Group.
2 to Left Group.
3 to D.T.M.O.
4 to S.C.R.A.
5 to R.A.Signal Officer.
6 to 38th.Division.
7 to V Corps R.A.
8 to V Corps H.A.
9 to 17th.D.A.
10 to 12th.D.A.
11 to 35th.D.A.
12 to V/V Corps H.T.M's.
13/14 War Diary.
15 File.

Table "A".

Serial No.	Time.	Unit.	Task.	Ammn.	Rate r.p.g.p.m.	Remarks.
1.	Z - 2 hrs. to Z - 5 mins.	1 How. Bty. Right Group	Search and sweep AVELUY WOOD in Q.35.c. and d. as far E. as the Rly.	BX.	$\frac{1}{2}$.	
2.	-do-	1 How. Bty. Left Group.	Huts and trenches in Q.35.b.	BX.	$\frac{1}{2}$.	
3	-do-	9. 6" T.M's. Right Group.	Trenches in Q.35.c. and b. Huts in Q.35.b.		1/3.	
4.	Zero to + 50 mins.	3. 18-pdr. Btys.) Right Group.	Search and sweep area W.4.b.8.3. - W.5.c.9.9. -	AX. BX.	Zero to + 35 3. + 35 to + 50. $1\frac{1}{2}$.	18-pdrs. fire 25% 106 fuze and 75% 101 fuze without delay.
5.	-do-	1. 4.5" How. Bty.) Right Group.	Q.35.d.0.0. - Q.35.c.0.3.	BX.	Zero to + 35 2/3. + 35 to + 50. $\frac{3}{4}$.	
6.	-do-	3. 18-pdr. Btys.) Left Group.	Search and sweep area Q.35.c.0.3. - Q.35.d.0.0. - Q.35.b.4.7. - Q.35.b.0.6. with special attention to trenches and huts.	AX.	As in serial No.4.	
7.	-do-	1. 4.5" How. Bty.) Left Group.		BX.	As in serial No.5.	
8.	-do-	9.6" T.M's. Right Group.	Trenches in Q.35.c. and b. Huts in Q.35.b.		Zero to + 50. $\frac{1}{2}$.	

Table "A" (Contd.)

Serial No.	Time.	Unit.	Task.	Amn.	Rate r.p.g.p.m.	Remarks.
9.	+ 3 hrs.50 mins. to + 3 hrs.55 mins.	2. 18-pdr.Btys.) Right Group	(Crossings over ANCRE. (V. 5.b.52.95. (Q.35.d.90.30. (Q.36.c.05.69. (Q.36.c.10.90. (Q.36.a.00.15. (Q.30.c.[illegible]. 35.15.	AX.	3.	1 Section on each crossing.
10.	-do-	1.4.5" How.Bty.)	(Search and sweep AVELUY (WOOD between rides "H" &"J".	BX.	2.	Front line will be reoccupied. Safety limits to be observed.
11.	-do-	2.18-pdr.Btys.) Left Group	(Crossings over ANCRE. (Q.30.c.[illegible]. 28.90. (Q.29.d.83.25. (Q.29.b.84.10. (Q.24.c.53.02. (Q.24.c.20.80. (Q.24.a.50.20.	AX.	3.	1 Section on each crossing.
12.	-do-	1.4.5"How.Bty.)	(Search and sweep AVELUY (WOOD N. of ride "J".	BX.	2.	Front line will be reoccupied. Safety limits to be observed.

To

Brigade Major
12 Div. Arty.

Ref. 12 DA Order No 10?.

Progress Report.

4 positions for 6" TMs. were found this morning in NEWTON RAVINE W3c, forward of existing positions. Work was begun on these at midday and is progressing well.
4 mortars and 300 rds. ammn. are being sent up by wagons tonight and will be carried to the positions in the morning.
There will therefore be 8 mortars with 500 rds. ready to shoot at W4c tomorrow night.
I have not been able to find any more positions which could be got ready quickly within reasonable distance of transport.

PR/9
18/6/18.

W. Poiblen (?)
.........Capt. R.F.
D.T.M.O. 12th Division

H.A.,V Corps.
S.G. 11/93.

SECRET.

Addenda No.1. to V Corps H.A.Instructions No.107 (S.G.11/91.)

1. Add :- TABLE "D"

Programme for 9.2" Gun on the 20th.June 1918.

Zero to Zero plus 1 hour. LONGUEVAL S.17.b.4.4. (Sheet 57-C.)

Rate of fire. One round per gun per five minutes.

Target should,if possible,be registered to-day 19/6/1918.

2. Add sub-para (c) to para 8. :-

Rate of fire 6" Guns.

Zero to Zero plus 50 minutes....................NORMAL

Zero plus 3 hours 50 minutes to
Zero plus 3 hours 55 minutes....................RAPID.

P.K. [signature]
Major R.A.
Brigade Major,V Corps Heavy Artillery.

19th.June.1918.

Issued to all recipients of H.A.Instructions No.107.

58th.Brigade R.G.A. to acknowledge.

H.A., V Corps.
S.G. 11/91.

S E C R E T.

V CORPS HEAVY ARTILLERY INSTRUCTIONS No.107.

1. On the 20th.June 1918, a feint attack will be made on the Southern portion of AVELUY WOOD.

2. The attack will be preceded by a preliminary bombardment which will be carried out by Corps Heavy Artillery, Field Artillery & Trench Mortars.
The Heavy Artillery programme from Zero minus 2 hours to Zero minus 5 minutes, is shown in TABLE "A" attached.

3. From Zero minus 5 minutes to Zero, all guns will be silent.

4. From Zero to Zero plus 50 minuts. The action of the Heavy Artillery is shown in TABLE "B" attached.

5. From Zero plus 50 minutes to Zero plus 3 hours 50 minutes. Counter Battery work will be carried out and any fleeting targets engaged.

6. From Zero plus 3 hours 50 minutes to Zero plus 3 hours 55 minutes, the action of the Heavy Artillery is shown in TABLE "C" attached.

7. The C.B., S.O., V Corps is drawing up a programme for Counter Battery work during the operations.

8. Rates of fire.

(a) From Zero minus 2 hours to Zero minus 5 minutes.

6" Hows. and 60-Pdrs.	One round per piece per two minutes.
Heavy Hows.	One round per piece per four minutes.

(b) Zero to Zero plus 35 minutes.

6" Hows. and 60-Pdrs.	One round per piece per minute.
Heavy Hows.	One round per piece per two minutes.

Zero plus 35 minutes to Zero plus 50 minutes.

6" Hows. and 60-Pdrs.	One round per piece per two minutes.
Heavy Hows.	One round per piece per four minutes.

Zero plus 3 hours 50 minutes to Zero plus 3 hours 55 minutes.

6" Hows. and 60-Pdrs.	One round per piece per minute
Heavy Hows.	One round per piece per two minutes.

9. HEATHCOTE BANK will be occupied by our Infantry. The Northern part of the Wood will be cleared back to PRINCES STREET - BRACKEN Trench and HORNET Trench to Q.29.c.6.0.

10. Ammunition. 6" and Heavy Hows. 106 fuzes, where safe.
60-Pdrs. Shrapnel.

11. Watches will be synchronised at 3-30 p.m. on the 19th.June, at these H.Qrs. Brigades concerned will send a representative.

12. Zero hour will be at 2 a.m. on the 20th.June 1918.

13. Brigades to acknowledge.

P. Rawlley [signature]
Major R.A.
Brigade Major, V Corps Heavy Artillery.

18th.June 1918.

Issued to :- 17th., 35th., 58th., 62nd., 93rd.Bdes.R.G.A.
Copies to :- R.A., V Corps. C.B., S.O., V Corps. Staff Captain H.A.
"O" Siege Park. 18 Ob.Group. Ammn.Officer H.A.
12th. & 38th.Divn. 12th. & 38th.Divn.Arty.
15 Squad.R.A.F. 18 Balloon Co.

H.A.,V Corps.
S.G. 11/91.

TABLE "A"

Heavy Artillery action from Zero minus 2 hours to Zero minus 5 minutes.

78th.S.Bty.	Area Q.35.a.95.30. - Q.35.b.50.00. - Q.35.d.45.65. - Q.35.c.80.90.
274th.S.Bty.	Trenches Q.35.b.40.65. to Q.35.b.25.40.
142nd.S.Bty.	Area W.4.c.80.40. - W.5.c.80.30. - W.5.c.30.00. - W.4.c.55.00.
112th.S.Bty.	Area W.4.b.25.35. - Q.35.d.00.00. - W.5.b.00.30. - W.4.d.00.85.
278th.S.Bty.	Area W.4.d.00.85. - W.5.b.00.30. - W.5.c.80.30. - W.4.c.80.40.
287th.S.Bty.	Area W.4.c.55.00. - W.5.c.60.00. - W.11.a.40.15. - W.10.a.35.70.
48th.S.Bty.	H.Qrs. W.10.b.70.10. - W.11.c.00.75.
248th.S.Bty.	Trenches W.10.b.40.60. - W.10.d.50.55.
135th.H.Bty.(2)	Search & Sweep North & South of Ride D from W.4.b.20.15.
13th.S.Bty.	Area W.5.c.50.75. - W.5.c.80.65. - W.11.a.55.85. - W.11.a.25.95.
56th.S.Bty.	Area W.5.a.35.75. - Q.35.d.00.00. - W.5.b.00.30. - W.5.a.55.20.

H.A.,V Corps.
S.G. 11/91.

TABLE "C".

Heavy Artillery action from Zero plus 3 hours 50 minutes to Zero plus 3 hours 55 minutes.

1. Bombard Areas in AVELUY WOOD as follows :-

112th.S.Bty.,278th.S.Bty. & 287th.S.Bty.
Area W.4.a.90.00. - W.5.a.00.00. to W.5.a.80.80. to W.5.central. to W.4.c.80.80.

274th.S.Bty. & 142nd.S.Bty.
Area W.4.c.80.80. to W.5.central. to W.5.c.70.50. to W.4.c.80.60.

51st.S.Bty.,248th.S.Bty.,48th.S.Bty.,13th.S.Bty.,& 56th.S.Bty.
Area W.4.c.80.60. to W.5.c.70.50. to W.11.a.40.20. to W.4.c.80.00.

2. Engage all approaches vide para 3 TABLE "B" sub para (i) to (xii)

N.B. Our Infantry will have returned to our Front Line.

H.A.,V Corps.
S.G. 11/91.

TABLE "B"

Heavy Artillery action from Zero to Zero plus 50 minutes.

1. (a) Zero to Zero plus 5 mins. Following batteries will form a barrage on line W.10.a.70.60. - W.4.a.80.00. as under :-

278th.S.B.	W.10.a.70.60. to W.4.c.70.00.
112th.S.B.	W.4.c.70.00. to W.4.c.75.30.
267th.S.B.	W.4.c.75.30. to W.4.c.80.60.
142nd.S.B.	W.4.c.80.60. to W.4.a.80.00.

(b) Zero plus 5 mins to Zero plus 35 mins. This barrage will move due East to the Railway Line in W.11.a. and W.5.c. lifting 150 yards every five minutes.

(c) Zero plus 35 mins. to Zero plus 40 mins.) Form a Protective Barrage along the Railway Line.

(d) Zero plus 40 mins to Zero plus 50 minuts. Bombard AVELUY WOOD in following Areas :-

278th.S.B.	Area W.10.a.70.60. - W.4.c.70.00. - W.11.a.40.30. to W.11.a.50.00.
112th.S.B.	Area W.4.c.70.00. - W.4.c.75.30. - W.5.c.55.30. - W.11.a.40.60.
267th.S.B.	Area W.4.c.75.30. - W.4.c.80.60. - W.5.c.60.60. - W.5.c.55.30.
142nd.S.B.	Area W.4.c.80.60. - W.4.a.80.00. - W.5.a.80.00. - W.5.c.60.60.

2. Bombard.
Zero to Zero plus 50 mins.

(i)	274th.S.B.	Q.35.b.central - Q.35.b.50.00.
(ii)	48th.S.B.	(1) Q.35.b.50.00. - Q.35.d.50.80.
(iii)	48th.S.B.	(2) W.5.a.50.80.
(iv)	248th.S.B.	Trenches & Sunken Road in W.10.b and d.
(v)	10 R.M.A.	AVELUY CHATEAU (10 rounds)

3. Search & Sweep.
Zero to Zero plus 50 mins.

(i)	111th.H.B.	(2) AVELUY - OVILLERS Road. W.18.a & b. X.13. X.7.
(ii)	111th.H.B.	(2) AVELUY - DONNET POST.
(iii)	2/1 Lancs.H.B.	(2) NAB VALLEY Road R.32. & X.2.
(iv)	2/1 Lancs H.B.	(2) Road W.6.c and d.
(v)	135th.H.B.	(2) THIEPVAL AVENUE.
(vi)	135th.H.B.	(2) CAMPBELL AVENUE.
(vii)	145th.H.B.	(3) Search & Sweep the Ridges South of AVELUY WOOD in W.10.a and b.
(viii)	122nd.H.B.	(3) Search & Sweep PIONEER VALLEY.
(ix)	58th.S.B.	(2) Rest Billets X.5.c.
(x)	58th.S.B.	(2) POZIERES - BAPAUME Road.
(xi)	409th.S.B.	(2) MIRAUMONT - ACHIET LE PETIT Rd.
(xii)	409th.S.B.	(2) MIRAUMONT - IRLES Road.

S E C R E T. C.B.S. 77.

Reference R.A. V Corps Instructions No. 158 of 16/6/18
and
V Corps Heavy Artillery Instructions No. 107.
for a CHINESE attack on AVELUY WOOD.

The following are the arrangements for C.B. work.

1. During the preliminary bombardment (i.e. zero minus 3 hours to zero minus five minutes)
Hostile Batteries detected active will be vigorously engaged.

To this end H.A.Brigades and 18 Observation Group, will make special efforts to identify active hostile batteries, and report to this office. 93rd, 62nd, and 17th H.A.Brigades will at once engage any batteries detected active in their normal zones, with whatever guns they may have available, reporting at once action taken to this office.

35th. H.A.Brigade will be prepared to assist in any zone, on being called upon from this office.

2. Period zero minus five minutes to zero:-
All guns will be silent.

3. Zero to zero plus 50 minutes, vigorous C.B. work will be carried out, with whatever guns are available, in accordance with a programme 'Appendix Z ' to these instructions, which will be issued later.

4. Period zero plus 50 minutes to zero plus three hours 50 minutes and onwards as may be required, hostile batteries detected active will be heavily engaged, as for the preliminary period (see para 1)

Six inch how gas shell will be used as far as possible during this period.

Divisional Artilleries, will be prepared to assist with 4.5" Hows, using gas shell if possible, on demand from this office.

5. When visibility permits, O.C. 15th Squadron R.A.F., will arrange for special Artillery Patrol Machines to report active hostile batteries by the N.F. system.
O.C., 18 Balloon Company will also report active batteries, or areas of activity.

J. Barring
Lt. Col. R.A.
Counter Battery Staff Officer V Corps.

18/6/18.

Issued to:-

17th. Bde. R.G.A.	34th. Bde. R.G.A.	ACKNOWLEDGE BY WIRE
35th. Bde. R.G.A.	58th. Bde. R.G.A.	
62nd. Bde. R.G.A.	78th. Bde. R.G.A.	
93rd. Bde. R.G.A.	17th. Div. Arty.	
12th. Div. Arty.	38th. Div. Arty.	
15th. Squadron.R.A.F.		
18 Balloon Co.	18 Obs. Group.	

R.A. V Corps.	V Corps H.A.	For Information.
35th. Div. Arty.	63rd. Div. Arty.	
C.B.S.O. III Corps.		
C.B.S.O. IV Corps.		

S E C R E T.

37TH INFANTRY BRIGADE ORDER NO.201

Copy No ..6.....

Ref:- 57D.S.E.1:40,000
and Trench Map 1:10,000

18th June, 1918.

1. A Chinese Attack will be made by the Right and Centre Divisions of the Corps on the Southern portion of AVELUY WOOD, accompanied by a heavy bombardment of the Northern portion of the Wood, on the 20th June. Zero hour will be at 2.00 a.m.

2. Time Table of Artillery bombardment and details of M.G. programme are attached.*
*To 37th Inf.Bde. Units only.

3. (a)The 35th, 36th and 37th L.T.M.Batteries(less Mortars of the 36th T.M.Battery which cannot safely be moved from their Battle position) will act as follows:-
(1) 0.00 to 0.03 Bombard trenches in West edge of Wood in W.4.c.
(2) 0.00 to 0.08 Bombard trenches North of W.4.central.
(3) 0.40 to 0.50 As in (1) and (2)
(4) 3.50 to 3.55 As in (1) and (2)
Ammunition as necessary, up to 200 rounds per mortar.

(b)Positions have been allotted to these Mortars, and details of the allotment of targets to each Battery will be notified separately to those concerned.

4. (a) During the period from Zero - 2.00 to Zero plus 0.50, trenches will be cleared as follows:-

6th Queen's
Left Coy. will withdraw 1 Platoon from Front Line (HEATHCOTE BANK) and occupy SAUCHIEHALL Support in localities not usually engaged by enemy artillery.

6th Buffs
The 2 Front Line Coys. will be disposed as follows:
Front Line:- 1 Platoon each.
PRINCES Support:- 1 platoon each(in localities not usually engaged by enemy artillery).
Remaining 2 platoons of each Coy.:- LOTHIAN TRENCH Q.33.c.

(b) Normal dispositions will be resumed as soon as practicable after Zero plus 0.50.

5. At Zero + 0.50 Officer Commanding 6th Buffs will arrange to send out fighting patrols to search selected portions of the area bombarded and obtain identifications and information as to results, as follows:-
(a) 1 Patrol to work down enemy front line on West edge of Wood in W.4.c.
(b) 1 Patrol to enemy work from W.4.c.6.7. towards suspected T.M. position about W.4.d.2.8.
(c) 1 Patrol along enemy front line from W.4.a.4.0. in Easterly direction.
(d) 1 Patrol to enemy sap, W.4.b.55.65. - 50.50.

These patrols will return to our lines not later than Zero plus 3.40.

6. Watches will be synchronized at 4.0 p.m. on the 19th instant at Brigade H.Q. An Officer from each Unit of 37th Bde. will attend.

7. ACKNOWLEDGE.

P.R.B.N. Nichols
Captain,
Brigade Major,
37th Infantry Brigade.

Issued through Signals at 7 p.m.

Distribution:-

Copy No. 1 6th Queen's
2 6th Buffs
3 6th R.W.Kent Regt.
4 37th T.M.Battery.
5 12th Division "G"
6 C.R.A.
7 D.T.M.O.
8 35th Inf.Bde.
9 36th Inf.Bde.
10 114th Inf.Bde.
11 315th Bde., R.F.A.
12 87th Field Coy., R.E.
13 37th Field Ambulance.
14 Bde. Signal Officer.
15 Staff Captain.
16 War Diary.
17 File.
19 121st Bn: M.G.Corps.

S E C R E T

12th Battalion, Machine Gun Corps. Copy No. 6

OPERATION ORDER No. 23.

18th June 1918

1. A Chinese attack will be made on AVELUY WOOD on 20th June. Zero 2 a.m.
2. The attack will be carried out by artillery as follows
   (a) Preliminary bombardment by heavy guns Zero minus 2 hours to Zero minus 5 mins.
   (b) All guns silent Zero minus 5 mins. to ZERO.
   (c) Creeping barrage and protective barrage Zero to Zero plus 50.
   (d) All guns silent (except counter-battery work and fire on observed movement) Zero plus 50 to Zero plus 3 hours 50 mins when 37th Inf. Bde. are sending out fighting patrols.
3. Machine Gun co-operation will be as per table below and as per Fire Organisation Orders issued separately to M.G. Coys.
4. No machine guns will open fire until the Field Artillery barrage commences at ZERO.
5. Watches will be synchronised by each M.G. Coy. at 37th Inf. Bde. H.Q. at 4 p.m. on 19th inst.
6. A C K N O W L E D G E.

R. Oakley

Lieut. Colonel.

Issued at 8.30 p.m. Comdg. 12th Bn., Machine Gun Corps.

TABLE.

Serial No	Time.	No. of M.G's.	Action.	Rate of fire etc.
1.	Z to plus 35	10.	Standing barrage from W.10.a.6.5. to W.10.b.9.5.	75 r.p.m. per gun.
2.	Z to plus 35	16.	Creeping barrage from line W.10.a.6.6. to W.4.a.8.0. Eastwards to line of Ride 7.	do do. Lift of 100 yds. every 4 mins.
3.	Z to plus 35	8	Standing barrages on trench W.10.c.3.7. Sunken Road in W.10.c. and W.9.d. and Fork Rds. W.10.d.9.7.	75 r.p.m. per gun.
4.	Z plus 37. Z plus 40. Z plus 44 Z plus 47. Z plus 49.	34.	Crashes on trenches W.5.central and W.5.c. & d. Rly. sgds. in W.11.c. Exits from AVELUY Village. Crossings over R. ANCRE in Q.5.d. Rds. & Rly. juncs. at W.17.a.2.3.	100 rds. per gun at each crash.
5.	Z plus 3 hrs 50 mins to Z plus 3 hrs. 55 min.	34.	As in Serial 4.	100 rds. per gun per min. in 5 crashes.

Copies to. 1. "A" Coy. 2. "B" Coy. 3. "C" Coy. 4. "D" Coy.
5. 12th Div. "G" 6. C.R.A. 7. 36th Inf. Bde.
8. 37th Inf. Bde. 9 C.M.G.O. 10. Office.

S E C R E T.

12th Divisional Artillery Order No. 107.

62nd Brigade R.F.A.
63rd Brigade R.F.A.
315th Brigade R.F.A.
12th D. A. Column
D. T. M. O.
and to 12th Divn. (C) and Sigs.)
12th Bn. M.G.C.) for
35th, 36, 37th Inf. Bdes.) information.
V Corps R.A. V Corps H.A.)

Ref. - 57D. S.E. 1/20,000. 13th June, 1918.

1. A Chinese Attack will be made on AVELUY Wood on 20th June. Zero Hour will be at 2 a.m.

2. The attack will consist of a preliminary bombardment a creeping barrage and a protective barrage. From Zero minus 5 minutes to Zero all guns will be silent - and again from Zero plus 50 minutes to Zero plus three hours 50 minutes; except that during the latter period all observed hostile movement will be engaged and Counter Battery work on active hostile batteries will continue.

3. At Zero plus 50 minutes the 37th Infantry Brigade are sending out fighting patrols to search selected portions of the area bombarded. They will return by Zero plus three hours 40 minutes. Front line trenches are being cleared as necessary.

4. The Artillery and 6 inch Trench Mortar tasks are shown on Tables A and B attached.

5. During the Operation A. and D. Batteries 62nd Brigade will be under the orders of O.C. 63rd Brigade and C. and B. Batteries 62nd Brigade will be under the orders of O.C. 315th Brigade R.F.A.

6. Rates of fire -

	18 pr.	4.5" How.
Zero to Zero plus 35 minutes.	3 R.P.G.P.M.	3 R.P.G.P.2 min.
Zero plus 35 mins. to Zero plus 50 mins.	3 R.P.G.P.2 mins.	3 R.P.G.P.4 min.
Zero plus 3 h.50 m. to Zero plus 3 h.55 m.	3 R.P.G.P.1 min.	2 R.P.G.P.1 min.

7. Watches will be synchronised at Headquarters 63rd Brigade R.F.A. (V 3 b 8 2) at 4.30 p.m. 19th June by the Reconnaissance Officer.

Please acknowledge.

Noel Chance
Major,
Brigade Major, 12th D. A.

18 Pounders.

TABLE A. - issued with 12th D.A. Order No. 107.

Phase	From	To	Unit	No. of guns	Target	Remarks.
1	Zero	Zero plus 3 minutes	63rd Brigade	22	W 10 a 40 60 to W 4 c 35 20	Ammunition. H.E. 50 % 106 Fuse and 50 % 101 Fuse without delay, as far as supplies will allow.
			315th Brigade	28	W 4 c 35 20 to W 4 a 30 00	
II	Zero plus 3 mins.	Zero plus 35 mins.	All guns creep ~~back~~ eastwards at rate of 50 yards per 2 minutes.			
III	Zero plus 35 mins.	Zero plus 40 mins.	63rd Brigade	22	Protective Barrage W 11 a 00 60 to W 5 c 20 20	
			315th Brigade	28	Protective Barrage W 5 c 20 20 to W 5 a 45 00	
IV	Zero plus 40 mins.	Zero plus 50 mins.	ALL GUNS		As per Phase I.	
V	Zero plus 3 hours 50 minutes	Zero plus 3 hours 55 minutes	63rd Brigade	2	Bridge at W 17 b 15 80	
				2	" " W 11 d 20 60	
				2	" " W 11 b 25 00	
				2	" " W 11 b 30 20	
				2	" " W 11 b 35 45	
			315th Brigade	2	" " W 5 d 60 20	
				2	" " W 5 d 70 45	
				2	" " W 5 d 95 70	
				2	" " W 5 d 95 85	
				2	" " W 5 b 95 00	
				2	" " W 5 b 95 10	
				2	" " W 5 b 88	

4.5 inch Hows. and 6 inch T.Ms.

TABLE B. - issued with 12th D.A. Order No. 107.

Phase	From	To	Unit	No. of guns	Target	Remarks
I	Zero	Zero plus 3 minutes	63rd Brigade	12	W 10 a 7 6 to W 4 c 65 50	150 yards East of 18 pr. barrage
			315th Brigade	6	W 4 c 65 50 to W 4 a 6 0	
II	Zero plus 3 mins.	Zero plus 35 mins.	All Howitzers and Trench Mortars		Creep ~~back~~ Eastward at 50 yds. per 2 minutes to protective barrage line.	
III	Zero plus 35 mins.	Zero plus 40 mins.	63rd Brigade	12	Protective Barrage W 11 a 0 6 to W 5 c 3 5	
			315th Brigade	6	Protective Barrage W 5 c 3 5 to W 5 a 45 00	
IV	Zero plus 40 mins.	Zero plus 50 mins.	All Howitzers and Trench Mortars		As for Phase I.	
V	Zero plus 3 hours 50 mins.	Zero plus 3 hours 55 mins.	All Howitzers and Trench Mortars.		Search trenches and strong points within limits of creeping barrage in Phase II.	

Note.- 6 inch Trench Mortars will be distributed over the front under orders of the D.T.M.O.

Amendment No. 1

to

18th Divisional Artillery Order No. 107.

Table A.	Phase II.	For "all guns creep back at" .... read "all guns creep EASTWARDS at" ......
Table B.	Phase II.	For "creep back at" .... read "creep EASTWARDS at" ......

Major,
18th June, 1918. Brigade Major 18th D. A.

Copies to all recipients of 18th D.A. Order No. 107.

Addendum No. 1

to

12th Divisional Artillery Order No. 107.

----

1. From Zero minus 2 hours to Zero minus 5 minutes -

4.5" Hows. 63rd Brigade - 12 Howitzers will bombard trenches in W 10 b and d.

315th Brigade - 6 Howitzers will search rides A, B and C East of line running N. and S. through W 4 central.

Rate of fire - 1 round per Howitzer per 2 minutes.

6" Newtons. Will co-operate under orders from D.T.M.O., firing 20 rounds per Mortar, leaving 30 rounds per Mortar for task in Table B. instead of 50.

2. From Zero plus 50 minutes to Zero plus 3 hours 50 minutes 4.5" Howitzers will be at disposal of C.B. S.O. for Counter Battery work if required, and will be prepared to use gas if conditions permit.

Noel Clarke(?)
Major,
Brigade Major 12th D. A.

18th June, 1918.

Copies to all recipients of 12th D.A. Order No. 107.

SECRET.

R.A. V Corps.

158/1

Reference Vth Corps Artillery Instruction No. 158 dated 16th June 1918 :-

The date will be 20th June.
Zero Hour will be 2 a.m.

R.A. Haining
Lt. Col. G.S.

June 18th 1918.

for B.G.,G.S., Vth Corps.

Copies to all recipients of V Corps A.I. No. 158.

S E C R E T.

C.B.S. 77/2.

APPENDIX 'Z' to C.B.S. 77 of 18/6/18.

1. The following guns are available for C.B. work and can bear on the area from which hostile fire may be expected.
They will engage targets as shewn against them, from zero to zero plus 50 minutes.

17th. Brigade. R.G.A.

51 Siege Battery (4 Hows. 6") X.13.b.35.55. and X W 9.
56 Siege Battery (3 Hows. 8") X W 12, X W 5 and X W 2.
13 Siege Battery (3 Hows.9.2") X W 1, X.13.a.20.80. and W.18.b.50.50.

35th. Brigade. R.G.A.

170 Siege Battery. (2 Hows 6") X W 7 and X.13.c.80.70.

62nd. Brigade. R.G.A.

126 Heavy Battery. (4 guns 60-pr) Northern Section:- X W 11 & X W 6.
Southern Section:- X W 17 and X.3.c.80.80.

224 Siege Battery. (2 Hows 6") X W 13.

76 Siege Battery. (3 Hows.9.2") X W 15, X W 16 and X W 18.

93rd.Brigade. R.G.A.

2/1 Lowland H.Bty.(2 guns 60-pr) X W 10 and R.31.d.80.20.

58th. Brigade. R.G.A.

431 Siege Battery.(2 Hows 12") North:- X.3.b.20.20. to X.3.b.60.60.

South:- X W 12 - X W 14 - X W 9.

Rates of fire 'Normal', except for 12" Hows. which will fire 10 rounds per how. during the period.

2. 67 Siege Battery and remaining guns of 93rd Brigade R.G.A. will stand by to engage any batteries detected active on which they can bear.

[signature]
Lt. Col. R.A.
19/6/18. Counter Battery Staff Officer V Corps.

Issued at 1 p.m. to all recipients of C.B.S. 77.

S E C R E T.

Amendment No. 2 to

12th Divisional Artillery Order No. 107.

---

1. Table B., Phase I should read - Target.

315th Bde.	6	Hows.	W 10 a 7 6 to W 4 c 60 00
63rd Bde.	12	..	W 4 c 60 00 to W 4 c 60 80

2. Table B., Phase V.

As the Infantry will have returned to their normal positions in our trenches, Howitzers and Trench Mortars will search trenches and strong points in W 4 d only.

3. It should be clearly understood that L.T.M. and strong Infantry posts will be situated in HEATHCOTE'S BANK W 3 d and sentry and Lewis Gun posts will be in our front line in W 4 a throughout the Operation. 6 inch T.Ms., especially those firing from temporary platforms, must bear this in mind when laying out lines of fire and selecting targets.

Noel Chenevix
Major,
Brigade Major 12th D. A.

19th June, 1918.

Copies to all recipients of 12th D.A. Order No. 107.

SECRET.

12th Division No. G.X. 2303

12th Div. Artillery.
35th Inf. Brigade.
36th Inf. Brigade.
37th Inf. Brigade.

Reference 12th Division No. G.X.2302 dated 19th June.
Corps H.A. notify that -
"During the Zero plus 3 hours 50 minutes Bombardment, the nearest target engaged by Heavy Artillery is W.4.a.90.00., 300 yards from our outposts line as shewn on the Map."

W. N. Pennie

Lieut-Colonel,
General Staff,
12th Division.

19th June, 1918.

SECRET and URGENT.

12th Division No. G.X. 2302

G.O.C., Corps Heavy Artillery.
12th Divisional Artillery.)
35th Inf. Bde.) For information.
36th Inf. Bde.)
37th Inf. Bde.)

Reference V Corps Artillery Instruction No. 158, Table C, Item (6).

Before the bombardment at Zero plus 3.50 commences, the Infantry will have resumed their ordinary position in the front line. This is indicated in the Column of Remarks, but I wish to make sure that it has been allowed for in allotting targets for this bombardment.

Please confirm.

N. R. Pinwill

Lieut.Colonel,
for Major-General,
Commanding 12th Division.

19th June, 1918.

Papers re Chinese Bombardment for War Diary

Raid
20/21st June
by
38th Div.

COPY No. 2 .....

SECRET

Vth CORPS ARTILLERY INSTRUCTION NO.162

18th JUNE 1918

1. At a date and at an hour to be notified later, the 38th Divn. will raid the enemy trenches and dug-outs from Q.35.b.55.50 to Q.23.d.55.00

2. The operation will be carried out under a protective barrage formed by the Field Artillery of the Divisions holding the Vth Corps front, and by the Vth Corps Heavy Artillery, as shown in 38th Divnl. Artillery operation Order No.63 of 17th June.

3. The C.B.SO., Vth Corps will arrange a Counter Battery programme in consultation with C.B.S.O., IVth Corps.

4. The date and time of the operation, together with the arrangements made for synchronisation, will be notified by B.G., R.A. 38th Division to all Artillery formations concerned.

5. Div.Artys. and C.H.A. to acknowledge.

R.H. Haining
Lt.Col.G.S.
For B.G., G.S., Vth Corps

Issuef at 7-30 p.m.

Copy No.1. 12th Div.
2. 12th D.A.
3. 17th Div.
4. 17th D.A.
5. 35th Div.
6. 35th D.A.
7. 38th Div.
8. 38th D.A.
9. Vth Corps H.A.
10. C.B.S.O., Vth Corps
11. Vth Corps "G"
12. S.C.R.A., Vth Corps
13. Amm.Offr.Vth Corps
14. 15th Squadron R.A.F.
15. 18 Balloon Coy.R.A.F.
16. III Corps
17. R.A.III Corps
18. IV Corps
19. R.A.IV Corps
20. R.A.Third Army
21. 63rd Division } For information.
22. 63rd D.A. }
23.- 28 File and Diary.

SECRET.

12th Division No. G.X. 2308

C.R.A.
C.R.E.
35th Inf. Bde.
36th Inf. Bde.
37th Inf. Bde.
12th Bn. M.G.C.
A.D.M.S.
"Q"

---

1. On the night 20th/21st June the 38th Division are carrying out a raid with 2 Battalions.
Objective - the line Q.35.b.5.5 - Q.23.d.5.0.

2. The raid will be carried out under Artillery and T.M. Barrage. The 12th Divisional Artillery is assisting under arrangements made by the C.R.A.

3. The hour of Zero will be notified in due course.

4. 37th Infantry Brigade will reduce the garrison of such front line trenches as may be necessary.
Orders regarding working parties on the night 20th/21st June will be issued later.

W. K. Pennell[?]

Lieut.Colonel,
General Staff,
12th Division.

19th June, 1918.

S E C R E T.

12th Division No. G.X. 2334.

C.R.A.
C.R.E.
35th Inf. Bde.
36th Inf. Bde.
37th Inf. Bde.
12th Bn. M.G.C.
5th Northants. Regt.
A.D.M.S.
"Q".

Reference 12th Division No. G.X. 2308 dated 19th June.

Zero hour will be 2.5 a.m.

Working parties from the Reserve Brigade and 5th Northants. Regt. will work as ordered, but will be W. of SENLIS not later than 1.45 a.m.

A C K N O W L E D G E.

Lieut.Colonel,
General Staff,
12th Division.

20th June, 1918.

S E C R E T.

Amendment No. 1 to

12th Divisional Artillery Order No. 108.

---

1. Para. 2, sub-para. (a). 315 Bde. Q 36 c 50 20 should read Q 30 c 50 20.

2. In same para. 63 Bde. - 6. 4.5" Hows. should read 62 Bde. 6 - 4.5" Hows.

Major,
Brigade Major 12th D.A.

19th June, 1918.

Addressed all recipients of above Order.

S E C R E T.

12th Divisional Artillery Order No. 108.

62nd)
63rd) Brigade R.F.A.
315th)
12th D.A. Column
and to 12th Divn. (G))
V Corps R.A.) for information
38th Div.Arty.)

Ref. - 57D. S.E. 1/20,000. 19th June, 1918.

1. The 38th Division are raiding the enemy trenches Q 35 b 55 50 to Q 23 d 55 00 on night 20/21st June. Strength of raiding party 7 Companies. They will remain in the enemy trenches until Zero plus 30 minutes, the signal for withdrawal being one Thermite Bomb burst over Q 29 central.

2. The Artillery will co-operate as follows -
From Zero to Zero plus 30 minutes -

(a)	63 Bde. R.F.A.	3 - 18prs.	Barrage	Q 36 a 8010 - Q 36 a 7550
	62	6 - ,,	..	Q 36 a 7550 - Q 30 c 5020
	315	3 - ,,	..	Q 30 c 5020 - Q 30 c 5040
	62	6 - 4.5"Hows.	..	Q 36 a 8010 - Q 30 c 5040
(b)	63	6 - 18 prs.	Search and sweep AVELUY WOOD East of line W 5 a 0 0 - W 5 a 4075	
	315	12 - ,,	Search and sweep AVELUY WOOD East of line W 5 a 4075 - Q 35 c 9080	

In neither case is the M.P.I. to be nearer than 300 yards to our trenches owing to splinters from trees.

(c) 63 Bde. R.F.A. 6 - 4.5"Hows. Smoke W 5 b 8040 - Q 36 c 2000 - Q 36 c 6520.

3. Rates of fire -

Zero to Zero plus 5 minutes.	18 prs.	3	R.P.G.P.M.	
	4.5"Hows.	2	,,	
Zero plus 5 to Zero plus 30 mins.	18 prs.	2	,,	
	4.5"Hows.	1	,,	
	,,	2	,,	(if smoke)

18 prs. fire 50 % A. and 50 % AX. (106 Fuse if available).

4. Watches will be synchronised at H.Q., 63rd Brigade R.F.A. by the Reconnaissance Officer 5 hours before Zero hour.

5. Zero hour will be notified later.

Please acknowledge.

Noel Chessre(?)
Major,
Brigade Major 12th D. A.

R.A.,38th.Div.No.G.S.1936/14.

S E C R E T.
XXXXXXXXXXX

20th.June 1918.

Reference 38th.D.A. O.O. No.63 para.7.

Zero hour will be 2.5 a.m. 21st.June.

38th.D.A.Units, 12th.D.A., 17th.D.A. and C.H.A. to ACKNOWLEDGE.

J. E. Evanston

Major R.A.

Brigade Major 38th.Divisional Artillery.

Issued at 11 a.m.

Copies to all recipients of O.O.63.

S E C R E T.
XXXXXXXXXXX

R.A.,38th.Div. No.G.S.1929/19.

19th.June 1918.

ADDENDUM No.1 to 38th.D.A.O.O. No.63.

---

1. At 3.30 a.m. 21st.June all batteries 38th.D.A. will fire for 5 minutes on their "S.O.S" lines unless the raid has been previously postponed.

2. All batteries 38th.D.A. will continue harassing fire as usual up to zero hour.

3. Reference para.4 the raid H.Q. of O.C. Raiding Party 2nd.R.W.F. will be Q.29.c.9.5. and not as stated.

4. In the event of the raid being postponed the code word "BLUE" will be sent.

J. E. Thurston [signature]

Major R.A.

Brigade Major 38th.Divisional Artillery.

Issued at 10 a.m.

Copies to all recipients of 38th.D.A.O.O. No.63.

12 Bde

Copy No. 5...

SECRET.

17th.Jun. 1918.

38th.DIVISIONAL ARTILLERY OPERATION ORDER No.63.

Ref. 57D. S.E. 1/20,000.
38th.D.A. Map "A" 1/10,000.

1. On night 20/21st.June 38th.Division is to raid the enemy's trenches in the MESNIL Sector.

2. INFANTRY ACTION.

(a) The Raiding Party is to consist of :-

3 companies 2nd.R.W.F. (115th.Inf.Bde.).
4 companies 14th.R.W.F.(113th.Inf.Bde.).

(b) The objective is the enemy trenches - emplacements and dug-outs on the line Q.35.b.55.50. to Q.23.d.55.00.

(c) Patrols are to be pushed out Eastward to the edge of the marsh.

(d) Bombing blocks are to be formed at Q.35.b.5.4. and Q.35.b.3.5. and Q.23.d.40.10.

(e) Raiding troops are to be formed up in "NO MAN'S LAND" immediately East of our front line at Zero - 15 mins.
The advance to the objectives starts at Zero.

(f) Raiders remain on the objective till Zero + 30.

(g) The Signal to the Raiding Party for withdrawal is a Thermite Bomb burst high in the air over Q.29.central - this signal will be repeated once.

3. ARTILLERY ACTION.

(a) The following Artillery will take part in the bombardment and covering barrages :-

6. 18-pdr. Batteries 2. 4.5" How. "	38th.D.A.
6. 18-pdr. Batteries 1. 4.5"How.Battery	D.A. on Right.
5. 18-pdr. Batteries 2. 4.5" How.Batteries	D.A. on Left.
22. 6" Hows. 6. 8" Hows. 2. 9.2" Hows. 6. 60-pdr. guns.	V Corps H.A.
12. 6" Newton Mortars.	38th.D.A.
5. L.T.M.Batteries (Stokes.)	

V Corps H.A. is arranging Counter Battery programme during the operation.

NOTE:- A Machine gun barrage of 116 guns is to be superimposed on the Artillery barrage.

(b) Owing to the proximity of the objective and the steepness of the slope there will be no preliminary bombardment of the area to be raided.

(c) Artillery tasks/

(c) Artillery tasks are shown in Appendix I and Map "A" attached.
(d) All batteries fire on the same targets throughout, except the 6" Southern group of 6" T.M's, which switch clear of the raiding party at Zero + 1 as shown detailed.
(e) The additional 6" T.M's are being installed in Right Group Sector. 38th.Divisional Artillery Group Commanders will sub-allot objectives to the 6" T.M's in their Sectors in consultation with D.T.M.O.

4. LIAISON.
38th.D.A. Groups will each find one Liaison Officer as under :-

RIGHT GROUP.	With O.C. Raiding Party 2nd.R.W.F. at his Raid H.Q. at Q.31.b.20.70.
LEFT GROUP.	With O.C.Raiding Party 14th.R.W.F. at his Raid H.Q. at Q.28.a.90.80.

These Officers will report at Zero - 2 hours.

5. R.A.Signal Officer will arrange for direct telephonic communication between the above Raid H.Q's and H.Q's of Right and Left Groups respectively.

6. The following are the arrangements for synchronization -

(a) A Staff Officer 38th.Division will be at Left Infantry Brigade H.Q. at 12 hours and 6 hours before zero.
The following will attend -
An Officer of 121 and 122 Brigades, D.T.M.O.
(b) An Officer of 38th.Division will visit H.Q. of 12th. and 17th.Divisions at 16 and 8 hours before zero for the purpose of synchronizing watches.
(c) H.A. will please arrange to synchronize at 12th. Division H.Q.

7. Zero hour will be notified later.

8. ACKNOWLEDGE.

ack rw

J.L. Marston
Major R.A.
Brigade Major 38th.Divisional Artillery.

Issued at 6.30pm

Copy No.1 to 121 Brigade.
2 to 122 Brigade.
3 to D.T.M.O.
4 to 17th.D.A.
5 to 35th.D.A.
6 to 12th.D.A.
7 to V Corps H.A.
8 to R.A.Signal Officer.
9 to 38th.Division.
10. to R.A. V Corps.
11 to S.C.R.A.
12/13 War Diary.
14 File.

Serial No.	Time.	UNIT.	TASK.	AMM.	REMARKS.
V CORPS HEAVY ARTILLERY (Contd.).					
12.	Zero to + 30.	2. 9.2" Hows.	Battalion H.Q. Q.24.a.20.60.		
13.	Zero to + 30.	2. 60-pdrs.	Enfilade Road R.19.c.00.40. - Q.24.a.30.50.		
		2. 60-pdrs.	Enfilade Road R.19.d.50.00. - R.19.a.00.80.		
		2. 60-pdrs.	Enfilade Road Q.18.b.20.20. - R.7.c.40.20.		
14.	T.M's. Zero to + 1.	9. 6" T.M's. (Right Group)	AREA - Q.35.d.00.80. Q.35.d.50.80. - Q.36.b.55.10. - Q.35.b.40.15.		RATES FOR T.M.'s Zero to + 1. 4 r.p.t.m. p.m + 1 to + 30. 1 r.p.t.m. p.m
15.	+ 1 to + 30.	9. 6" T.M's. (Right Group).	Lift on to Q.35.c.70.10. - Q.35.d.30.10. - Q.35.d.50.80. - Q.35.d.00.80.		
16.	Zero to + 30.	3. 6" T.M's. (Left Group).	AREA - Q.23.b.10.00. - Q.23.d.50.80. - Q.23.b.60.10. - Q.23.b.30.30.		
17.	At Zero + 30		All Field and Heavy Artillery & 6" T.M's Cease Fire.		

APPENDIX I.

Serial No.	Time.	Unit.		Task.	Amn.	Remarks.
ARTILLERY OF 38th.DIVISION.						
1.	Zero to + 30.	3 18-pdr.Btys.	Right Group.	(1) Q.35.b.10.30. - Q.35.d.50.90. - Q.36.c.00.75. (2) Q.35.a.80.20. - Q.35.d.45.70. (3) Q.36.a.00.75. - Q.35.d.95.25.	A AX	18-pdr. will fire 50% "A" and 50% AX (106 fuze) except where stated. 4.5" Hows. BX. except 1 How.Bty.Right Div.Artillery, which will fire Smoke if wind is suitable.
2.		1 4.5" How.Bty.		Q.36.c.55.40. - Q.36.a.80.10.		RATES. Rds.per gun per min.
3.	Zero to + 30.	3 18-pdr.Btys.	Left Group.	(1) Q.23.d.50.40.- Q.23.d.00.80. (2) Q.23.d.00.75.- Q.23.a.75.60. (3) River Crossings. 2 guns Q.30.c.35.15. 2 guns Q.30.c.30.90. 2 guns Q.30.a.50.95.	"A"	Zero to + 5. / + 5 to + 30. 18-pdrs. 3. / 2. 4.5" Hows. 2. / 1.
4.		1 4.5" How.Bty.		Q.23.b.00.10. - Q.23.d.55.85.		
ARTILLERY OF DIVISION ON RIGHT.						
5.	Zero to + 30.	3 18-pdr.Btys		Q.36.a.80.10.- Q.30.c.50.40.		
6.		3 18-pdr.Btys.		Search and sweep AVELUY WOOD W.4.b.40.00.- W.5.b.20.00.- Q.35.d.40.60. - Q.35.a.70.10.		
7.		1 4.5" How.Bty.		W.5.b.80.40. - Q.36.c.20.00.- Q.36.c.05.20.	Smoke.	If smoke is used. 2. / 1½.

Contd.

Appendix 1 (Contd.)

Serial No.	Ti e.	Unit.	Task.	Am.n.	Remarks.
ARTILLERY OFDIVISION ON LEFT.					
8.	Zero to + 30.	5 18-pdr.Btys.	(1) 1 Battery. Q.23.a.80.60. - Q.17.d.4.2. (2) 2 Batteries. Q.17.c.90.90. - Q.18.c.50.10. (3) 2 Batteries. Q.18.c.70.50. - Q.17.b.30.30.	As above	As above
9.	Zero to + 30.	2 4.5" How.Btys.	On Trenches in area Q.23.b.60.10. - Q.24.a.00.30. - Q.18.c.40.00. - Q.24.b.40.95.		
V CORPS HEAVY ARTILLERY.					
10.	Zero to + 30.	6 6" Hows. 4 6" Hows. 6 6" Hows. 2 6" Hows. 2 6" Hows. 2 6" Hows.	Q.36.b.00.30. - R.25.a.40.20. Q.30.d.00.30. - R.25.a.20.80. Q.30.c.60.50. - Q.30.b.90.90. Triangle Q.30.b.10.80. - Q.24.d.30.00. - Q.24.d.00.30. R.19.c.00.50. - Q.24.b.60.30. The MOUND Q.24.a.70.80. - Q.18.c.70.20.		
11.	Zero to + 30.	2 8" Hows. 2 8" Hows. 2 8" Hows.	W.6.a.20.60. Q.36.c.50.20. Q.25.b.50.20.		

Contd.

SECRET. C.B.S. 79.

COUNTER BATTERY INSTRUCTIONS.

Reference V Corps H.A. Instructions No. 109.
In connection with a Raid to be carried out by 38th. Division on the enemy trenches in the MESNIL Sector.

1. The following guns are available for C.B. work, and will engage targets from zero as shown against them.

17th. Brigade. R.G.A.

51st S.B.	(2 Hows. 6")	X W 5.
56th.S.B.	(1 How. 8")	X W 2.
13th.S.B.	(1 How. 9.2")	W.12.a.90.20. to W X 1.

35th. Brigade. R.G.A.

170th.S.B.	(2 Hows. 6")	X W 2.

62nd. Brigade. R.G.A.

122nd. H.B.	(3 guns 60-prs)	X W 16, X W 18 and X.3.c.3.7.
128th. H.B.	(3 guns 60-prs)	R.26.d.50.30, R.31.b.50.90.
76th. S.B.	(1 How. 9.2")	R Y 3 to R.26.c.90.20.
67th. S.B.	(1 How. 8")	R.25.b.90.90.

93rd. Brigade. R.G.A.

231st.S.B. forward Section	(2 Hows 6")	R.20.a.80.90. to R W 5 R.14.d.30.60.
232nd.S.B. forward Section	(2 Hows 6")	R Y 5 and X W 18.
124th.S.B.	(2 Hows. 9.2")	R Y 6 and R.21.a.70.00.
215th.S.B.	(2 Hows. 8")	R Y 1 and R.26.b.90.30. to R.27.a.20.20.
2/1 Lowland H.B.	(2 guns 60-pr)	X W 10 and X W 13.
35th. H.B.	(2 guns 60-pr)	R Y 6, R Y 7.

58th. Brigade. R.G.A.

58th. S.B.	(3 guns 6")	X W 9, X W 14 and X W 12.
409th. S.B.	(3 guns 6")	X W 16, X W 17 and X W 18.
431st. S.B.	(2 Hows 12")	North:- X W 17. South:- X W 9.

Rate of fire 'NORMAL' till zero plus 30 minutes, then half that rate pending orders from this office.

2. IV Corps are engaging batteries in the Northern part of the area.

3. H.A.Brigades and 18 Observation Group will make the usual special arrangements to keep this office informed of hostile activity.

4. H.A.Brigades and 18 Observation Group, acknowledge by wire.

F. O. Barry [signature]
Lt. Col. R.A.
20/6/18. Counter Battery Staff Officer V Corps.

Issued at 2 p.m. to:-

17th., 35th., 62nd., 93rd and 58th. Bdes. R.G.A. and 18 Observation Group.

Copies for Information to:-
R.A. V Corps. V Corps H.A. 15th. Squadron. R.A.F.
18 Balloon Company. 38th., 12th., and 17th. DIV. ARTYS.
C.B.S.O. IV Corps.

H.A.,V Corps.
S.G. 11/96.

S E C R E T.

V CORPS HEAVY ARTILLERY INSTRUCTIONS No. 109.

1. On the night 20th./21st.June 1918,the 38th.Division is to carry out a raid on the enemy's trenches in the MESNIL Sector.

2. (a) The objective is the enemy's trenches - emplacements - and dug-outs on the line Q.35.b.55.50. to Q.23.d.55.00.
(b) The raiding troops will be formed up in "No Man's Land" immediately East of our front line at Zero minus 15 minutes.
(c) The raiders will remain on the objective until Zero plus 30 minutes.
(d) The Signal for re-call will be a THERMILE Bomb burst high in the air over Q.29.central. This signal will be repeated once.

3. The raid will be supported by all the Divisional Artilleries & Corps H.A.

4. The action of the Corps H.A. is given in TABLE "A" attached.

5. Rates of fire.

Zero to Zero plus 5 minutes...... All natures..... RAPID.
Zero plus 5 mins. to Zero plus 30 minutes. .... All natures..... NORMAL.

6. Ammunition. Howitzers. H.E. 106 fuzes where safe.
60-Pdrs. Shrapnel.

7. Watches will be synchronised on the afternoon of the 20/6/18. Brigades concerned will send a representative to H.A.,H.Qrs. Exact time will be notified later.

8. The C.B.,S.O.,V Corps is arranging a Counter Battery programme.

9. Zero hour will be notified later.

10. Brigades to acknowledge.

[signature]
Major R.A.
19th.June.1918. Brigade Major,V Corps Heavy Artillery.

Issued to :- 17th.,35th.,58th.,62nd.,93rd.Bdes.R.G.A.

Copies to :- C.B.,S.O.,V Corps. R.A.,V Corps. IV Corps H.A.
Staff Capt.,H.A. 38th.,12th.,17th.,Divisions.
Ammn.Officer H.A. 38th.,12th.,17th.,Divn.,Arty.
Signal Offr.,H.A. "O" Siege Park. 18 Obs.Group.
15 Squad R.A.F. 18 Balloon Co. 12th.Wing R.A.F.

H.A.,V Corps.
S.G. 11/96.

TABLE "A"

Action of V Corps Heavy Artillery from Zero to Zero plus 30 minutes.

51st.S.Bty.(2)	Trenches	Q.36.b.00.30. to Q.36.b.40.60.
248th.S.Bty.(2)	..	Q.36.b.40.60. to Q.30.d.70.20.
248th.S.Bty.(2)	..	Q.30.d.00.30. to Q.30.b.70.20.
274th.S.Bty.(2)	..	Q.30.b.70.20. to R.25.a.20.80.
267th.S.Bty.(4)	..	Q.30.c.80.50. to Q.30.b.20.20.
142nd.S.Bty.(4)	..	Q.30.b.20.20. to Q.30.b.90.90.
224th.S.Bty.(2)	Triangle	Q.30.b.10.80. - Q.24.d.30.00. - Q.24.d.00.30.
231st.S.Bty.(2)		R.19.c.00.50. to Q.24.b.60.30.
232nd.S.Bty.(2)	MOUND.	Q.24.a.70.80. to Q.18.c.70.20.
13th.S.Bty.(2)	Area	W. 6.a.05.75. - W. 6.a.30.75. - W. 6.a.30.40. - W.6.a.05.40.
56th.S.Bty.(2)		Q.36.c.50.20.
67th.S.Bty.(2)		Q.23.b.50.20.
76th.S.Bty.(2)	Bn.H.Qrs.	Q.24.a.20.60.
35th.H.Bty.(2)	Enfilade Road	R.19.c.00.40. - Q.24.d.00.70.
126th.H.Bty.(2) (P.11.a.)	.. ..	R.19.a.80.20. - R.19.a.00.80.
122nd.H.Bty.(2)	.. ..	Q.18.c.60.50. - R. 7.c.40.20.
111th.H.Bty.(2)	Search & Sweep THIEPVAL WOOD from Western edge to Trench Q.30.d.20.20. to R.25.a.30.80.	

Zero plus 30 minutes. Cease firing.

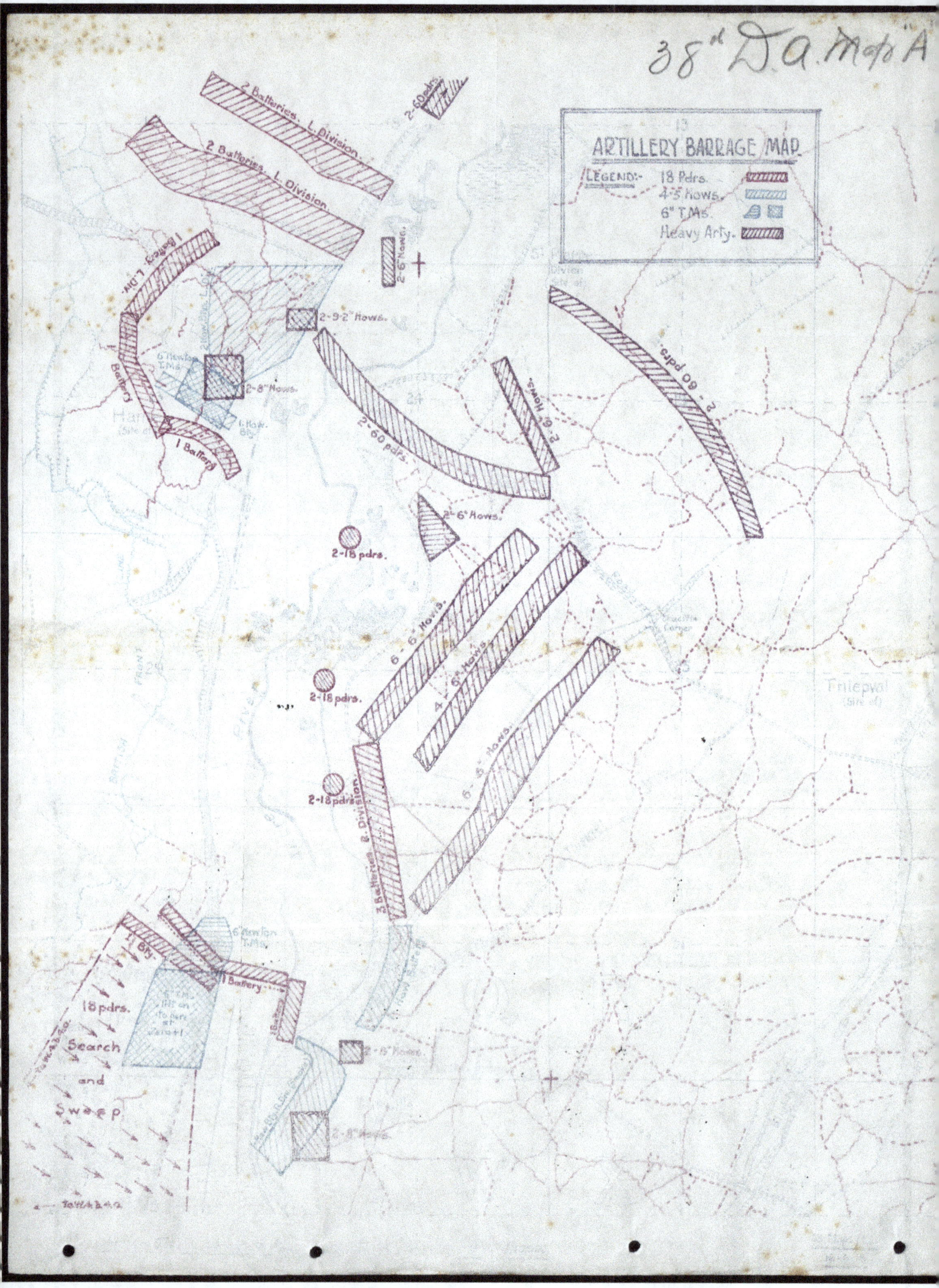

38th D.A. Map "A"
ARTILLERY BARRAGE MAP
LEGEND:-
18 Pdrs.
4·5 Hows.
6" T.Ms.
Heavy Arty.
2 Batteries. L. Division.
2 Batteries. L. Division.
2-60 pdrs.
2-6" Hows.
2-9·2" Hows.
2-8" Hows.
1 Battery L. Div.
1 Battery
1 Battery
2-60 pdrs.
2-60 pdrs.
2-6" Hows.
2-6" Hows.
2-18 pdrs.
2-18 pdrs.
2-18 pdrs.
6-6" Hows.
4-6" Hows.
6-8" Hows.
3 Batteries 8. Division
1 Bty.
1 Battery
18 pdrs.
Search
and
Sweep
2-8" Hows.
2-8" Hows.
Thiepval
(Site of)

38th Raid

War Diary

S E C R E T.

12th Division No. G.X. 2431.

18th Division.
35th Inf. Bde.)
36th Inf. Bde.)
37th Inf. Bde.)   for information.
C.R.A.)
C.R.E.)
12th Bn. M.G.C.)

---

1. The 12th Division will carry out a minor operation as shown on the attached map with a view to occupying and consolidating the line shown in BLUE. Two Battalions of the 37th Infantry Brigade - each less 1 Company - will be used.

It is understood that the 18th Division is prepared to co-operate by occupying and consolidating the enemy's Front and Support Lines South of the Inter-Divisional Boundary.

2. The proposed date is the 30th June - Zero hour to be about an hour before dusk, say 8 p.m.

3. The operation will be carried out under a barrage of Artillery, L.T.Mortars and Machine Guns: smoke to be used for masking hostile Machine guns if the wind is suitable.

4. It is suggested that for the purposes of the operation the boundary between the 12th & 18th Divisions be BOUNDARY Street inclusive to the 12th Division: and the point of junction in the enemy's line W.15.d.77.00

5. Will you please inform me if you agree to the above proposals.

H.W. Higginson

Major-General,

Commanding 12th Division.

22nd June, 1918.

S E C R E T.

12th Division No. G.X. 2413

C.R.A.
35th Inf. Bde.
36th Inf. Bde.
37th Inf. Bde.
12th Bn. M.G.C.

---

1. In view of a probable operation in the near future the enemy wire will be cut at intervals along the Divisional front, special attention being paid to W.15.d. where the wire is reported to be thick. It is essential that this wire be properly cut. Cutting will be proceeded with daily.

2. The C.R.A. will arrange details with the Brigadiers concerned; these details will include the use of L.T.M's where suitable and the clearing of trenches when necessary during wire cutting.

3. The Brigades in the line will be responsible for preventing the enemy from repairing damage by means of M.G. and L.G. fire at night.

4. Special efforts will be made to gain all possible information regarding the enemy wire in W.15. a. and d.

Lieut-Colonel,
General Staff,
12th Division.

22nd June, 1918.

SECRET.

12th Division No. G.X.2430

C.R.A.
C.R.E.
35th Inf. Bde.
36th Inf. Bde.
37th Inf. Bde.
12th Bn. M.G.C.
12th Div. Signals.
5th Northamptonshire Regt.
"Q".
A.D.M.S.

OPERATION W.15.d. - Memo.No.1.

1. The 37th Infantry Brigade will carry out an operation with a view to :-

(a) occupying and consolidating the line as shown in BLUE on attached Sketch (issued to 37th Inf. Bde., C.R.A. and 12th Bn.M.G.C. only):

(b) raiding the areas shown in BLUE on sketch. The occupation by us of the line indicated will deprive the enemy of valuable observation points.

The 18th Division has been asked to co-operate by occupying and consolidating a portion of the enemy's front and support lines S. of W.15.a.7.2. The boundary between 12th and 18th Divisions will be BOUNDARY Street (inclusive to the 12th Division) and thence to W.15.d.7.2.

2. The following will carry out the operation :-

2 Battalions, 37th Inf. Bde. (each less 1 Coy.left as garrison of the present front system).
1 Coy. 5th Northamptonshire Regt. for clearing and joining up C.Ts.
A Detachment R.E. for wiring posts.

3. The operation will be carried out under Artillery, Machine gun and L.T.M barrages. Probable date 30th June - proposed Zero Hour 8 p.m.

4. The following are the arrangements for reliefs.

(a) 37th Inf. Bde. will relieve 36th Inf. Bde. (less 2 Coys on the night 29th/30th June.
(b) The 2 Coys. 36th Inf. Bde. will hold the portion of the Right Brigade Front from Road junction W.15.a. 45.75. (exclusive) to the Brigade Northern Boundary till relieved after completion of the operation by the 37th Inf. Bde.: details to be arranged by Brigadiers concerned.

5. A practise ground is being laid out under Divisional arrangement just W. of SENLIS.

[signature]
Lieut-Colonel,
General Staff,
12th Division.

22nd June, 1918.

S E C R E T.

12th Division No. G.X. 2464

C.R.A.
C.R.E
35th Inf. Bde.
36th Inf. Bde.
37th Inf. Bde.
12th Bn. M.G.C.

12th Div. Signals.
5th Northamptonshire Regt.
A.D.M.S.
"Q".

Operation W.15.d. - Memo No. 2.

1. In view of a forthcoming operation, the following action will be taken. All arrangements will be taken in hand at once and completed as soon as possible.

2. Working Parties - Reserve Brigade.

From the 25th June (inclusive) till the conclusion of the operation, working parties will be found by the Reserve Brigade as under.

(a) Under C.E. V Corps (G.X.2142) - 1 Company strength 100.
(b) Under C.R.E. 12 th Division (G.X.2280) - 1½ Companies strength 150.
(c) Under O.C. Signals (G.X.2293) - 1 Company strength 100:
½ Coy. 5th Northants. Regt. strength 50.

3. Carrying Parties for Ammunition, R.E. Stores, etc.

(a) L.T.M. Ammunition will be dumped by each Infantry Brigade for its own guns taking part in the operation. Ammunition for 3 extra Batteries asked for (24 Mortars) by 37th Inf. Bde.

(b) M.G. Ammunition will be dumped by 12th Batln. M G.C. for all guns taking part: 4 extra Companies have been asked for.

(c) R.E. Stores, Wire, Stakes, etc., Water and Reserve S.A.A. will be dumped by 37th Inf. Bde.

4. (a) Assembly trenches and C.T's.
The 36th Inf. Bde. will in consultation with 37th Inf. Bde. prepare the necessary assembly trenches and sites for dumps and will construct any additional Battle H.Q. required in the forward areas and as far West as COBURN TRENCH (inclusive).
The C.R.E. will deepen and improve C.T's. as necessary.
(b) Medical.
The A.D.M.S. will arrange with 37th Inf. Bde. as to Medical Arrangements and will construct any additional accommodation required.
(c) Communication.
The O.C. Signals will draw up the plan of signal communication and carry out any work required.
(d) Stragglers Posts and the disposal of Prisoners will be dealt with by 37th Inf. Bde.

5. All arrangements made in connection with the operation will be reported to Divisional Headquarters as soon as possible. Full details are required for transmission to Corps i.e. position of dumps and amounts of Ammunition etc. in them, location of Battle H.Q., means of communication, etc.

Lieut.Colonel,
General Staff,
12th Division.

24th June, 1918.

S E C R E T.

HEADQUARTERS
R.A. 790.
12th DIVISIONAL ARTILLERY

62nd)
63rd) Brigade R.F.A.
93rd)
Sig. Offr. R.A.
and to 12th Dn. (G) & Sigs.) for
35th,36th,37th Inf. Bdes.) information.

Ref. 57D. S.E.
1/20,000.

Warning Order.

24th June, 1918.

1. On or about the 30th instant the 37th Infantry Brigade are carrying out an operation to raid and hold parts of the enemy system in W 15 b and d.

2. 18 pr. batteries of Brigades will occupy temporary positions to support the operation in the areas shown on the attached tracing which also shows the zones they will be required to barrage.

3. Brigades will reconnoitre these areas forthwith and send location statements showing proposed Battery positions to Divisional Artillery H.Q. by last D.R. on the 25th instant.

4. The operation will last about 6 hours and 300 (two-thirds A.) rounds per gun will be required at the temporary positions.

5. Lieut-Colonel R.G. THOMSON, C.M.G., D.S.O. will be in command of the Artillery during the operation.

6. On completion of the operation Brigades will successively occupy their normal positions under orders from O.C. 63rd Brigade R.F.A. commencing with 63rd Brigade, then 62nd Brigade and finally 93rd Army Brigade.

[signature]
Major,
Brigade Major 12th D. A.

Identification Trace for

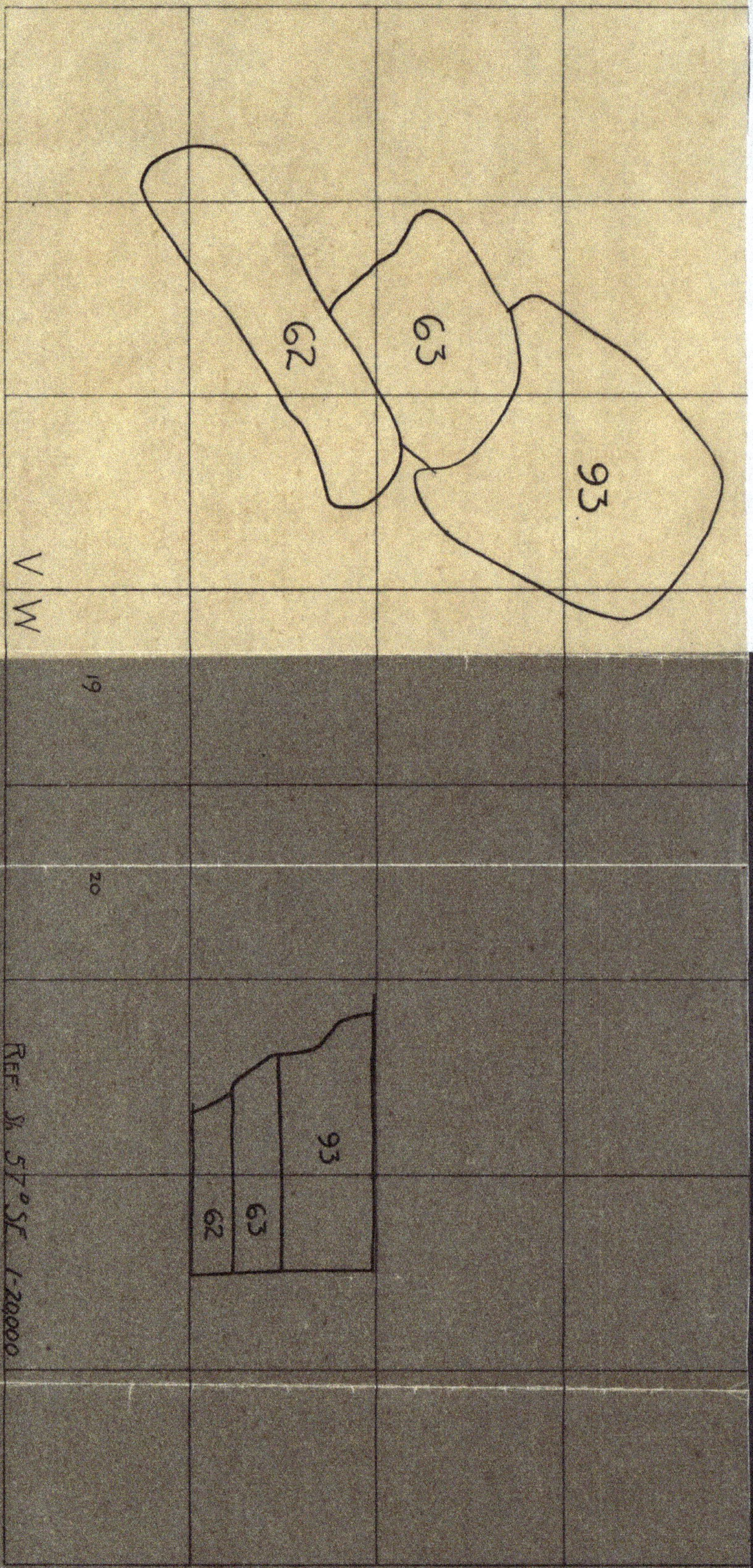

NOTE.—(1). These traces are intended to facilitate the communication of information as to the position of targets, which have b

(2). The squares on this trace are 500 yards in length on the 1/10,000 scale, 1,000 yards in length on the 1/20,000 s on the 1/40,000 scale.

(3). The squares on the trace are fitted to the squares of the map showing the targets, which are then dra letters and numbers must also be added to enable the recipient to place the trace in the correct position on hi may also be traced, but this is not essential. The name and scale of the map to which the trace refers must can be used for the 1/10,000, 1/20,000, or 1/40,000 scale.

G.S.G.S. 3023

S E C R E T.

C O P Y No. 8

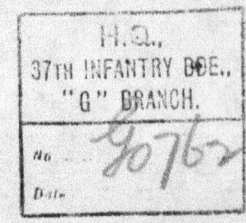

H.Q.
37TH INFANTRY BDE.,
"G" BRANCH.
No. G0762
Date

37th Infantry Brigade
Operations in W.15.
Instructions No.1

Ref: 57 D. S.E. 1/20.000.

1. Battle H.Q.
(a) The 2 attacking Battalions, 6th Queen's and 6th R.W.Kent Regt, will establish Battle H.Q. together in the Sunken road at W.13.a.3.6. Adv. battle report centre for both battalions to be situated in vicinity of Bank in W.14.a. Exact location to be decided by Battalions and notified to this office.

(b) Adv. Brigade Headquarters will be established at Support Battalion Headquarters, V.12.c.6.1.

2. Medical arrangements.
(a) During the operations R.A.P. for both Battalions will be situated at W.13.d.7.6; walking wounded will proceed to R.A.P. where they will be given further instructions.
(b) Adv. R.A.M.C. bearer posts in bank at W.14.b.2.2. Relay post at R.A.P.

(c) Stretcher cases will be evacuated by ambulance from point on HEDAUVILLE ROAD just W. of BOUZINCOURT, to A.D.S. HEDAUVILLE.

3. PRISONERS.
All prisoners will be sent immediately to adv. Brigade Headquarters at V.12.c.6.1. where they will be taken over by the A.P.M., a receipt being obtained. All captured M.G's, Mortars and trophies will also, in first case, be sent to adv. Brigade Headquarters.

4. Stragglers Posts.
Stragglers posts will be established as follows:-
(a) Entrance to C.T. off bank at W.14.b.4.4.
(b) Just N. of Battalion Headquarters in Sunken road - W.13.a.4.7.
These posts will be manned from Zero minus 1 hour onwards by 6th Buffs.

5. Control Posts.
For control of traffic in C.T. (QUARTZ) during hour of assembly and during the operation, 6th Buffs will detail 2 Officers to be posted as follows:,
One at junction of C.T. and SAUCHIEHALL Reserve W.14.c.6.9
One at junction of C.T. and DRAGON TRENCH W.14.b.85.10.

6. Dumps.
Forward dumps will be established under Brigade arrangements as follows :-

(a)	Right Battalion Dump	W.15.d.20.40.
(b)	Left -do-	W.15.a.70.30.
(c)	Emergency Dump	W.15.a.35.10.
(d)	Adv. Brigade dump	W.14.b.35.40.

Each of (a) (b) and (c) will contain the following :-

20 boxes S.A.A.
15 Boxes No. 36 grenades
2 boxes Very Lights 1" white
1 box "S.O.S" signals
500 sandbags
20 picks
20 shovels
12 tins water
12 rolls concertina wire
6 rolls barbed wire
20 long screw pickets
20 short --do--

Adv. Brigade dump will be made up of double the amount laid down for (a) (b) and (c).

7. Equipment.
(a) All ranks engaged in operation will carry full fighting order, including 1 days rations plus iron rations and full water bottle.

(b) 1st wave, including "Moppers up" and 2nd wave will carry 2 bombs apiece, including proportion of "P" bombs, and Very Pistols on a scale of 1 per Platoon. Of every 3 men in these waves, 2 will carry S.A. wire cutters and 1 a hand wire cutter to be tied to the man.

(c) All raiding and "mopping up" Platoons will have their bombing squads fully equipped with an adequate supply of bombs.
Blocking parties will carry 6 sandbags a man, and 2 picks and 2 shovels.

(d) Consolidators will carry 4 sandbags a man, 50% shovels, 50% picks, 220 rounds S.A.A., and 3"S.O.S." signals per platoon.

(e) All officers will carry compasses.

8. Distinguishing Marks.
(a) All ranks engaged in the operations, including Pioneers and R.E., will wear a piece of 4 by 2 sewn on each shoulder in continuation of, and below, the shoulder strap.

(b) Carrying parties will wear 2 pieces of 4 by 2 sewn on as above on each shoulder.

P.B.B. Nichols
Captain.
Brigade Major.
25-6-18. 37th Infantry Brigade.

Copy No. 1 6th Queen's
2 6th Buffs
3 6th R.W.Kent Regt.
4 37th T.M.Batty.
5 12th Division, G.
6 12th Division, Q.
7 C.R.E. 12th Division
8 C.R.A. -do-
9 A.D.M.S.
10 D.T.M.O.
11 A.P.M.
12 35th Inf.Bde.
13 36th Inf.Bde.
14 54th Inf.Bde.
15 12th Bn.M.G.Corps
16 5th Northants Regt (Pioneers)
17 70th Field Coy, R.E.
18 63rd Bde. R.F.A.
19 H.A.Liaison Officer
20 37th Field Amb.
21 Bde Signal Officer
22 Bde Transport Officer
23 Bde Supply Officer
24 Staff Captain
25 War Diary
26 File.

37th Infantry Brigade No. G.O.771.

S E C R E T.

Copy No.........8

37th Infantry Brigade
Operations in W.15.
Instructions No.2.

Ref. Part of
Sheet 57D. SE
1/10.000

1. L.T.M. Co-operation.

Numbers.

(a) 6 L.T.M. Batteries will take part in the operation; 3 Batteries of the 12th Division and 3 Batteries of the 17th Division which are being made available. One Battery of the 17th Division is being attached to each Battery of the 12th Division for purposes of co-operation.

Distribution.

(b) Batteries will be distributed as follows:-

(I) Covering 37th Infantry Brigade Front during the operation:-
36th Trench Mortar Battery.
37th Trench Mortar Battery
2 Batteries 17th Division.

(II) Firing from positions in Left Brigade Sector:-
35th Trench Mortar Battery.
1 Battery 17th Division.

Positions and Targets.

(c) (I) Positions in and around WELSH TRENCH of 4 Batteries covering the 37th Infantry Brigade front will be *as* shown in attached Map B*.
Targets of these Batteries are the German Front Line and saps within the following limits:-

*To units of
37th Inf. Bde,
35th Inf. Bde.
36th Inf. Bde.
12th Divn.
D.T.M.C. only.

"A" L.T.M. Batty. W.15.d.00.70 - W.15.d.60.40
17th Division
37th L.T.M. Batty.W.15.d.60.40.- W.15.d.33.72
"B" L.T.M. Batty. W.15.d.33.72 - W.15.b.09.02.
17th Division
36th L.T.M. Batty.W.15.b.09.02 - W.15.a.86.42.

These targets are shown on map B*.
Special attention will be paid by 36th Trench Mortar Battery to Sap at W.15.a.75.40. Our troops are assembling in the western side of trench loop at N. of SHELL HOLE TRENCH in order that Stokes bombardment of this sap may not be interfered with.

(II) The 35th T.M.B. from emplacements in HEATHCOTES BANK are bombarding enemy position in W.4.c.; "C" L.T.M. Battery, 17th Division, from emplacements in W.3.d. are bombarding enemy trenches in W.9.b. and d; orders for these bombardments will be issued separately.

P.T.O

Action.

(d) The 4 Batteries covering 37th Infantry Brigade front will open a hurricane bombardment on targets as in para. (c) (I) above at Zero hour and continue to Zero plus 5 minutes when fire will cease. Further fire will depend on the situation. S.C. Batteries will have positions ready in SHELL HOLE TRENCH from which fire can be brought to bear to cover the line of consolidation, and assist in breaking up any counter-attack. S.C. Batteries will be prepared to push Mortars up into the old German Front Line if the situation requires. Further orders as to the number of guns required forward & zones will be issued to those concerned.

Ammunition.

(e) Emplacements for all Batteries have been prepared, and ammunition on a scale of 100 rounds per Mortar for Batteries in 37th Infantry Brigade area, and 200 rounds per mortar for Batteries in Left Brigade area is being dumped; this ammunition is in excess of normal reserves.

Occupation of Positions.

(f) (I) The 37th L.T.M. Battery will occupy their positions during the night 28th/29th June and will come under the orders of the G.O.C., 36th Infantry Brigade.

(II) The 3 L.T.M. Batteries of the 17th Division will occupy their positions during the night 29th/30th June and will withdraw on the 1st July and night 1st/2nd July.

(III) L.T.M. Headquarters in the 37th Infantry Brigade Sector during the operation will be at W.14.b.3.3.

2. Signal Communication.

(a) Telephonic.

The Brigade will be responsible for telephonic communication up to Battalions Report Centre in Bank in W.14.b.

Each Battalion will arrange to extend one line from a suitable Company H.Q. - this line will be extended to the front line before Zero. These lines will go back to Battalion Report Centre, and if considered necessary may be earth return. Light cable is available for this purpose.

(b) Visual.

Battalions will combine visual communications and consolidating party from each Battalion will take with them one Lucas Lamp and will signal direct back to Battalion H.Q.

Battalion H.Q. will have visual communication with Advanced Brigade Headquarters via Transmitting Station at W.7.c.1.9.

(c) Power Buzzers.

A Power Buzzer and amplifier will be sent with consolidating party from each Battalion and will gain communication with a set which will be established at the Battalions Report Centre. This set will be in communication with a set at Advanced Brigade Headquarters.

During the operation all Power Buzzer messages may be sent in clear.

(d) <u>Pigeons.</u>

6 Pigeons will be supplied to each Battalion for use on the morning of Zero plus 1 day if required.

(e) <u>Message Carrying Rockets.</u>

8 message carrying rockets will be issued to each Battalion for use between advanced troops and Battalions Report Centre, and if necessary, from there back to Battalion Headquarters.

P.B.B. Nichols
Captain,
Brigade Major,
37th Infantry Brigade.

<u>Distribution:</u>

As for 37th Infantry Brigade
Instructions No. 1, less
A.P.M., 12th Division.

S E C R E T.

12th Division No. G.X.2486.

C.R.A.
C.R.E. 12th Div. Signals.
35th Inf. Bde. 5th Northamptonshire Regt.
36th Inf. Bde. A.D.M.S.
37th Inf. Bde. "Q".
12th Bn. M.G.C. 18th Division.

Operation W.15.d. - Memo. No. 3.

1. Distribution of L.T.M.Batteries.

L.T.M.Batteries taking part in the operation will be distributed as follows :-

Unit.	Objective.	Emplacements.
(a) 35th T.M.Bty.	Barrage trenches in W.4.c.	Heathcotes Bank.
(b) 36th T.M.Bty.) 37th T.M.Bty.) 2 L.T.M.Btys.) (additional))	Barrage W.15.a, b & d.	WELSH Trench.
(c) 1 L.T.M.Bty. (additional).	Barrage trenches in W.9.b & d.	To be selected.

Detailed selection of positions will be made as follows :-

(a) by 35th Inf. Bde.) The D.T.M.O. will
(b) by 36th and 37th Inf.Bdes.in consultation) be available to
(c) -do- -do- -do-) assist in co-ordinating the L.T.M. arrangements.

Ammunition for L.T. Mortars.

For (a) and (c) above - 200 rounds per mortar.
For (b) above 100 rounds per mortar.

Existing dumps in the forward area may be made use of but normal reserves maintained at the battle position of L.T.M's are not to be depleted.

2. The following programme of night harassing fire is issued by the 18th Division. 12th Bn. M.G.Corps will not fire on enemy wire in W.15.a., b. & d. during the hours when patrols of the 18th Division are out. Actual times for M.G.harassing fire on this wire will, subject to the above, be arranged between the Brigadier and M.G.Bn.

Night Harassing fire 18th Division.

Date.	Harassing fire.	Patrolling.	Harassing fire.
25/26	9.30 - 10 p.m.	10 p.m. - 12.30 a.m.	12.30 a.m. onward
26/27	Nil.	all night	Nil.
27/28	Nil.	Up to 12.15 a.m.	12.15 a.m. onward.
28/29	Up to 11.30 p.m.	11.30 p.m. - 1 a.m.	1 a.m. onward.
29/30	9.25 p.m. - 10 p.m.	10 pm - 1 a.m.	1 a.m. onward.

W. R. Pennell

Lieut.Colonel,
General Staff,
12th Division.

25th June, 1918.

Copy to DTMO

SECRET.

12th Division No. G.X. 2620

ADDENDUM No. 2.

to

12th DIVISION ORDER No. 261 dated 28th June, 1918.

1. (a) The 4 6" T.M's and 2 Coys. M.G.C. detailed from the 35th Division are not now available to take part in the operation.

These Units are being supplied by the 17th Division.

(b) The following amendments to 12th Division Order No. 261 will be made.

para.2 (c)
for "with 2 Companies each of the 17th and 35th Battalions M.G.Corps (attached)."
read "with 4 Companies 17th Battalion M.G.Corps (attached)."

para 2 (d)
for "(with 4 6" T.M's 35th Division attached)."
read "(with 4 6" T.M's 17th Division attached)."

para 8 (b)
for "17th and 35th Battalions M.G.C."
read "17th Battalion M.G.C."
add "The 8 Machine guns in 'Mobile Reserve' to the 17th Division will rejoin their Division on the conclusion of the operation should the situation admit, i.e. on the morning of the 1st July.

para 8 (c)
for "35th Division"
read "17th Division."

2. Synchronisation of Watches (para 9.)

(a) 12th D.A.) at 12th Divisional Headquarters
C.R.E.) at 10. 0 a.m., 30th June.

(b) Infantry Bdes.)
12th Bn. M.G.C.) at Headquarters 37th Inf. Bde. at
5th Northampton-) 10.45 a.m., 30th June.
shire Regt.)

(c) V CORPS is arranging to synchronise watches of -

Corps H.A.
18th Division.
38th Division.

3. Acknowledge.

29.6.18

[signature]

Lieut-Colonel,
General Staff,
12th Division.

To all recipients of 12th Division Order No.261.

S E C R E T.

12th Division No. G.X.2583.

ADDENDUM No. 1
to
12th DIVISION ORDER No. 261 dated 28th JUNE, 1918.

1. Para. 5. complete as follows :-

(a) The S.O.S. Signal for the operation will be a rifle grenade rocket bursting into RED / RED / RED /. This is the Normal S.O.S. Signal of the 18th Division and will apply to the 12th Division Front as far North as W.15.a.46.77 from Zero till the operation is complete and the present S.O.S. Signal (GREEN / RED / GREEN) has been distributed to troops in the captured position. The Brigadier 37th Infantry Brigade will notify 12th Division, C.R.A., 12th Bn. M.G.C. and Flank Brigades by priority wire the time at which the normal (GREEN / RED / GREEN) S.O.S. Signal will be brought into use again.

(b) In addition to the S.O.S. Signal the 18th Division is making use of the following Light Signals.

(1)	1st objective gained. 2nd do. 3rd do.	Succession of White Very Lights.
(2)	Artillery and M.G. support required.	- Succession of Green Very Lights.
(3)	Lengthen barrage.	- Succession of Red Very Lights.
(4)	Artillery and M.G's cease fire.	- Succession of White Very Lights.
(5)	Consolidation complete and covering parties withdrawn.	- Pairs of Red and Green Very Lights sent up in succession.

(N.B. The above signals do not apply to the 12th Division).

2. Para. 3. Add new sub-paras 3 (d) and (e).

(d) The 18th Division is putting down a smoke screen with 4" Stokes Mortars at Zero minus 10 minutes.

(e) The Heavy Artillery supporting the 18th Division will open "Counter preparation" on the 1st July about 2.15 a.m.

3. Add new para. 11.

11. Zero hour will be notified by Divisional Headquarters to all concerned before 12 noon on the 30th June.
It will be between 9.15 p.m. and 10 p.m. 30th June.

4. A C K N O W L E D G E.

W. R. Pauwels (signature)
Lieut.Colonel,
General Staff,
12th Division.

28th June, 1918.

Copies to :- All recipients of 12th Division Order No. 261.

S E C R E T.

Copy No. 2

12th DIVISION ORDER No. 261.

Ref. Map: 57.D. S.E. 1/20,000. 28th June, 1918.

1. (a) The 12th Division will carry out an operation on the night 30th June/1st July with a view to

(1) occupying and consolidating the line W.15.d.78.00 - 78.68 - b.52.00 - b.00.45 - a.50.65.

(2) raiding occupied areas in W.15.b. and along the line of the road W.15.d.95.00 - W.15.b.95.25.

(b) The 18th Division is co-operating on the right by occupying and consolidating the enemy trenches from W.15.d.78.00 - W.21.b. 50:00 - W.21.d.00.85 - W.21.a.77.10.

(c) The 38th Division is co-operating on the left by bringing fire of Artillery, T.M's. and Machine Guns to bear on portions of AVELUY WOOD

2. Troops Engaged.

(a) 37th Infantry Brigade.
3 Sections R.E.
2 Coys. 5th Northamptonshire Regt. (each less 1 platoon).
36th T.M.Battery and 2 L.T.M.Batteries 17th Divn. (attached).

The above will carry out the operation referred to in para. 1 (a) under orders of the Brigadier, 37th Infantry Brigade.

(b) 35th T.M.Battery and 1 T.M.Battery, 17th Divn. (attached), will co-operate by bombarding the enemy trenches in W.9.b. and d. and W.4.a. and c. under arrangements made by the Brigadier, 35th Infantry Brigade.

(c) The 12th Bn. M.G.Corps, with 2 Companies each of the 17th and 35th Battns. M.G.Corps (attached) will cover the operation under arrangements made by the O.C. 12th Bn. M.G.Corps in consultation with the Brigadier, 37th Infantry Brigade.

(d) The 12th Divisional Artillery (with four 6" T.M's. 35th Divn. attached) and Corps Heavy Artillery will cover the operation under arrangements made by the C.R.A. 12th Division.

3. (a) Time Table.

Zero Time.	Action.
Zero.	Artillery, Machine Guns and Stokes Mortars open fire. Infantry leaves assembly trenches and advances up to barrage.
plus 3 mins.	Stokes Mortars cease fire.
plus 5 "	Field Artillery Barrage lifts forward at rate of 100 yards in 2 minutes.
plus 13 "	Field Artillery Barrage reaches S.O.S. Line.
plus 15 "	" " " searches forward 200 yards.
plus 19 "	" " ceases fire and stands by for S.O.S.
	Machine guns stand by for S.O.S.: fire bursts at irregular intervals till Zero + 4 hours or ordered to stop.

/ (b)

3. (continued)

(b) The signal for Machine Guns and Stokes Mortars to open fire at Zero will be the opening of the Field Artillery barrage.

(c) Corps Heavy Artillery opens fire at Zero and continues firing till Zero plus 4 hours or until ordered to stop.

4. Consolidation.

The line to be consolidated will be organized in posts which will be constructed at the following points :-

W.15.d.77.00. W.15.b.51.00.
W.15.d.74.28. W.15.a.98.47.
W.15.d.79.71.

The 3 Sections R.E. attached to 37th Inf. Bde. will be used for laying out (not digging) and wiring these posts.

Two Communication Trenches will be dug to connect the captured position with our present Front Line.

5. (a) The S. O. S. Signal for the operation will be a rifle grenade rocket bursting into

(details later)

6. (a) Distinguishing Marks. All ranks engaged in the operation - including R.E., Pioneers, M.G. and L.T.M. personnel moving forward to the present front line and beyond - will wear a piece of flannellette (4" x 2") sewn on each arm just below the shoulder strap: carrying parties will wear two pieces similarly sewn on.

7. (a) Prisoners will be sent back under escort to Advanced Brigade H.Q. at V.12.c.6.1, where they will be taken over by the A.P.M. The Intelligence Officer 12th Division will be at Advanced Brigade H.Q. and will conduct the preliminary examination.

(b) Stragglers Posts will be established by the 37th Infantry Brigade as follows from Zero - 1 hour :-

(1) Entrance to C.T. off bank at W.14.b.4.4.
(2) At Cross Roads V.12.c.5.4.

(c) Medical Arrangements during the Operation.

(1) R.A.P. for both assaulting Battalions at W.13.d.7.6. (near the ALBERT - BOUZINCOURT Road).

(2) Walking wounded to R.A.P. as in (1) above whence they will proceed to A.D.S. HEDAUVILLE.

(3) Advanced R.A.M.C. bearer post in bank at W.14.b.2.2: Relay Post at R.A.P. as in (1) above.

/ (d) Communications..

7. (continued)

(d) Communications. The following special arrangements have been made :-

(1) Lines. From Advanced Brigade H.Q. (V.12.c.6.1) to Battalion Report Centre in W.14.a.
Each assaulting Battalion will lay a line forward to the vicinity of the front line before Zero: these lines will be extended forward after Zero.

(2) Visual. Each assaulting Battalion will take one Lucas Lamp for communication to Battalion H.Q. (W.13.a.).

(3) A Power Buzzer and Amplifier will be carried by each assaulting Battalion: these will work to Battalion Report Centre (W.14.a.) which will be in connection with Battalion H.Q. (W.13.a.) and Advanced Brigade H.Q. by Power Buzzer and Amplifier.

(4) Pigeons: 6 per assaulting Battalion. These will not be liberated before dawn on the 1st July.

(5) Message carrying rockets: 3 to each assaulting Battalion. Rockets will be fired to Battalion Report Centre (W.14.a.) after dawn if necessary.

(6) Runners and Runner Relay Posts will be arranged by 37th Infantry Brigade.

(e) (1) Contact Aeroplane.

A Contact Aeroplane will fly over the captured position at dawn on the 1st July. Troops will show their position by displaying in the trench a piece of white cloth 2'6" x 1'.

(2) Counter-attack Aeroplanes will patrol the front before dawn and at dusk on the 1st July.

8. Withdrawl of Attached Units.

(a) L.T.M. Batteries attached for the operation will be withdrawn should the local situation admit under the orders of the Brigadiers 35th and 37th Infantry Brigades after 12 midnight 30th June/1st July. They will be accommodated for the night by the Infantry Brigades to which they are attached, rejoining their Divisions on the 1st July.

(b) Machine Gun Companies of the 17th and 35th Battalions M.G.C. will be withdrawn under the orders of the 12th Battn. M.G.C. on the night 1st/2nd July.

(c) The four 6" T.M's. 35th Division will be withdrawn as soon as circumstances admit under orders of the C.R.A. 12th Division.

9. Synchronization of Watches on the 30th June.

12th D.A. and Corps H.A.) C.R.E.)	at 12th Divisional H.Q. by a Divisional Staff Officer.
Infantry Brigades.) 12th Bn. M.G.C.) 5th Northants. Regt.)	at H.Q. 37th Infantry Brigade by a Divisional Staff Officer.

/ a Staff,,,,

9. (continued)

A Staff Officer from 12th Divisional H.Q. will visit the 18th and 38th Division H.Q. to synchronize watches, unless this is arranged by V Corps.

Times for the above will be notified later.

10. Advanced Divisional H.Q. will open at V.1.c.1.1 at 8.30 p.m 30th June and will close at 6 a.m. 1st July if the situation admits.

Lieut.Colonel,
General Staff,
12th Division.

Issued at 8 a.m.

Copies to :-

1. "Q".
2. C.R.A.
3. C.R.E.
4. 35th Infantry Brigade.
5. 36th Infantry Brigade.
6. 37th Infantry Brigade.
7. 12th Bn. M.G.C.
8. 12th Div. Signals.
9. 5th Northamptonshire Regt.
10. 17th Division.
11. 35th Division.
12. 18th Division.
13. 38th Division.
14. 15th Squadron, R.A.F.
15. V Corps.
16. - 22. G.S. and Records.
23. A.D.M.S.
24. A.P.M.
25. Camp Commandant.
26. Div. Gas Officer.

S E C R E T.

12th Division No. G.X. 2619.

C.R.A.
C.R.E.
35th Inf. Bde.
36th Inf. Bde.
37th Inf. Bde.
12th Bn. M.G.C.
12th Div. Signals.
5th Northamptonshire Regt.
A.D.M.S.
A.D.C.
"Q".

---

1. In view of a possible counter-attack by the enemy on the morning 1st July, the 36th Infantry Brigade (in Reserve) will send 1 Battalion from the BROWN Line to the PURPLE Line in the vicinity of V.12.c.-V.18.a. to be in position by 2.30 a.m. 1st July.

2. The remainder of the 36th Infantry Brigade (less 2 Companies attached to 37th Infantry Brigade if not relieved in the line) will be ready to move at 15 minutes notice from 2.30 a.m. 1st July.

3. A C K N O W L E D G E.

W. R. Pinwill

Lieut-Colonel,
General Staff,
12th Division.

29th June, 1918.

SECRET.

Addendum No. 1 to

12th Divisional Artillery Order No. 110.

----

1. The following amendments will be made -

(a) Table A., Phase V. Rate of fire will average 1 round P.G.P.M.

(b) Table B. 38th Divl. Arty. will continue SMOKE barrage until Zero plus 1 hour 30 minutes.

(c) 1 - 18 pr. gun of B/62 will enfilade line of shell holes W 4 c 10 00 to W 4 c 25 15 from Zero to Zero plus 2 hours.

(d) Table C. Two additional Mortars will fire from Zero to Zero plus 3 minutes -
One Mortar on W 15 d 75 30
.. .. W 15 b 05 80

2. At 3,15 a.m. 1st July 18 pr. batteries will open on the E. protective barrage line for 2 minutes, then search forward in five 2 minute lifts of 100 yards each, coming back to the protective barrage line in four irregular jumps of 2 minutes each, ceasing fire at 3.35 a.m.
Batteries on the N. flank protective barrage line will at the same time search Eastwards from the line W 15 b 00 30 - W 9 d 00 20
Rate of fire - 3 rounds P.G.P.M.
D/62 will search down the Ravine in W 9 d.
D/63 will bombard road W 15 b 85 60 to W 9 d 95 45.

3. Watches will be synchronised at H.Q., 63rd Brigade R.F.A. at 10.45 a.m. tomorrow when an officer from each Brigade and the D.T.M.O. will attend.
V Corps is arranging to synchronise watches of -
Corps H.A.
18th Division.
38th Division.

Please acknowledge.

Issued at 7.30 p.m.

Noel Cheyne(?)
Major,
Brigade Major 12th D. A.

29th June, 1918.

Copies to all recipients of 12th D.A. Order No. 110

S E C R E T.

12th Divisional Artillery Order No. 110.

5 62nd)
10 63rd) Brigade
4 93rd) R.F.A.
1 315th)
1 12th D.A.Column.
1 D. T. M. O.
and to 12th Divn. (G) & Signals)
V Corps R.A. & H.A.) for
3+ 35th.36th.37th Inf. Bdes.) information.
18th and 38th D. As. (5))

Ref. 57D. S.E. 1/20,000. 28th June, 1918.

1. A combined operation will be carried out on night 30th June/1st July by the Division and 54th Infantry Brigade (18th Division) on our right.

2. The Division will capture and hold the enemy line W 15 d 78 00 - 78 68 - b 52 00 - b 10 45 - a 50 65; and simultaneously will raid areas in W 15 b and along the line of the road W 15 d 95 00 - W 15 b 95 25.

3. The 54th Infantry Brigade will capture and hold the German front line system from W 21 d 1 7 to W 15 d 8 0.

4. The G.O.C. 37th Infantry Brigade (H.Q. - V 12 c 6 1) will command the troops carrying out the operation referred to in para. 2.
Lieut-Colonel R.G.THOMSON, C.M.G., D.S.O. will be his Artillery Liaison Officer.

5. The attack of the Division will be supported by the following Field Artillery -

62nd Brigade	3 - 18 pr. Batteries.
	1 - 4.5"How. ..
63rd Brigade	3 - 18 pr. ..
	1 - 4.5"How. ..
93rd Brigade	3 - 18 pr. ..
315th Brigade	3 - 18 pr. ..
	1 - 4.5"How. ..
38th Divl. Arty.	3 - 18 pr. ..
	1 - 4.5"How. ..

6. The action of the Field Artillery and 6 inch Trench Mortars will be as shown in Tables A. B. C. and Tracing 'A' attached.

7. The Heavy Artillery are bombarding selected targets and carrying out counter-battery work. A copy of their orders will be sent to 37th Infantry Brigade and Lieut-Colonel R.G.THOMSON, C.M.G., D.S.O.

8. The S.O.S. signal for the operation will be a rifle grenade rocket bursting into RED/RED/RED (the normal S.O.S. signal of the

the 18th Division). Should this be sent up batteries will open on the barrage line shown in Red on the tracing 'A'.

9. Should the normal S.O.S. signal (GREEN/RED/GREEN) be sent up batteries whose normal S.O.S. lines are North of a line running due East and West through W 15 a 46 77 will fire on their normal S.O.S. targets. The 315th Brigade will be at the disposal of O.C. 63rd Brigade who will issue orders as to the S.O.S. lines South of that line.

10. The 54th Infantry Brigade is making use of a number of other Light signals which do <u>not</u> apply to this Division.

11. O.C. 63rd Brigade will detail any Liaison Officers required by the Infantry.

12. Zero hour will be notified to all concerned before 12 Noon 30th June.

It will be between 9.15 p.m. and 10 p.m. 30th June.

13. Orders as regards the s ynchronisation of watches will be issued later.

14. Advanced Divisional H.Q. will open at V 1 c 1 1 at 8.30 p.m.30th June and will close at 6 a.m. 1st July if the s ituation admits.

<u>PLEASE ACKNOWLEDGE.</u>

[signature]

Major,
Brigade Major 12th D. A.

Issued with 12th Divl. Artillery Order No. 110.

TABLE A.

18 Pr. Tasks.

Phase	Time	Unit	No. of guns	Task	Remarks.
I	Zero to Zero plus 3 minutes	62nd Bde.	16	As per Tracing 'A'.	100 % AX. Rate - 3 rds. P.G.P.M
		63rd Bde.	16	do. do.	do. do.
		93rd Bde.	8 6 2	do. do. Enfilade W 15 b 10 55 - 70 30 Enfilado W 15 b 90 25 - 85 75	do. do.
		315th Bde.	8 6	As per Tracing 'A'. Search slope from W 10 c 30 80 - W 10 a 00 25 for 400 yds. East.	do. do.
		38 Div. Arty.	12 6	As per tracing attached Smoke Square W 10 a	60%A:40%AX. do. Unless wind is N.E.
II	Zero plus 3 minutes to Zero plus 16 minutes	62nd Bde.	16	Same as Phase I.	100 % A. Rate - 3 rds.P.G.P.M.
		63rd Bde.	16	do. do.	100 % A. do.
		93rd Bde.	14 2	As per Tracing 'A' Enfilade W 15 b 90 25 - 85 75 TILL Zero plus 8 minutes. THEN STOP.	100 % A. do.
		315th Bde.	8 6	Same as Phase I. do. do.	100 % AX. do.
		38 Div. Arty.	18	do. do.	60%A:40%AX. do.

TABLE A. (Sheet 2)

Phase	Time	Unit	No. of guns	T a s k	Remarks
III	Zero plus 16 minutes to Zero plus 20 minutes	62nd Bde.	16	Search forward 200 yds. beyond S.O.S. lines in Tracing 'A'	100% AX. 2 rds. P.G.P.M.
		63rd Bde.	16	do. do.	100% AX. do.
		93rd Bde.	6	do. do.	100% AX. do.
			8	Stand on North flank S.O.S. barrage	100% A. do.
		315th Bde.	6	Search forward 200 yds. E. of S.O.S. line in Tracing 'A'	100% AX. do.
			6	Same as Phase I.	
		38th Div. Arty.	2	Enfilade [illegible] 10 b 5 5 to [illegible] 4 c 45 25	60%A:40%AX. do.
			6	Search and sweep slope in [illegible] 10 a	60%A:40%AX. do.
			6	Smoke as for Phase I	Stop at Zero plus 30 mins.
IV	Zero plus 20 minutes to Zero plus 50 minutes	ALL		As per Phase III	Ammunition as per Phase III. Short bursts at frequent intervals to average one round per gun per minute.
V	Zero plus 50 minutes to Zero plus 2 hours	ALL		As per Phase III	Ammunition as per Phase III, averaging ½ round per gun per minute.

NOTE.- In Phases IV and V. ammunition 60 % A: 40 % AX. except Northern flank barrage which will be 100 % A.

Issued with 13th Divl. Artillery Order No. 110.

TABLE B.

4.5 inch How. Tasks.

Phase	Time	Unit	No. of hows.	Task	Remarks.
I	Zero to Zero plus 3 minutes	62nd Bde.	3 2	W 15 b 10 70 to W 9 d 25 20 Trench W 9 d 22 90	101 Non-delay. 2 R.P.H.P.M. do. do.
		63rd Bde.	6	Trench W 15 d 99 to W 15 b 8 6	do. do.
		315th Bde.	2 2	W 15 d 90 70 W 15 d 95 80	do. do. do. do.
		38th Div. Arty.	6	Smoke slope W 10 a and b	
II	Zero plus 3 minutes to Zero plus 9 minutes	62nd Bde.	3 2	W 9 d 4 3 to W 9 d 80 45 Trench W 9 d 22 90	106 Fuse. 2 R.P.H.P.M. 101 Fuse. do.
		63rd Bde.	6	As per Phase I.	101 Fuse. do.
		315th Bde.	4	W 16 c 85 30 to W 16 c 85 80	106 Fuse do.
		38th Div. Arty.	6	As per Phase I.	
III	Zero plus 9 minutes to Zero plus 30 minutes	62nd Bde.	5	As per Phase II	1½ R.P.H.P.M.
		63rd Bde.	(2 (2 (2	W 16 a 60 45 W 16 c 70 30 W 9 d 95 55	do.
		315th Bde.	4	As per Phase II.	do.
		38th Div. Arty.	6	As per Phase II	STOP at Zero plus 30 mins.
IV	Zero plus 30 mins. until ordered to STOP.	62nd Bde.) 63rd Bde.) 315th Bde.)		As per Phase III.	30 rds. per How. per hour.

Issued with 12th Divl. Artillery Order No. 110. TABLE 'C'

6 inch Newton T. Ms.

Phase	Time	No. of Mortars	Tasks	Remarks
I	Zero to Zero plus 3 minutes	1 1 1 1 4	W 15 b 1 6 (A) W 9 b 55 00 W 9 b 55 15 W 3 d 95 00 W. edge of AVELUY WOOD W 10 a 40 80 - W 4 c 40 50.	Intense rate of fire
II	Zero plus 3 to Zero plus 20 minutes	8	Same as Phase I, but (A) moves to W 9 d 40 35	Rapid
III	Zero plus 20 minutes to Zero plus one hour.	8	As per Phase II.	Slow

Issued with Divn Order No 110 Table A

18 pdr CREEPING BARRAGE

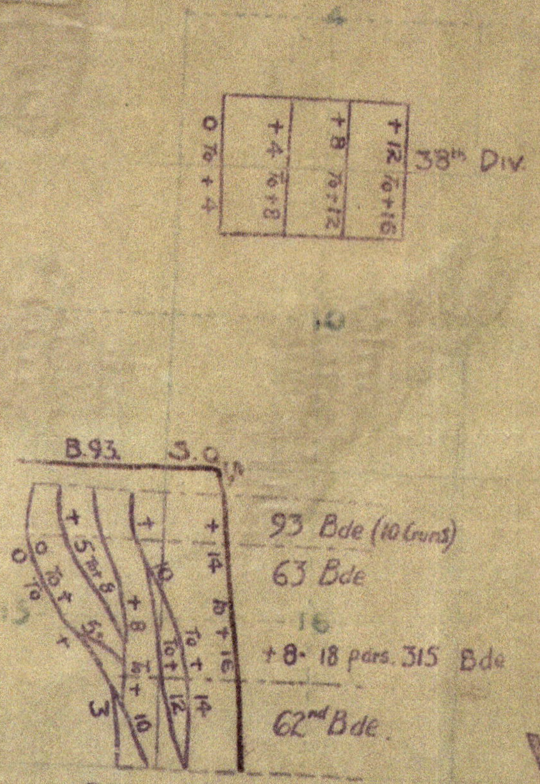

REF. 57°SE Scale 1-20,000.

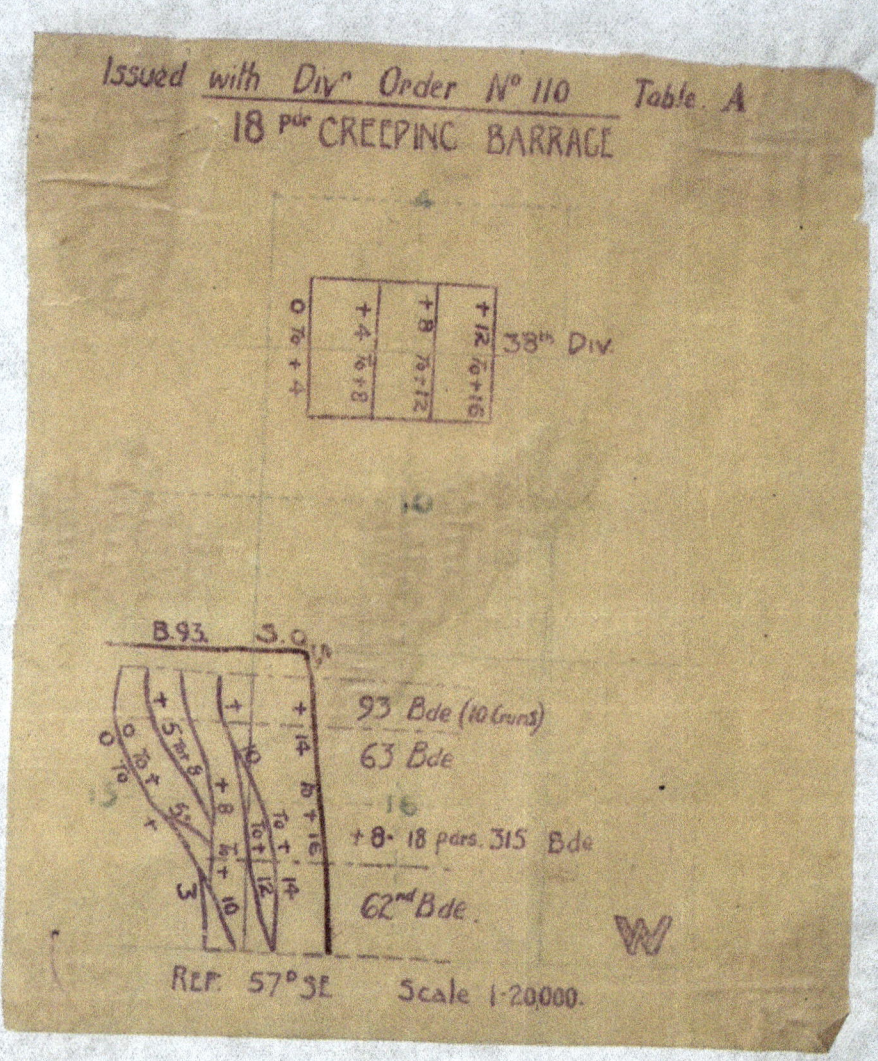

Copy 2 29

SECRET.

18th DIVISIONAL ARTILLERY OPERATION ORDER No. 133.

1. A combined operation will be carried out by the 12th Division on our left, and the 54th Infantry Brigade of the 18th Division, on a date to be notified separately.

2. The 54th Infantry Brigade will capture, and hold, the German front line system from W.21.d.1.7 to W.15.d.8.0 shewn (dotted blue) in attached Map "A".

3. The 12th Division objective is the line of the road from W.15.d.3.0 to W.15.a.8.4 (approximately).

4. Chinese attacks will be carried out by 58th Division, and 53rd Infantry Brigade.

5. The attack will be preceded by a smoke barrage put down by No. 1 Special Company, and artillery standing barrages.

6. The attack of the 54th Infantry Brigade will be supported by :-

LEFT GROUP.	4	18-pdr. batteries.
	1	4.5" how. battery.
RIGHT GROUP.	1	18-pdr. battery will be lent to the Left Group for the operation, and will come under orders of the O.C., Left Group at 6 p.m. on the 29th instant. It will return to the Right Group 24 hours after the operation takes place.
III CORPS H.A.	2	9.2" Hows.
	2	8" Hows.
	12	6" Hows.
	8	60-pounders.

There will also be a protective Mac-hine Gun barrage.

The remaining two 18-pdr. batteries and one 4.5" howitzer battery of the Right Group will be at the disposal of the Right Infantry Brigade for the Chinese attack.

7. The action of the artillery will be as shewn on Tables (A), (B), (C) and (D), and Map "A".

8. At Zero plus 6 minutes all guns will be laid on the protective barrage shewn on Map "A", and be prepared to open fire immediately artillery support is asked for by the Infantry.

9. On the night 29th/30th June, B/82 and B/83 will be moved forward to positions near the ORCHARD in V.19.a., and V.12.d., or 18.b., respectively.

They will remain in these positions for 48 hours after the operation has taken place.

P.T.O.

10. SIGNAL ARRANGEMENTS.

The f-ollowing light signals will be used in addition to the S.O.S., and will be repeated by all Light Signal Stations :-

(a) 2nd Objective gained.) Succession of WHITE Very Lights.
3rd Do. do.)

(b) Artillery and M.G.) Succession of GREEN Very Lights.
sup-port required.)

(c) Lengthen range. Succession of RED Very Lights.

(d) Artillery and M.Gs.) Succession of WHITE Very Lights.
cease fire.)

Signal.	Meaning of Signal.	By whom sent up.	By whom repeated.
Pairs of red and green Very lights sent up in succession.	Consolidation completed, all covering parties withdrawn.	Assault Coy. Commander, 2nd Bedfords.	Assault Coy. Commander, 6th North'n.R. All Light Signal Stations.

11. LIAISON & OBSERVATION.

Right and Left Groups will keep their O.Ps. about CAREY and MURRAY TRENCHES manned throughout the night.

O.C., Left Group will detail a F.O.O. to go forward to the captured trench, as early as possible after daylight, to report on the visibility from the new trench. He will lay a telephone line and be prepared to engage any movement during the day.

12. In order to anticipate a hostile counter-attack, Counter Preparation wi-ll be carried out on the morning and evening of 1st July in accordance with Table (D).

The Zero hour for Counter Preparation will be issued from this office.

13. Watches will be synchronised at 54th Infa-ntry Brigade Hd. Qrs. V.20.d.4.4 at 3 p.m. June 30th.

Left and Right Groups, and 85th Brigade R.G.A., will send representatives with reliable watches.

14. Zero hour will be notified later.

15. ACKNOWLEDGE.

[signature] Major

Major R.A.
B.M., R.A., 18th Division.

27th June, 1918.

To :

	Copy No.		Copy No.
Right Group	1 to 5	18th Div'l.Artillery	29
Left Group	6 to 11	58th DivisionalArty.	30
85th Brigade R.G.A.	12 to 21	53rd Inf. Bde.	31
82nd Brigade R.F.A.	22	54th Inf. Bde.	32
18th Div'l.Amm.Col.	23	55th Inf. Bde.	33
18th D.T.M.O.	24	Staff Captain	34
169th B.A.C.	25	Reconnaissance Officer	35
18th Division	26	Signal Officer, 18th D.A.	36
III Corps R.A.	27	War Diary	37
III Corps H.A.	28	File.	38

<u>SECRET</u>. <u>18th D.A., No.S.L.455</u>.

<u>Reference 18th D.A. O.O. No. 133.</u>

Herewith amended Tables (A), (B), (C) and (D), and Map "A", which cancel Tables and Map issued with Operation Order No. 133 dated 27th instant.

<u>6" Newton Trench Mortars</u>.

6" Newton Trench Mortars will take part in the operation. Tasks are shown on Table (B) and Map "A".

<u>RIGHT GROUP</u>.

Reference para. 6, III Corps H.A.

12 6" Hows. and 1 12" How. are available for the Chinese attack of the 53rd Infantry Brigade.

Tasks are shown on Table (C) and Map "A".

<u>S.O.S</u>.

After the signal given in para. 10 (pairs of red and green Very Lights) has been sent up, the S.O.S. Signal <u>RED over RED over RED</u> will come into force.

ACKNOWLEDGE.

for Major R.A.

29th June, 1918. B.M.,R.A., 18th Division.

Copies to all recipients of 18th D.A. O.O. No. 133.

18th D.A. O.O. No. 133.

Amended TABLE (A).

18-pdr. TASKS.

Serial No.	Unit.	No. of guns.	Time.	OBJECTIVE. Co-ordinates.	Task.	Rate of fire.	Ammunition.	Remarks.
1.	LEFT GROUP.	10	0 to 0 plus 2	W.21.b.8.6 to W.21.b.75.75.	A.1.GREEN	Rapid	A & AX	
	Do.		0 plus 2 to 0 plus 4	W.21.b.90.75 to W.22.a.00.65	A.3.GREEN	do.	do.	
2.	Do.	4	0 to 0 plus 4	W.15.d.75.15 to W.15.d.90.00	A.2.GREEN	do.	do.	
3.	Do.	6	0 to 0 plus 1	W.21.b.75.35 to W.21.b.55.15	A.4.GREEN	do.	do.	
4.	Do.	4	0 to 0 plus 5	W.21.d.20.25 to W.21.d.10.05	A.5.GREEN	do.	do.	
5.	Do.	6	0 plus 6 to 0 plus 120	See TABLE (C)	C.3.RED	Slow.	A d	In bursts.
6.	Do.	4	do.	do.	C.5.RED	do.	A	do.
7.	Do.	4	do.	do.	C.4.RED	do.	A	do.
8.	Do.	2	do.	do.	C.2.RED	do.	A	do.
9.	Do.	8	do.	W.22.a.&.c.	A.6.&.7 GREEN	do.	A	On Trench; Sunken Road, and areas shewn on Map "A"
10.	Do.	All 18-pdrs.	0 to plus 120	W.22.c.00.00 to W.16.c.5.0	Protective Barrage line VIOLET.	S.O.S. Rates.	A	All guns on protective barrage line.

18th D.A. O.O. No. 133.

Amended TABLE (B).

4.5" How. TASKS.

Serial No.	Unit.	No. of Hows.	Time.	OBJECTIVE. Co-ordinates	Task.	Rate of fire.	Remarks.
1	LEFT GROUP.	2	0 to 0 plus 120	W.22.a.25.05 - W.22.a.15.30	B.1.BLUE	Slow.	M.Gs. and Trench Junctions.
2.	Do.	4	0 plus 2 to 0 plus 120	W.22.a.25.05 to W.22.a.15.30 W.22.a.30.15 to W.22.a.65.15	B.1.) B.2.) BLUE	do.	

6" Newton T.M. TASKS.

1.	6" Newtons.	1	0 to 0 plus 10	W.27.c.50.87.	E.1.BLACK.	Normal.	Trench junctions and Sunken Road.
2.	Do.	2	0 to 0 plus 8	W.22.a.25.85.	E.4.BLACK.	do.	Protective barrage lines.
3.	Do.	2	do.	W.22.a.15.65.	E.3.BLACK.	do.	
4.	Do.	1	0 to 0 plus 10	W.22.a.20.05.	E.2.BLACK.	do.	

At Zero plus 120, 4.5" hows. and 6" Newtons will be ready to open fire at S.O.S. rates on above tasks.

1 Stn. A. O.O. No. 133.

Amended TABLE (C)

HEAVY ARTILLERY TASKS.

Serial No.	Unit.	No. of hows. or guns.	Time.	OBJECTIVE. Co-ordinates	Tasks.	Rate of fire.	Remarks.
1.	6" Hows.	2	0 plus 2 to 0 plus 6	W.22.c.6.6.	C.1.RED	Rapid.	Trench junction and Sunken Road.
			0 plus 6 to 0 plus 120	do.		Slow.	
2.	Do.	4	0 plus 2 to 0 plus 6	W.27.b.3.8. to	C.2.RED	Rapid.	Trench junction and trench.
			0.plus 6 to 0 plus 120	W.27.b.8.9		Slow.	
3.	Do.	4	0 plus 2 to 0 plus 6	W.22.d.35.80 to	C.5.RED	Rapid	Brickworks.
			0 plus 6 to 0 plus 120	W.22.d.50.99		Slow	
4.	Do.	2	0 plus 2 to 0 plus 6	W.22.a.45.45 to	C.3.RED	Rapid	Brickworks.
			0 plus 6 to 0 plus 120	W.22.a.45.75		Slow	
5.	Do.	12	0 to 0 plus 10	E.3.central to E.3.a.95.80	C.6.RED	Rapid	Trench.
6.	9.2" hows. 8" hows.	2 2	0 plus 2 to 0 plus 120	W.27.b.8.9 to W.22.c.3.7	C.4.RED	Slow	On trench, M.Gs. and Coy.Hd.Qrs.
7.	60-pdrs.	8	0 plus 2 to 0 plus 60	W.16.c; 22.b. and 22.d.	D.1.to 6 BROWN	Normal	Trench and communications as per Map "A"
			0 plus 60 to 0 plus 120			Slow	
8.	12" How.	1	4 p.m.30/6/18.	E.3.b.30.15.	C.7.RED	6 rounds	Cutting and bridge
			0 to 0 plus 120			4 rounds	(one round at Zero)

At Zero plus 120, Heavy Artillery will be ready to open at S.O.S. rates on the above tasks.

18th D.A. O.O. No. 133.

Amended TABLE (D).

COUNTER PREPARATION ON MORNING AND EVENING OF 1st JULY.

Serial No.	Unit.	Time.	Objective.	Rates of fire.
1.	All 18-pdrs., 4.5" hows. and Heavy Artillery.	Zero to Zero plus 2. Zero plus 2 to Zero plus 7.	Protective barrage lines. Search forward 500 yards due East at 100 yards per minute.	Normal.
2.	Do.	Zero plus 15 to Zero plus 22.	Do. do.	do.
3.	Do.	Zero plus 1 hr.5 mins. to Zero plus 1 hr.12 mins.	Do. do.	do.
4.	Do.	Zero plus 1 hr.45 mins. to Zero plus 1 hr.52 mins.	Do. do.	do.
1.	Do.	9 p.m. to 9.02 p.m. 9.02 p.m. to 9.07 p.m.	Do. do.	do.
2.	Do.	9.15 p.m. to 9.22 p.m.	Do. do.	do.
3.	Do.	9.40 p.m. to 9.47 p.m.	Do. do.	do.
4.	Do.	10 p.m. to 10.7 p.m.	Do. do.	do.

Map 'A'.
Block
Enemy Block
A.1
A.2
A.3
A.4
A.5
A.6
A.7
B.1
B.2
C.1
C.2
C.3
C.4
C.5
C.6
C.7
D.1 1 Gun.
D.2 1 Gun
D.3 1 Gun
D.4 2 Guns
D.5 1 Gun.
D.6 2 Guns.
E.1
E.2
E.3
E.4
21
22
27
3
W
E
LEGEND.
18prs shewn in Green.
4·5" Hows. " " Blue.
60pdrs " " Brown.
6" Hows &c. " " Red.
T.Ms. " " Black.
18/pdr Protective Barrage Violet.
18th D.A. No 38. 29-6-18.
Ref. III Corps Sheet No 84: 1/10,000

S E C R E T.

Copy No.......77....

37th Infantry Brigade
Order No. 204.

28/6/18.

Ref. 57D SE
1/20.000 and
V. Corps Topo.
No. D.33
d/- 25/6/18.

*Issued to
Units of
37th Inf.
Bde.
12th Divn.
35th Inf.Bde.
36th Inf.Bde.
54th Inf.Bde.
12th Bn.MGC.
70th Coy. RE
63rd Bde RFA
5th Northants

1. The 37th Infantry Brigade will carry out on the night of June 30th/July 1st the following operation :-

(a) The capture and consolidation of the line W.15.d.80.00. - 78.68. - b.52.00. - b.00.45. - a.50.65.

(b) The raiding of the following objectives as shown in Map "A"*

(1) Objective "A". Area of Nissen Huts and M.Gs. round W.15.b.1.7.
(2) Objective "B". Area of M.Gs. and trenches about W.15.b. central.
(3) Objective "C". Area of M.Gs, and trenches about W.15.b.8.6.

(c) Raiding along the line of Road W.15.d.95.00. - W.15.b.95.25.

2. The 54th Infantry Brigade on our right will simultaneously capture and consolidate the enemy trenches from W.15.d.80.00. - W.21.b.50.00. - W. 21.d.00.85. - W.21.a.77.10.

3. The 38th Division is co-operating on the left by bringing fire of Artillery, T.Ms., and M.Gs. to bear on portion of AVELUY WOOD.

4. GENERAL PLAN of INFANTRY ATTACK.

(i) The attack will be carried out under an Artillery, M.G. and L.T.M. Barrage, with the 6th Queen's on the right and the 6th R.W. Kent Regt. on the left. Battalion boundaries of attack are given in Map "A". German C.T. from W.15.d,30.70 - 80.75. is inclusive to 6th R.W. Kent Regt.

(ii) The 6th Buffs, less 210 men acting as carrying parties, will be in support.

(iii) Each Battalion will attack on a two Company frontage, and each front Company, with the exception of Left Company, Left Battalion, which will deal with Objectives "A" "B" and "C", will be on a two platoon front.

(iv) At Zero the Infantry will move forward from their trenches keeping as close under the barrage as possible.

The 1st Wave will go to the 3rd objective.
The "Moppers up" will go to the 1st & 2nd objectives.
The 2nd Wave will go to the 2nd objective.
Two platoons from each Battalion will remainto

P10

garrison British Front Line.
The platoon detailed for consolidation will halt in "No Man's Land" at a point clear of any hostile barrage on our Front Line.

(v) Boundaries of objectives are as given on Map "A"; and attacking formations, assembly positions, and times and routes to Assembly Positions are given in Appendix "A".

(vi) 1st and 2nd waves, including "Moppers up", but excluding Raiding Parties for "B" and "C", will advance in extended order. All other troops including raiding parties for B and C will move in small colu
(vii) There will not be a greater distance than 30 yards between successive waves - "Moppers up" will not be more than 10 yards behind the wave they "mop up" for.

(viii) Raiding Parties for objectives "A" and "B" will be one platoon strong, for objective "C" 2 platoons. These parties will not vacate the area of their objective until Zero plus 45 minutes.

On vacating these areas they will form a flank covering party to the Consolidating Troops along the AVELUY ROAD between British Front Line and Cross Roads at W.15.b.99.25. at which point communication will be established with the left of Right Company Left Battn.

(ix) Direction during the attack will be assisted by the flanking men of the 1st and 2nd wavesof each Battalion running out a tape from the British Front Line as they advance.

(x) Throughout the operation Lewis Guns will be worked in pairs.

(xi) Sappers for demolition purposes will accompany 2nd wave; details will be notified later.

(xii) O.C. 6th Queen's will ensure that the closest touch is maintained with the left of the 54th Infantry Brigade. A special party under an Officer will be detailed to establish and maintain touch.

A similar party is being detailed by the 54th Infantry Brigade to keep touch with us.

(xiii) Until touch has been established with Units on right and left, blocks will be formed by Battalions on th flanks of each objective.

5. COVERING TROOPS.

Covering Troops will push patrols well out to obtain warning of any counter-attack being developed by the enemy. Points to be specially guarded are :-

(a) Sunken Road W.15.d.95.00.
(b) Cross Roads at W.15.b.95.25.

Blocks will be formed by the Left Battalion at the following points :-

W.16.c.87.00.
W.15.b.05.60.

Special Intelligence men will be detailed by Battalions to accompany raiding and covering troops to search and examine enemy dead and wounded.

6. CONSOLIDATION. (i) At Zero plus 10 minutes the consolidating parties will cross the German Front Line and will move forward at once to construct strong points on and supporting BLUE LINE (line as shewn on Map "A") at approximately the following points :-

Right Battn.
(a) W.15.d.80.00*
(b) W.15.d,74.28*
(c) W.15,d,79.71.*
(d) W.15.d.60.30.

Left Battn:-
(e) W.15.b.51.00*
(f) W.15.b.30.25
(g) W.15.a.98.47*
(h) W.15.d.30.75

* Sections R.E. will lay out and wire, but not dig, these posts, as follows :-

(a) and (b) 1 Section R.E.
(c) and (e) 1 Section R.E.
(g) 1 Section R.E.
(see para. 12)

Blocks will be formed by

Right Battn. at W.15.d.84.78.
Left Battn. at W. 15.b.05.53.

(ii) Mopping up parties proceeding to 1st objective will be responsible for consolidating the German Front Line, and for covering all approaches between it and the line of consolidation by L.G. fire.

7. WITHDRAWAL.

(i) Withdrawal of covering troops will commence at 2.10 a.m. and will be completed by 2.30 a.m, and concerns only those troops in front of the line of consolidation.

(ii) Covering troops will be preceded by small advanced guards who will warn consolidating troops and will also be provided with Red Flash Lamps to distinguish them from enemy troops.

(iii) Foremost troops will be withdrawn first covered by those in rear, the last to withdraw being covered by the garrison of the new line.

(iv) The covering troops (2 Companies per Battalion) will after withdrawal take up positions as follows :-

P.T.O.

1 Coy. each Battn.	GLASS SUPPORT & WELSH TRENCHES	Within Battn. Boundaries.
1 Coy. " "	COBURN TRENCH	

Each Battalion will then hold the new line on a two Company frontage, Companies disposed in depth.

8. COUNTER-ATTACK. The new Line will be held at all costs. In the event of the enemy breaking through at any point, supporting platoons of front line Companies will counter-attack immediately without waiting for orders.
Supporting Companies will reconnoitre approaches and be prepared to counter-attack on order from O.C. Battalion concerned.

9. ARTILLERY BARRAGE & PROGRAMME (i) Appendix "B" giving Time-Table of Barrages and Map showing the Field Artillery Barrage will be issued shortly to all concerned.

(ii) Corps Heavy Artillery will form successive barrage lines in rear and neutralize selected areas. Fire will be opened at Zero and continue till Zero plus four hours or until ordered to stop.

10. STOKES MORTARS. From Zero to Zero plus 3 minutes a Stokes Mortar Barrage will be put down on German Front Line. Detailed instructions as to the action of Stokes Mortars during the operation have already been issued to all concerned.
The signal for Stokes Mortars to open fire at Zero will be the opening of the Field Artillery Barrage.

11. MACHINE GUNS. (i) A map shewing the M.G. Barrage will be issued shortly to all concerned - 2 Companies each of the 17th and 35th Battn. M.G. Corps are assisting the 12th Division M.G. Corps to cover the operation.

(ii) 4 Machine Guns will cover the new line from forward positions; two will be attached to the 6th Queen's and two to 6th R.W. Kent Regt.

(a) The two guns to be attached to 6th R.W. Kent Regt. are situated at W.15.a.40.85. and will not move.

(b) The two guns attached to 6th Queen's will move forward on instructions from O.C. 6th Queen's, to strong point on Sunken Road at W.15.d.74.28. These two guns will report to O.C. 6th Queen's on the morning of Zero day.

12. R.E. COOPERATION. Three R.E. Sections will take part in the operation, and will lay out and wire Strong Points as detailed in para. 6 above.
Each R.E. Section will be provided with a carrying party of 1 Officer and 50 Other Ranks of the 6th Buffs. Assembly of R.E., and Carrying Parties is given in Appendix "A".
Orders for these troops to move up will be issued by Battalions through Officer in command of R.E. detachment, who will be situated at Advanced Battalions' Report Centre.

On completion of their work R.E. and Carrying Parties will return to their Units.

13. PIONEERS. Each Battalion will have placed at its disposal 1 Company (less 1 platoon) 5th Northamptonshire Regt. (Pioneers) to dig communication trenches across "No Man's Land" as follows :-

Right Battn.

(i) Open up old trench from junction of BOUNDARY TRENCH with Front Line to Sap at W.15.d.62.30. in German Front Line.

Left Battn.

(ii) From British Front Line at W.15.c.80.95. to German Front Line at W.15.a.95.05.

Assembly Positions are given in Appendix "A" These troops will move up under orders of Os.C. Battalions concerned.

On completion of work they will return to their Unit.

14. CARRYING PARTIES. O.C. 6th Buffs will detail a carrying party of 1 Officer and 30 Other Ranks for each Battalion. These parties will carry materials in Battalion Dumps forward to new positions under instructions from Os.C. Battalions concerned.
They will assemble in ADELAIDE TRENCH astride QUARTZ TRENCH.
Party for 6th Queen's South of QUARTZ TRENCH,
Party for 6th R.W. Kent Regt. North of QUARTZ TRENCH. and will report to Battalions concerned on morning of Zero day.

On completion of work they will return to their Unit.

15. AEROPLANE PROGRAMME. (i) A contact aeroplane will fly over the captured position at dawn on the 1st July. Troops will show their position by displaying in the trench a piece of white cloth 2'6" x 1'.

(ii) Counter-attack aeroplanes will patrol the front before dawn and dusk on the 1st July.

16. LEWIS GUN DUMPS. Battalions will make dumps of L.G. drums in the British Front Line on Zero day, the position of which will be known to all concerned, in order that drums may be obtained quickly when required.

17. A.A. LEWIS GUNS. After the operation each Company in close support in German and British Front Lines will detail two of their Lewis Guns as Anti-Aircraft.

18. SYNCHRONISATION.

Watches will be synchronised at Advanced Brigade Headquarters V.12.c,6.1. on 30th June. An Officer

P.T.O.

with a reliable watch from each Unit of 37th Infantry Brigade and 70th Company R.E. will attend. Time will be notified later.

19. **S.O.S.** S.O.S. Signal for operation will be notified later.

20. **INSTRUCTIONS.**
All Administrative, Medical, Signal, and L.T.M. arrangements have already been issued in previous Instructions, together with orders on equipment, distinguishing marks and Battle Headquarters.

21. **ZERO.** Zero hour will be notified later.

22. ACKNOWLEDGE.

R.B.B. Nichols
Captain,
Brigade Major,
37th Infantry Brigade.

Issued through Signals at
4·30 p.m.

Distribution:-

Copy No. 1/2 6th Queen's
2/3 6th Buffs.
4/5 6th R.W. Kent Regt.
6/7 37th L.T.M. Batty. (one for attached Battery)
8/9 12th Division "G"
10 C.R.E., 12th Division.
11 C.R.A., 12th Division.
12 D.T.M.O.
13-15 35th Inf. Bde. (2 for L.T.M. Batteries)
16-18 36th Inf. Bde. (ditto)
19 54th Inf. Bde.
20 12th Battn. M.G.C.
21 5th Northamptonshire Regt, (Pioneers)
22 70th Field Company, R.E.
23 63rd Brigade R.F.A.
24 H.A. Liaison Officer.
25 37th Field Ambulance.
26 Brigade Signal Officer.
27 Brigade Transport Officer.
28 Brigade Supply Officer.
29 Staff Captain.
30 War Diary.
31 File.

Appendix "A".

28/6/18.

Table of Attacking Formations
and Assembly Positions.
To accompany 37th Infantry Brigade Order No. 204.

Serial No.	Wave	Composed of (1.Right Bn.) (2.Left Bn.)	Assembly Positions	Route to Assembly Positions.	Time new C.T. is open between BOUZINCOURT TR. and Front Line for moving troops to assembly positions,	Objectives	Remarks
1.	1st	(1) 4 Platoons	SHELL HOLE TRENCH	6th Queen's. Now C.T. - QUARTZ ST. up to WELSH TRENCH. Right handed down WELSH TRENCH - BOUNDARY ST. 6th R.W. Kent Regt. New C.T. - QUARTZ - direct through to Front Line; also GLASS SUPPORT and GORDON STREET.	6th Queen's. Zero minus 6 hours to Zero minus 4 hours. 6th R.W. Kent Regt. Zero minus 4 hours to Zero minus 2 hours.	Sunken Road (3rd Objective)	
		(2) 6 Platoons (including raiders)	2 SHELL HOLE TR. 4 Front Line from GORDON ST. South.			Sunken Road and "A" "B" & "C".	
2.	Moppers up to 1st Wave.	(1) 4 Platoons	SHELL HOLE TRENCH.			German Front & Support Lines (1st & 2nd objectives)	
		(2) 2 Platoons	ditto (W. side of trench loop only used).			German Front Line.	
3.	2nd	(1) 2 Platoons	SHELL HOLE TRENCH.			German Support Line	
		(2) 2 Platoons	ditto.			ditto.	
4.	Consol-idators	(1) 4 Platoons	WELSH TR.			Occupy and consolidate line to be held.	
		(2) 4 Platoons	GLASS SUPPORT and WELSH TRS.				

PTO

Serial No.	Wave	Composed of (1. Right Bn.) (2. Left Bn.)	Assembly Positions	Route to Assembly Positions.	Time new C.T. is open between BOUZINCOURT TR. & Front Line for moving troops to Assembly Positions.	Objectives,	Remarks.
5.	Troops to hold British System.	(1) 2 Platoons	BOUNDARY TR. (W. of WELSH TR.)				
		(2) 2 Platoons	QUARTZ ST. (W. of GLASS TR.)				
6.	-	3 Sections R.E. 150 carriers 5th Buffs.	COBURN TR. (from W.14.d. 25.70. to junction of QUARTZ).	BOUZINCOURT AV. - New C.T.	-	-	To pick up carrying parties at Support Battalion H.Q. at Zero minus 2 hours. To be in position Zero minus 1 hour
7.	-	2 Coys. (each less 1 platoon) 5th Northants (Pioneers).	COBURN TR. (from W.14.c. 70.10. - W.14.d.25.70)	ditto.	-	-	Head of column to be at junction of BOUZINCOURT AV. and BOUZINCOURT TR. W.13.a.90.00 at Zero minus 2 hours. To be in position Zero minus 1 hour.

S E C R E T.

37th Inf.Bde.No.G.O.794.

CRA

Herewith Addendum and Amendment No.1 to 37th Inf.Bde. Order No.204, together with Appendix B, ~~Field Artillery and M.G.Barrage Maps.~~

P.Bist Nichols

Captain.

Brigade Major.

37th Infantry Brigade.

29.8-18.

S E C R E T.

Copy No ....

ADDENDUM and AMENDMENT NO.1
to
37TH INF.BDE. ORDER NO. 204

Amendment.

1. Para.4 (viii).

Delete lines 3 and 4, and substitute
"These parties will all have vacated the area of their objectives by Zero plus 75 minutes."

Addenda

1. Add to Para. 4 (ix).

"The 54th Inf.Bde. are firing tracer bullets which will give direction to their left flank; this will assist in giving direction to right of 6th Queen's".

2. Add to Para.9 following sub-para (iii):-

(iii) The Heavy Artillery supporting the 18th Division on our right will open "Counter Preparation" on the 1st July about 2.15 a.m.

3. Add to Para. 13

O.C., Pioneers will be situated at Adv. Battalions' Report Centre - W.14.b.4.4.

4. Add to Para. 14

Carrying parties will wear same equipment as Raiders and Covering troops.

5. Add to Para. 19

(a) The S.O.S. Signal for the operation will be a rifle grenade rocket bursting into RED / RED / RED /. This is the normal S.O.S. Signal of the 18th Division and will apply to the 12th Division Front as far North as W.15.a.46.77. from Zero till the operation is complete and the present S.O.S. Signal (GREEN / RED GREEN) has been distributed to troops in the captured position.
Bde. H.Q. will notify all concerned, including 12th Divn., C.R.A., 12th Bn. M.G.C. and Flank Brigades by priority wire the time at which the normal GREEN/RED/GREEN S.O.S. Signal will be brought into use again.

(b) In addition to the S.O.S. Signal the 54th Inf.Bde. is making use of the following light Signals.

(1) 1st Objective gained)
2nd do.) Succession of White Very Lights.
3rd do.)

(2) Artillery and M.G. Support required. - Succession of Green Very Lights.

(3) Lengthen Barrage. - Succession of Red Very Lights.

(4) Artillery and M.G's cease fire. - Succession of White Very Lights.

P.T.O.

(5) Consolidation complete and) - Pairs of Red and Green Very
covering parties withdrawn) Lights sent up in succession.

(N.B. The above Signals do not apply to the 37th Inf.Bde.)

6. Add new Para. 23 -

23. SMOKE The 18th Division on our right, is putting down a Smoke screen with 4" Stokes Mortars at Zero minus 10 minutes.

Our troops will be warned not to confuse this Screen with Zero.

7. Add new Para. 24.-

24. Battalions will be responsible within their boundaries for cutting our own wire, and masking the gaps, on the night 29th/30th June.

P.B.B. Nichols
Captain,
Brigade Major,
37th Infantry Brigade.

29.6.1918.

Copies to all recipients of 37th Inf.Bde. Order No. 204

Appendix "B"

Time Table of Barrages.

Zero Time	Action.
Zero	Artillery, Machine Guns and Stokes Mortars open fire. Infantry leaves assembly trenches and advances up to Barrage.
Plus 3 minutes	Stokes Mortars cease fire.
Plus 5 minutes	Field Artillery Barrage lifts forward at rate of 100 yds. in 3 mins. opposite Left Battalion Front.
Plus 8 minutes	Field Artillery Barrage lifts forward at rate of 100 yds. in 2 mins. opposite Left Battalion Front.
Plus 10 minutes	Field Artillery Barrage lifts forward at rate of 100 yds. in 2 mins. opposite whole Front.
Plus 12 minutes	Field Artillery Barrage lifts forward at rate of 100 yds. in 2 mins. opposite line of SUNKEN ROAD, W.15.d.95.00. - W.15.b.95.25.
Plus 14 minutes	Field Artillery Barrage reaches S.O.S. Lines.
Plus 16 minutes to Zero plus 2 hours	Field Artillery searches country forward.

Machine Guns stand by for S.O.S.; fire bursts at irregular intervals till Zero plus 4 hours or until ordered to stop.

37th Infantry Brigade No. G.O. 785.

SECRET.

Copy No........8...

37th Infantry Brigade
Operations in W.15.
AMENDMENT to INSTRUCTIONS No. 1.

Para 4. STRAGGLERS POSTS.

Delete 3rd line and substitute :-

(b) At Cross Roads V.12.c.8.4.

Para. 7. EQUIPMENT.

Sub-para. (b) last word of first line -

For 2 read 1.

Sub-para. (d)

For 50% shovels, 50% picks

read 66% shovels, 33% picks.

Add sub-para.

(f) All raiding and covering troops will discard their packs and bayonet scabbards, and generally go over as light as possible.

R.W. Nichols
Captain,
Brigade Major,
37th Infantry Brigade.

27/6/18.

Distribution:-

As for 37th Infantry Brigade Instructions No. 1.

S E C R E T.

Copy No........11.....

ADDENDUM and AMENDMENT No. 2
to
37th INF.BDE. ORDER NO. 204.

1.

Add to para. 4 (ix)

"Line of Junction between 6th Queen's and 6th R.W. Kent Regt. will be shewn occasionally by the firing of Thermite Shells by the Artillery."

2. Para. ii. Lines 2 and 3.

<u>for</u> "2 Coys. each of the 17th and 38th Battns. M.G. Corps"

<u>read</u> "4 Coys. 17th Battn. M.G. Corps."

3. Add to Appendix "A" Column 6.

"All C.Ts. are closed to down traffic from Zero minus 7 hours to Zero."

4. Add to para. 18.

"Time of synchronisation - 12 noon."

5. Add new para. 25.

Captain P.A. WILKINSON, M.C. "D/63" will be Liaison Officer at attacking Battalions H.Q. W.13.a.3.6. during the operation.

6. Add new para. 26.

Adv. Brigade Headquarters will open at V.12.c.6.1. at 4.0 p.m. 30th June - Date and time of closing will depend on the situation.

P.G.S. Nichols
Captain,
Brigade Major,
37th Infantry Brigade.

29th June 1918.

Distribution:

Copies to all recipients of 37th Inf. Bde. Order No. 204.

S E C R E T.

Copy No 11

ADDENDUM and AMENDMENT No.3
to
37TH INF. BDE. ORDER No.204

1. Para. 4 sub-para (iv) - line 6

   For "2nd Wave will go to the Second Objective."

   read "The 2nd Wave will take the Second Objective and will be prepared to support the 1st Wave if necessary."

2. Add to Para.6 sub-para (i)
   "Blocks will be formed by Right Battn. at W.15.d.82.22.

3. Para. 8 - last 2 lines.

   For "be prepared to counter-attack on order from O.C. Battalion concerned"

   read "be prepared to counter-attack on their own initiative without waiting for orders of O.C. Battalion concerned."

4. Para. 21

   Zero hour will be 9.35 p.m.

5. ACKNOWLEDGE.

Norman Smithers
Captain,
a/Brigade Major,
37th Infantry Brigade.

30/6/1918.

Distribution:-
Copies to all recipients of 37th Inf.Bde. Order No. 204.

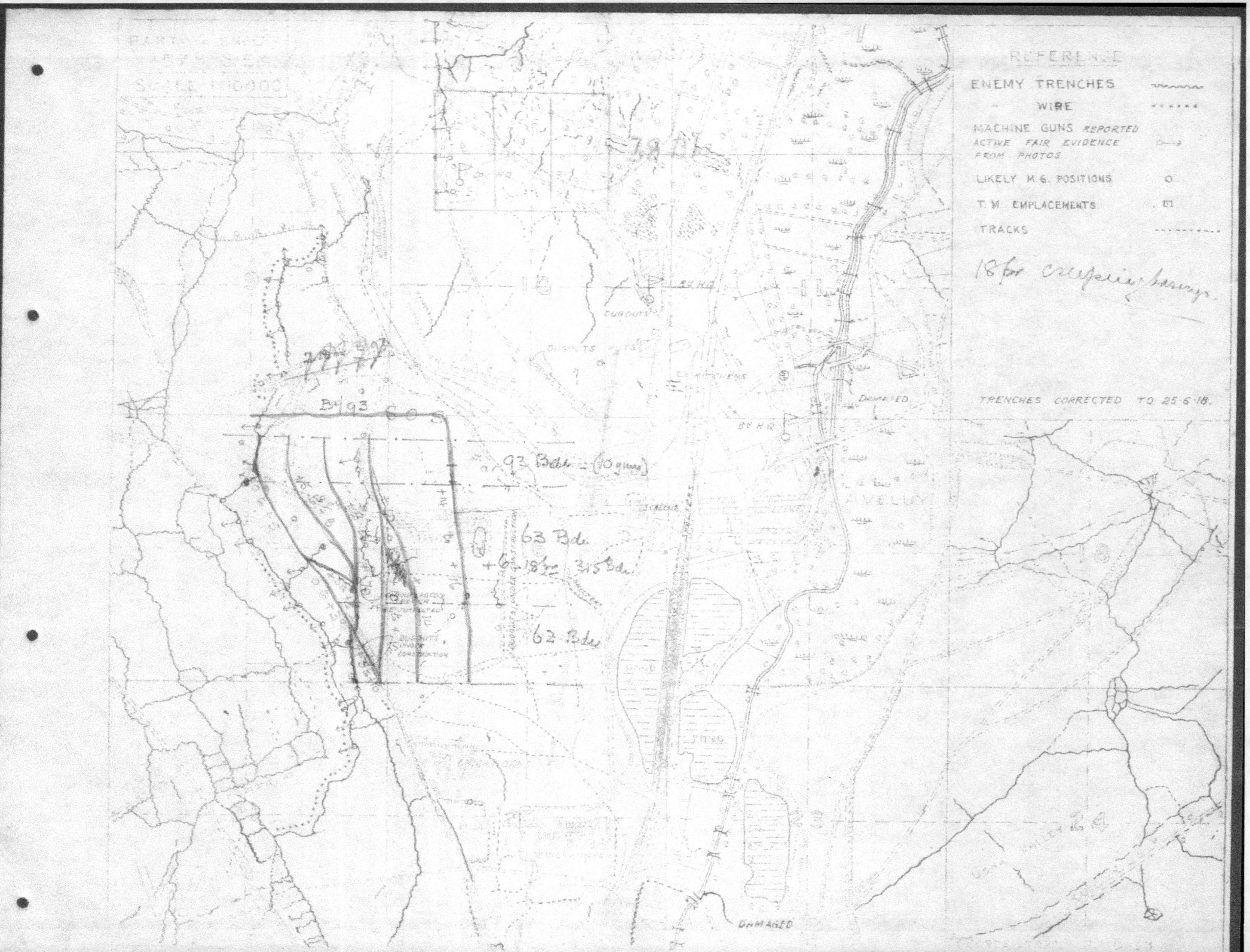
REFERENCE
ENEMY TRENCHES
WIRE
MACHINE GUNS REPORTED ACTIVE FAIR EVIDENCE FROM PHOTOS
LIKELY M.G. POSITIONS
T.M. EMPLACEMENTS
TRACKS
18 pr Creeping barrage
TRENCHES CORRECTED TO 25.5.18.
SCALE 1:10000
DUGOUTS
Bn H.Q.
DAMAGED
AVELUY
93 Bde (10 guns)
63 Bde
62 Bde
Bn 93
DUGOUTS UNDER CONSTRUCTION

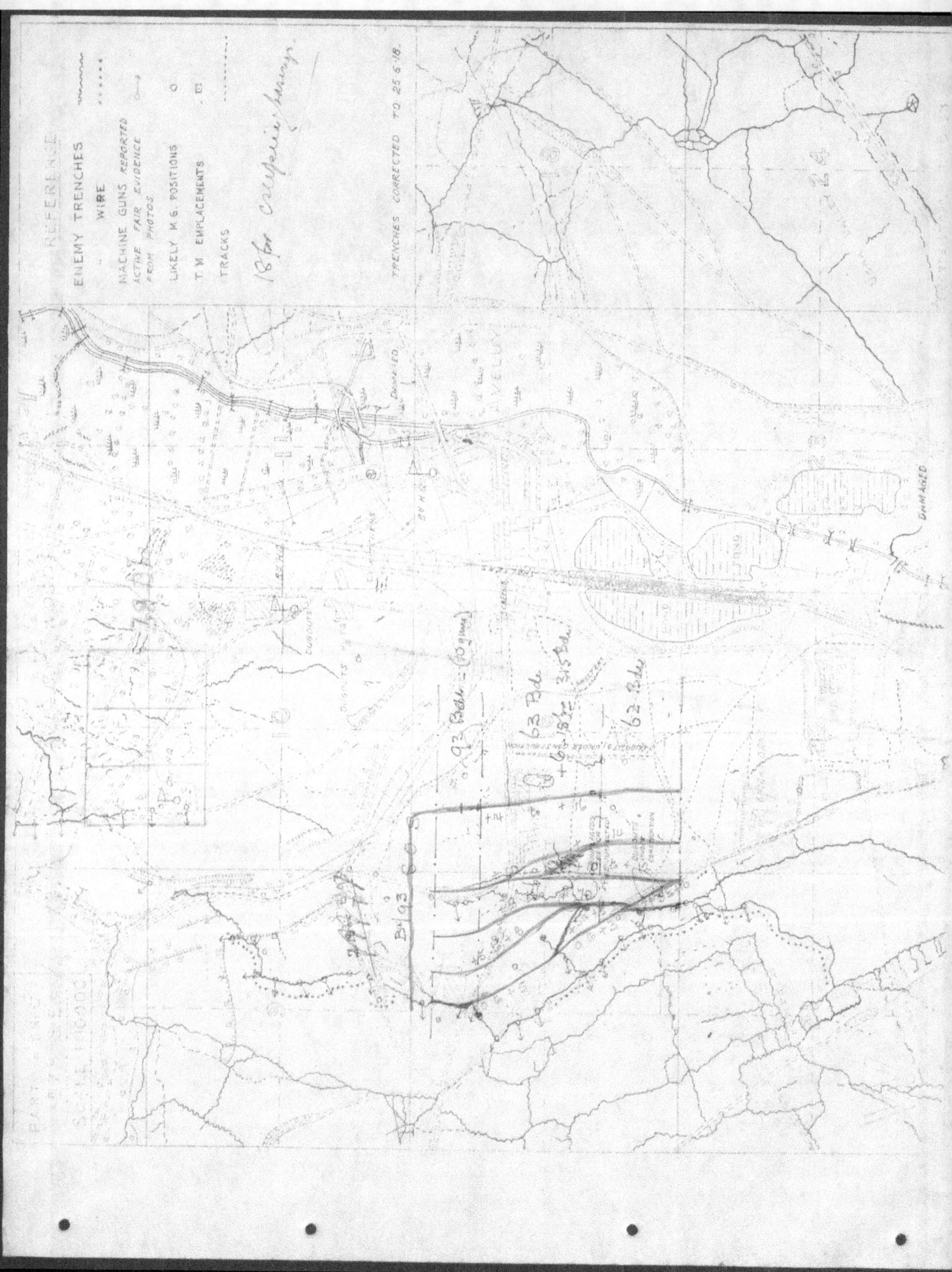

S E C R E T.
XXXXXXXXXXX 15

Copy No.......

29.6.1918

38th.DIVISIONAL ARTILLERY OPERATION ORDER No.66.

Ref. 57D. S.E. 1/20,000.)
Tracing "X" attached.)

1. (a) 12th.Division and 54th.Infantry Brigade (18th.Divn.) are carrying out a minor operation on night 30th.June/1st.July.
(b) Objective to be attacked and held is the line W.21.d.1.7. to W.15.d.8.0. (54th.Infantry Brigade). W.15.d.78.00. - 78.68.- b.52.00.- b.10.45.- a.50.65. (12th.Division).
(c) Inaddition areas in W.15.b. and along the line of the road W.15.d.95.00. - W.15.b.95.25. are to be raided by 12th.Division.

2. (a) The following Field Artillery is supporting the operation :-

12th.D.A.
93rd. and 315th.(Army) Brigades.
38th.D.A. 18- 18-pdrs. 6. 4.5" Hows.

(b) C.H.A. is bombarding selected targets and carrying out C-B work.

3. Action of Field Artillery and 6" T.M's is shown in 12th.D.A. Order No.110, two copies of which are forwarded herewith for each 38th. D.A.Group.

4. (a) Action of 38th.D.A.Batteries is shown in Table "X" and Tracing "X" attached.
(b) Following guns will take part :-

"A"/121 - 6.
"B"/121. - 2.
"B"/122. - 6.
"C"/122. - 4.
"D"/122. - 6.

5. (a) The "S.O.S" Signal for the operation is a rifle grenade rocket bursting into RED over RED over RED. Should this be sent up certain batteries are to open on a special Barrage line. This does not effect 38th.D.A.
(b) Should the normal S.O.S. Signal (GREEN over RED over GREEN) be sent up all 38th.D.A. batteries will open on their normal S.O.S. lines.
(c) 18th.Division is making use of a number of other Light Signals. These do NOT apply to 12th.Division or to 38th.D.A.

6. Arrangements for synchronization of watches will be notified later.

7. Zero hour will be notified later. It will be between 9.15 p.m. and 10.00 p.m. 30th.June.

8. RIGHT and LEFT Groups to ACKNOWLEDGE.

J.E. Marston
Major R.A.
Brigade Major 38th.Divisional Artillery.

Issued at 6 PM

Copy No.1 - 4 Right Group.
5 - 7 Left Group.
8 D.T.M.O.
9. S.C.R.A.
10 - 11 38th.Division.
12. R.A.,V Corps.
13 H.A. V Corps.
14 - 15 12th.D.A.
16 63rd.D.A.
17 - 18 War Diary.
19 File.

TABLE "X".

Serial No.	Unit	Time	Target	Ammunition	Rate rds.p.g.p.m.	Remarks
1.	B/122 (6) C/122 (4) B/121 (2)	Zero to + 16 min.	As per Tracing "X"	60% A 40% AX	3.	
2.	B/122 (6)	+ 16 to + 50	Search & sweep slope in W.10.a.	-do-	+ 16 to + 20 2	+ 20 to + 50 short bursts at frequent intervals averaging 1 rd p.g.p.m.
3.	B/121 (2)	+ 16 to + 50	Enfilade W.10. b.5.5. - W.4.c. 45.25.	-do-	-do-	-do- -do-
4.	"A"/121 (6)	Zero to + 90 min.	Square W.10.a.	Smoke.	Zero to + 30 3. +30 to + 90 1.	If wind is N.E. Ammn.will be as for Serial No.1
5.	"D"/122 (6)	Zero to + 90 min.	Slope W.10.a. and b.	Smoke.	1.	If wind is N.E. "BX" will be used.
6.	"B"/122 (6) "B"/121 (2)	+ 50 to + 2 hrs.	As in serial Nos.2 and 3.	60% "A" 40% "AX"	½.	Irregular bursts averaging ½ r.p.g.p.m.
7.	"B"/122 (6) "B"/121 (2)	+ 2 hrs to + 4 hrs.	AVELUY WOOD South of Ride "D".	-do-		Searching and sweeping with irregular bursts.

Issued with 58th D.A.O.O. No.66. Tracing X

18 pdr CREEPING BARRAGE.

SECRET.

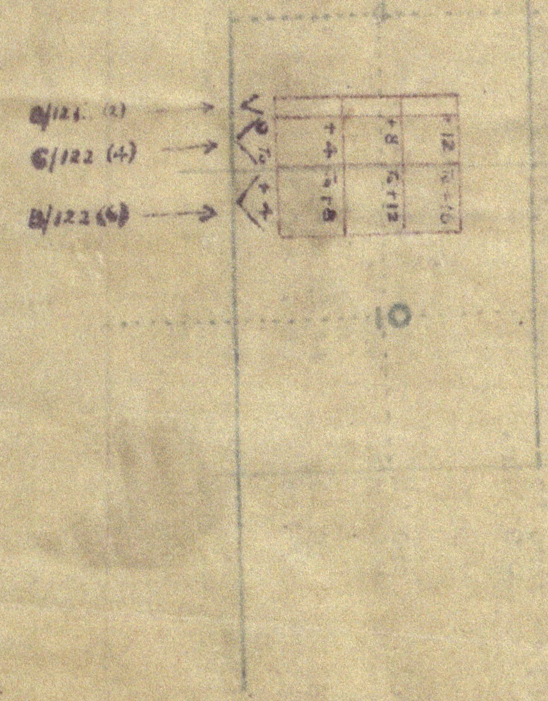

Ref. 57c S.E.
1:20000

SECRET

Copy No. 17

29.6.18.

38th DIVISIONAL ARTILLERY OPERATION ORDER NO 65.

Ref. 57.d.S.E. 1/20000.

1. (a) Right Division V Corps is carrying out a minor operation in the near future.

(b) In order to assist in mystifying the enemy, Centre and Left D.A's are to fire smoke and gas at certain times on 29th and 30th.

2. Action of 38th D.A will be as follows.

3. On 29th June.

(a)

Time	Target
6.25 - 6.40.p.m.	Q.36.c.85.40.-Q.36.d.15.25.
9.40.- 9.55.p.m.	Q.30.c.80.35.- Q.30.d.20.25.
11.15.- 11.30.p.m.	Q.23.b.83.40.- Q.24.a.10.60.

(b) D/121 forward section to fire BNC
D/122 forward section to fire Smoke.

(c) Rate 2 rounds per Howitzer per minute. Fire in each case to begin with a section salvo.

(d) Forward Sections of 18-pdrs will fire bursts of shrapnel on the above targets during each gas and smoke bombardment, and will harass the same targets during the night.

4. On 30th June.

(a)

Time	Target
12.35.- 12.50.p.m.	Q.30.c.80.35 - Q.30.d.20.25.
4.10 - 4.25.p.m.	Q.23.b.83.40.- Q.24.a.10.60.
8.25.- 8.40.p.m.	Q.36.c.85.40.- Q.36.d.15.25.

(b) All forward sections 18-pdrs to fire smoke.
Both forward sections 4.5" Hows to fire BNC.

(c) Rates 18-pdrs 3 rounds per gun per minute.
4.5" Hows 2 rounds per gun per minute.
Fire in each case to begin with a section salvo.

5. If weather conditions are unfavourable for gas, the code word BLINK will be wired from this office and BX with 106 fuze will be substituted for BNC.

6. Watches will be synchronised by telephone .
(a) To-day 29th at 5.p.m.
(b) Tomorrow 30th at 11.30.a.m.

7. Right and Left Groups to ACKNOWLEDGE.

Issued at 12-30pm.

J. E. Marston
Major R.A.
Brigade Major 38th Div.Arty.

For distribution see over.

Copy No.1 to 5	Right Group.
6.to 10	Left Group.
11.	D,T.M.O.
12	S.C.R.A.
13,14.	38th Div."G"
15.	R.A Vth Corps.
16.	H.A.Vth Corps.
17	12th D.A.
18.	63rd D.A.
19,20.	War Diary
21.	File.

SECRET.   Copy No.....7

17TH DIVISIONAL ARTILLERY ORDER No. 204.

29th June 1918.

1. In order to assist the 18th Division in an operation which will shortly take place a portion of the 17th Div. Trench Mortars will come under orders of the 12th Div. Arty. from to-night.

2. The following party will proceed by lorry to-day:-

1 Officer
4 detachments.
4.6" Newtons with all stores for firing.
(beds and sub-beds will be found by 12th D.A.)

The party will report on arrival at the H.Q. of 12th Div. T.Ms at U.10.d.8.2. Rations for the 29th and 30th inst will be taken.

3. Two lorries for this party will be at the Cross Roads T.13.d.7.9 at about 5.0 p.m. to-day to convey the party.

4. D.T.M.O. to acknowledge.

Major, R.A.,
Brigade Major,
17th Divisional Artillery.

Issued at 1.5 p.m.

Copies to :- No. 1 D.T.M.O.
2 17th Divn. "G")
3 17th Divn. "Q") for information
4 Staff Capt.)
5-6 File & War Diary.
7. 12 DA 1

H.A.,V Corps.
S.G. 11/118.

S E C R E T.

V CORPS HEAVY ARTILLERY INSTRUCTIONS No. 125.

1. A combined operation will be carried out on the night 30th.June/ 1st.July 1918, by the 12th.Division and the 54th.Infantry Brigade (18th.Division) on our Right.

2. The 12th.Division will capture and hold the enemy line W.15.d. 78.00. to 78.68. to W.15.b.52.00. to 10.45. to W.15.a.50.85. & will simultaneously raid area in W.15.b. and along the line of the road W.15.d.85.00. - W.15.b.95.25.

3. The 54th.Infantry Brigade will capture and hold the German Front Line System from W.21.d.1.7. to W.15.d.8.0.

4. The action of the V Corps H.A. in support of the operation is shown in TABLES "A" and "B" attached.

5. The C.B.,S.O.,V Corps is issuing orders for Counter Battery work during the operation,and ~~also a special gassing programme of hostile batteries for the night 29th./30th.June 1918.~~

6. A special S.O.S. signal on the front of the operations during the night 30th.June / 1st.July will be a rifle grenade rocket bursting into RED / RED / RED.
Should this signal be sent up subsequent to the conclusion of the operation, batteries will immediately open fire on their targets,vide TABLE "A" , and continue firing until ordered to cease.

7. Rates of fire.

T A B L E " A ".

	Zero to Zero plus 15 mins.	Zero plus 15 mins. to Zero plus 45 mins.	Zero plus 45 mins until ordered to cease.
60-Pdrs. & 6" Hows.	RAPID	RAPID	NORMAL
8" & 9.2" Hows.	RAPID	NORMAL	SLOW
12" & 15" Hows.	RAPID	NORMAL	NORMAL

T A B L E " B "

All natures. NORMAL

8. Ammunition;- All Hows. 106 fuzes where safe.
60-Pdrs. Shrapnel.

9. Zero hour will be notified later.

10. Watches will be synchronised at H.A.,H.Qrs. at 11 a.m. on the 30th. June 1918. Brigades will send representatives.

11. Brigades to acknowledge.

Major R.A.
Brigade Major,V Corps Heavy Artillery.

29th.June.1918.

Issued to :- 17th.,35th.,58th.,62nd.93rd.Brigades R.G.A.
Copies to :- 12th.Divn. 12th.Divn.Arty. (3) R.A.,V Corps.
C.B.,S.O.,V Corps. Staff Captain H.A.
Ammn. Officer,H.A. Signal Officer,H.A.
"O" Siege Park. 54th.Infnatry Brigade
III Corps H.A. 18th.Division. 18th.Div.Arty.

S E C R E T.

H.A., V Corps.
S.G. 11/118

T A B L E "A".

Action of V Corps H.A.,
From Zero until ordered to ' Cease Fire '.

Zero to Zero plus 5 mins.	112th.S.Bty. (2 guns)	W.15.b.90.45. to W.15.b.85.80.
Zero plus 5 mins. until ordered to cease firing	112th.S.Bty. (2 guns.)	BANK. W.16.a.70.30. to W.16.a.70.00.
Zero until ordered to cease firing.	6" Hows.	
	173rd.S.Bty.(4)	W.10.a.50.40. to W.10.c.80.60.
	199th.S.Bty.(6)	W.10.c.80.60. to W.10.d.60.00.
	207th.S.Bty.(4)	W.10.d.90.10. to W.10.d.90.70.
	207th.S.Bty.(2)	W.16.a.85.60. to W.16.b.00.45.
	142nd.S.Bty.(4)	BANK. W.16.a.85.00. to W.16.c.85.20.
	112th.S.Bty.(2)	BANK. W.16.a.70.30. to W.16.a.70.00.
	278th.S.Bty.(2)	Railway Embankment. W.17.a.15.40. to W.17.a.15.25.
	278th.S.Bty.(2)	Trench. W.10.b.40.20. to W.10.d.35.50.
	9.2" Hows.	
	48th.S.Bty.(3)	Trench. W.10.b.40.20. to W.10.d.35.50.
	13th.S.Bty.(3)	AVELUY W.17.a.50.30. to W.17.a.80.30.
	12" Hows.	
	431st.S.Bty.(1)	AVELUY CHATEAU W.11.c.95.00.
	15" Hows.	
	10 R.M.A.	H.Qrs. W.10.b.75.00. to W.10.d.95.75.
	60-Pdrs.	
	145th.H.Bty.(2)	Southern Edge AVELUY WOOD in W.10.a and b.
	122nd.H.Bty.(3)	PIONEER VALLEY. W.10.c.4.3. to W.16.b.3.6.
	111th.H.Bty.(2)	Road W.16.a.70.30. Sweep Eastwards to Railway.

T A B L E "B".

Action by V Corps H.A. at 3 -15 a.m. on the 1st.July 1918.

3 -15 a.m. to 3-30 45 a.m.	Batteries will open fire on the same targets on which they were firing at the conclusion of the operation, vide TABLE "A", except as under :-
10 R.M.A.	On CRUCIFIX CORNER.

SECRET. C.B.S. 35.

COUNTER BATTERY INSTRUCTIONS.

For a minor operation to be carried out by 12th Division (in conjunction with 18th Division III Corps) S.E. of BOUZINCOURT on the night 30th June/1st July. 1918.

(vide R.A. V Corps Instructions No. 168 and V Corps H.A.)
(Instructions No. 125)

1. Heavy Artillery as under is available for C.B. work and can bear on the area required.

These Batteries will engage targets against them, from Zero onwards.

93rd.Brigade. R.G.A.

2/1 Lowland H.Bty.	(2 60-prs)	R Y 8 - X W 10.
231st. Siege Bty.	(2 6" Hows)	R Y 7.
232nd. Siege Bty.	(3 6" Hows)	X W 18 - X W 15.

62nd.Brigade. R.G.A.

224th. Siege Bty.	(2 6" Hows)	X W 10 - R Y 8.
274th. Siege Bty.	(2 6" Hows)	X W 1 - X.13.a.20.70.
136th. Heavy Bty.	(4 60-prs)	X W 13 - X W 18 - W.12.a.90.20 to W X 1 and W.18.b.50.60.
67th. Siege Bty.	(3 8" Hows)	X W 2 - X W 3 - X.8.a.70.60.
78th. Siege Bty.	(3 9.2" ")	X W 16 - X W 17 - X.3.a.70.70.

35th.Brigade. R.G.A.

170th. Siege Bty.	(2 6" Hows)	X W 2 - X W 3.
257th. Siege Bty.	(4 6" Hows)	W.18.b.50.60. - X W 7 - W X 1 to W.12.a.90.20. and W X 2 to W.18.c.60.95.
111th. Heavy Bty.	(2 60-prs)	X W 15 - X W 17.

17th.Brigade. R.G.A.

51st. Siege Bty.	(4 6" Hows)	X W 12 - X W 14 and X W 9 (2 hows)
248th. Siege Bty.	(4 6" Hows)	X W 11 - X W 13 - X W 4 - X W 6. and X.13.c.80.70.
56th. Siege Bty.	(3 8" Hows)	X W 17 - X W 5 - X.13.b.90.70.
2/1 Lancs.H. Bty.	(5 60-prs)	X W 4 - X W 6 - X W 7 - X W 8(2 guns)
135th. Heavy Bty.	(6 60-prs)	X W 11 - X W 10 - XW 13 - X W 14 - X W 5 (2 guns)

58th. Brigade. R.G.A.

58th. Siege Bty.	(2 guns 6")	Sweep along line of batteries X W 9 to X W 3.
409th. Siege Bty.	(2 guns 6")	Sweep along line of batteries X W 2 - X W 17 - X W 19.
431st. Siege Bty. (North)	(1 12" How)	Stand by to re-inforce any required area.
343rd. Siege Bty.	(1 12" How)	Stand by to re-inforce any required area.

6" Hows will fire gas shell from zero to zero plus **15 minutes**, and 50% gas shell subsequently, to be fired in bursts between bursts of H.E. - 60 prs and 6" guns will fire 50% shrapnel.

To sheet 2.

Shoot 2.

2. Rates of fire zero to zero plus 15 minutes RAPID.
zero plus 15 minutes onwards NORMAL. (until information regarding hostile shelling is obtained, when further instructions will be issued from this office)

3. Remaining guns of 93rd Brigade R.G.A., will stand by prepared to carry out any C.B. work required in the Northern part of the area.

4. H.A.Brigades and 18 Observation Group will take special steps to keep this office informed of all hostile shelling - especially with regard to the area affected.

5. 15th Squadron R.A.F., will arrange for special Artillery Patrols from daylight 1st July, and 18 Balloon Company, will report areas of hostile activity as well as individual batteries, if possible.

6. III Corps are carrying out a C.B. programme on Batteries in their area likely to fire on the area of operations.

7. Brigades R.G.A., 15 Squadron R.A.F., 18 Balloon Company, and 18 Observation Group, acknowledge by wire.

Lt. Col. R.A.

29/6/18. Counter Battery Staff Officer V Corps.

Issued to:- 17th., 35th., 58th., 62nd., and 93rd Brigades.R.G.A.
15th. Squadron R.A.F.
18 Balloon Company.
18 Observation Group.
R.A., V Corps.
V Corps H.A.
12th. Division.
12th. Div. Arty. (4 copies)
C.B.S.O. III Corps.

SECRET.

AMENDMENT No. 2. to VTH CORPS ARTY. INSTN. No. 168
dated 29th JUNE 1918.

1. Paragraph 3. Line 2 - for "Division Order No. 261," read " Divisional Artillery Order No. 110."

2. Paragraph 5. Line 1.- for " 3 a.m. " read " 3-15 a.m. "

3. Paragraph 6. Line 3. after "AVELUY WOOD" insert "until Zero plus two hours" -
Line 4.- for "Zero plus four hours" substitute "Zero plus 90 minutes"-

R.H. Haining

Lt. Col. G.S.

June 29th 1918. for B.G.,G.S., Vth Corps.

Addressed all recipients of A.I. No. 168,
dated 29-6-18.

SECRET.

R.A. V Corps.

994.

38th Division.
63rd Division.

The Right Division will be carrying out a minor operation in the near future.

In order to assist in mystifying the enemy, the Centre and Left Divisional Artilleries will each fire smoke and gas mixed for a period of about 15 minutes on three occasions on the 29th inst. and on three occasions on the 30th inst.

This fire will be directed on such parts of the hostile forward system as may be selected by the Divisions concerned.

The times of firing will be as arranged by Divisions, but on each day one of the periods should be between 10 p.m. and 11-30 p.m.

Left and Centre Div. Artys. to acknowledge, and to forward details of shoots to R.A. Vth Corps.

R.H. Manning[?] for Lt Col
Brigadier General, G.S.
Vth Corps.

June 28th 1918.

Copies to :- 12th Divn.
12th Div. Arty.
38th Div. Arty.
63rd Div. Arty.
Ammn. Off. V Corps.
V Corps "G"
S.C. V Corps.

SECRET.

R.A. V Corps.

975

38th Division.
63rd Division.

In order to divert the attention of the enemy from the intended operation on the front of the 12th Division, the 38th and 63rd Divisions will arrange to carry out forthwith wire cutting along the whole of their respective fronts.

June 27th 1918.

for B.G., G.S., Vth Corps.

copies to :-
12th Division.
12th Div. Arty.
17th Division.
17th Div. Arty.
35th Division.
35th Div. Arty.
38th Div. Arty.
63rd Div. Arty.
III Corps.
R.A. III Corps.
IV Corps.
R.A. IV Corps.
V Corps H.A.
C.B.S.O. V Corps.

COPY No......28

SECRET

Vth CORPS ARTILLERY INSTRUCTION NO.168

29th JUNE 1918.

1. The 12th Division will carry out a minor operation SOUTH EAST of BOUZINCOURT on the night of June 30/July 1st, at an hour which will be notified later.
The 18th Division, III Corps, will continue the operation on the right.

2. The attacking Infantry of Vth Corps will be covered by :-

(a) The three Brigades of Field Artillery at present covering the 12th Division and the 315th Army Brigade R.F.A. from G.H.Q. Reserve, which has been placed under orders of B.G.,R.A.12th Division for this purpose.

(b) The Corps Heavy Artillery at present covering the 12th Divn., and in addition by the three 6" Howr.Batteries 34th Bde.R.G.A. from Mobile Reserve and three 6" Howr.Batteries 54th Bde.R.G.A. temporarily detached from IVth Corps.

3. The action of the Artillery will be as detailed in 12th Division Order No. 201 dated 28th June 1918.
In addition to the Heavy Artillery targets shown on the map accompanying the Divisional orders, the Heavy Artillery will bombard the railway cutting at W.17.a.1.3. and the road W.10.d.8.1. to W.10.d.9.7.

4. The C.B.S.O. will, in conjunction with the C.B.S.O.III Corps, arrange :-

(a) a vigorous neutralizing programme from zero onwards of all hostile batteries bearing on the area of the operation.

(b) a programme for the gassing of the hostile batteries (referred to in 4 (a)) throughout the night of 29/30th June. 4.5" Howrs. of Divisional Artillery will co-operate with Corps H.A. in this programme.

5. At 3 a.m. on 1st JULY the Field Artillery supporting the operation will open on their S.O.S.Lines, search forward to the railway in lifts of 100 yards every two minutes, and come back irregularly to the S.O.S.line at an average rate of 100 yards per minute.
The Heavy Artillery concerned will during this time,search PIONEER VALLEY and all hostile assembly positions and dug-outs opposite the front of 12th Division.

6. The 38th Divisional Artillery will assist in the operation under arrangements made by the B.G.,R.A.12th Division and will, in addition, continue to fire bursts of fire on AVELUY WOOD and to maintain the smoke barrage until ZERO plus four hours.

7. Four 6" Trench Mortars, with detachments, of 17th Division have been placed at the disposal of 12th Division for the operation.

8. ZERO hour will be notified to all concerned by 12th Division before 12 noon on 30th JUNE.

9. Watches will be synchronized as laid down in Vth Corps Order No.217 of 28th June 1918.para 7.

10. Div.Artys. inthe line and C.H.A. to acknowledge to R.A.V.Corps.

R.H. Haining
Lieut.Colonel
For B.G.,G.S.Vth Corps

Issued at 11 a.m.

Distribution overleaf.

DISTRIBUTION OF A.I.168.

-----*-----

No.1. 12th Division
2. 12th D.A.
3. 17th Division
4. 17th D.A.
5. 35th Division
6. 35th D.A.
7. 38th Division
8. 38th D.A.
9. 63rd Division
10. 63rd D.A.
11. Vth Corps H.A.
12. C.B.S.O., Vth Corps
13. Vth Corps "G"
14. Vth Corps "Q"
15. S.C., R.A. Vth Corps
16. Ammn. Offr. Vth Corps
17. 15 Squadron R.A.F.
18. 18 Balloon Coy. R.A.F.
19. A.D.Sigs. Vth Corps
20. III Corps
21. R.A. III Corps
22. IV Corps
23. R.A. IV Corps
24. R.A. Third Army
25 - 32 File and Diary.

SECRET.
12th Division No. G.X. 2632

"Q". 12th Bn. M.G.C.
C.R.A. 12th Div. Signals.
C.R.E. Camp Commandant.
A.D.M.S. A.D.C.

Composition, etc., of Advanced Divisional H.Q.
Night 30th June/1st July.

1. Composition. The following Officers only will move to V.1.c.1.1. :-

G.O.C.	G.S.O.(1).	C.R.A.	O.C.Signals.	4 American
A.D.C.	Intell.Offcr.	Bde. Major.	1 Officer.	Officers.
	(1 Clerk.)	(Clerk and		
	(1 Orderly.)	Signals)		

2. Vehicles and cars moving to Advanced Div. H.Q. during daylight will proceed via VARENNES or by Cross Country Track from the CONTAY - VARENNES Rd. at U.6.a.

~~3~~. The Road running North from WARLOY to VARENNES past the aerodrome will not be used.

3. Advanced Divisional H.Q.opens at V.1.c.1.1. at 8 p.m. 30th June and closes, circumstances admitting, at 6 a.m. 1st July.

W. P. Pu[illegible]
Lieut-Colonel, G.S.
12th Division.

29th June, 1918.

SECRET.

12th Division No. G.X.2669.

C.R.A.
35th Inf. Bde.
36th Inf. Bde.
37th Inf. Bde.
12th Battn. M.G.C.
18th Division.

Reference Division Order No. 261, para 7 (c).

1. The Counter-attack aeroplane will signal as follows :-

(a) By wireless sending LL. or S.O.S. call to the Artillery according to circumstances.

(b) By dropping a parachute flare which breaks into long smoke streamers over the enemy troops which are counter-attacking or are assembled for the purpose.

2. The Counter-attack Plane working with the 18th Division will fly over our lines sounding the Klaxon horn and will then fly in the direction of the enemy troops firing a white parachute light over them.

Lieut-Colonel,
General Staff,
12th Division.

30th June, 1918.

HEADQUARTERS
RA. 790/5
12TH DIVISIONAL ARTILLERY

SECRET.

12th Division No.G.X.2641.

"Q"	5th Northamptonshire Regt.
C.R.A.	17th Division.
C.R.E.	18th Division.
35th Inf. Bde.	38th Division.
36th Inf. Bde.	15th Squadron R.A.F.
37th Inf. Bde.	V Corps.
12th Bn. M.G.C.	A.D.M.S.
12th Div. Signals.	A.P.M.
	A.D.C.

Reference 12th Division Order No. 261.

1. The hour of ZERO will be 9.35 p.m., 30th June, 1918.

2. ACKNOWLEDGE by wire. ✓ack

62
63
93
315
ST.O.O.

[signature]

Lieut-Colonel,
General Staff,
12th Division.

30th June, 1918.

12th Divisional Artillery Daily Summary.

(From 6 am. 30th June to 6 am. 1st July 1918).

OPERATIONS. Batteries registered and calibrated and engaged fleeting targets whenever these presented themselves.

Movement on roads in W 18 a was engaged from time to time with good results, several parties being dispersed and casualties inflicted.

6 inch Newtons fired a further 81 rounds on enemy wire in W 15 b and d with good effect, wire and stakes being blown up.

8.10 pm. N.F. call on W 18 b 3 4 was answered and engaged.

At 9.35 pm. all batteries opened out on their various tasks as laid down in 12th D.A. Order No. 110.

At Zero plus 2 hours 10 mins. order to cease fire was given.

At 2.2 a.m. in reply to heavy barrage and special S.O.S. (Red over Red over Red) all batteries opened out on protective barrage lines and continued to fire until 2.30 a.m. No Infantry action followed.

At 3.15 a.m. batteries fired on counter-preparation targets as laid down in Addendum No. 1 to 12th D.A. Order No. 110. There was no reply from the enemy.

HOSTILE ACTIVITY. Hostile artillery was quiet during the morning and afternoon of the 30th inst.

During the morning a few 10.5 cms were fired at a working party in V 3 a. Between 2 and 2.30 pm. a few H.T.Ms fell in W 3 d.
Hostile barrage came down about 6 minutes after zero and was mainly directed against the division on our right but extended as far north as MARTINSART WOOD. It was composed of 15 cm, 10.5 cm & 7.7 cm. It was never very heavy and by 10.15 pm. consisted almost entirely of 7.7 cm. By zero plus 1 hour barrage had ceased.
At 2.2 am. the enemy put down a heavy barrage on the captured trenches for about 20 minutes. No infantry action followed.

GENERAL. The line now held by our infantry is reported to be as follows, W 15 d 8 0 along enemy's support line to W 15 d 3 7 to W 15 d 5 9 - W 15 d 3 7 - W 15 a 8 4, with strong points at W 15 d 8 7 and W 15 d 5 9 which are wired. Two C.Ts. across No Man's Land have been dug.

The infantry were satisfied with the barrage and no short shooting occurred.

Response to hostile barrage and our S.O.S. at 2.2 a.m. was very prompt.

Casualties (which were considerable) were almost entirely caused by M.G. fire from W 15 b 3 7 and W 15 b 2 7 (apparently)

The wire was well cut and offered no obstacle. 6 inch T.Ms. fired 408 rounds during the operation.

Captain,
for C.R.A., 12th Division.

1st July, 1918.

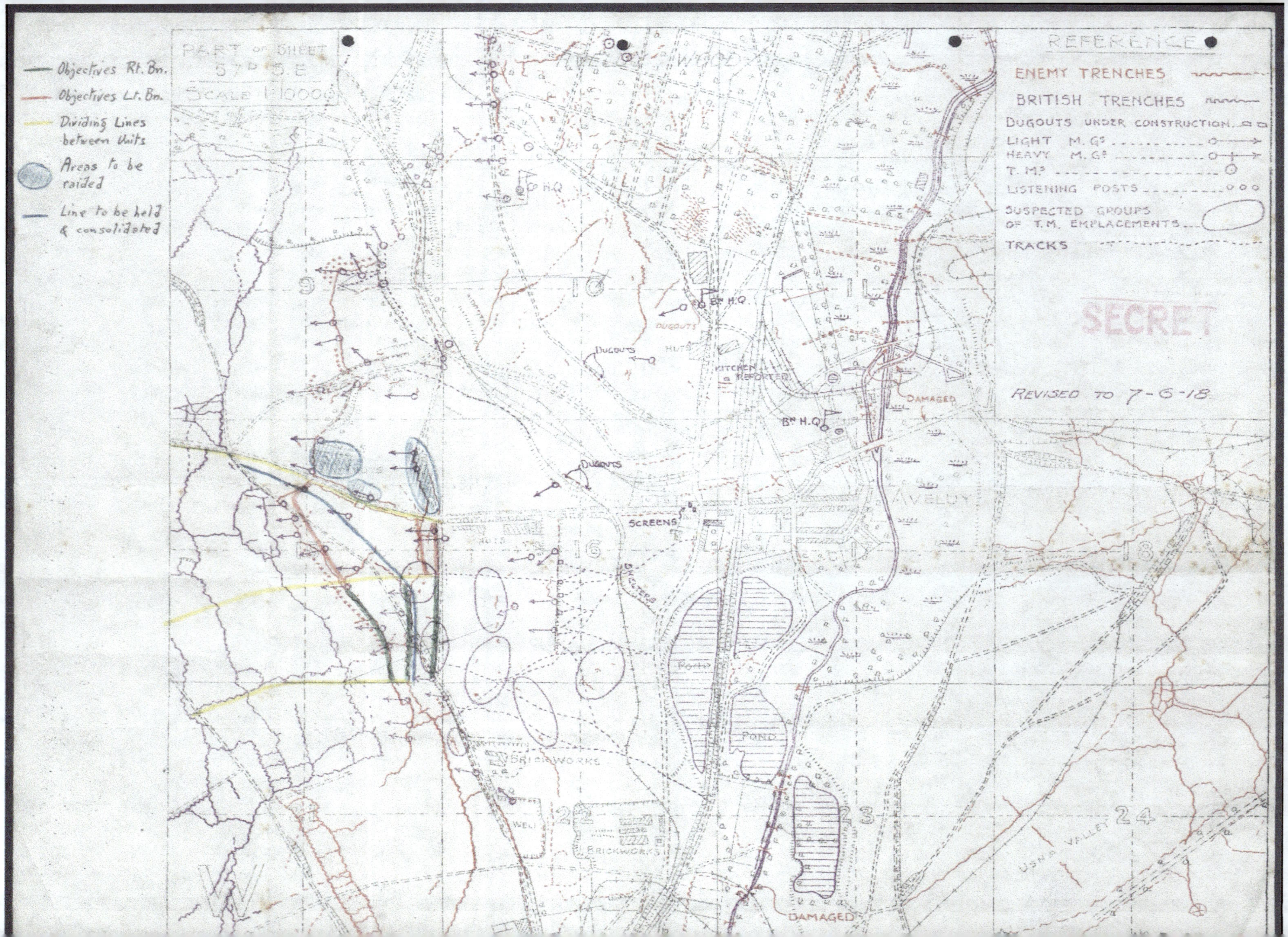
Objectives Rt. Bn.
Objectives Lt. Bn.
Dividing Lines between Units
Areas to be raided
Line to be held & consolidated
PART OF SHEET 57D S.E.
SCALE 1:10000
REFERENCE
ENEMY TRENCHES
BRITISH TRENCHES
DUGOUTS UNDER CONSTRUCTION
LIGHT M.Gs
HEAVY M.Gs
T.Ms
LISTENING POSTS
SUSPECTED GROUPS OF T.M. EMPLACEMENTS
TRACKS
SECRET
REVISED TO 7-6-18
WOOD
Bn H.Q
DUGOUTS
HUTS
KITCHEN REPORTED
DAMAGED
Bn H.Q
DUGOUTS
AVELUY
SCREENS
SHELTERS
POND
POND
BRICKWORKS
WELL
BRICKWORKS
USNA VALLEY
DAMAGED
9
10
11
16
18
22
23
24

K
L
Q
R
Miraumont
Beaumont-Hamel
Auchonvillers
Hawthorn Ridge
Beaucourt sur Ancre (Site of)
Grandcourt
St Pierre Divion
Hamel
Thiepval Wood
Thiepval (Site of)
Mesnil
Hill 142
Englebelmer
Vitermont
Vitermont Mill (Site of)
Serre
CORPS TOPO. SECTION. REFERENCE.
Scale 1:20,000

PART OF SHEET 57D S.E.
SCALE 1:10000
REFERENCE
ENEMY TRENCHES
WIRE
MACHINE GUNS REPORTED ACTIVE FAIR EVIDENCE FROM PHOTOS
LIKELY M.G. POSITIONS
T. M. EMPLACEMENTS
TRACKS
TRENCHES CORRECTED TO 25.6.18.
WOOD
SMOKE
AVELUY
POND
POND
DAMAGED
DAMAGED
KITCHENS
DUGOUTS
SCREENS
BRICKWORKS
CAMOUFLAGED TRENCH T.M.S. SUSPECTED
DUGOUTS UNDER CONSTRUCTION
9
10
11
16
17
18
22
23
24

12th Div. Arty.

C. R. A.,

12th DIVISION,

J U L Y 1 9 1 8.

CONFIDENTIAL.

Vol 38

W A R D I A R Y

Headquarters, 12th Divisional Artillery,

July, 1918.

Vol. XXXIII.

Instructions regarding War Diaries and Intelligence Summaries are contained in F. S. Regs., Part II. and the Staff Manual respectively. Title pages will be prepared in manuscript.

July 1918
Vol XXXVIII

WAR DIARY
or
INTELLIGENCE SUMMARY.
(Erase heading not required.)

HQ. 12 Div. Arty — Sheet I

Army Form C. 2118.

Place	Date	Hour	Summary of Events and Information	Remarks and references to Appendices
TOUTENCOURT Sheet 57D SE. 1.20.000	1		Enemy attacked our new post at W.15.d.84 under an artillery barrage. The S.O.S. went up at 11.55p. Throughout the night the forward posts were attacked and counter attacked ending in our line running along the enemy front line with 2 forward posts at W.15.d.7.7. The H.A. cooperated in counter attacks at 12 midnight & 1.5 a.m. very successfully & the counter battery work was exceptionally good. The S.O.S. barrages came down promptly & accurately on all occasions.	
	2nd		Orders were issued for the completion of yesterdays task. This was going to consist of consoliding and holding the Enemy trench from W 21 b 78.85 to our block at W 15 D 65 80 the portion allotted to the 37th Inf Brigade being between W 15 D 80.00 and W 15 D 65 80. ~~Rep~~ This attack never materialised however as the Enemy at 9.30 pm launched a very determined counter attack and forced back our troops from the positions recently captured to the original British front line. At 9.20 pm his barrage was put down and at almost the same moment our guns opened on their S.O.S lines: Previous to this - at 9 pm 2 18pr batteries opened on Infantry reported at W 15 b 9.4 and on M.G's reported active. At 9.15 pm further movement was reported & fire was accordingly increased and continued till the S.O.S went up. It soon became evident that the right of the Divisional front was alone being attacked and batteries on the left stopped and "Assisted Right".	
	9th		Special precautionary period commenced throughout Division in view of possible attack on this ~~Orders received at 7.30 pm that the Division was being transferred~~	
	~~10~~ 10 to 12th		~~to 3rd Corps~~. front. All very quiet however and the Infantry of the Division were relieved by the 17th Division. Command of the Artillery passed to C.R.A 17th Division on completion of infantry relief during night 10th/11th. On morning of 11th 12th Div. Arty moved to RUBEMPRE.	

(A7092). Wt. W12839/M1293. 750,000. 1/17. D. D. & L., Ltd. Forms/C.2118/14.

WAR DIARY
or
INTELLIGENCE SUMMARY.
(*Erase heading not required.*)

Army Form C. 2118.

Instructions regarding War Diaries and Intelligence Summaries are contained in F. S. Regs., Part II. and the Staff Manual respectively. Title pages will be prepared in manuscript.

July 1918
Vol XXXIII

HQ 12th D A. Sheet [redacted]I

Place	Date	Hour	Summary of Events and Information	Remarks and references to Appendices
RUBEMPRE sheet 57° SE	12	7.30pm.	Orders received that Division was being transferred to 22nd Corps. During night 62nd & 63rd Bdes were relieved by 17th Div. Arty – forward sniping and anti tank guns being left "in situ".	
	13	2pm	D.A & 62nd & 63rd Bdes marched to RENANCOURT – 2 miles West of AMIENS	
LOEUILLY. (Ref SHEET AMIENS 17)	14	7.30	D.A & 62nd & 63rd Bdes moved to LOEUILLY, NEUVILLE-SOUS-LOEUILLY area. The division is not in XXII Corps but is in reserve to two French Corps d'armées and administered by IX Corps.	
	19th	–	Orders received that the 62nd and 63rd Brigades RFA are to move into the line – probably opposite MOREUIL – on the IXth (French) Corps front on the night 20th/21st July, and to come under the orders (tactically) of the IXth (French) Corps.	
	20th		Proposed move postponed 24 hours, and orders received that no round should be fired without orders being received to that effect from General GARNIER DUPLESSIX Cmdg IX (French) Army Corps. Registration thereby rendered impossible. Thorough reconnaissance of probable positions conducted by Div Arty HQ, Brigade Commanders and Battery officers. Everything satisfactory except that no information is available as to rôle expected of 12th Div Arty and no indication as to zone of probable targets. Reconnaissance of positions must therefore be incomplete.	
	21st.	8.30 pm	Brigades left Wagon lines and came into action. 62nd Bde South of BOIS des RAYONS 63rd Bde between DOMMARTIN and REMIENCOURT. Advanced Div Arty HQ opened at GUVINCOURT at HQ of 66th (Fr) Div. Arty.	

(A7092). Wt. W12839/M1293. 75,000. 1/17. D. D. & L., Ltd. Forms/C.2118/14.

Instructions regarding War Diaries and Intelligence Summaries are contained in F. S. Regs., Part II. and the Staff Manual respectively. Title pages will be prepared in manuscript.

July 18
Vol XXXIII

WAR DIARY
or
INTELLIGENCE SUMMARY.
(Erase heading not required.)

12th D.A. ~~HQ~~.

Army Form C. 2118.

Sheet ~~[illegible]~~

Place	Date	Hour	Summary of Events and Information	Remarks and references to Appendices
GUYENCOURT	22nd		12th Div Arty comes under orders of 66th (French) Division, commanded by General BRISSAUD - DESMAILLET. 66th (French) Divisional Artillery is under Colonel DIETRICH. Five thousand rounds of smoke shell brought up to 62nd Bde during the night.	
Ref SHEET FPD MOREUIL	23rd		15th (French) Division (on right of (66th/Fr) Division) attacked at 5·30 a.m. 62nd Bde RFA provided smoke barrages as requested from 6·30 to 7·30 am and from 7·30 am to 8·30 a.m. Weather favourable & screens satisfactory. French attack successful and special thanks given us by them for smoke barrages without which they say operation would not have been brought to successful finish. The second smoke barrage was repeated at 6·30 pm but wind was strong and very gusty.	
		8 pm	66th (Fr) Division attacked after 75 minutes intensive preparation by their own artillery from Zero -15 minutes to Zero + 50 mins 12th Div Arty put down protective barrage fire to S.W of MORISEL. During remainder of night 12 D A harassed all roads from MORISEL to MOREUIL, as it was thought that the enemy were probably withdrawing across the AVRE River.	
			The operations as a whole were completely successful and resulted in capture of all objectives and some 2000 prisoners, 40 guns and 350 machine guns.	
			12th Div Arty fired during the 24 hours over 9500 rounds of ammunition. The French express themselves as being very pleased indeed with the part played by us. "Entente" very strong.	
			During night 23/24th all batteries replenished ammunition - up to 200 rounds per gun.	

WAR DIARY
or
INTELLIGENCE SUMMARY.
(Erase heading not required.)

Army Form C. 2118.

Instructions regarding War Diaries and Intelligence Summaries are contained in F. S. Regs., Part II. and the Staff Manual respectively. Title pages will be prepared in manuscript.

July 18 V.L. XXXIII

12th D.A. HQ Sheet IV.

Place	Date	Hour	Summary of Events and Information	Remarks and references to Appendices
GUYENCOURT Ref Sheet FP.D MOREUIL	23rd	10pm	Enemy started harassing roads and tracks near 62nd Bde RFA, causing slight delay to teams replenishing ammunition, but about 11 p.m. fire ceased. Enemy artillery response throughout the ~~operations~~ was remarkably small, and confined ~~almost~~ almost entirely to French front line system. 12th Div. Arty casualties — NiL.	
	24th		Day very quiet. At night all batteries withdrew to wagon lines. Unexpended ammunition returned via D.A.C to Railhead, and every battery position cleared of empty cartridge cases etc. Advanced Div Arty HQ returned to LOEUILLY 9 a.m. 25/7/18	
LOEUILLY Sheet AMIENS 17.	25th	2.30 pm	General BRISSAUD - DESMAILLET Comdg 66e (F) Division came to LOEUILLY and presented the undermentioned nine officers and men with the Croix de Guerre (cités à l'ordre de la Division). Lieut a/Major T. H. G. STAMPER M.C Comdg B/62nd Bde RFA — No 73059 Sgt. F.G. BURTON D/63 Capt a/Major J. S. C MUNRO M.C Comdg D/63rd Bde RFA — No 95242 Sgt. A.E. BRAINE A/62 Lieut a/Major J CAMPBELL M.C Comdg A/62nd Bde RFA — No 8543 Cpl. J. WATERS C/62 Lieut a/Capt A. J. JOHNSON Comdg D/63rd Bde RFA — No 8354 Br. H BENN B/63 Captain a/Major C.N. RONEY-DOUGAL a/Brigade Major. "For devotion to Duty and GOOD WORK."	

(A7092). Wt. W12839/M1293. 75,000. 1/17. D. D. & L., Ltd. Forms/C.2118/14.

Instructions regarding War Diaries and Intelligence Summaries are contained in F. S. Regs., Part II. and the Staff Manual respectively. Title pages will be prepared in manuscript.

July 18
Vol XXXIII

WAR DIARY
or
INTELLIGENCE SUMMARY.
(Erase heading not required.)

12th D.A. HQ
Sheet Y

Army Form C. 2118.

Place	Date	Hour	Summary of Events and Information	Remarks and references to Appendices
LOEUILLY. Ref SHEET AMIENS 17.	27th		Warning Order received that 12th Division will shortly take over portion of line from 37th (Fr) Division and come under orders of Australian Corps, Fourth Army.	
	28th		Orders received that 12th Division will NOT now take over portion of line from 37th (Fr) Division.	
			Major H.W.L. WALLER D.S.O. M.C. joined, on being posted as Brigade Major vice Major N. CHANCE M.C. (gone home).	
		5.30pm	The Divisional Commander presented decorations to N.C.O.s and men of 12th Div. Arty.	
	29		Orders received placing 12th Div Arty under orders of 4th Australian Div.	
	30		C.R.A. B.M. Brigade & battery commanders reconnoitred front of 37th French Div. C.R.A. transferred 4th Australian Div & Australian Corps.	
	31.		12th Div. Arty less HQrs moved to BOVES area.	

H.W.L. Waller Major
Brigade Major,
12th Divisional Artillery.

1 8 17

(A7092). Wt. W12839/M1293. 750,000. 1/17. D. D. & L., Ltd. Forms/C.2118/14.

12th Div. Arty.

C. R. A.,

12th DIVISION,

AUGUST 1918.

Lt[illegible] 76 12

WAR DIARY
or
INTELLIGENCE SUMMARY.
(Erase heading not required.)

Army Form C. 2118.

Instructions regarding War Diaries and Intelligence Summaries are contained in F. S. Regs., Part II. and the Staff Manual respectively. Title pages will be prepared in manuscript.

Aug 1918
Vol. XXXIV

August

HQ 12 Divl. Arty

Sheet 1

Place	Date	Hour	Summary of Events and Information	Remarks and references to Appendices
CAGNY	1	–	HQ 12th Div Arty moved to CAGNY	Vol ~~4~~ 39
Ref. 62 D			12th Divl Arty plus 23rd Army Bde RFA relieved artillery of 37th (French) Div and covered 4th Australian Divn	
1/40,000	2	10 am	CRA 12th Div took over from CRA 37th (French) Div	
			The day passed very quietly on both sides. During the evening the weather and visibility improved, enabling batteries to register with detached guns and sections.	
			The night passed quietly	
			One section per battery of 8th Canadian Army Bde RFA relieved 23rd Army Bde RFA.	
	3		Very quiet day. Batteries carried out some harassing fire during the night	
			Relief of 23rd Army Bde RFA by 8th Canadian Army Bde RFA completed	
	4	3 am	Enemy put down a brisk barrage on front line in C 4 for 10 mins, later raided 4 posts and succeeded in occupying 3 of them, but left 10 dead & one prisoner. Some of our men are missing. At 4 am at request of Infantry Right Group opened on SOS lines and continued firing until 4.20 am: the rest of the day passed quietly	
	5		The day passed particularly quietly on both sides also the night. One section per battery moved to forward positions in O 28 and O 34.	
	6		Another quiet day nothing unusual happening. During the night the relief of the 12th DA was completed and guns taken up to forward positions in O 28 and O 34.	
			Personnel was withdrawn to wagon lines	
35 a 80	7		Y. day. 12 DA HQ moved to forward HQ at N 35 a 80 (62 D) and during the evening gun detachments went forward to battery positions and laid out lines of fire etc.	
			The night passed quietly.	
	8	4.20 am	(Z day). All batteries fired on their barrage lines according to time table. Everything proceeded satisfactorily and during the barrage only 2 casualties were sustained in the two Brigades – 2 Gunners wounded	

D. D. & L., London, E.C.
(A10266) Wt W5300/P713 750,000 2/18 Sch. 52 Forms/C2118/16.

Instructions regarding War Diaries and Intelligence Summaries are contained in F. S. Regs., Part II. and the Staff Manual respectively. Title pages will be prepared in manuscript.

Aug. 1918
Vol XXXIV

WAR DIARY
or
INTELLIGENCE SUMMARY.

(*Erase heading not required.*)

HQ 12th Div. Arty

Army Form C. 2118.

Sheet 2

Place	Date	Hour	Summary of Events and Information	Remarks and references to Appendices
			Teams left wagon lines at Zero plus [illegible] and proceeded to assembly places in the vicinity of BOIS de TRONVILLE (O 34 c). Owing to congestion of traffic on the roads times of arrival at places of assembly varied from about 10.30 am to 12.30 pm. Teams were ordered to forward to battery positions at [illegible] and by 2.30 pm all batteries had moved forward to take up defensive positions on the line O 16 central. All batteries were in action at 4 pm.	
MARCELCAVE			At 4 pm HQ 12 DA moved to WATER TOWER in MARCELCAVE.	
V11 d 8 0	9	9am	HQ 12th DA moved to V11 d 8 0. At [illegible] am 63rd Bde RFA came under orders of 2nd Canadian DA. 2 batteries being placed under orders of O.C. 5th Bde CFA & 2 [illegible] 6th.	
	10	11am	62nd Bde RFA moved into positions of readiness in W 27.	
	11		During the afternoon orders were received for 62nd & 63rd Bdes RFA to relieve 179th & 10th Army Bdes RFA and cover 12th C.I.B. Relief was carried out satisfactorily, 62nd Bde being in position in F 21 and 63rd Bde in F 15. HQ 12 DA moved to F 13 a 7 8.	
E 23 c 2 2	12	8am	HQ 12th DA moved to E 23 c 2 2. At 5pm 62nd & 63rd Bdes formed into 12th DA Group to cover left sector 4th Can. Dn front. During the night 12th C.I.B. accompanying this sector was relieved by Bde of 2nd Can. Dn. & 12th DA Group passed to the command of 2nd Can. Dn.	
	13		The day passed quietly. After dark all batteries except B & C 168 moved forward of Section to battle positions in F 23 and 29.	
	14		During the morning with all calibres enemy artillery fairly active round CHILLY. 10th Army Bde RFA joined 12th DA Group.	
E 23 c 2 2	15		Normal day. Hostile artillery quiet during the day with exception of MAUCOURT, but was active harassing forward and back areas during the night. Hostile aircraft active during the night bombing. All guns in forward battle positions were withdrawn during hours of darkness owing to attack being temporarily postponed. Batteries carried out harassing fire in view of possible enemy divisional relief.	

D. D. & L., London, E.C.
(A10266) Wt W5300/P713 750,000 2/18 Sch. 52 Forms/C2118/16.

Instructions regarding War Diaries and Intelligence Summaries are contained in F. S. Regs., Part II. and the Staff Manual respectively. Title pages will be prepared in manuscript.

Aug 1918
Vol XXXIV

WAR DIARY
or
INTELLIGENCE SUMMARY.
(Erase heading not required.)

H.Q. 12th Div Arty

Army Form C. 2118.

Sheet 3

Place	Date	Hour	Summary of Events and Information	Remarks and references to Appendices
E23 a 22	16		Quiet morning except for 15 cm Hows shelling MEHARICOURT	
		4.30pm	12th DA put down a smoke screen to hide infantry patrols from CHAULNES. This operation was suddenly ordered in order to conform with French attack in direction of ROYE. Battn patrols were sent out with the idea of taking up positions on the railway line in A 15, 21 & 27 but met with strong resistance. Posts were eventually established at A 14 b 10.25 – d 10.70 – 30.80 – c 75.50 – d 20.10. A 20 b 55.95 – 72.72 – d 65.65.	
		6pm	Hostile Artillery shelled forward system and villages with all calibres in reply to our operations	
		8.30pm 12 am	Area in F 23 c & d – F 29 a & b shelled fairly heavily with all calibres. Direction of fire from N E. Hostile Artillery exceptionally quiet.	
	17		Normal day	
		4.30am	A heavy bombardment was heard N. of Divisional boundary. The night passed unusually quietly. Hostile aircraft did no bombing. Upon an enemy plane crossed our lines & set one of our balloons on fire in F 16	
	18		VIPER WOOD in F 28 d was shelled by 15 cm for 1½ hours. Also MAUCOURT and MEHARICOURT. Hostile light T.Ms were very active on Australian front opposite POLYGON WOOD also on our front opposite HALLU. At dawn this morning two fires were observed East of HATTENCOURT. 5.30 am One of our planes while crossing enemy lines was hit by enemy A.A. Gun and crashed	
	19		Hostile artillery very active during the day but quiet during the night.	
		4-5pm	The Left Battn Left Bde of the 2nd Canadian Dn carried out a local operation and advanced 500 yds. Posts were established forthwith. The enemy barrage in retaliation was weak, mostly light guns: 4 prisoners taken	
		6pm	The enemy made an attempt to gain back the lost ground but were repulsed with heavy losses. Prisoners stated our 18 pr. barrage very effective & was right on top of them & so prevented them doing anything	
		8.30pm	Our batteries opened up on S.O.S. lines and rates in answer to S.O.S. signal on our front. Ceased firing at 8.50 pm: nothing occurred. MAUCOURT & MEHARICOURT were shelled at intervals during the day by all calibres. VRELY was shelled with 10 cm H.V. for 1 hour at 2pm. Aerial activity normal: no bombs dropped during the night.	

D. D. & L., London, E.C.
(A10266) Wt W5300/P713 750,000 2/18 Sch. 52 Forms/C2118/16.

Instructions regarding War Diaries and Intelligence Summaries are contained in F. S. Regs., Part II. and the Staff Manual respectively. Title pages will be prepared in manuscript.

WAR DIARY
or
INTELLIGENCE SUMMARY.
(Erase heading not required.)

Army Form C. 2118.

Sheet 4

Place	Date	Hour	Summary of Events and Information	Remarks and references to Appendices
E22C 22	20		Normal day, nothing unusual occurred. Hostile shelling on DEHARICOURT + DAUCOURT and CHILLY intermittently throughout the day by all calibres. [illegible] in A19d + 25a were shelled with 7.7 cm + 10.5 cm for 30 minutes. Aerial activity below normal. 3 balloons (hostile) ascended East of HALLU G.B. 89°, 103°, 112°. Visibility Good. No movement seen. Hostile shelling during the night 'Nil' + no bombing done.	
	21		Hostile shelling more than usual. DEHARICOURT and DAUCOURT being places of interest during the hostile intermittent shelling all day. CHILLY also received attention. Back areas and our front line were shelled by all calibres at odd times for periods of 20 to 30 minutes each time. Hostile aerial activity normal: occasional E.A crossed our line. [illegible] movement: none seen. Visibility for the day Good. One hostile balloon brought down in flames by one of our scouts. G.B. 123°	
		2pm	Our Field Guns harassed the enemy all night on tracks, C.T. roads + BROWNING WOOD.	
	22		Hostile artillery not so active today. DEHARICOURT, DAUCOURT, CHILLY received the usual shelling by all calibres. LIHON and QUARRY WOOD + DEHARICOURT WOOD were shelled by 10.5 and 15 cm from 11 am till Noon.	
		3.30pm	CHILLY was shelled heavily for 10 minutes with 7.7 cm in retaliation for our concentration on enemy front and support line + their C.Ts which we concentrated on + on BROWNING WOOD from 3pm – 5pm with 5 minute bursts each time. Aerial activity normal. Visibility Good. No movement seen.	
		9pm	During the night till 1pm hostile bombing machines active on our back areas. We carried out harassing fire with field guns + 4.5" Hows. on enemy back areas, cross roads, trench junctions, woods + bridges.	
	23		Hostile shelling fairly active throughout the day. DEHARICOURT, DAUCOURT + CHILLY and DEHARICOURT WOOD intermittently shelled by all calibres.	
		5pm	CHILLY and vicinity were heavily shelled in retaliation for our concentration on enemy trenches at 1-2pm. During the concentration 6 Germans were seen to be blown into the air. Visibility good. We harassed the enemy intermittently during the night on his cross roads, C.Ts, trench junctions. Aerial activity normal. 5 hostile balloons ascended opposite our front during the day. One Section of D + B/62 were relieved by one Battery of "75" of the 35th French Division. Relief was completed at 1am 24th.	
	24.		Hostile shelling much quieter. DAUCOURT, DEHARICOURT + CHILLY were shelled intermittently during the afternoon by 10.5 and 15 cm. Hostile artillery harassed DAUCOURT + ROSIERES from 10pm till midnight and again at dawn for a short period. Our Artillery carried out harassing fire during the night till dawn on enemy back areas, roads and tracks as usual.	

D. D. & L., London, E.C.
(A10266) Wt W5300/P713 750,000 2/18 Sch. 52 Forms/C2118/16.

Instructions regarding War Diaries and Intelligence Summaries are contained in F. S. Regs., Part II. and the Staff Manual respectively. Title pages will be prepared in manuscript.

Aug. 1918
Vol XXXIV

WAR DIARY
or
INTELLIGENCE SUMMARY.
(Erase heading not required.)

HQ 12th Div. Arty.

Army Form C. 2118.

Sheet 5

Place	Date	Hour	Summary of Events and Information	Remarks and references to Appendices
E22 c 2 2	25	6 am	3 E.A. patrolled our front. Relief of the 63rd Bde and remaining batteries of the 62nd Bde commenced at night during the hours of darkness by the 34th & 35th French Divisions and completed at midnight. On completion the 62nd & 63rd Bde batteries marched to their respective wagon lines in areas around HARCOURT COURCELLES and DERNAIN. 62nd Bde in V 28 c & d, V 29 c, D 4, D 5 c & d, D 10 a & b & D 11 a. 63rd Bde in V 26 b & d, V 27, D 2 b and d, D 3, D 8 b, D 9 a and b. DAC & 12th Coy 12th Divl Train also after relief by the French went moved to their lines in V 25 c & d, V 26 a and c, D 1, D 2 a & c, D 7 a & b, D 8 a.	
D 26 b 8 3			At 9.30 am 12 D.A. HQ moved to D 26 b 8 3 & established HQ in the wood. 62nd & 63rd Bdes 12th DAC & Divisional Train marched at 9 am through MARCELCAVE VAUX VERRE to HEILLY and wagon lines in the vicinity.	
	26		12th D.A. rested and refitted.	
		9 am	63rd Bde RFA moved forward and relieved the 69th A.F.A. Bde (under orders from 18th D.A.) who were covering the 12th Division Infantry holding the line in A 2, 8 & 14. Relief completed by 9 am on 27th. 62nd Bde HQ at F 16 d 0 5. A/62 F 12 a 1 1. C/62 A 7 b 4 7, C/62 F 16 d 0 5. D/62 A 7 b 6 9.	
J 3 b 1 5	27		12 D.A. HQ moved their HQ to LE PETITE CHATEAU in RIBEMONT in J 3 b 1 5 & established their as their Rear HQ. Forward HQ at E 28 b 0 3.	
		3 pm	63rd Bde moved forward and relieved the 9th Bde A.F.A. in A 14 a 66 68 7 d 25 75. 14 a 44 – 14 a 45. 63rd Bde HQ A 13 b 9 8 (Sheet 62 D).	
	28		The day was quiet. Our Bdes the 62nd & 63rd RFA are under CRA 18th Division	
HIDDEN WOOD	29	11 am	12 D.A. HQ moved forward and established their HQ in HIDDEN WOOD. Batteries of 12 D.A. came under command of CRA 47th Division	

Sgd. A. Steel Lieut.
for Brigade Major 12 D.A.

D. D. & L., London, E.C.
(A10266) Wt W5300/P713 750,000 3/18 Sch. 52 Forms/C2118/16.

12th Divisional Artillery

C. R. A.

12th DIVISION,

AUGUST, 1918.

CONFIDENTIAL.

W A R D I A R Y

Headquarters, 12th Divisional Artillery,

August, 1918.

Vol. XXXIV

Army Form C. 2118.

WAR DIARY
or
~~INTELLIGENCE SUMMARY.~~
(Erase heading not required.)

Instructions regarding War Diaries and Intelligence Summaries are contained in F. S. Regs., Part II. and the Staff Manual respectively. Title pages will be prepared in manuscript.

Aug 1918 VOL XXIV — H.Q. 12th Div. Arty — Sheet I

Place	Date	Hour	Summary of Events and Information	Remarks and references to Appendices
CAGNY Reference 62D 1/40,000	1	-	H.Q. 12th Div. Arty. moved to CAGNY. 12th Div. arty plus 23rd Army Bde R.F.A. relieved artillery of 37th (French) Div. as per 12th D.A.W.Order No 1. and covered 4th Australian Div.	App: I
	2	10 am	CRA 12th Div. took over from CRA 37th French Div. The day passed very quietly on both sides. During the evening the weather and visibility improved, enabling batteries to register with detached guns & sections. The night passed quietly. One section per battery of 8th Canadian Army Bde RFA relieved corresponding sections of 23rd Army Bde RFA as per 12th DA Order No 114.	
	3		Very quiet day. Batteries carried out some harassing fire during the night. Relief of 23rd Army Bde RFA by 8th Canadian Army Bde RFA completed.	
	4	3 am	Enemy put down a brisk barrage on front line in C.4. & 10 mins later raided 4 posts and succeeded in occupying 3 of them but left 10 dead & one prisoner. Some of our men are missing. At 4 am at request of infantry Right group opened on S.O.S lines and continued firing until 4 am. The rest of the day passed quietly.	
	5	-	The day passed particularly quietly on both sides, also the night. One section per battery moved to forward	

(A7092). Wt. W12839/M1293. 750,000. 1/17. D. D. & L., Ltd. Forms/C.2118/14.

Army Form C. 2118.

Instructions regarding War Diaries and Intelligence Summaries are contained in F. S. Regs., Part II. and the Staff Manual respectively. Title pages will be prepared in manuscript.

Aug 1918
VOL XXIV

WAR DIARY
or
~~INTELLIGENCE SUMMARY~~.
(*Erase heading not required.*)

H Q 12th Div. Arty

Sheet 2

Place	Date	Hour	Summary of Events and Information	Remarks and references to Appendices
CAGNY	5	-	to forward positions [in O28 + O34] as per 12th DA order No 116.	App. I
	6		Another quiet day, nothing unusual happening. During the night the relief of the 12th DA Bty as per 12th DA 116 was completed and guns taken up to forward positions [in O28 + O34]. Personnel was withdrawn to the wagon lines.	
N35 a 80	7	-	Y day. 12th D.A. H.Q. moved to forward HQ at N35 a 80 (62 D) × during the evening gun detachments went forward to battery positions and laid out lines of fire &c. The night passed quietly.	
	8	4.20am	(Zero day) All batteries fired on their barrage tasks according to time table ~~[illegible]~~. Everything proceeded satisfactorily & during the barrage only 2 casualties were sustained in the two Bdes ~~[illegible]~~, 2 gunners wounded. Teams left wagon lines at Zero plus 4 and proceeded to assembly places in vicinity of BOIS de TRONVILLE (O34 C). Owing to congestion of traffic on the roads, times of arrival at place of assembly varied from about 10.30 am to 12.30 pm. Teams were ordered to proceed to battery positions at 11 am and by 2.30 pm all batteries had moved forward to take up defensive positions on the line V16 central [to V22 central]. All batteries were in action at	
MARCELCAVE			at 4 pm HQ 12th DA moved to WATER TOWER in MARCELCAVE.	

(A7092). Wt. W12839/M1293. 750,000. 1/17. D. D. & L., Ltd. Forms/C.2118/14.

Army Form C. 2118.

WAR DIARY
or
~~INTELLIGENCE~~ SUMMARY.
(Erase heading not required.)

Instructions regarding War Diaries and Intelligence Summaries are contained in F. S. Regs., Part II. and the Staff Manual respectively. Title pages will be prepared in manuscript.

Aug 1918.
Vol XXIV.

HQ 12th Div. Arty

Sheet 3

Place	Date	Hour	Summary of Events and Information	Remarks and references to Appendices
V11d80	9	9am	HQrs 12th D.A. moved to V11d80. At am 63rd Bde RFA came under orders of 2nd Canadian D.A. 2 batteries being placed under command of OC 5th Bde CFA & 2 batteries " " " OC 6th Bde. "	
			62nd Bde moved into position of readiness in W27.	
	10	11am	During the afternoon orders were received for 62nd & 63rd Bdes RFA to relieve 179th & 104th army Bdes RFA & cover 12th C.I.B. Relief was carried out satisfactorily. 62nd Bde being in position in E21 and 63rd Bde in F15.	
	11.		HQ 12th DA moved to F13a78.	
			HQ 12th DA moved to E23c22	
	12.	8am	At 5pm 62nd & 63rd Bdes formed into 12th DA group to cover left sector of 4th Can Div front. During the night 12th CIB covering this sector was relieved by Bde of 2nd Can Div & 12th DA group passed to the command of 2nd Can Div.	
	13	-	The day passed quietly. After dark all batteries except B & C 63 moved forward / action to battle positions in F23 & 29.	
	14.		Enemy artillery fairly active round CHILLY during the morning with all calibres.	
		7am	104th Bde (Army) RFA joined 12th DA group.	

(A7092). Wt. W12839/M1293. 750,000. 1/17. D. D. & L., Ltd. Forms/C.2118/14.

Army Form C. 2118.

WAR DIARY
or
~~INTELLIGENCE SUMMARY.~~
(Erase heading not required.)

Instructions regarding War Diaries and Intelligence Summaries are contained in F. S. Regs., Part II. and the Staff Manual respectively. Title pages will be prepared in manuscript.

Aug. 1918
Vol: XXXIV

H.Q. 12th Div Arty

Sheet 2

Place	Date	Hour	Summary of Events and Information	Remarks and references to Appendices
E23c22	15	-	Normal day; hostile artillery quiet during the day with exception of MAUCOURT but was active harassing forward and back areas during the night. Hostile aircraft active during night bombing.	
			All guns in forward battle positions were withdrawn during hours of darkness, owing to attack being temporarily postponed.	
			Batteries carried out vigorous harassing fire in view of possible enemy Divisional relief.	
	16	-	Quiet morning, except for 15cm Hows shelling MEHARICOURT.	
		4.30pm	12th D.A. put down a smoke screen to hide infantry patrols from CHAULNES. This operation was suddenly ordered in order to conform with French attack in direction of ROYE. Battle patrols were sent out with the idea of taking up position on the railway line in A15, 21 & 27, but met with strong resistance. Posts were eventually established at A14 b 10-35, d 10-70, 30-80, c.75-50, d.25-10, A.20.b.55-95, 72-72, d.65-65.	
E23c22		6pm	Hostile artillery shelled forward system & villages with all calibres in reply to our operations.	
		8/30pm to 4 am	Area in F23c & d & F29a & b shelled heavily with all calibres. Direction of fire from N.E.	
	17.		Normal day. Hostile artillery exceptionally quiet.	
		4/30am	A ~~heavy~~ bombardment was heard North of Divisional boundary. The night passed unusually quiet. Hostile Aircraft did no bombing. 6pm. An Enemy plane crossed our lines & set one of our balloons on fire in E16. The two observers descended safely.	
E22c22	18.		VIPER WOOD, in F.28d, was shelled by 15 c.m. for 1½ hours, also MAUCOURT and	

Instructions regarding War Diaries and Intelligence Summaries are contained in F. S. Regs., Part II. and the Staff Manual respectively. Title pages will be prepared in manuscript.

WAR DIARY
or
~~INTELLIGENCE SUMMARY.~~
(Erase heading not required.)

Army Form C. 2118.

Aug. 1918 Vol. XXXIV

HQ 12 Div Arty Sheet 5

Place	Date	Hour	Summary of Events and Information	Remarks and references to Appendices
E22C22	18.		MEHARICOURT Hostile light T.M's were very active on Australian front opposite POLYGON WOOD also on our front opposite HALLU at dawn this morning. ~~5 a.m.~~ Two fires were observed East of HATTENCOURT. 5.30 a.m. One of our planes while crossing over the enemy line on reconnaissance work was hit by an enemy Anti Aircraft gun & crashed.	
"	19.		Hostile ~~activity~~ artillery very active during the day, but quiet in the night.	
		4 p.m. & 5 pm.	The left battalion (Left Bde) of the 4th Canadian carried out a local operation & advanced 500 yds. Posts were established forthwith. The Enemy barrage in retaliation was weak, mostly light guns. 4 Prisoners were taken.	
		6 pm.	The enemy made three attempts to gain back the lost ground but were repulsed with heavy losses. The prisoners stated our 18 prs barrage was very effective & was right on ~~top~~ of them so preventing ~~them~~ doing anything.	
		8/30 pm	Our Batteries opened up on S.O.S. lines & rates in answer to S.O.S. signal on our front. Ceased firing at 8/50 pm. nothing occurred. MAUCOURT & MEHARICOURT were shelled at intervals during the day by all calibres. VRELY was shelled with 4.2 H.V. for 1 hour at 2 pm. Aerial activity normal. No bombs were dropped during the night.	
"	20		Normal day nothing unusual occurred. Hostile shelling on MEHARICOURT & MAUCOURT & CHILLY intermittently throughout the day by all calibres. Trenches in A19d & A25a were shelled with 7.7 cm & 10.5 cm for 30 minutes. Aerial activity below normal. 3 hostile balloons ascended East of Hallu G.B. sq. 103° 112° visibility good. No movement seen. Hostile shelling during the night nil, & no bombing done.	
"	21.		Hostile shelling more than usual. MEHARICOURT & MAUCOURT being the chief places of interest during the hostile intermittent shelling all day. CHILLY also received attention. Back areas & our front line were shelled by all calibres at odd times for periods of 20 minutes to 30 minutes each time. Hostile aerial activity normal, occasional EA crossed our line. Movement none seen. Visibility for the day good. One hostile balloon brought down	

Instructions regarding War Diaries and Intelligence Summaries are contained in F. S. Regs., Part II. and the Staff Manual respectively. Title pages will be prepared in manuscript.

Army Form C. 2118.

WAR DIARY
or
~~INTELLIGENCE SUMMARY.~~
(Erase heading not required.)

Aug. 1918
Vol XXXIV

HQ 12 Div Arty Sheet 6

Place	Date	Hour	Summary of Events and Information	Remarks and references to Appendices
E22c22	21.	2pm	in flames by one of our scouts G.B. 123°.	
			Our Field guns harassed the enemy all night on Tracks, C.T. Roads, & Browning Wood.	
E22c22	22.		Hostile shelling not so active today. MEHARICOURT, MAUCOURT, CHILLY, received the usual shelling by all calibres. LIHON & QUARRY WOOD & MEHARICOURT WOOD were shelled by 10.5 cm & 15 cm. from 11 am till noon	
		3.30pm	CHILLY was shelled heavily for 10 minutes with 7.7 cm in retaliation to our concentration crashes on Browning wood & enemy front & support line & their C.T.s which we concentrated on from 3pm. to 5pm, 5 minute bursts each time.	
			aerial activity normal. Visibility good. No movement was seen	
E22c22		9pm	during the night till 1pm Hostile bombing machines active on our back areas.	
			We carried out harassing fire with field guns & 4.5 Howtz on enemy back areas, cross roads, Trench junctions & woods, & bridges.	
E22c22	23		Hostile shelling fairly active throughout the day. MEHARICOURT, MAUCOURT & CHILLY & MEHARICOURT WOOD were intermittently shelled by all calibres.	
		5pm	CHILLY & vicinity were heavily shelled in retaliation to our concentration on enemy trenches at 1.2pm	
			during this concentration 6 germans were seen to be blown in the air. Visibility good. We harassed the enemy intermittently during the night on the cross roads & C.T.'s & Trench junctions.	
			aerial activity normal. 5 Hostile Balloons ascended opposite our front during the day.	

Army Form C. 2118.

WAR DIARY
or
~~INTELLIGENCE~~ SUMMARY.
(Erase heading not required.)

Instructions regarding War Diaries and Intelligence Summaries are contained in F. S. Regs., Part II. and the Staff Manual respectively. Title pages will be prepared in manuscript.

Aug 1918 Vol. XXXIV — H.Q. 12 Div. Arty Sheet 9

Place	Date	Hour	Summary of Events and Information	Remarks and references to Appendices
E22c22	23	Midnight	One section of D & B/62 were relieved by one Battery of 75" of the 35th French Division. Relief was completed at 1 Am. 24th.	
E22c22	24.		Hostile shelling much quieter. MAUCOURT, MEHARICOURT & CHILLY were shelled intermittently during the afternoon by 10.5 cm & 15 cm. Hostile artillery harassed MAUCOURT & ROSIERES from 10 am till midnight and again at dawn for a short period. Our artillery carried out harassing fire during the night till dawn on enemy back areas, Roads & tracks as usual.	
		6am – 7am	3 E.A patrolled our front. Relief of the 63rd Brigade & remaining batteries of the 62nd Brigade commenced at night during the hours of darkness by the 34th & 35th French Divisions & completed at Midnight. On Completion the 62nd & 63rd Bde. batteries marched to their respective Wagon Lines in areas round IGNAUCOURT, COURCELLES & DEMAIN. 62nd Bde in V28c. and d, V29c, D4, D5a, c and d, D10a and b, & D11a. 63rd Bde in V26b and d, V27, D2b and d, D3, D8b, D9a and b. DAC and No 1. CO 12th Divisional Train also after relief by the French will march to their lines in V25c and d, V26a and c, D.1, D.2.a and c, D7a & b, D.8a.	
~~[illegible]~~	25.			
E22c22	25		at 9.30am 12th DA HQ moved to D26b 8.3 & established HQ in the wood. 62nd & 63rd Bdes. RFA & DAC & Divisional Train marched at 9 a.m. through MARCELCAVE, VAUX, VERRE, HEILLY & wagon lines in the vicinity.	
D26b83	26.		12th DA rested & refitted	
	~~27~~	9am	62nd Bde RFA moved forward and relieved the 169th Bde AFA (under orders from 25th DA) who were covering the 12th Divisional Infantry ~~hold~~ the line in A2, 8 & 14. Relief Completed by 9 am on 27th. 62nd Bde H.Q. at F18b 0.5 A/62 in F12a 18 – B/62 A7b 4.7 – C/62 F1d 0.5 – D/62 A7b 6.9	
J3b15	27.		12th DA HQ moved their H.Q. to ~~La Petite~~ CHATEAU in RIBEMONT in J.3 b 1.5 & established this as their rear HQ. Forward H.Q. at E23b 0.8	
		2pm	63rd Bde moved forward & relieved the 179th Bde AFA in A14a 6.6 – A7d 45.75 – A14a 4.4 – A14a 5.5. 63rd Bde HQ A13b 9.8. (Sheet 62 D).	

(A7092). Wt. W12839/M1293- 750,000. 1/17. D. D. & L., Ltd. Forms/C.2118/14.

Instructions regarding War Diaries and Intelligence Summaries are contained in F. S. Regs., Part II. and the Staff Manual respectively. Title pages will be prepared in manuscript.

Army Form C. 2118.

WAR DIARY
or
~~INTELLIGENCE~~ SUMMARY.
(Erase heading not required.)

Aug: 1918 Vol: XXXIV — H.Q. 12 Div. Arty — Sheet 8

Place	Date	Hour	Summary of Events and Information	Remarks and references to Appendices
J3 d 15	28		The day was quiet. Our Bdes. the 62nd & 63rd R.F.A. are under the Command of the C.R.A. 25th Div. The D AC & No1 sec train moved to area near MEAULTE in E27 & 22	
J3 d 15	29		Again a normal day	
Hidden Wood F10 central	30	11am	The 12th ~~D A~~ H.Q moved forward & established their H.Q in HIDDEN WOOD. The D AC & No1 sect. A S C Train moved to lines in 98 a 58 & 92 c 44 DAC H.Q. in A20 d 40.95. The 12 D A came under the Command of C.R.A. 47th D A	
HIDDENWOOD	31		Quiet day nothing unusual occurred.	

~~act~~
Lieut.
for Brigade Major 12 D A

(A7092). Wt. W12839/M1293- 750,000. 1/17. D. D. & L., Ltd. Forms/C.2118/14.

Appendix I

War Diary
H.Q. R.A. 12th Division

August 1918

W. Diary.

S E C R E T.   Copy No. 13

12th Divisional Artillery Warning Order No. 1.

Reference Map AMIENS 1/100,000
and 62D 1/40,000.   29th July, 1918.

1. The 4th Australian Division will relieve the 37th French Division from CACHY to Riv. de LUCE (inclusive) on night August 1/2nd.

2. The 12th Divisional Artillery and 23rd (Army) Brigade R.F.A. (less one 18 pr. battery) will cover this Sector from positions to be selected. Probable distribution as under -

(a) Right Group. Covering Right Infantry Brigade.
O.C. Lt.Col. H.E.S.WYNNE, D.S.O. — 62nd Brigade R.F.A. 2 - 18 pr. batteries 23rd (Army) Brigade, R.F.A.

(b) Left Group. Covering Left Infantry Brigade.
O.C. Major J.S.G.MUNRO, M.C. — 63rd Brigade R.F.A. 1 - 4.5" How. Battery, 23rd (Army) Brigade R.F.A.

3. Relief will be carried out as follows -
One Section per Battery night 31st July/1st August.
Remainder night 1st/2nd August.
Sections will march from their present Wagon Lines under Brigade arrangements, straight into action. New Wagon Lines in the vicinity of BOVES are being selected and will be notified to all concerned.
Orders for move of 12th D.A. Column and Trench Mortars will be issued later.

4. Following ammunition will be dumped at or near the guns -
18 pr. 300 rounds per gun.
4.5" How. 250 .. .. ..

5. (a) No registration is to be carried out before dawn on August 2nd.

(b) As little movement as possible will be carried out during daylight.

6. The B.G. R.A. will probably assume responsibility for the defence of the 4th Australian Division front at 8 a.m. on the 2nd August - H.Q., T 1 a 8 5 (Sheet 62D).

H W L Wallis.
Major,
Brigade Major 12th D. A.

Copy No. 1. Australian Corps.
2. 12th Divn. (6).
3. 62nd Bde. RFA (4 spare)
4. 63rd Bde. RFA (4 spare)
5. 12th D.A.C.
6. D. T. M. O.
7. 12th Divn. (Q).
8. 12th Divn. Signals.
9. S.C., R.A., 12th Divn.
10. R.A. Sigs., 12th Divn.
11. R.E. Offr. i/c. R.A. Works.
12. No. 1 Coy. Train.
13.14. War Diary.
15.16. Spare.
17. 37th French Division.
18. A.D.M.S., 12th Divn.
19. 23rd Army Bde. R.F.A.
20 4 Aust. Divn

W Diary

SECRET. Copy No.

12th Divisional Artillery Warning Order No. 2.

4th August, 1918.

1. Relief of the 62nd Brigade R.F.A., 63rd Brigade R.F.A. and 8th Canadian Army Brigade R.F.A. by an Artillery Brigade of the 3rd, 1st and 2nd Canadian D.A. respectively will be carried out -
One Section in main positions night 5/6th August.
Remainder of Battery night 6/7th August.
Details to be arranged between Group and Brigade Commanders concerned.

2. Batteries will retain their own guns. Ammunition at the guns (i.e., 300 rounds 18 pr. and 250 rounds 4.5" How., per gun and howitzer) will be handed over, also telephone lines, maps, etc.

3. (a) Command of Batteries will not pass until the whole relief of the Battery is complete.
(b) Command of Groups will pass as arranged mutually between Group Commanders.
(c) H.Q., 63rd Brigade R.F.A. will be withdrawn from the line when the reorganisation of Groups detailed in 12th Divisional Artillery Order No. 115, para. 4 (c) takes effect.
The O.C. 63rd Brigade R.F.A. is responsible for establishing communications between Batteries of his Brigade and the Groups to whom they are affiliated, and that Group Commanders concerned are satisfied.
He will hand over his H.Q. complete to the O.C. 2nd Brigade, Canadian F.A. (1st Canadian Division) and will assist him with any information, guides, etc. he can give him.

4. The B.G. R.A., 12th Divisional Artillery will hand over responsibility for the defence of the Sector at 10 a.m. August 7th.

5. Groups please acknowledge.

L H Gow Captain,
for Major,
Brigade Major 12th D. A.

Copy No. 1. Canadian Corps R.A.
2. 2nd Canadian Divn. (G).
3. Right Group.
4. Left Group (1 copy spare for 63rd Bde.RFA).
5. 12th D.A.C.
6. Staff Captain, 12th D.A.
7. R.A. Signal Officer.
8. 2nd Canadian D.A. (1 spare).
9. 1st ,, ,, (1 ..)
10. 3rd ,, ,, (1 ..)
11-14 War Diary & File.

w Diary

SECRET. Copy No. 11.

12th Divisional Artillery Order No. 114.

Reference Map - Sheet
62D, 1/40,000. 31st July, 1918.

1. The 8th Canadian Army Brigade R.F.A. will relieve the 23rd Army Brigade R.F.A. in the Left Group as under -
   One Section per Battery night 2/3rd August.
   Remainder night 3/4th August.

2. All ammunition at the guns, telephone lines, maps, etc. will be taken over.

3. Colonel J.C. STEWART, D.S.O., 8th Canadian Brigade will assume command of the Left Group on completion of the relief.
   Command of Batteries will pass on completion of the relief of the Battery.

4. At 12 Noon, 4th August, one 18 pr. Battery 63rd Brigade, now in Left Group, will pass to tactical control of O.C. Right Group. Details to be arranged between Group Commanders.

5. Progress and completion of relief to be notified to R.A. H.Q.

6. Destination of 23rd Army Brigade R.F.A. on relief will be notified later.

7. Brigades please acknowledge.

H W L Waller
Major,
Brigade Major 12th D. A.

Copy No. 1. 4th Aust: Divn. (G).
2. Australian Corps.
3. 62nd Brigade R.F.A.
4. 63rd Brigade R.F.A.
5. 23rd Army Bde. R.F.A.
6. 8th Canadian Army Bde. R.F.A.
7. 12th D.A. Column.
8. R.A. Signals, 12th Divn.
10-13. War Diary and File.
9. Staff Captain 12th D.A.

HEADQUARTERS
R.A. 867.
12TH DIVISIONAL ARTILLERY

SECRET.

H.Q. Right Group.
H.Q. Left Group.
H.Q. 8th Canadian Army Bde.)
4th Aust. Division (G)) for information.
2nd Australian D. A.)

2nd August 1918.

1. On the night 2/3rd August the 4th Australian Infantry Brigade (4th Australian Division) will extend to the left and relieve the 2nd Australian Division (6th Aust. Inf. Bde.) up to and including the VILLERS BRETONNEUX - CHAULNES Railway. Relief to be complete by 3 a.m.

2. On completion of relief the Northern boundary between 2nd and 4th Australian Divisions will be - From front line at V 1 b 8 6, along North side of Railway to O 36 a 7 0 - thence West along Grid Line through O 34 central to N 32 central - N 30 c 6 0 - N 29 d 0 0.

3. The 2nd Australian D.A. will continue to cover this front until the relief of the Battery covering this portion of the line by the 32nd Battery (8th Canadian Brigade R.F.A.) is completed on night 3/4th August. Responsibility will then pass to O.C. Left Group.

4. Completion of this relief will be reported to this office.

5. Right and Left Groups please acknowledge.

Major,
Brigade Major 12th D. A.

VERY SECRET. W. Diary Copy No. 13

12th Divisional Artillery Order No. 115.

Reference - Map Sheet 62D, S.W.
1/20,000. 4th August, 1918.

1. The 4th Australian Division will be relieved in the present Sector by the 2nd and 3rd Canadian Divisions between the 4th and 6th August.
  (a) 2nd Canadian Division. From present North Boundary at V 1 b 6 6 to U 16 d 1 4.
  (b) 3rd Canadian Division. From U 16 d 1 4 to present Southern Boundary about C 9 b 0 7.

2. (a) On night 4/5th August, 13th Australian Infantry Brigade will take over the whole of the present Divisional Front.
  (b) On night 5/6th. 4th Canadian Brigade will take over the 2nd Canadian Divisional Front (para. 1 (a) above).
  (c) On night 5/6th. 8th Canadian Brigade will take over the 3rd Canadian Divisional Front (para. 1 (b) above).
N.B. - Reliefs (b) and (c) to be completed by 1 a.m.

3. Command of the Sector will pass to the G.O.C. 2nd Canadian Division at 10 a.m. on 5th August.

4. Artillery arrangements.
  (a) Artillery now covering the Front will remain in position.

  (b) As a temporary measure, from the hour on night 4/5th August at which the G.O.C. 13th Australian Infantry Brigade takes over the whole Divisional Front until 1 a.m. on night 5/6th August, O.C. Right Group will assume tactical control of both Right and Left Groups.

  (c) From 1 a.m. on the night 5/6th August, the distribution of Artillery covering the Sector will be -
  (i) RIGHT GROUP. (covering 3rd Canadian Div. Front).
    O.C. Lt.Col. WYNNE, D.S.O. — 62nd Brigade R.F.A.
    H.Q. - T 4 a 0 0 — 2 - 18pr. Batteries, 63rd Brigade R.F.A.
  (ii) LEFT GROUP. (covering 2nd Canadian Div. Front)
    O.C. Lt.Col. STEWART, D.S.O. — 8th Canadian Army Bde.
    H.Q. - N 35 c 2 2 — 1 - 18pr. and 1-4.5" How. Battery, 63rd Bde. R.F.A.

N.B. - The transfer of 1 - 18 pr. Battery 63rd Brigade from Left to Right Group to be arranged between Group Commanders.

5. Groups please acknowledge.

H W L Waller
Major,
Brigade Major 12th D. A.

Issued at a.m.

Copy No. 1. Australian Corps R.A.
2. Canadian Corps R.A.
3. 4th Aust. Divn. (G).
4. 2nd Canadian Divn. (G).
5. Right Group.
6. Left Group (1 spare for 63rd Bde.)
7. 12th DA.C.
8. Staff Capt., 12th D.A.
9. R.A. Signal Officer.
10-13. War Diary and File.

War diary

SECRET. Copy No. 12

12th Divisional Artillery Order No. 116.

Ref. Map Sheet 62D S.W. 1/20,000. 4th August, 1918.

1. 12th Divisional Artillery Warning Order No. 2 is confirmed. Reliefs will be carried out as indicated therein. Guns, 12th Divl. Artillery, will, on relief, move direct to new positions already allotted to Brigade Commanders.

2. On completion of Relief, the distribution of Artillery covering the Sector will be -

(a) RIGHT GROUP. (Covering the 3rd Canadian Divn. Front.)

O.C., 10th Bde. C.F.A.
H.Qrs. T 4 a 0 0

10th Bde. C.F.A.
2 - 18 pdr. batteries,
2nd Bde. C.F.A.
Total 5 - 18 pdr. Batts.
1 - 4.5"How.Batty.

(b) LEFT GROUP. (Covering the 2nd Canadian Divn. Front.)

O.C., 5th Bde. C.F.A.
H.Qrs. N 35 c 2 2

5th Bde. C.F.A.
1 - 18 pdr. and
1 - 4.5"How. Battery,
2nd Bde. C.F.A.
Total 4 - 18 pdr. batterys
2 - 4.5"How. Battys.

3. No movement will be made forward of BOVES before 9 p.m.

4. Progress of and completion of all reliefs to be notified 12th Divl. Artly. H.Qrs. BOUTILLERIE.

5. The 3rd Canadian Division are arranging direct telephone communication between these H.Qrs. and the Right Group by 10 a.m. 6th August.

6. 12th Divl. Artly. Wagon Lines will remain as at present.

7. Groups and D.A.C. please acknowledge.

H W L Waller
Major,
Brigade Major, 12th Divl. Artillery.

Issued to all recipients of 12th D.A. Warning Order No. 2.
In addition 3rd Canadian Divn. (G).

<u>SECRET.</u>

R.A. 303.

62nd)
63rd) Brigade R.F.A.
108th)
12th D.T.M.O.
12th D.A.C.
Officer i/c. R.A. Sigs.

1. The 4th Canadian Division is relieving the 2nd Canadian Division on nights 16/17th and 17/18th August.
The 2nd Canadian Divl. Artillery are being withdrawn on the above nights. 5th C.F.A. Bde. will be relieved by the 179th Army Bde. 6th C.F.A. Bde. will be withdrawn without relief.

2. 12th Divl. Artillery and 108th Army Bde. pass to 4th Canadian Divn. at Noon August 17th.

3. The 179th and 8th Army Bdes. are being grouped for defensive and offensive purposes under command of O.C. 179th Army Bde. - H.Q. - F 7 b 8 0. This Group will superimpose its fire on the S.O.S. lines covered by the 4th Canadian D.A. and the 12th D.A. Groups covering the Divisional Front.

16th August, 1918.

Major,
Brigade Major 12th D. A.

S E C R E T. R.A. 833/1.

W. Diary

62nd)
63rd) Brigade R.F.A.
104th)
12th D.T.M.O.
12th D.A.C.
Officer i/c. R.A. Sigs.

Reference R.A. 833 dated 15th August 1918, para. 3 -

1. The transfer of the 179th Army Brigade R.F.A. to the Left Division has been cancelled.

2. The H.Q. 5th C.F.A. Bde. will be withdrawn on night August 16/17th and H.Q. 6th C.F.A. Bde. on night August 17/18th.

3. On withdrawal of H.Q. 5th Bde. C.F.A., O.C. 8th Army Bde. C.F.A. will assume command of the Group. The fire of this Group will be superimposed on the whole Divisional Front.

16th August, 1918.

Major,
Brigade Major 12th D. A.

S E C R E T. R.A. 333/2.

62nd)
63rd) Bde. R.F.A.
104th)
18th D.T.M.O.
Offr. i/c. R.A. Sigs.) for
4th Can. D.A.) information. 16th August 1918.

In continuation of No. R.A. 333 dated 16th August 1918.

1. At Noon 17th August, Artillery covering the 4th Canadian Division Front will be grouped as under -

(a) RIGHT GROUP (covering Right Infantry Bde. in the Line).
O.C. Lt.Col. J.A.McDonald, D.S.O., 3rd and 4th Brigades, C.F.A.

(b) LEFT GROUP. (covering Left Infantry Brigade in the Line).
18th Divisional Artillery. -
62nd Bde. R.F.A. covering Right Battalion in the Line.
63rd Bde. R.F.A. " Left " "

(c) Army Brigades under direct orders of 4th Canadian D.A. will remain silent except in case of confirmed S.O.S. 104th Army Bde. will superimpose its fire on the Left Group Zone.

2. Left Group Boundaries -
(a) Northern Divisional Boundary - Line of the railway through A 8 central.
(b) Southern. A 26 a [illegible] - A 26 c 3 7 through [illegible] central.
(c) Boundary between 62nd and 63rd Brigades an East and West Grid line through point of junction of Right and Left Battalions.

3. Liaison will be maintained as at present -
(a) O.C. 62nd Bde. R.F.A. with G.O.C. Left Infantry Bde. ([illegible]).
(b) Battalion Liaison Officers -
62nd Bde. with Right Battalion.
63rd Bde. with Left Battalion.

4. D.T.M.O., 18th Division, will arrange in consultation with D.T.M.O., 4th Canadian Divn. to place one Battery 6" Newtons in the line on the Left Group Front distributed in depth as under -
(a) 2 - 6" Newtons active for wire cutting.
(b) 2 - 6" Newtons silent covering ROUVROY - [illegible] - [illegible] line.
(c) 2 - 6" Newtons silent covering the old French Front line (approx. [illegible] through [illegible] central).

5.(a) Each battery will have detached guns for sniping and harassing purposes.
(b) Each of the Army Bdes. will push forward one detached gun or section for the same purpose.
(c) Any retaliation required will, if possible, be done with these detached guns.

6. Main positions will be kept as silent as possible.
Battery positions will be protected against gas, and, as time permits, splinter proof for guns and protection for ammunition will be provided.

7. Strict supervision will be maintained over ammunition dumped in battle positions, and weather protection constructed as soon as possible.

8. The above policy and distribution of batteries and zones will come into effect coincident with the assumption of command by G.O.C. 4th Can. Divn., 12 Noon 17th inst.

9. Brigades please acknowledge. [illegible signature] Major
[illegible]

12th Div. Arty.

C. R. A.,

12th DIVISION,

S E P T E M B E R 1 9 1 8.

C o n f i d e n t i a l.

W A R   D I A R Y

Headquarters, 12th Divisional Artillery.

September 1918.

Vol.XL..

Instructions regarding War Diaries and Intelligence Summaries are contained in F. S. Regs., Part II. and the Staff Manual respectively. Title pages will be prepared in manuscript.

Sept 1918
Vol XL

WAR DIARY
or
~~INTELLIGENCE SUMMARY~~.
(Erase heading not required.)

Army Form C. 2118.

H.Q 12th Div. Arty.

Sheet 1

Place	Date	Hour	Summary of Events and Information	Remarks and references to Appendices
F10 central	1	-	No change in situation batteries still under command of CRA 47 Div.	
	4		H.Q 12th D.A. moved to COMBLES.	
	5	6.30am	CRA 12th Div. took over from a/CRA 18th Div. & assumed command of 12th & 18th Div. Artys.	
		6.45am	All batteries fired barrage, as per BM I 4/9/18 in support of Infantry attack on NURLU Ridge. Infantry met with considerable resistance, wire and MGs being the obstacles. Hostile shelling was slight. During the day batteries fired numerous concentrations on MGs. trenches and also Germans seen dribbling up to trenches in V22 b & d:	
			from 7pm - 8.15pm Heavies bombarded high ground in V29 a also D5b, c & d. Infantry resumed attack on NURLU with field artillery support but not much progress was made. Heavy and field arty carried out harassing fire during the night.	
	6	8am	attack on NURLU was resumed supported by 62nd, 63rd, 82nd & 83rd Bdes RFA ~~as per BM 64 [illegible]~~ attack proved very successful and the line D11a56 - D5b50 - V29b20 - V22b62 was quickly captured: 62nd, 63rd & 82nd Bdes were ordered to move their batteries east of Canal in support of their respective Inf. Bdes. at noon 36th Inf. Bde received orders to advance to line LIERAMONT - SORREL WOOD, 35th Inf Bde to form defensive flank SORREL WOOD to junction with 21st Div. Position remained obscure for some time but this line was captured some time	

Army Form C. 2118.

WAR DIARY
or
~~INTELLIGENCE~~ SUMMARY.
(*Erase heading not required.*)

Instructions regarding War Diaries and Intelligence Summaries are contained in F. S. Regs., Part II. and the Staff Manual respectively. Title pages will be prepared in manuscript.

Sept '18
VOL XL

H.Q 12th Div Arty

Sheet 2

Place	Date	Hour	Summary of Events and Information	Remarks and references to Appendices
			during the afternoon.	
U29a38.	6th	6pm	12th D.A. H.Q moved to U29a38.	
			Field and Heavy artillery carried out harassing fire during the	
			night: 82nd, 62nd & 63rd Bdes were ordered to move to positions within 4000 yards of trench [system W28a – GUYENCOURT]	
			108th Army Bde RFA relieved 83rd Bde RFA.	
	7th		108th Army Bde RFA continued to advance	
		8am	37th Inf Bde supported by 82nd & 108th Bdes RFA ~~[illegible]~~. Everything proceeded	
			under a barrage ~~[illegible]~~ satisfactorily and eventually we held the line E5c60 – E5a60 –	
			W29d10 – W29d33 thence north along trench: during the evening that 174th Inf Bde 58th Div	
			would pass through 37th Inf Bde 12th Div at 7.30 am. orders were received	
	8th	7.30am	82nd & 108th Bdes RFA passed command of 12th Div arty Bdes &	
			to CRA 58th Div:	
	9th – 15th		HQ remained at U29a38 in rest	
	16th		HQ 12th Div. Arty moved to D16c09 in anticipation of attack in	
			conjunction with 18th Div. on the right and 58th Div on the left.	see 12th D.A. order 120 16/9/18
			Artillery was allotted and grouped as follows.	
			Covering 58th Div. 63rd Bde RFA and 108th Army Bde RFA	
			" 35th Inf Bde 62nd Bde, 231st Bde & 112th Bde RFA	
			" 36th " " 83rd Bde RFA. Div Boundaries and objectives	
			are shown on Tracing A. attached, also 18pdr barrage & 4.5" How tasks.	

A5834 Wt. W4973/M687 750,000 8/16 D. D. & L. Ltd. Forms/C.2118/13.

Army Form C. 2118.

WAR DIARY
or
~~INTELLIGENCE SUMMARY.~~
(Erase heading not required.)

Instructions regarding War Diaries and Intelligence Summaries are contained in F. S. Regs., Part II. and the Staff Manual respectively. Title pages will be prepared in manuscript.

VOL XL

HQ 12th Div. Arty

Sheet 3.

Place	Date	Hour	Summary of Events and Information — Sept 1918 — Sept 1918.	Remarks and references to Appendices
D16 c 0 9	17th		CRA. visited Bde Commanders. Considerable shelling during night & early morning.	
	18th	5·20am.	Barrage was put down in support of Infantry attack as per 12 DA. Instructions No 1 and appendices: from the start attack proved unsuccessful owing to the villages of EPEHY & PEIZIERE not being cleared of the enemy: 36th Inf Bde made progress to begin with and in consequence Batteries of 63rd Bde RFA moved forward to positions in W 30 a & c. These batteries had to be withdrawn during the night owing to their being about 1100 from the front line. & the presence of MGs which were still holding out in PEIZIERE & the vicinity. By 11 am 62nd Bde batteries were in action in E17 b & E5 d: The attack on the Red line was postponed until 3·30 pm owing to the obscurity of the situation. Barrage was fired by 62nd & 63rd groups but no progress was made and at 7 pm the situation was as follows:— ~~[illegible]~~ line F8c 36 – up trench to X25c80 was held by our Infantry. Harassing fire was carried out by field & heavy artillery during the night. During the night 35th Inf Bde improved their position and held line F2 central – E end of TETARD WOOD – CHESNUT AVENUE.	
	19	11am	a barrage was put down by all batteries in support of Infantry attack on the line BRAETON POST – BIRD TRench – MULE TRench – X28c C00 – OCKENDEN TR & ROOM TR. No information was received for over an	

A5834 Wt. W4973/M687 750,000 8/16 D. D. & L. Ltd. Forms/C.2118/13.

WAR DIARY
or
~~INTELLIGENCE SUMMARY.~~
(Erase heading not required.)

Army Form C. 2118.

VOL XL HQ 12th Div Arty Sheet 4.

Place	Date	Hour	Summary of Events and Information (Sept 1918)	Remarks and references to Appendices
DIBCOQ	19	–	an hour when it was reported that little progress had been made. During the afternoon sections of B/62 and A/112 engaged MULE TR, OCKENDEN TR & NO 12 Copse and drove the enemy out of these points. By night fall our line ran as follows POPLAR Trench - ROOM TR - OCKENDEN TR - down DEELISH AVENUE to OLD COPSE thence across to DOSE TR in F10c: Harassing fire was carried out by field and heavy arty. during the night	
	20		The morning passed quietly except for some shelling of EPEHY. Our infantry improved their positions and batteries engaged various fleeting targets: by field and heavy artillery Harassing fire was carried out during the night. 62nd Bde & 112th Bde artillery was regrouped as follows. 62nd Bde & 112th Bde covering right Inf Bde (37th) and 63rd & 231st Bde covering 36th Inf Bde. (Left)	
	21.	5.40am	Barrage in support of Infantry attack on ~~[illegible]~~ Blue line was put down by all batteries. Progress was made on the right Bde front who reached BRAETON & HEYTHORP posts and just west of LITTLE PRIEL FARM. No news was received from 58th Div on our left.	
		12 noon	Germans were reported counter attacking on 18th Div left Bde front in F11. 62nd Bde engaged enemy with observed fire:	

Instructions regarding War Diaries and Intelligence Summaries are contained in F. S. Regs., Part II. and the Staff Manual respectively. Title pages will be prepared in manuscript.

WAR DIARY
or
~~INTELLIGENCE SUMMARY.~~
(Erase heading not required.)

Army Form C. 2118.

Vol XL — HQ 12th Div Arty — Sheet 5

Place	Date	Hour	Summary of Events and Information (Sept 1918)	Remarks and references to Appendices
DIGC 19	21		Orders were given to 62 + 63. Bdes to bombard RED LINE with observed fire. Guns were registered in daylight and bombardment was carried on for 3 hours. ([illegible]) Barrage as ordered [illegible] was put down at midnight and attack proved successful, all objectives being taken.	
	22		The day passed quietly, nothing unusual occurring. Batteries continued to carry out observed shoots on targets seen with excellent results. Batteries carried out harassing fire and fired Counter preparation as ordered by III Corps RA.	
	23		Bombardment of approaches and strong points by field and heavy artillery continues. Orders were received that 231st Bde RFA would be withdrawn after dark. This was done: 44th Bde RFA relieved 108th Army Bde RFA (under arrangements made by 58th DA, + were transferred to 12th DA group) When 36th Inf Bde took over front held by 117th Inf Bde (58th Div) Harassing fire and Counter preparation was fired by all batteries. In addition bursts were fired to coincide with attack by 18th Div on EGG POST (F11C):	
	24		Bombardment as on previous days continued.	
		11.30 am.	Enemy put down heavy barrage on Div. front + attacked in vicinity of LITTLE PRIEL FARM but was ejected. All batteries	

(A7092). Wt. W12839/M1293 750,000. 1/17. D. D. & L., Ltd. Forms/C.2118/14.

Instructions regarding War Diaries and Intelligence Summaries are contained in F. S. Regs., Part II. and the Staff Manual respectively. Title pages will be prepared in manuscript.

WAR DIARY
or
~~INTELLIGENCE SUMMARY~~.
(Erase heading not required.)

Army Form C. 2118.

VOL XL — HQ 12th Div Arty — Sheet 6

Place	Date	Hour	Summary of Events and Information	Remarks and references to Appendices
			Sept 1918	
	24.		fired on S.O.S lines for an hour. Harassing fire was carried out by all batteries during the night.	
	25.	5am.	Enemy put down barrage in vicinity of BRAETON post in FSC. Batteries fired on S.O.S lines until 5.40 am, & enemy was ejected having suffered heavily. The rest of the day passed comparatively quietly, little movement or hostile activity being recorded. Harassing fire was maintained by field & heavy artillery during the day and night.	
	26	12.50 am	Batteries cooperated with gas bombardment by special Coy RE as per 12th DA Order 124. This did not bring down much retaliation. At 3 am batteries assisted an infantry attack on DADOS LOOP & LANE. This proved successful but at about 5.30 am after heavy shelling by 15 & 10.5 cm enemy retook ground gained by us at 3 am. Counter preparation was fired between 5 & 6 am. Orders were received and issued to groups dealing with tasks for 27th inst. Gas bombardment with B.B. gas shell was carried out at times & on targets detailed in 12th D.A Instructions No 3. Harassing fire was carried out by field and heavy artillery.	
	27	-	At 5.30 am creeping barrage as laid down in 12th D.A. Instructions No 4 & "Tracing A" was fired.	

(A7092). Wt. W12839/M1293. 750,000. 1/17. D. D. & L., Ltd. Forms/C.2118/14.

Instructions regarding War Diaries and Intelligence Summaries are contained in F. S. Regs., Part II. and the Staff Manual respectively. Title pages will be prepared in manuscript.

WAR DIARY
or
~~INTELLIGENCE~~ SUMMARY.
(Erase heading not required.)

Army Form C. 2118.

Vol XL HQ 12th Div Arty Sheet 7

Place	Date	Hour	Summary of Events and Information Sept 1918	Remarks and references to Appendices
D16 C19.	27	-	Our Infantry again captured DADOS LOOP & LANE but were again driven out. 27th American Div captured the KNOLL, & reached all objectives, but were driven out by strong German counter attack. Subsequent attacks improved their position but final objective was not reached. The night passed quietly. 62nd Bde RFA went up into action during the evening into positions in F14 & 15.	
	28		Wire cutting and bombardments were continued throughout the day and harassing fire including gas concentrations were fired during the night. Hostile artillery was quiet during the entire day.	
		6		
	29	5.50	Barrage as per 12th DA order no 127 was put down. From reports received at 7.10 am all appeared to be going well, both as regards our own Infantry and also on either flank: after the barrage was fired, numerous targets consisting of parties of the enemy, machine guns & forward guns were engaged successfully.	
		11.15 am.	Our left battalion was reported to be where they started from, and likewise the Div on our left. Right battalion however had captured the QUARRIES including 150 prisoners & trench	
	do	1.50 pm	TINO ~~Trench~~ support was reported to be in our possession & touch gained with 18th Div. on our right	

(A7092). Wt. W12839/M1293. 750,000. 1/17. D. D. & L., Ltd. Forms/C.2118/14.

Army Form C. 2118.

WAR DIARY
or
~~INTELLIGENCE SUMMARY.~~
(Erase heading not required.)

Instructions regarding War Diaries and Intelligence Summaries are contained in F. S. Regs., Part II. and the Staff Manual respectively. Title pages will be prepared in manuscript.

VOL XL

HQ 12th Div Arty. Sheet 8

Place	Date	Hour	Summary of Events and Information	Remarks and references to Appendices
			Sept 1918.	
D16C19.	29.		From this time onward nothing much was done except to engage movement &c with observation. The situation on the right was extremely obscure, the 27th American Division being out in front in vicinity of LE CATELET & GOUY while the line held by 3rd Australian Div was KNOLL Trench & line of trenches running South from this point: Harassing fire by field and heavy artillery was arranged and counter preparation was fired in the morning.	
	30		Firing on targets observed was again the order of the day. Our infantry continued to make steady progress and the artillery assisted them in every way they could by engaging parties of the enemy, MGs and guns in action. Orders were received during the afternoon that the 12th Div less (artillery) would be relieved that night by the 18th Div and that 62nd & 63rd Bdes. would come under the 18th Div. Arty on completion of infantry relief. Relief was completed during the early hours of the morning of the 1st inst. HQrs 12th DA remained at D16C19.	

L.H.G.W. Capt.
for Brigade Major
Brigade Major 12th D.A.

(A7092). Wt. W12839/M1293. 750,000. 1/17. D. D. & L., Ltd. Forms/C.2118/14.

"A" Form
Army Form C. 2121
(In pads of 100.)

MESSAGES AND SIGNALS.

No. of Message............

Prefix............Code..............m.	Words	Charge.	This message is on a/c of:	Recd. at......m.
Office of Origin and Service Instructions	Sent		............................Service.	Date..............
	At ....m.			From ....
	To			
	By		(Signature of "Franking Officer")	By................

TO			
62 Bde	83 Bde		
63 Bde	12 [illegible] G		
82 Bde			

Sender's Number.	Day of Month.	In reply to Number.	AAA
BM 1	4-9-16		

Artillery Bde. will fire Barrage
morning Sept 5th aaa Zero
hour 6.45 am aaa Start
Line ~~[illegible]~~ 18 pr 62 and
83 Bdes V 27 c 0 5.15
V 21 c 0.0 aaa 62 and 82
Bdes V. 21 c 0 c 15 V. 21 a 0 6
aaa Boundaries E and W Grid
Lines aaa Both Bdes superimposed
on First [illegible] aaa On start
Line Zero 15 Zero plus 20
then Creep 100 yds in
Four minutes 15' Grid through
V. 23 V 29 Central aaa
4.5 Hows Creep 300 yds East
of 18 prs aaa Rates of fire
Normal [illegible] Rapid when

From			
Place			
Time			

The above may be forwarded as now corrected. (Z)
....
Censor. Signature of Addressor or person authorised to telegraph in his name

* This line should be erased if not required.

a.21.d95.

Order No. 1625. Wt. W3253/ P 511 27/2 H. & K., Ltd. (E. 2634).

"A" Form (In pads of 100.)

MESSAGES AND SIGNALS.

No. of Message............

Prefix.............Code..............m. Office of Origin and Service Instructions	Words	Charge.	This message is on a/c of:	Recd. at......m.
....	Sent		........................Service.	Date..............
....	At ....m.			From ....
....	To		....	
....	By		(Signature of "Franking Officer")	By................

TO— [illegible]

Sender's Number.	Day of Month.	In reply to Number.	AAA
*			

[illegible]

From

Place [illegible]

Time [illegible]

The above may be forwarded as now corrected. (Z)

....

Censor. Signature of Addressor or person authorised to telegraph in his name [illegible]

* This line should be erased if not required.

Order No. 1625. Wt. W3253/ P 511. 27/2 H. & K., Ltd. (**E. 2634**).

"A" Form

Army Form C. 2121
(In pads of 100.)

MESSAGES AND SIGNALS.

No. of Message..........

Prefix..........Code..........m. | Words | Charge.

Office of Origin and Service Instructions

War Diary

Sent

At ....m.

To ....

By ....

This message is on a/c of:

..........Service.

....

(Signature of "Franking Officer")

Recd. at......m.

Date..........

From ....

By..........

TO: 62 Bde RFA — 12 Div G
63 Bde — 82 Bde
108 Bde —

Sender's Number.	Day of Month.	In reply to Number.	AAA
BM 43.	6 Sept.		

Bombardment morning Sept 7th aaa Zero to Zero plus 60 18pdrs and 4.5 Hows on Trenches GUYENCOURT inclusive through E 3b – W. 27d – W 28 a to W 22 c. 4. 0 aaa aaa Rates of fire Zero to Zero plus 30 Slow Zero plus 30 to Zero plus 60 Normal aaa At Zero plus 60 lift to Line Trenches from E 11 a 8 6 to ~~W 28 d~~ W. 22 d 0. 9 till Zero plus 110 when ~~fire~~ bombardment fire will cease aaa Rates ~~[illegible]~~ Normal to be fired in bursts aaa 62 Bde to keep JACQUENNE Copse under constant fire till Zero plus 110. aaa Boundaries

From			
Place			
Time			

The above may be forwarded as now corrected. (Z)

....
Censor.

....
Signature of Addressor or person authorised to telegraph in his name

* This line should be erased if not required.

Order No. 1625. Wt. W3253/ P 511. 27/2 H. & K., Ltd. (E. 2634).

"A" Form
Army Form C. 2121
(In pads of 100.)

MESSAGES AND SIGNALS.
No. of Message...........

Prefix.........Code..............m.	Words	Charge.	This message is on a/c of:	Recd. at......m.
Office of Origin and Service Instructions			.......................Service.	Date...............
	Sent At ....m.			From ....
	To			
	By		(Signature of "Franking Officer")	By................

TO Page 2

Sender's Number.	Day of Month.	In reply to Number.	AAA

63rd Bde Southern Div Boundary
to E & W Grid through W 27 d 5 0
aaa 62 Bde E & W Grid through
W 27 d 50 to Northern Div
Boundary aaa 108 Bde Superimposed
on 62 Bde & 63 Bdes front till
Zero plus 60 when it will
be free to advance aaa
82 Bde will ~~[illegible]~~ act
throughout as already ordered
by 37 Inf Bde and
acknowledge aaa addressed
62 63 82 108 Bde
repeated 12 Div G

From 12 Div G
Place
Time

The above may be forwarded as now corrected. (Z) [signature]

Censor. Signature of Addressor or person authorised to telegraph in his name

* This line should be erased if not required.

Order No. 1625. Wt. W3253/ P 511. 27/2 H. & K., Ltd. (E. 2634).

VERY SECRET. Copy No. 13

12th Divisional Artillery Order No. 120.

Ref: Map.-1/20,000.
Sheets - 57C S.E. & 62C N.E.

15th September, 1918.

1. At Zero hour on Z day - 12th Division will take part in an attack on a wide front - 18th Division is attacking on the right of the 12th Division and a Division of the Vth Corps on the left.

2. 35th Infantry Brigade will attack on the Right, 36th Infantry Brigade on the left, passing through troops of the 58th Division now in the line.

Boundary line between 35th and 36th Infantry Brigades is as follows:- Bend in trench at E.6.b.6.2. - South Eastern corner of FISHERS KEEP at F.1.a.15.15 thence along road to the T of WEEDON POST and the prolongation of this road to the grid line between X.25. and F.1., thence due East along this grid line.

3. Objectives are shown on the attached tracing.

First Objective ... the GREEN LINE.
Second Objective ... the RED LINE.
Line of exploitation ... the BLUE LINE.

There will be a pause of about an hour on the GREEN LINE, after which 37th Infantry Brigade will pass through 35th and 36th Infantry Brigades, and will attack and capture the RED LINE.

Protective barrage will remain in front of this line for half an hour, after which the 37th Infantry Brigade will exploit success as far as the BLUE LINE, the object being to secure the RED LINE and such positions in front of it as will give observation and assist our further advance.

4. Artillery Arrangements will be given in Artillery Instructions to be issued later.

5. Four tanks will be available. Two tanks each are allotted to 35th and 36th Infantry Brigades, but they will not go East of the line MALASSISE FARM - trench in F.2.c - F.1.b. - X.25.c and X.25.a.

6. The importance of secrecy must be impressed on all ranks.

Many old buried cables exist in the area, which make it easy for the enemy to pick up telephone conversations by means of Listening sets which are, no doubt, already installed in the HINDENBURG LINE.

Officers and men must not expose themselves when reconnoitring.

After troops are in position telephone will not be used for communication within the Division previous to the attack, except in cases of urgent necessity.

7. The Division will go into position for the attack on Y Day.

8. ACKNOWLEDGE.

H W L Waller
Major.
Brigade Major R.A., 12th Division.

For distribution see reverse.

Copy No. 1 to 12th Division "G".
2 to 62nd Brigade R.F.A.
3 to 63rd Brigade R.F.A.
4 to 108th A.F.A. Brigade.
5.to 112th Brigade R.F.A.
6 to 12th D. T. M. O.
7 to 12th D. A. Column.
8 to R.A. Signal Officer.
9 to S.C., R.A., 12th Divn.
10-13 War Diary & File.

S E C R E T. Copy No. 17.....

12th Divisional Artillery Instructions No.1 -
issued with 12th D.A.Order No. 120 -

14th September,1918.

1.(a) The Artillery available for covering the attack of the 12th Division is - 12th Divisional Artillery, 108th Army Brigade, and 112th Brigade R.F.A.

2. Those will be grouped as under:-

(a) Right Group - Covering attack of 35th Infantry Brigade-

O.C.,-Major C.N.RONEY-DOUGAL. 62nd Bde., R.F.A.	62nd Brigade R.F.A.
H.Q., with 35th Infantry Bde.	112th Brigade R.F.A.

(b) Left Group - Covering attack of 36th Infantry Brigade.

O.C.,-Lt-Colonel R.G. THOMSON, C.M.G., D.S.O.	63rd Brigade R.F.A.
63rd Brigade R.F.A.	108th Army Bde.,R.F.A.
H.Q., with 36th Infantry Brigade. E.3.c.0.8.	

3.(a) Batteries 108th Brigade should be sited as far forward as possible with a view to their carrying the Barrage up to the protective Barrage on the RED LINE from those positions so as to cover the advance of the remaining Brigades.

(b) Batteries 112th Brigade will also be sited weåll forward to carry on the Barrage during the advance of the 62nd Brigade R.F.A.

(c) During the Pause on the Proxtective Barrage of the 1st Objective - 62nd & 63rd Brigades must advance and be ready to open fire when the Barrage commences to advance to the Second Objective. This move must be carried out as rapidly as possible.
From their new positions they will be required to carry the Barrage up to the Protective Barrage on the Second Objective and if required up to 500 yards East of the BLUE LINE.

4. At a time in the Barrage to be notified later the 112th Brigade will revert to the control of O.C., 112th Brigade R.F.A. and will then be Grouped with the 37th Infantry Brigade and be prepared to advance in close support in accordance with the wishes of the G.O.C., 37th Infantry Brigade.
O.C., 112th Brigade will establish his H.Q., near H.Q., 37th Infantry Brigade on Y Day.

5. Os.C., 62nd & 63rd Brigades will arrange for Officers Patrols to keep close touch with the Infantry situation on our own front and the immediate Flanks. These patrols should also reconnoitre for Positions and the safest route to them as soon as the situation permits.

6. Ammunition -

6. Ammunition.-

(a)The following ammunition will be dumped at the guns -

(i) 18-Pounders.- 400 rounds per gun (60% A 40% AX) During the Barrage one round in 15 will be Smoke - Orders regarding amounts to be dumped will be issued later.

(ii) 4.5"Hows. - 300 rounds per How., B.X. | Dumping of Ammunition may be commenced forthwith.

(b)In addition, whenever possible, small extra dumps of boxed ammunition should be made somewhere near the position to facilitate refilling after Batteries have advanced. These Dumps must be carefully camouflaged.

7. The Tracing issued with O.O. No. 120 (to Artillery Brigades only) shews objectives, Start Lines, and the general idea of the Barrage. This should be taken as a general guide only and is liable to alteration.

8.(a) The D.T.M.O. will select positions for 6" Newton T.Ms. to fire on PEIZIERES and EPEHY during the opening phase of the Barrage.

(b) The four Mobile German Minenwerfers are allotted to the 37th Infantry Brigade. Officers in charge should get into touch with H.Q., 37th Infantry Brigade (U 29 d 8 4) forthwith. The Guns will join the 37th Infantry Brigade on Y Day.

9. On Y/Z night 62nd & 63rd Brigades will be responsible for the defence of their respective Infantry Brigade fronts. 63rd Brigade will only fire in the event of S.O.S.

10. ACKNOWLEDGE.

H W L Waller.

Major,
Brigade Major R.A., 12th Division.

Copy No. 1 to 12th Division "G".
2 to IIIrd Corps R.A.
3 to 62nd Brigade R.F.A. (4 spare)
4 to 63rd Brigade R.F.A. (4 spare).
5 to 108th Army Brigade R.F.A. (4 spare).
6 to 112th Brigade R.F.A. (4 spare).
7 to 12th D. T. M. O.
8 to 12th D. A. Column.
9 to R.A. Signals.
10 to S.C., R.A., 12th Division.
11 to 35th Infantry Brigade.
12 to 36th Infantry Brigade.
13 to 37th Infantry Brigade.
14 to 58th Divisional Artillery.
15-18 War Diary & File.

S E C R E T.   Copy No.16.....

12th Divisional Artillery Order No. 121.

Ref: Map, 1/20,000.   16th September,1918.
Sheets - 57C S.E. & 62C N.E.

1. 12th Divisional Artillery Order No. 120 and Artillery Instructions No.1 issued with above Order are cancelled.

2.(a)At Zero hour on Z day - 12th Division will take part in an attack which is being made on a wide front.

(b)18th Division is attacking on the right of 12th Division: 58th Division will be on the left of 12th Division as far as the GREEN LINE; forward of the GREEN LINE 21st Division will be on the left of the 12th Division.

3. The attack on the GREEN LINE will be carried out by 36th Infantry Brigade (less one Battalion) on the right; 35th Infantry Brigade on the left.

The main attack of the 35th Infantry Brigade will be in a North-Easterly direction from the approx. line E.12.d.8.7. to E.12.a.6.7.

The 35th Infantry Brigade is detailing two companies to advance on the right of 58th Division to deal with FISHERS KEEP and WEEDON POST.

36th Infantry Brigade (less one Battalion) will detail sufficient troops to move on the right of 35th Infantry Brigade to clear the area as far East as railway line in F.7.a., b and c. and F.1.d.

The Brigade will be formed up on the line of the railway ready to advance on the GREEN LINE at Zero plus 90 minutes.

37th Infantry Brigade will move forward in rear of 35th and 36th Infantry Brigades. It will be formed up close to the barrage ready to advance on the RED LINE at Zero plus 190 minutes.

The main objective of the attack of this Brigade is the LITTLE PRIEL FARM spur including theo Farm itself, and the KILDARE POST spur.

The Brigade will capture and consolidate the RED LINE and exploit to the BLUE LINE.

Reconnoitring Patrols will be pushed forward from the BLUE LINE to Canal and through VENDHUILLE Village to ascertain if the enemy is still West of the canal and if there are any means of crossing it.

4. Boundary Lines of Zone of Attack 12th Division , and objectives are shown on Tracing 'A' issued Artillery Brigade Commanders.

5. Artillery Instructions and Instructions regarding Communications are being issued separately.

6. Two tanks are available. They will start with 35th Infantry Brigade and will mop up the village of EPEHY: they will then move to DEELISH POST, keeping on the Southern side of the ridge which runs from EPEHY towards LEMPIRE. After mopping up the trenches in the neighbourhood of DEELISH POST, they will return via valley in F.7.d. and 13.a., mopping up on the way.

7. Contact aeroplanes will fly over the Corps front at the following hours :- Zero plus 2 hours 15 minutes: Zero plus 5 hours: Zero plus 7 hours.

8. A Counter-attack plane will be up continuously from daylight with the sole mission of detecting enemy Counter-attacks. The plane will fly in the direction of the enemy troops and drop a white parachute flare as near to the Counter-attack troops as possible.

The 3rd and Australian Coprs S.O.S. Signal will be :- rifle grenade bursting into 3 stars RED over RED over RED.

The 5th Corps S.O.S. will be :- rifle grenade bursting into 3 stars GREEN over RED over GREEN.

9. Watches will be -

9. Watches will be synchronized at present 36th Infantry Brigade H.Q., at V.28.c.3.1. at 7 p.m. on the 17th instant.
All Artillery Brigades will send a representative.

10. At Zero hour Headquarters will be as follows:-

12th Division & Divl. Artillery H.Q.	-	D.15.d.8.8.
35th Infantry Brigade approx.	-	E.3.d.2.7.
36th Infantry Brigade ..	-	E.3.c.0.7.
37th Infantry Brigade ..	-	E.3.c.2.7.

11. The importance of secrecy must be impressed on all ranks.
Many old buried cables exist in the area, which make it easy for the enemy to pick up telephone conversations by means of listening sets which are, no doubt, already installed in the HINDENBURG LINE.
Officers and men must not expose themselves when reconnoitring.
After troops are in position telephone will not be used for communication within the Division previous th the attack, except in cases of urgent necessity.

12. In the event of hostile guns being reported captured, information will at once be passed to D.A., H.Q., giving location of guns - nature - and amount of ammunition with guns.
On no account are spare parts, sights, etc., to be removed as souvenirs.

13. A C K N O W L E D G E.

H W L Waller

Major,
Brigade Major R.A., 12th Division.

Copy No.1 - IIIrd Corps R.A.
2. - 12th Division "G".
3. - 62nd Brigade R.F.A. (4 spare).
4. - 63rd Brigade R.F.A. (4 spare).
5. - 108th A.F.A.Brigade.(4 spare).
6. - 112th Brigade R.F.A.(4 spare).
7. - 83rd Brigade R.F.A. (4 spare).
8. - 12th D. T. M. O. (1 spare).
9. - 12th D. A. Column.
10.- R.A., Signal Officer.
11.- S.C., R.A., 12th Divn.
12.- 89th Brigade R.G.A.
13.- 139th H.B., R.G.A.
14-17 - War Diary & File.
18 231 Bde RFA (4 spare)

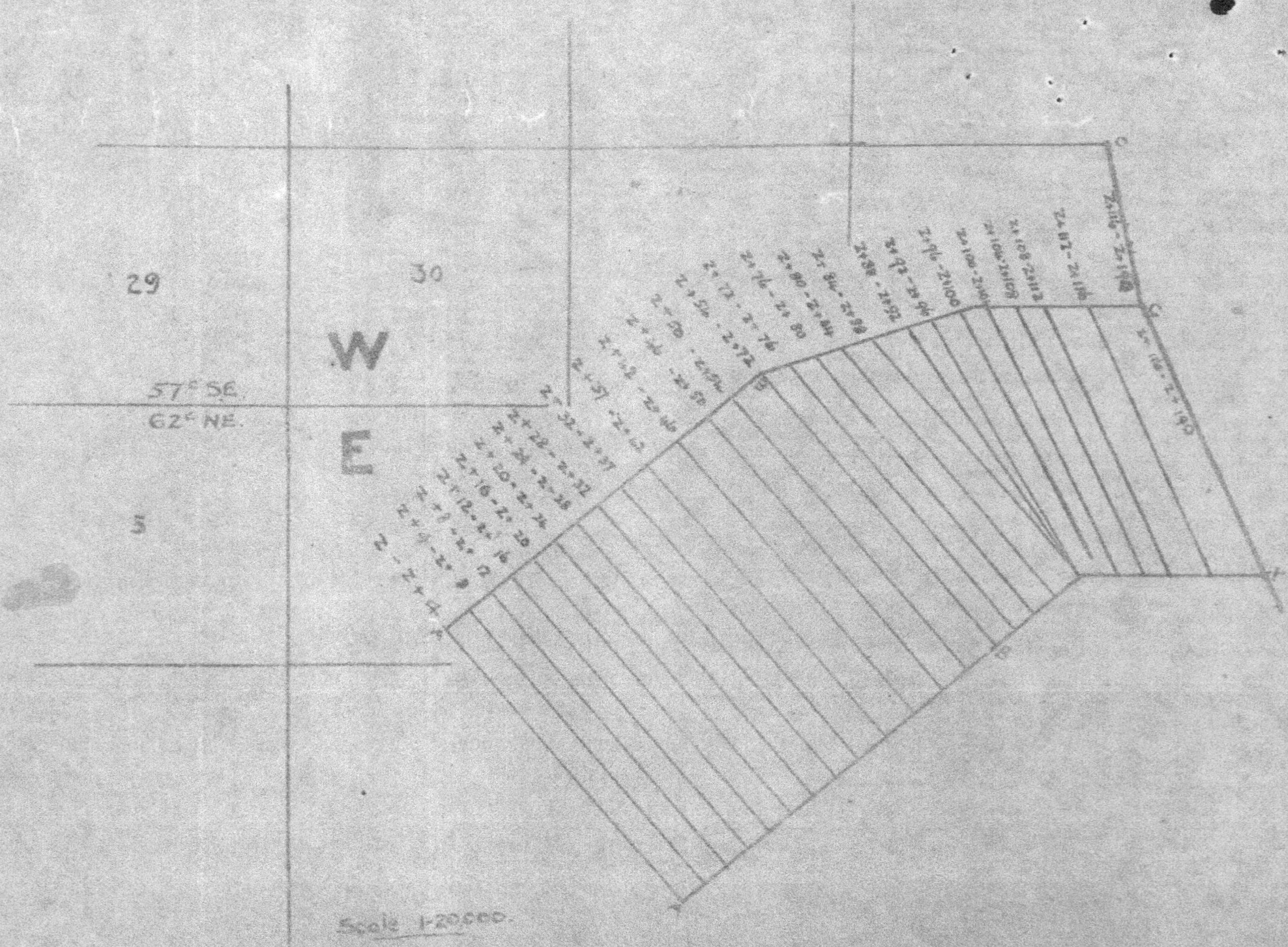
29
30
5
W
E
57° SE
62° NE
Scale 1-20,000

S E C R E T.

Amendment No. 1 to 12th Divisional Artillery Instructions
issued with 12th Divisional Artillery Order No.121.

1. Instructions No.1 - para. 5, at end add.-

"Cs.C., 62nd and 63rd Brigade Groups will arrange that one forward Artillery Intelligence Officer and Party from their Group accompanies respectively the Right and Left assaulting Battalion 37th Infantry Brigade."

2. Instructions No.1 - para 11(a).

The 4.5" Howitzer Batteries 231st Brigade and 108th Brigade will be the Batteries detailed to answer "LL" Calls during the Barrage.

3. Appendix "A".

Para.1. An amended Barrage Tracing for 62nd and 112th Brigade's Barrage up to the protective Barrage on the 1st Objective, is issued herewith to all concerned.

4. Appendix "A".

106 Fuzes will not be fired in the Barrage to be fired by 83rd Brigade and 2 Batteries 63rd Brigade Group detailed in para.3.

5. Appendix "B".

(a) 112th Brigade R.F.A. Tasks -

Delete " Target No.9" and substitute "9a. Z plus 20 to Z plus 42 1 R.F.G.P.M. - MALASSIS FARM - F 2 d 0 0.

(b) 231st Brigade R.F.A. Tasks.-

Line 2 - before "Z plus 37" add words "4 guns" - and at end add New Target " 2 guns - Z plus 37 to Z plus 80 - MALASSIS FARM - F 2 d 0 0 at Z plus 80 those guns will join 4 guns on COPSE Trenches, Etc., in F 3 b till Z plus 190".

(c) 83rd Brigade R.F.A. Tasks - at end add.

(i) Occasional rounds of H.E. will be fired at all three Areas allotted as Smoke Targets - These rounds will be in addition to the Smoke rounds ordered above.

(ii) This Barrage will only be fired if the wind is blowing from any point/ between S.S.W. and N.W. - Should the wind be unfavourable the whole programme will be carried out with H.E.

(iii) An officer will be posted where he can watch this Smoke Barrage and regulate the rate of fire as appears necessary.

H W L Waller.
Major.

16th Septr., 1918. Brigade Major R.A., 12th Division.

Copies to all recipients of 12th D.A. Insts. No. 1.

S E C R E T.

Copy No. 21

12th Divisional Artillery Instructions No. 1 - Issued with 12th Divl. Artillery Order No. 121.

16th September, 1918.

1. The total Artillery available for covering the attack of the 12th Division during various phases is - 12th Divisional Artillery, 108th Army Bde., R.F.A., 112th Brigade R.F.A., 83rd Brigade R.F.A. and 231st Brigade R.F.A. Periods during which these Brigades function under 12th Divisional control is given in para. 2 below.

2. (a) Groups as under -

(i) 83rd Brigade R.F.A. Covering the attack of 36th Infantry Brigade.
O.C. - Major OMMANNY - 83rd Brigade R.F.A.
H.Q., with 36th Infantry Brigade.

(ii) 62nd Brigade Group. Covering the attack of 35th Infantry Brigade.-
O.C. - Major C.N. RONEY-DOUGAL — 62nd Brigade R.F.A.
H.Q., with 35th Infantry Brigade. — 112th Brigade R.F.A.
231st Brigade R.F.A.

(iii) 63rd Brigade Group. Under orders of and covering the attack of 58th Division.
O.C. - Lt.Col. R.G. THOMSON, C.M.G., D.S.O. — 63rd Brigade R.F.A.
108th Brigade A.F.A.
H.Q. - E 3 c 0 8.

(b) On the completion of the barrage up to the Protective Barrage on the First Objective (GREEN LINE) -

(i) The 83rd Brigade R.F.A. will be transferred from the 12th Division to the 18th Division.

(ii) 63rd Brigade R.F.A. and 108th A.F.A. Brigade will come under orders of the 12th Division.

(c) As 231st Brigade R.F.A. will not arrive in time to take part in the Barrage they will be prepared to fire the Protective Barrage on the First Objective from X.27.c.40 to F.$.b.5.3 - and carry the creeping Barrage on to Second Objective with one 18-Pdr., Battery.
62nd and 112th Brigades will thus be free to advance by batteries on arrival on the Prontective Barrage on First Objective.

3. (a) Special Instructions for 18-Pounder Barrage are given in Appendix 'A' and Barrage Tracings to be issued later - attached Tracing is an advanced copy which should be taken as a general guide until confirmed.

(b) Special Tasks for 4.5" Howitzers are given in Appendix 'B' - to be issued later.

4. Orders for the advance of Brigades will be issued later.

5. Orders regarding Officers Patrols, and Forward Intelligence Officers have been already issued - The greatest latitude must be allowed Os.C. Brigades as to the distance they will advance their batteries, as they must be guided by the situation at the moment.

6. One Section -

6. One Section of 87th Company R.E. will report at H.Q., 62nd Brigade R.F.A. on Y Day to arrange with Os.C., 62nd and 112th Artillery Brigades assistance in preparing routes of advance for their Brigades.

7.(a)The D.T.M.O. will arrange to bombard FISHERS KEEP (vicinity of F.1.a.1.15.) from Zero to Zero plus 16 with 6" Newton T.Ms. now in position.

(b)The four German MINENWERFERS are allotted to the 37th Infantry Brigade and will join the 37th Infantry Brigade on Y Day.

8. On Y/Z Night 62nd Brigade R.F.A. will be responsible for the defence of the front - 112th Brigade will have its lines superimposed on the front, but will not open fire except in case of confirmed S.O.S.

9. Instructions regarding dumping of ammunition have been issued separately.

10. S.O.S.

In the case of an S.O.S. Call being received from the air or from the ground during the barrage programme all Artillery Brigades in the Divisional Area affected will at once switch one Battery per Brigade on to the threatened area for 5 minutes at the rate of 4 rounds per 18-pounder per minute. Then for 5 minutes at the rate of 3 rounds per 18-pounder per minute. After 10 minutes the fire will be slowed down and return to the barrage programme as the situation permits.

If the Call is near a Divisional Boundary the flank Brigade will co-operate as detailed above.

11.(a)During the Barrage LL Calls/will only be answered by Divisional Artillery as under.-

One 18-pounder Battery per Brigade.
Two 4.5" Howitzer Batteries per Division, these will not be detailed for Special Smoke Barrages.

These Guns and Howitzers will be detailed beforehand.

LL Calls. -

will be answered by three salvoes immediately on the receipt of the call. If the Call is repeated after a reasonable interval the bursts will be fired again.

ANTI-TANK GUNS.

If an enemy gun is observed from the air obviously firing on Tanks and within 1,200 yards from the Tanks it will be reported by the Call "LLNF" and answered as for other LL Calls.

(b)After the completion of the Barrage Programme.

NF Calls.

Will be answered by the batteries allotted to Counter Battery work.

GF Calls.

Will be answered by a section of all Field and Heavy Artillery Batteries that can bring fire to bear.

LL Calls.

Will be answered by all Heavy Artillery batteries in the zone allotted to their group and all Field Artillery Batteries that can bring fire to bear on the Target with the exception of one 18-pounder battery of each Brigade which will remain covering the zone allotted to that Brigade.

GF & LL Calls. -

S E C R E T.

APPENDIX "A".

Issued with 12th D.A. Instructions No.1.

Reference Maps - Barrage Tracing -
57C S.E. & 62C N.E.

1. 18-pdr. Barrage will be fired in accordance, on Lines and at Times shown on Tracing, issued to all concerned.

35th Inf. Bde. Barrage. 2. At Zero the 18-pdrs of 62nd and 112th Brigades will open on the Start Line shown marked A - A (i.e. E 6 d 1 3 to F 7 c 8 3) - at Zero plus 4 it will commence to creep at 100 yards every 4 minutes (except 8th & 9th Lifts which are 100 yards in 5 minutes) up to line B - B where it pauses from plus 54 to plus 72 minutes to allow our Infantry to occupy PRINCE RESERVE. Very special care must be taken to avoid shorts during this pause.
The Barrage then advances to the Protective Barrage Line CX - 231st Brigade R.F.A. will then take up the Protective Barrage so as to permit 62nd and 112th Brigades to advance.

36th Inf. Bde. Barrage. 3(a) At Zero - 18-pdrs of 83rd Brigade R.F.A. will open on the line F 2 d 0 6 - F 7 d 2 0 as shown on tracing. They will continue to fire on this line until Z plus 90. At Z plus 90 Barrage will commence creeping as shewn - 100 yards every 3 minutes until the protective Barrage is reached at Z plus 138.

(b) At Z plus 80 two 18-pdr Batteries of 63rd Brigade Group are being released by 58th Division, and will then superimpose their fire over the whole front on which the 83rd Brigade R.F.A. are firing - they will conform to the Barrage until the Protective Barrage Line is reached when they will stop and be free to advance.

(c) The O.C., 83rd Brigade will arrange to drop one 18-pdr gun of his Brigade on each of the following three trenches as the Creeping Barrage passes - (1) F 8 d 4 3, (2) F 9 c 0 5, (3) F 9 c 4 7 - They will continue on these until - (1) Z plus 150, (2) Z plus 156, (3) Z plus 160 - when they will stop firing.

Protective Barrage. 4. Protective Barrage on 1st Objective will be fired as under so as to release 62nd, 63rd, and 112th Brigades for their advance.

(a) 108th A.F.A. Brigade from Northern Divl. Boundary to E & W Grid through X 27 c 4 0 from Z plus 116 to Z plus 190.

(b) 231st Brigade R.F.A. from E & W Grid through X 27 c 4 0 to Southern Divisional Boundary from Z plus 116 to Z plus 190.

Fire on this line will remain stationary from Z plus 116 - Z Z plus 121, after which it will search to a depth of 500 yards by bursts of fire of 5 minutes duration every 15 minutes.
Rates of fire on Protective Barrage
While Stationary. - Slow.
During Bursts of Searching Fire.- Normal.
From Zero plus 187 to Zero plus 190 - Rapid.

Advance of 37th I.B. to RED LINE. 5. At Zero plus 190 - Two 18-pdr Batteries from each of 62nd and 63rd Brigade Groups will commence Creeping from Line D - D and C - C respectively. Remaining Batteries will remain in observation until the line E - E is reached - when the whole front will be again covered and continued up to the Protective Barrage Line. Boundary between groups an East & West line through X 29 c 2 6.
Fire will be continued on the Protective Barrage until Z plus 235 and will then cease. Rate of fire on Protective Barrage - SLOW.

Advance to Blue Line.

Advance of 37th I.B. to BLUE LINE.

6. Artillery fire required by 37th Infantry Brigade to cover their advance to the BLUE LINE will be arranged direct with O.C., 112th Brigade R.F.A. who will be in close touch with G.O.C., 37th Infantry Brigade.

7. AMMUNITION.

(a) Shrapnel will be fired at Ranges up to 5000 yards except that each 18-pdr Gun of 62nd and 112th Brigades will fire one round of Smoke in Every 15 rounds - up to first objective.

(b) Rates of fire normal throughout except where special orders to the contrary are given.

8. A C K N O W L E D G E.

H W L Waller.
Major,
Brigade Major R.A., 12th Division.

Copies to All recipientsof 12th D.A. Insts. No. 1.

S E C R E T. Appendix "B".

4.5" HOWITZER TASKS.

Issued with 12th Divl. Artillery Insts. No. 1.

62nd Brigade R.F.A.

Target No.	Time.	Rates of Fire.	Remarks.
2	Zero to Z plus 16.	2 rds. P.G.P.M.	for first 5 mins. then 1 R.P.G.P.M.
4.	Z 16 to 20.	1 R.P.G.P.M.	
5.	Z 20 to 24.	1 R.P.G.P.M.	
10.	Z 24 to 37.	1 R.P.G.P.M.	
14.	Z 37 to 46.	1 R.P.G.P.M.	On trench.
18.	Z 46 to 72.	½ rd. P.G.P.M.	Creep through wood and stop on E. edge. Z 72 to 88.
22.	Z 88 to 190.	½ R.P.G.P.M.	Creep Eastwards and stop on E. half.
25.	Z 190 to 202.	1 R.P.G.P.M.	
29.	Z 202 to 234.	½ R.P.G.P.M.	
37.	Z 234 to 286.	½ R.P.G.P.M.	Protective Barrage.

63rd Brigade R.F.A.

Target No.	Time.	Rates of Fire.	Remarks.
30.	Z 190 to 202	1 R.P.G.P.M.	
34.	Z 202 to 230	1 R.P.G.P.M.	
32.	Z 230 to 242.	1 R.P.G.P.M.	
42	Z 242 to 286.	½ R.P.G.P.M.	Protective Barrage.

108th A.F.A. Brigade.

Target No.	Time.	Rates of Fire.	Remarks.
31	Zero plus 190 to 222	½ R.P.G.P.M.	1 Section walk up Rd. keeping 300x E. of 18pr. barrage. 4 Guns
35	Z 190 to 222	-do-	
	Z 222 to 286	-do-	On STONE TRENCH. 23c + 29a

112th Brigade, R.F.A.

Target No.	Time.	Rates of Fire.	Remarks.
1	Z to plus 12	1 R.P.G.P.M.	
3	Z 12 to 20	-do-	
9	Z 20 to 42	½ R.P.G.P.M.	
13	Z 42 to 50	1 R.P.G.P.M.	
17	Z 50 to 100	½ R.P.G.P.M.	
21	Z 100 to 184	-do-	
24	Z 184 to 206	-do-	
28	Z 206 to 238	-do-	
32	Z 238 to 242	1 R.P.G.P.M.	
36 and 40	Z 242 to 286	½ R.P.G.P.M.	Protective Barrage. include LARK POST.

231 Brigade, R.F.A. will take over 112th Brigade, R.F.A. How. targets when it has moved thus freeing 112th Brigade.

231st Brigade, R.F.A.

Target No.	Time.	Rates of Fire.	Remarks.
8	Zero to plus 37	½ R.P.G.P.M.	On VAUGHANS BANK.
	Z 37 to 190	½ R.P.G.P.M.	On COPSE TRENCHES & SUNKEN ROAD in F 3 b

When the Brigade has moved it will take over the programme arranged for 112th Brigade, R.F.A.

83rd Brigade, R.F.A.

Target.	Time.	Rates of Fire.
Smoke targets A, B and C.	Zero to Zero plus 90	3 rds. per gun per min. for 1 min. afterwards 1 rd. per gun per 2 mins. unless screen requires thickening.

Tracing 'B' showing Targets is attached.

H W L Waller

Major.
Brigade Major R.A., 12th Division.

16th September, 1918.

Copies to all recepients of 12th D.A. Artillery Instructions No.1.

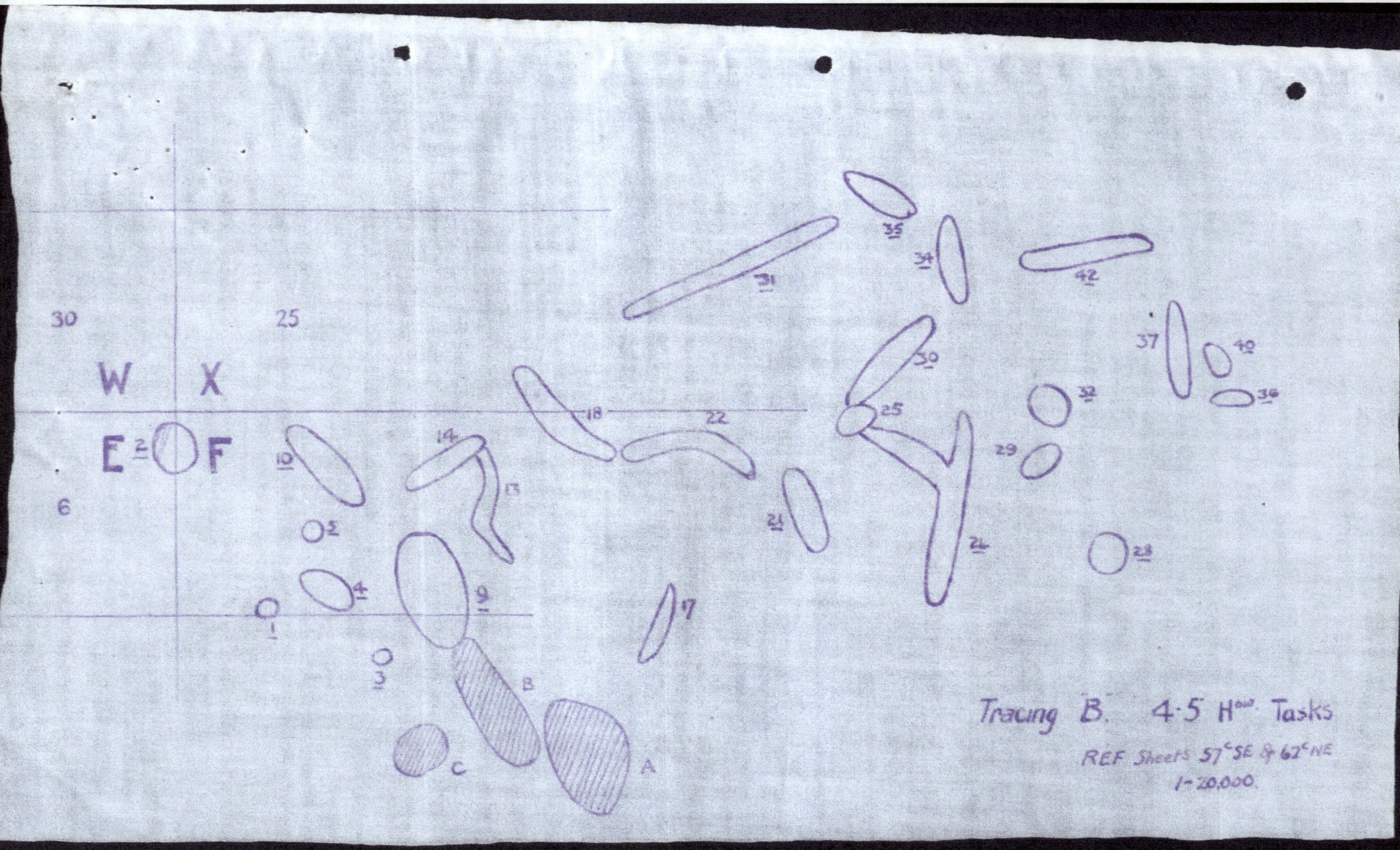
30
25
W
X
E
2
F
6
1
2
3
4
9
10
13
14
17
18
21
22
24
25
28
29
30
31
32
34
35
36
37
40
42
A
B
C
Tracing B. 4·5 How. Tasks
REF Sheets 57C SE & 62C NE
1-20,000.

S E C R E T.   Copy No. ......

12th Divisional Artillery Instructions No.2.

The Advance.

1. As soon as the Barrage reaches the protective Barrage on the 1st Objective -

(a) 112th Brigade R.F.A. passes from the control of O.C., 62nd Brigade Group to command of O.C., 112th Brigade R.F.A. and is free to advance.

(b) 62nd and 63rd Brigades are also free to advance at once.

2. As soon as the situation becomes clear, and 62nd and 63rd Brigades are established in their forward Positions, 231st and 108th Brigades will advance under instructions of Os. C. 62nd and 63rd Brigade Groups respectively.

3. As soon as the Barrage Programme is finished - O.C., 112th Brigade will have a call on both 62nd and 63rd Brigade Groups and will arrange direct with them any Artillery Support required by the G.O.C., 37th Infantry Brigade to cover his attack on the BLUE LINE or any other operation.

O.C., 112th Brigade will inform 12th D.A., H.Q., what special Heavy Artillery Support he requires at any time.

Os.C., 62nd and 63rd Brigade Groups are responsible for maintaining touch with O.C., 112th Brigade (who will be with Headquarters, 37th Infantry Brigade).

4. The attack on the BLUE LINE will probably be carried out about Zero plus 7 hours.

5. A C K N O W L E D G E.

H W L Waller.

Major.

16th September, 1918.   Brigade Major R.A., 12th Division.

Copies to all recipients of 12th D.A. Insts. No.1

SECRET.   Copy No. ....

12th Divisional Artillery Instructions No.3 - issued with 12th Divisional Artillery Order No.121.

---

1. S.O.S.

(a) Signal -

i. IIIrd and Australian Corps - Rifle Grenade bursting into 3 stars - RED over RED over RED.

ii. Vth Corps - Rifle Grenade bursting into 3 stars - GREEN over RED over GREEN.

(b) S.O.S. Rates in rounds per Gun per minute after Barrage Programme is finished -

	18-pdrs.	4.5"Hows.
First 5 minutes	4	2
Second 5 minutes	2	1
Third 5 minutes	1	½

- at the end of 15 minutes fire will cease, unless the S.O.S. Signal is repeated, or in the opinion of the Group, or Brigade Commander further fire is required.

(c) Ammunition.-

18-pounders 75% T.S. 25% H.E.
4.5" Howitzers H.E. 106 Fuze.

2. COUNTER PREPARATION.

(a) This will be divided under two headings -

"A" C.P. along the whole front.
"B" C.P. Annihilating Fire.

(b) C.P. "A" will be fired along the whole front in bursts, fire being concentrated by Groups or independent Brigades on portions of their front likely to be used by the enemy for concentrating for attack.
Field Artillery will deal with area - S.O.S. Line to 1000 yards East.

Rates of fire -

Rate "X" - 60 rounds per hour.
Rate "Y" - 30 .. .. ..

Fire to be in bursts at irregular intervals.

(c) i. C.P. "B" Concentrated fire by Groups or Independent Brigades on any given Map Square.

18-pdrs. will open on West Grid of Square at Zero - Rest for 2 minutes, and then creep 100 yards every 2 minutes for 500 yards through the square or squares ordered.
4.5" Howitzers will fire on line 200 yards East of 18-pdr line.

ii. Rates of fire unless other rates are especially ordered at the time -

18-pdrs. 3 R.P.G.P.M.
4.5"Hows. 2 R.P.G.P.M.
Ammunition 18-pdrs. 50% T.S. - 50% H.E.

3. If a C.P. "B" is -

3. If C.P. "B" is ordered ~~on a square through which the S.O.S. line passes~~ - ~~18-pdrs.~~ will open on a line 100 yards East of the S.O.S. line and then creep for 500 yards as above.

4.(a) Should it be found impossible to send Zero hour by D.R. at any time and the telephone have to be resorted to; the hour will be sent as plus or minus "Standard Hour".

(b) Standard hour until further orders will be 5 a.m.

Example - Zero Hour 6.45 a.m. -

Message would be "Zero Hour - Standard plus 1 hour ~~45 minutes.~~

5. A C K N O W L E D G E.

Hugh Walker.
Major.
Brigade Major R.A., 12th Division.

Copies to - No.1 IIIrd Corps R.A.
2 12th Division "G"
3 62nd Brigade R.F.A. (4 spare)
4 63rd Brigade R.F.A. (4 spare)
5 108th A.F.A. Brigade (4 spare)
6 112th Brigade R.F.A. (4 spare).
7 231st Brigade R.F.A. (4 spare)
8 35th Infantry Brigade.
9 36th Infantry Brigade.
10 37th Infantry Brigade.
11 R.A. Signal Officer.
12 H.A. Liaison Officer.
13-17 War Diary & File.

H.Q.
ROYAL ARTILLERY.
12TH DIVISION.
No. RA 958
Date..........

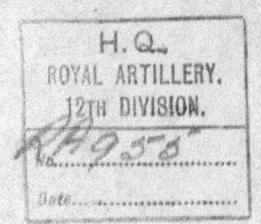

62nd Brigade.R.F.A.
63rd Brigade R.F.A.
109th A.F.A. Brigade.
112th Brigade R.F.A.
231st Brigade R.F.A.

Following extracts from Addendum No. 2 to 12th Division Order No. 253 are forwarded for your information. -

"2. As soon as it is known that 37th Infantry Brigade have established themselves on the RED LINE, 35th Infantry Brigade will take over the whole of the defence of the GREEN LINE from the Divisional Boundary at F 9 c 5 9 to E 26 c 9 9.

On relief, 36th Infantry Brigade (less one Battalion) will be withdrawn into Divisional Reserve South and West of EPEHY about Squares E.6. & 12.

Headquarters for 35th and 36th Infantry Brigades will be established close to each other about E 5 d., E 11., or E 12.

"3. The protective barrage on the RED LINE will remain for 20 minutes and will then stop.

60 pounders will fire on the QUARRIES till Zero plus 300 and will then fire on OSSUS WOOD for 6 minutes and will then stop.

Patrols will be sent out as soon as the Protective Barrage lifts.

If the BLUE LINE is found to be held the advance from the RED LINE will begin at Zero plus 420 minutes.

Special arrangements will be made by 37th Infantry Brigade for obtaining information as to whether our patrols have been able to make good the BLUE LINE.

This information will be sent back by runner and visual to 37th Infantry Brigade Command Post, and will also be sent by pigeon.

It is very important that the message should reach the Brigade as early as possible to enable them to inform the Artillery regarding the Barrage.

The Barrage will be ordered by G.O.C., 37th Infantry Brigade and arrangements made by him with Colonel QUERIPEL.

It has been arranged that Colonel QUERIPEL will be in touch with and have a call on all five Field Artillery Brigades for this operation.

"5. The following success signal will be fired as soon as troops have established themselves on the GREEN and RED LINES :-

Rifle Grenade bursting into 3 stars - WHITE over WHITE over WHITE.

"6. The following signals between Tanks and Infantry must be impressed on all ranks :-

<u>Tanks to Infantry</u>

Green and White Flag	-	Come on, all clear.
Red and Yellow Flag	-	I am broken down: go on.
Red, White and Blue, Tricolour.	-	Tank is coming back to refill.

"7. If an enfilade barrage is likely to be arranged for the BLUE LINE troops must be reminded that they cannot get as close to an enfilade barrage as they can to an overhead barrage."

[signature]

Major.

17/9/18. Brigade Major R.A., 12th Division.

CO-OPERATION TASKS FOR 150th H.B., R.G.A.

Target No.	Target.	Rate of Fire.	Remarks.
1.	3 Guns - [illegible] TRENCH F 4 a 2 7 to F 4 a 1 0.20.	Zero to Zero plus 10 - Rapid.	50% Shrapnel.
2.	2 Guns - Trench Junction in F 4 d 90 90.	Zero plus 10 to Zero plus [illegible] - SLOW.	
3.	3 Guns on [illegible] FARM in X 28 c.	Zero plus [illegible] to Zero plus [illegible] - SLOW.	50% Shrapnel.
4.	3 Guns - Trench X 29 d 4 4 to X 29 d 4 7	Zero plus 280 to Zero plus [illegible] - SLOW.	50% Shrapnel - fire to be distributed so as to cover the Communication trenches.
5.	3 Guns - [illegible] ROAD in X 30 b and X 30 c.	Zero plus 300 to Zero plus [illegible] - RAPID.	All H.E.

Total expenditure not to exceed [illegible] rounds.

N.B. - At Zero plus 200 2 guns will advance to their forward position on receiving orders from here.

17th September,1918.

Major,
Brigade Major R.A., 18th Division.

Copy to 150th H.B., R.G.A. thro' (50th Bde.,R.G.A.) (2 copies).
18th Division "G".
97th Infantry Brigade.
112th Brigade R.F.A.
File.

S E C R E T. Copy No. 12..

12th Divisional Artillery Order No. 122.

18th Septr., 1918.

1. The line is being consolidated and held tonight by 36th Infantry Brigade on Right, and 35th Infantry Brigade on Left.
37th Infantry Brigade is being withdrawn into Reserve ready to attack on morning of 19th Septr., 1918.

2. At Zero hour on the 19th Septr., 1918, 12th Division will attack - Objective - Line BRAETON POST - BIRD TRENCH - MULE TRENCH - X 28 c 0 0 - OCKENDEN TRENCH - ROOM TRENCH.

3.(a) 37th Infantry Brigade will attack on the Right, passing through 36th Infantry Brigade. 35th Infantry Brigade will attack on the Left.

(b) Dividing Line between Infantry Brigades - Railway at F 2 c 0 8 - Trench F 2 c 8 8 - Trench at F 3 b 2 3.

4. Artillery Groups. -

(a) 112th Brigade Group - Covering 37th Infantry Brigade Front.

O.C. - Lt-Colonel QUERIPEL. 112th Bde., R.F.A.	112th Bde., R.F.A. 63rd Bde., R.F.A.

(b) 62nd Brigade Group - Covering 35th Infantry Brigade.

O.C. - Major RONEY-DOUGAL. 62nd Bde., R.F.A.	62nd Bde., R.F.A. 231st Brigade R.F.A.

5.(a) Northern Divisional Boundary will be notified later.

(b) Southern Divisional Boundary - Present Southern Divisional Boundary.

(c) Inter-Group as for between Infantry Brigades.

6.(a) 18-Pounder Barrage will rest from Zero to Z plus 20 on the Start Line. At Z plus 20 it will move forward at rate of 100 yards in 4 minutes - after a certain distance (not yet decided) it halts again for 20 minutes - after which it again advances at Rate of 100 yards in 4 minutes.
As each gun reaches a point 300 yards beyond objective it halts, and forms a Protective Barrage - 30 minutes after whole Barrage has reached Protective Line Fire Ceases.

(b) 4.5"Howitzer Barrage will creep throughout, 300 yards East of 18-pr Barrage. Groups will arrange that Howitzers walk up any Trenches or Sunken Roads in their Zones.
D/231 has been allotted Special Smoke Task.

7. To facilitate description of Barrage by wire Lines will be referred to by the number of the line from the "Start Line" - Thus "Start Line" (Zero to Z plus 20) will be "Line 1" - Z plus 20 to Z plus 24 "Line 2", etc.

8. Rates of fire -

(a) Last two minutes before Barrage moves on after each 20 minute pause - RAPID.

(b) 30 minutes on Protective Barrage - SLOW.

Remainder NORMAL throughout.

(9).

9. Ammunition.-

(a) 18-pdr - Shrapnel up to 5000 yards then AX.
4.5" Howitzers - BX.

(b) 106 Fuzes will only be used by Batteries whose line of Fire is at Right Angles to Line of Advance.

10. ZERO HOUR - 11 a.m.

11. Watches will be synchronised with Infantry Brigades.

12. Artillery Brigades please ACKNOWLEDGE.

H W L Waller
Major.
Brigade Major R.A., 12th Division.

Issued at 3.30 a.m. 19/9/18.

Copy No.1 - 12th Division "G". ./.
2 - 62nd Bde., R.F.A. (9 spare) ./. for 231 Bde
3 - 63rd Bde., R.F.A. (4 spare)
4 - 112th Bde., R.F.A. (4 spare)
5 - 35th Infantry Brigade. ./.
6 - 36th Infantry Brigade.
7 - 37th Infantry Brigade ./.
8 - 139th Battery R.G.A.
9 - 98th Brigade R.G.A.
10- Liaison Officer H.A.
11- R.A., Signal Officer.
12-15 War Diary & File.

./. Smoke Barrage Programme attached.

Appendix "A".

Issued with 18th Divisional Artillery Order No. 182.

D/82nd Brigade R.F.A. SMOKE.

Task I. 3 Guns on ROOM Trench F 3 a 5 6 - Z plus 10 - Z plus 30.

Task II. 3 Guns on DUBLIN Trench F 3 c 0 7 - Z plus 10 to Z plus 30.

Task III. 3 Guns on HEWENORP POST - F 4 b 7 6 - Plus 30 to plus 100.

Task IV. 3 Guns on Trenches and Quarries in X 29 d - Plus 30 to plus 100.

In each case each area 300 yards on either side of point will be SMOKED.

SMOKE will only be fired if wind is blowing from any Point between N.W. through West to South.

Rate of fire - 1 Round per gun per 2 minutes.

An officer will watch this barrage from an O.P. and make any necessary corrections.

S E C R E T. Copy No.

12th Divisional Artillery Order No.123.

Ref. Map.- 1/20,000.
ST. EMILE Shoot.

23rd September,1918.

1. (a) The Front of the Division will be re-adjusted on night of 23rd/24th Septr., and will be in accordance with Boundaries shown on attached tracing (issued to Group Commanders only).

(b) On the night 24th/25th Septr., a further re-adjustment will be made in the Southern Divisional Boundary which will be notified later.

2. (a) From 6 p.m. today the Boundary between the 112th and 63rd Brigade Groups will be an E & W Grid Line through X 29 c 0 3.

(b) From 6 p.m. today 112th Brigade Group Southern Boundary will be the Divisional Southern Boundary as shown on the tracing - at the same hour 231st Brigade R.F.A., will pass to the tactical Control of O.C., 112th Brigade Group.

(c) 63rd Brigade Group Northern Boundary - from the hour the G.O.C., 36th Inf: Bde: assumes Command of the Sector taken over from the 58th Division - will be the Divisional Northern Boundary as shown on the tracing as far as X 23 c 0 6 - thence due East

At the same hour the 44th Brigade R.F.A. will come under Tactical Control of O.C., 63rd Brigade Group.

3. The following further transfers and reliefs of Artillery will take place shortly - Dates will be notified later :-

(a) 112th Brigade R.F.A. to the 27th American Division, Australian Corps. They will in all probability remain in their present positions.

(b) 231st Brigade R.F.A. will be withdrawn and transferred to IXth Corps.

(c) 62nd Brigade R.F.A. will be relieved by 117th Brigade R.F.A. and will rest in their present Wagon lines.

4. (a) Distribution of Artillery covering the Divisional Front from the hour at which G.O.C., 36th Infantry Brigade assumes Command of the 58th Divisional Sector is given in Appendix "A".

(b) Distribution of Artillery after withdrawals and transfers mentioned in para. 3 (a) & (b) is given in Appendix "B".

5. Groups and Brigades to ACKNOWLEDGE,

Hugh Waller
Major.
Brigade Major 12th Divl. Arty.

Issued at -

For distribution see reverse.

Distribution :- Copy No. 1.- R.A., IIIrd Corps.
2.- 12th Divn. "G".
3.- 63rd Bde., Group.
4.- 112th Bde., Group.
5.- 62nd Bde., R.F.A.
6.- 231st Bde., R.F.A.
7.- D.T.M.O.
8.- 12th D.A.Column.
9.- R.A. Signals.
10.- S.C., 12th D.A.
11.- 58th D.A.(1 Spare for 44th Bde).
12-15.- War Diary & File.

APPENDIX "A".

(a) 112th Bde., Group-Covering Front of 35th Infantry Brigade -

O.C. 112th Bde., R.F.A. — 112th Bde., R.F.A.; 62nd Bde., R.F.A.; 231st Bde., R.F.A.

(b) 63rd Bde., Group -Covering Front of 36th Infantry Brigade -

O.C. 63rd Bde., R.F.A. — 63rd Bde., R.F.A.; 44th Bde., R.F.A.

APPENDIX "B".

(a) Right Group - Covering Front of Right Infantry Brigade in the Line.-

O.C. 62nd Bde., R.F.A. — 62nd Bde., R.F.A.; 2 B'tys - 44th Bde., R.F.A.

(b) Left Group - Covering Front of Left Infantry Brigade in the Line.-

O.C. 63rd Bde., R.F.A. — 63rd Bde., R.F.A.; 2 B'tys - 44th Bde., R.F.A.

S E C R E T.

Addendum No.1 to 12th Divisional Artillery
Order No. 123.

Reference Para. 3 (c) -

1. 62nd Brigade R.F.A. will be relieved in the line on the 26th September, by the 117th Brigade R.F.A. - All details to be arranged direct between Brigade Commanders.

2. On relief the 62nd Brigade R.F.A. will march to area U 30 b & d (VAUX WOOD).

3.(a)Command of Batteries will pass when the whole relief of the Battery is complete.

(b)Command of the Right Group, 12th Division, as given in Appendix "B", will pass to O.C., 117th Brigade R.F.A. atv an hour to be arranged mutually between Brigade Commanders and notified Right Infantry Brigade in the Line and 12th D.A.,H.Q.

4. Completion of relief will be wired 12th D.A., H.Q., using the word "PESHAWAR".

5. 62nd Brigade R.F.A. and 74th Divisional Artillery please ACKNOWLEDGE.

H W h Waller

Major,
23rd September,1918. Brigade Major R.A., 12th Division.

Copies to all recipients of 12th D.A. Order No.123.

S E C R E T.

Addendum No. 2 to 12th Divisional Artillery
Order No. 123.

---

1. At 10 a.m. on Sept., 25th the Southern Divisional Boundary will become the East and West Grid Line between F 5 and F 11.

2. At the same hour the 112th Brigade R.F.A. passes to the Australian Corps Control - and Artillery Grouping as ordered in Appendix "B" of above order will come into force.

3. Brigades to ACKNOWLEDGE.

H W L Waller.

Major,
24th September, 1918. Brigade Major R.A., 12th Divn.

Copies to all recipients of 12th D.A. Order No. 123.

S E C R E T.   Copy No. 9....

12th Divisional Artillery Order No. 124.

Ref. Map. 1/20,000
ST. EMILE Sheet.

24th September, 1918.

1. In the event of wind being favourable, "D" Special Coy., R.E., will carry out a gas projection on LARK POST on the night 25th/26th September. Zero Hour will be at 12.50 a.m.

2. The projectors will be installed at F 4 c 95 95. One hundred rounds will be fired. After the first projection at Zero there will be no subsequent firing.

3. Artillery will cover the noise and flash of the projection as under -

Zero minus 2 minutes to Zero plus 5 minutes -

(a) 4.5" Howitzer Batteries of both Groups to be concentrated on LARK POST and vicinity -
Rate - First 3 minutes RAPID.
Remaining 4 minutes NORMAL.

(b) 18-pdrs.
Right Group - Trenches in F 6 a.
Left Group - Trenches in X 29 d.
Rates - NORMAL.

4. Troops east of a N & S Line through F 4 c 9 9 will wear box respirators from Zero minus 5 minutes to Zero plus 15 minutes or until told to remove them by an Officer.

5. The R.E. Officer in charge of the projection will have his H.Q. at approximately F 4 c 9 4.

6. The following Code will be used.

Operation will take place..........BILL.
Operation will not take place......BERT.
Operation Completed................ALF.

7. Groups please ACKNOWLEDGE.

H W L Waller
Major.
Brigade Major R.A., 12th Divn.

Copy No. 1 to III Corps R.A.
2 to 12th Division "G".
3 to Right Group (3 spare).
4 to Left Group (3 spare).
5 to D.T.M.O.
6 to S.C., R.A., 12th Divn.
7 to 139th B'ty., R.G.A.
8 to 11 War Diary & File.

S E C R E T.   Copy No.......

12th Divisional Artillery Order No. 125.

Ref. Map: 1/20,000.   25th September, 1918.
St. EMILE Shoot.

1. On the 25th September, 83rd Brigade R.F.A. will move into action, and will come under Tactical Control O.C., Left Group (63rd Bde., R.F.A. H.Q. E 4 c 4 1)
Two 18-Pounder Batteries will relieve B & C Batteries 44th Brigade R.F.A., at W 29 b 7 0 and W 29 b 5 5 respectively. All details of relief to be arranged between Brigade Commanders concerned.

2. B & C Batteries 44th Brigade R.F.A., will, on relief, move to positions selected today. The whole 44th Brigade R.F.A. will then be concentrated under Command of O.C., 44th Brigade R.F.A. and will be grouped for Tactical Purposes under O.C., Right Group (present H.Q. - E 12 d 8 2).

3. On the 26th September, 82nd Brigade R.F.A. will move to position being reconnoitred today in Right Group Area, and will come under the Tactical Control of O.C., Right Group.

4.(a) Location of all new positions to be reported as soon as possible to this office.

(b) Arrival in action and completion of relief to be reported to this office.

5. Brigades please ACKNOWLEDGE.

H W L Waller
Major,
Brigade Major R.A., 12th Division.

Copy No.1 to IIIrd Corps R.A.
2 to 12th Division "G".
3 to 62nd Brigade R.F.A.
4 to 63rd Brigade R.F.A.
5 to 44th Brigade R.F.A.
6 to 117th Brigade R.F.A.
7 to 82nd Brigade R.F.A.
8 to 83rd Brigade R.F.A.
9 to 12th D. T. M. O.
10 to 12th D. A. Column.
11 to R.A. Signals Officer.
12 to S.C., 12th D. A.
13 to H.A. Liaison Officer.
14 to IIIrd Corps H.A.
15 to 74th D. A.
16 to 18th D. A.
17-20 War Diary & File.

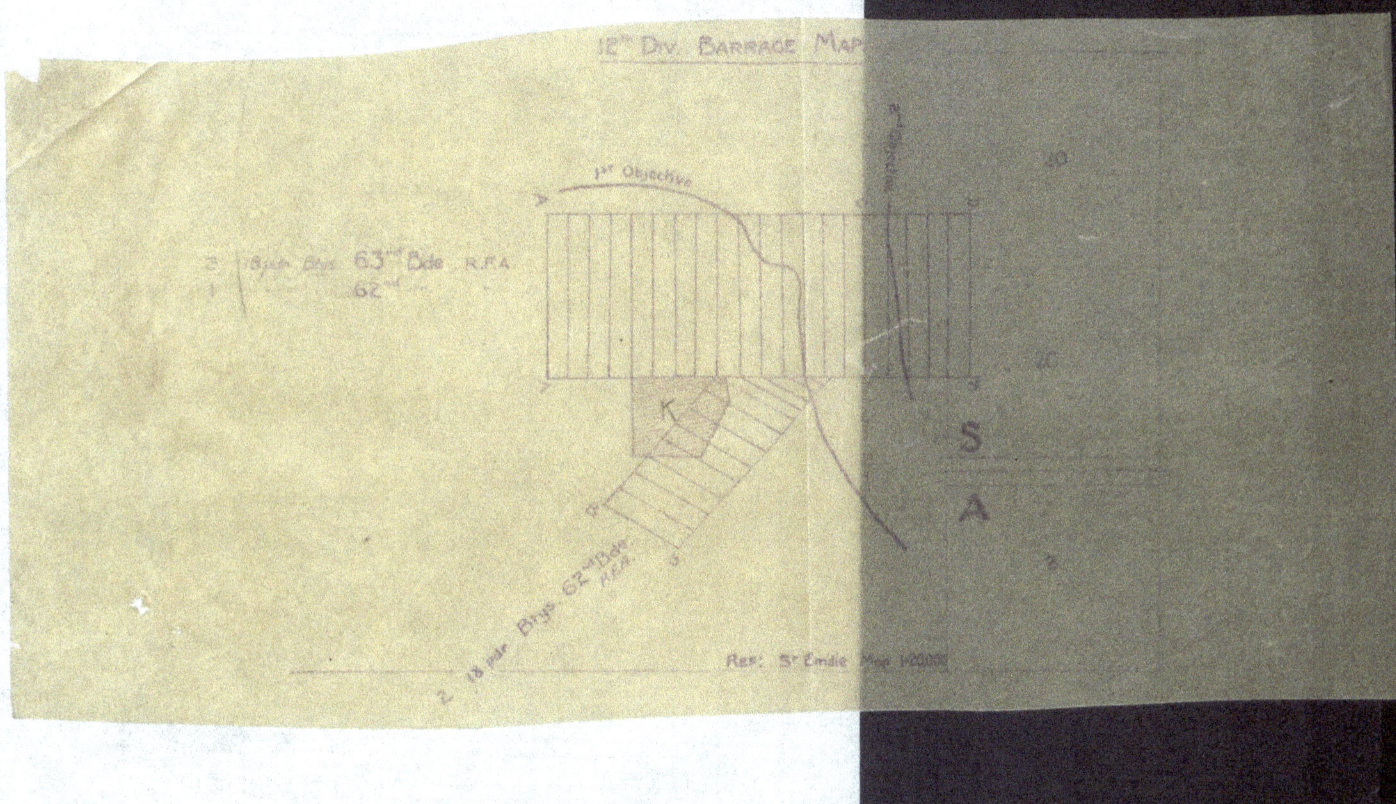

12th Div. Barrage Map
1st Objective
3 18pdr Btys 63rd Bde R.F.A.
1 62nd
K
2 18 pdr Btys 62nd Bde R.F.A.
S
A
Ref: St Emilie Map 1/20,000

Very Secret.   Copy No......

12th Divisional Artillery Order 126.

Ref. Map - 1/20,000   25th September, 1918.
St. EMILE Sheet.

1. At Zero hour on "Z" day the Division on our Right will attack the KNOLL (F 12 a) and the BLUE LINE South of it.

2. The 12th Division will co-operate as follows - Final Objective approximately the Line - TOMBOIS SUPPORT (about A 1 c 2 5) - TINO Trench to F 6 a 5 9 - Trench through F 6 a 2 9 - BIRDCAGE - SWALLOW Trench - STONE Trench to about X 23 c 5 7.

3.(a) 37th Inf. Bde., chiefly bombers and Lewis Gunners will follow the creeping barrage down Trenches leading to the objective.

(b) Other troops of 37th Inf. Bde. will be held in readiness to follow and exploit success.

(c) Should the Advanced assaulting parties be unable to penetrate the enemy's line a regular attack will be delivered by the Division later.

4. Artillery Arrangements will be given in Artillery Instructions to be issued later.

5. Brigades ACKNOWLEDGE.

H W L Waller

Major,
Brigade Major R.A., 12th Division.

Copy No. 1 - IIIrd Corps R.A.
2 - 12th Division "G"
3 - 62nd Brigade R.F.A.
4 - 63rd Brigade R.F.A.
5 - 44th Brigade R.F.A.
6 - 117th Brigade R.F.A.
7 - 82nd Brigade R.F.A.
8 - 83rd Brigade R.F.A.
9 - 12th D. T. M. O.
10 - 12th D. A. Column.
11 - R.A. Signals Officer.
12 - S.C., 12th D. A.
13 - H.A. Liaison Officer.
14 - IIIrd Corps H. A.
15 - 74th D. A.
16-19 War Diary and File.

S E C R ET.

Amendment No. 1 to 12th D.A. Order No. 126 and Instructions.

---

1. Order No. 126 - para. 1 line 1 for "Z" Day" read "X" Day".

2. Instructions No. 2 para. 4 (b) Line 1 and Line 2 for "Z" Day" read "X" Day".

3. Instructions No. 3 Para. 2 - at end add fresh Targets-

   "(j) Approaches both sides of Canal to Bridge at A 3 a 55.

   (k) H.Q. at S 25 d 5 C."

4. Instructions No. 3 para 3 Line 1 - for "320 rounds" read "260 rounds".

Major,
Brigade Major R.A., 12th Divn.

26th September, 1918.

Copies to all recipients of 12th D.A. Order No. 126 plus 35th, 36th and 37th I.Bs.

SECRET.   Copy No..........

2nd Amendment to 12th Divisional Artillery Order No.126 and Instructions.

---

1. Reference Barrage Tracing "A" issued with Instructions No.4 para.1 -
Boundaries are now as follows :-

(a) Right Group - South Boundary.

Line F 5 d 0 5 00 to F 6 c 25 00 thence through A 2 Central.

North Boundary.

East and West Line through X 29 c 50 60.

(b) Left Group - 63rd Brigade R.F.A. South Boundary.

East and West Line through X 29 c 50 60

North Boundary - as before.

2. Instructions No. 4.

(a) Para. 1 Line 2 for "3-18.pdr Batteries" read "2-18.pdr. Batteries.

(b) Para. 4. Batteries 63rd Brigade R.F.A. will not fire the Special Tasks therein allotted - but are allotted as below.

(c) At the end of Instructions add fresh para -

"63rd Brigade R.F.A. and one 18-pdr. Battery, 83rd Brigade R.F.A. are placed at the disposal G.O.C., 36th Infantry Brigade for a special operation. All details regarding barrage to be arranged direct between O.C. Left Group (63rd Brigade R.F.A.) and the G.O.C., 36th Infantry Brigade - and notified 12th D.A., H.Q."

3. Instructions No. 2 - para.2(a).
Line 2 - for "O.C., Br-General L.J. HEXT, C.M.G." read "O.C., Lt-Colonel Robertson, D.S.O." 44th Brigade R.F.A."

4. Instructions No. 4 para. 4 (d).
Line 3 for "Zero plus 120" read "Zero plus 18" and add "From Zero plus 18 the Western limit of the Smoke Barrage will conform to the creeping barrage line till the Zero plus 21 - 24 Line is reached (X 30 c 0 4). The Smoke Barrage will then continue till Z plus 120 between points X 30 c 0 4 and X 30 c 9 5."

H W L Walker

Major.
Brigade Major R.A., 12th Division.

26th September,1918.

Copies to all recipients of 12th D.A. Order No. 126 plus 35th, 36th and 37th I.Bs.

S E C R E T. Copy No. 17.

12th Divisional Artillery Instructions No.1 issued with 12th D.A. Order No.126.

---

1. The Bombardment will consist of :-

(a) Intensive Harassing Fire.
(b) Special Gas (B.B.) Bombardment.
(c) Cutting Lanes in Hostile Wire Defences.
(d) Counter Battery work and Bombardment of Strong Points and Localities by H.A.

2. HARASSING FIRE.

(a) From now, until "Z" day the enemy position will be continuously harassed - special attention being paid to the following :- LARK Trench - TINO Trench - The New Trench running from TINO Trench at F 6 a 5 9 to F 6 a 2 9 thence as shown on map to FALCON AVENUE (X 30 a 1 1) - The QUARRIES - The BRIDCAGE - Junctions of STONE Trench with STONE LANE and CATELET Trench - also special attention to any M.G. nests which may be located.

(b) INTENSIVE HARASSING FIRE.

This will commence at 6 a.m. on "X" Day.

The keynote of its application should be variety and surprise, and plans must be so framed that throughout the 24 hours of the day and night, the enemy should be permitted no immunity or security from shell fire.

Facilities of observation must be fully exploited in order to limit the area on which unobserved harassing fire will have to be maintained by day. Areas over which no observation is possible must receive special attention.

In shelling roads, H.E. with delay action fuzes are NOT to be employed.

3. SPECIAL GAS (B.B.) BOMBARDMENT.

(a) This bombardment will be carried out by 18-pdrs. and 6" Hows., firing "BB" gas shells in combination with H.E. during intermittent periods between 10 p.m. on "W" day and 6 a.m. on "X" day.

The objectives will be the hostile defensive system and Artillery positions along the whole front so far as the range of Guns permit.

Subsequent to 6 a.m. on "X" day, no "BB" gas shell will be fired without the authority of the ARMY.

(b) During the hours of daylight Smoke Shell will be mixed with Gas Shell in all gas concentrations within the range of 18-pdrs., and 4.5" Howitzers.

4. WIRE CUTTING.

This will commence at 6 a.m. on "X" Day and will be carried out principally with 4.5" Hows. and 6" Hows (with instantaneous fuzes), and, where feasible, with 6" Newton Mortars. Lanes once cut must be kept open by means of rifle and machine gun fire.

5. The Bombardment of strong points is commencing at 6 a.m. on "X" Day.

4

6. The 18-pdr. Air Recuperator Guns will be grouped in Batteries - Location in action of these Batteries will be reported as soon as possible to this office.

7. AMMUNITION.

(a) In addition to all echelons being full the following amounts will be dumped :-

18-pdrs............500 rounds per Gun.
4.5"Hows...........500 .. .. ..

(b) 3000 rounds 18-pdr. "BB" Gas shell are available, and will be allotted to Batteries taking part in special Gas (BB) Bombardments.

(c) All special shell will be included in the amounts to be dumped given in para. 7 (a) above.

(d) As much ammunition as possible will be kept boxed at all dumps.

8. Brigades please acknowledge.

H.W.L. Waller
Major.
Brigade Major R.A., 12th Division.

Copies to all recipients of 12th D.A. Order No. 126.

S E C R E T. Copy No. 20.

12th Divisional Artillery Instructions No.2 issued with 12th D.A.Order No.126.

---

1. The Artillery available to cover the 12th Divisional Front is 12th, 18th and 74th Divisional Artilleries.

2. GROUPING.

(a) Right Group.-

C.C. Br-General L.J.HEXT, C.M.G.	74th Divisional Arty. 82nd Brigade R.F.A.

(b) Left Group.-

C.C. Lt-Colonel R. THOMSON, C.M.G., D.S.O.	63rd Brigade R.F.A. 83rd Brigade R.F.A.

N.B. - Orders regarding Grouping and Tasks of 62nd Brigade R.F.A. will be issued later.

3. Group Boundary.

(a) Right Group.-

Southern - E & W Grid between F 5 & F 11.
Northern - E & W Grid through X 29 c 0 3.

(b) Left Group.-

Southern - E & W Grid through X 29 c 0 3.
Northern - E & W Grid through X 23 c 0 6.

4. TASKS.

(a) Prior to Zero hour "Z" Day Brigades will carry out Harassing and Bombardment Tasks in their respective Group Zones.
Both Groups will detail Batteries to take part in special (B.B) Gas Bombardments - details of which will be issued as soon as possible.

(b) Barrage on "Z" Day.

Brigades of 74th and 18th Divisional Artilleries will be allotted Lanes for the Barrage on "Z" Day.
63rd Brigade R.F.A. will be superimposed on the Front and will work in close co-operation with the attacking Infantry. O.C., 63rd Brigade R.F.A. will be free to take any of his Batteries out of the Barrage to assist the Infantry with close observed shooting should the necessity arise - or to engage fleeting opportunity Targets.

5. 6" Newton T.Ms. and German Minenwerfers are being placed in position to assist in the Bombardment.

6. Brigades please ACKNOWLEDGE.

H W h Walker
Major,
Brigade Major R.A., 12th Division.

Copies to all recipients of 12th D.A. Order No. 126 plus 35th, 36th & 37th I.Bs.

S E C R E T.

Copy No........

12th Divisional Artillery Instructions No. 3 issued with 12th D.A. Order No. 126.

Reference Instructions No.1 para 3.

1. A "BB" Gas Bombardment will be carried out between 10 p.m. on "W" Day and 6 a.m. on "X" Day.

2. The areas to be engaged by 18-pdrs. of the 12th Division are -

(a) Headquarters and Banks about S 25 b 2 5.
(b) Eastern approaches to VENDHUILE Bridges at S 26 b 5 0.
(c) Western approaches to VENDHUILE Bridge at S 26 b 5 0.
(d) Northern approaches to Bridge at S 26 a 7 3.
(e) Southern approaches to Bridge at S 26 a 7 5.
(f) Headquarters at S 26 a 9 8.
(g) HARGIVAL FARM about A 3 b 1 9.
(h) RICHMOND COPSE about S 28 a 0 0.
(i) RICHMOND QUARRY about S 28 a 2 8.

3. Total of 320 rounds "BB" and 320 rounds H.E. will be fired on each Target in four bursts at -

10 p.m. to 10.15 p.m.
12.25 p.m. to 12.40 a.m.
2.40 a.m. to 2.55 a.m.
4.15 a.m. to 4.30 a.m.

Ammunition allotted to be divided equally between each burst - one round of H.E. will be fired for each round of "BB" Gas Shell.

4. A map showing areas to be engaged has been issued to each Group Commander.

5. Batteries detailed for these Tasks will draw 320 rounds "BB" Gas Shell forthwith from the 12th A.R.P. - E 2 d 5 8.

6. Watches will be synchronised at 44th Brigade H.Q.,R.F.A. - E 12 c 7 3 at 4 p.m. tonight - 26th instant.

7. Groups please ACKNOWLEDGE.

H W H Waller.
Major,
Brigade Major R.A., 12th Division.

Copies to all recipients of 12th D.A.Order No. 126 plus 35th, 36th and 37th I.Bs.

S E C R E T. Copy No........

12th Divisional Artillery Instructions No. 4 issued with 12th D.A. Order No. 126.

Reference 12th D.A. Instructions No. 2 para. 4(b) - Barrage on "X" Day.

1. A Creeping Barrage will be fired by 9-18.pdr Batteries Right Group and 3-18.pdr Batteries 83rd Brigade R.F.A. in accordance with tracing "A" issued to all concerned.

2(a) The Barrage will rest 3 minutes on the Start Line - it will then creep at the rate of 100 yards every 3 minutes to the Protective Barrage Line in accordance with Tracing "A". 4.5" Howitzers in Barrage will creep 100 yards in advance of 18-pdr. Barrage throughout.

(b) Ammunition 18-pdr. 50% Shrapnel 50% H.E.

3. PROTECTIVE BARRAGE.

After reaching Protective Barrage Line all Batteries will search East for 500 yards for 5 minutes every 15 minutes until Zero plus 75 minutes.

4. SPECIAL TASKS.

(a) One 18-pdr. Battery 83rd Brigade and one 4.5" How. Battery Right Group will bombard LARK TRENCH from LARK POST to F 5 b 9 9., and from F 6 a 3 3 to F 6 b 9 2.

The fire of these Batteries will commence creeping as follows:-

18-pdrs. When Creeping Barrage reaches it.

4.5"Hows. 100 yards in advance of 18-pdr. Barrage.

(b) Two 18-pdr. Batteries 83rd Brigade R.F.A. will bombard STONE Trench from Zero till an hour to be notified later.

(c) One 4.5" How. Battery, Right Group, will enfilade BIRD LANE - keeping 100 yards East of the 18-pdr. Creeping Barrage.

(d) 4.5" How. Battery, 83rd Brigade R.F.A., will form a Smoke Screen from X 29 d 5 4 to X 30 c 9 5 - from Zero to Zero plus120.

An officer will be put in charge of this screen. He will be stationed where he can best observe the effect and will regulate the rate of fire.

(e) The 4.5" How. Battery, 83rd Brigade R.F.A., will fire the Barrage on the 83rd Brigade Lane - keeping 100 yards East of the 18-pdr. Barrage.

5. Rates of Fire -

Zero to Zero plus 3 RAPID.
Zero plus 3 to End NORMAL.

6. Orders for -

6. Orders for S.O.S. Calls during the Barrage Programme - Calls from the Air - Fleeting Targets - will be as issued for previous operations in IIIrd Corps.

7. Groups Please ACKNOWLEDGE.

H W L Waller

Major,
Brigade Major R.A., 12th Division.

Copies to all recipients of 12th D.A. Order No. 126 plus
35th, 36th & 37th I.Bs.

1

SECRET.

12th Divisional Artillery INSTRUCTIONS No. 5

issued with 12th D.A. Order No. 126.

---

1. On "X" Day, 6" Newton T.Ms. will bombard the QUARRIES in X 29 d from Zero to Zero plus 20. At Zero plus 20 they will stop.

2. The German Minenwerfers are placed at disposal of G.O.C., 36th Infantry Brigade to support operations on "X" day.

3. D.T.M.O. to acknowledge

H W L Walker
Major,

26th Sept. 1918. Brigade Major R.A., 12th Division.

Copies to 35th Infantry Bde.
36th Infantry Bde.
37th Infantry Bde.
62nd Brigade, R.F.A.
63rd Brigade, R.F.A.
44th Brigade, R.F.A.
117th Brigade, R.F.A.
82nd Brigade, R.F.A.
83rd Brigade, R.F.A.
12th D.T.M.O.

SECRET.   Copy No..........

12th Divisional Artillery Instructions No. 6

1. On completion of the operation detailed in 12th D.A. Instructions No. 4 for the 27th September - the Artillery will continue the bombardment of the HINDENBURG LINE as laid down in 12th D.A. Instructions No. 1.

2. HARASSING FIRE.

(a) Field Artillery have been allotted the area as far East as a N & S Grid through A 4 c 0 0 for Harassing purposes.

(b) This area is divided into two Group lanes as under for harassing purposes. Groups will further sub-divide this into Brigade Lanes and should notify them to this office.

(c) Right Group Lane.
Southern Boundary - Corps Boundary - Grid between F 5 and F 11 to F 6 c 2.0 - A 2 Central, thence due East.
Northern Boundary - Northern Boundary - an E & W Line through X 29 a 0 2.

Left Group Lane.
Southern Boundary - an E & W Line through X 29 a 0 2
Northern Boundary - North Corps Boundary - an E & W Line through X 23 c 0 6.

The above Inter-Group Line will also be the Boundary for Defence of the Line and S.O.S. purposes from 3 p.m. today.

(d) Harassing Fire will be carried out in those lanes by 18-pdr. Guns firing bursts of fire at irregular intervals.
Three bursts per hour will be fired and each burst will consist of 6 rounds per gun. So that Harassing Fire may be continuous - the Brigade Task per hour will be fired by one third of the guns - while detachments of the remaining two thirds rest.
Group Commanders will ensure that the whole area allotted them is harassed - particular attention being paid by day to areas over which direct observation cannot be obtained and by night to approaches.
As much as possible of this Harassing Fire Task should be done with observed fire.

3. WIRE CUTTING.

Lanes in the wire will be cut by 4.5" Howitzers, using 106 Fuze, as follows :-

(a) Right Group - Wire in A 1 b, A 2 a & b.

(b) Left Group - Wire in X 30 a & c.

4. 4.5" HOWITZER TASKS.

(a) Gas bombardment with CG and NC Shell of trenches from A 2 b 3 0 to S 25 d 9 2, This will be ordered whenever atmospheric conditions are favourable, This will be ordered by the Code wire "VIOLETS", TASK "A" - ZERO Hour, ".

(b) On night -

(b) On night 27th/28th September - Gas Concentrations will be fired on PUTNEY (S 26 b and S 27 b c) by D/117 and D/82 firing CG and NC Gas.

Each Concentration will be of five minutes duration commencing at 12.55 a.m. - 2.10 a.m. - and 5.5 a.m.

Rates of Fire - RAPID.

(c) The amount of 4.5" Howitzer ammunition to be fired during the bombardment is 200 rounds per gun per 24 hours.

5. A C K N O W L E D G E. (Groups only)

H W h Waller
Major,
Brigade Major R.A., 12th Division.

Copy No. 1 to IIIrd Corps R.A.
2 12th Division "G".
3. Right Group.
4 44th Brigade R.F.A. (4 spare)) Through
5 82nd Brigade R.F.A. (4 spare)) Right
6 117th Brigade R.F.A. (4 spare)) Group.
7 Left Group.
8 63rd Brigade R.F.A. (4 spare)) Through Left
9 83rd Brigade R.F.A. (4 spare)) Group.
10 12th D. T. M. O.
11 12th D. A. Column.
12 R.A. Signal Officer.
13 S.C., 12th D. A.
14 H.A., Liaison Officer.
15 62nd Brigade R.F.A. (4 spare)
16 74th Divl. Arty. ✓
17 27th American Division. ✓
18 H.A., IIIrd Corps. ✓
19 27th Brigade R.F.A. ✓
20-23 War Diary & File.
24 18 Divl Arty ✓

Tracing A

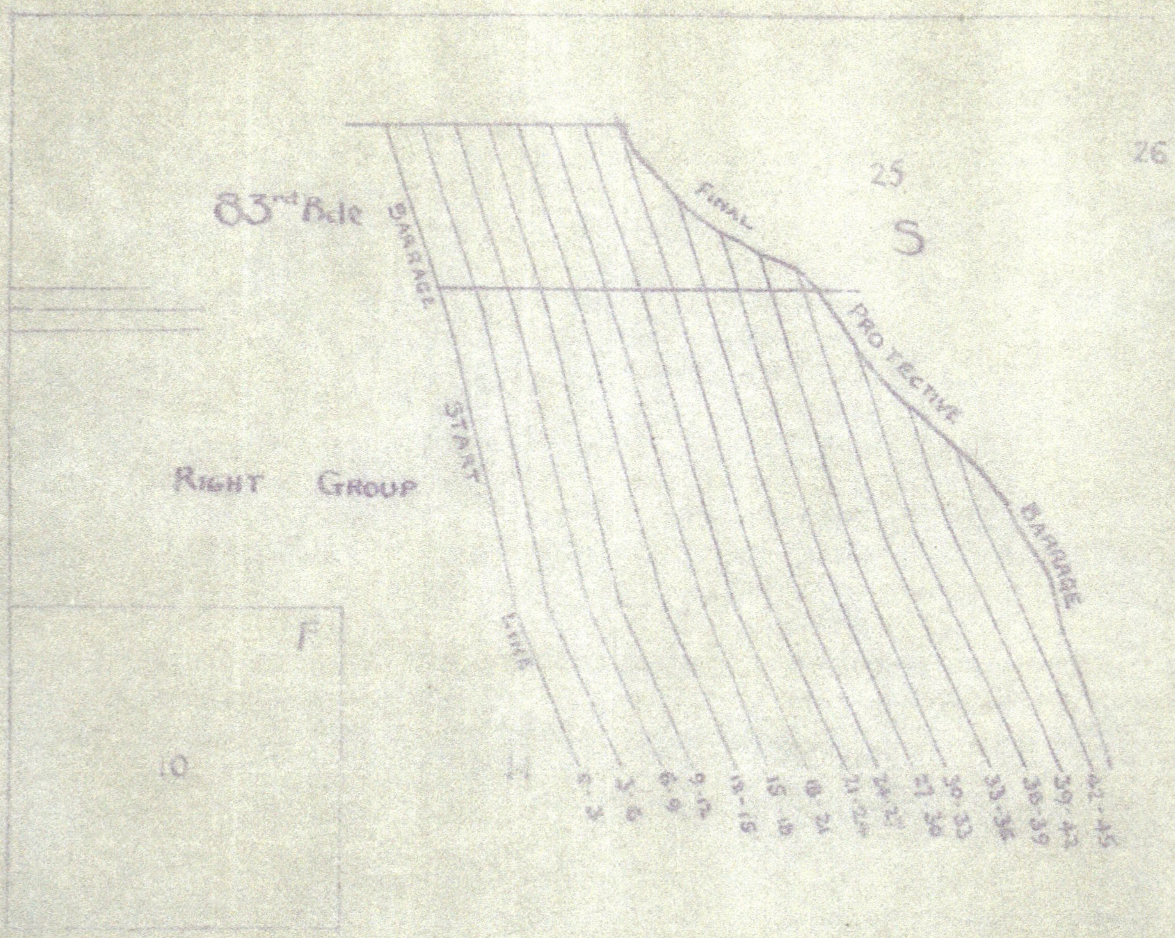

Ref St Emilie Sheet
1-20000

SECRET.

Copy No. 8

12th Divisional Artillery Order No. 127.

Ref. Map - 1/20,000
St. EMILE Sheet.

28th September, 1918.

1. The Fourth Army is advancing at Zero hour on "Z" Day. Troops are crossing the canal where it runs in a tunnel, then turning north to move up the Eastern bank.

18th Division is covering the Left Flank of this movement on the Western bank of the canal.

2. On "Z" Day at an hour to be notified later, which will probably be about Zero plus 5 hours, 12th Division will carry out an operation with the following objects :-

(a) to cover the Left Flank of the 18th Division.

(b) to mop up the area between the present front and the canal.

(c) In the event of the Division on our left not being able to advance simultaneously, to form a defensive flank along LARK SPUR facing Northwards towards OSSUS.

3. The advance of the 18th Division begins at Zero hour. Their Left Flank will be on the line - F 6 a 4 0 to S 25 b 8 0 when our advance begins. This line is also the dividing line between 12th and 18th Divisions.

If the attack of the 33rd Division on our left is successful, 33rd Division will be advancing to the canal side by side with us.

4.(a) 37th Infantry Brigade will do the attack.

(b) 35th Infantry Brigade will hold the present front line with one Battalion.

(c) 36th Infantry Brigade will have two Battalions holding the present front line.

5.(a) The Objectives are shown on the barrage tracing.

(b) The advance of 12th Division from 1st to 2nd Objective will synchronise with the advance of the 18th Division.

(c) A line of exploitation, forming a bridgehead East of the Canal will be notified later. The canal will not be crossed until the troops on the East bank have passed north of our Sector, when footbridges will be laid. The troops exploiting Northwards on the Eastern bank of the canal are timed to pass the Line S 27 d 5 0 - S 27 Central - S 29 Central - S 29 d 9 0 at 11 a.m.

6.(a) Artillery Arrangements will be notified in Artillery Instructions.

(b) Orders regarding S.O.S., Calls from the Air, etc., during Barrage are as for previous operations and repeated in Instructions No. 2. (issued Bdes., only).

7.(a) Contact aeroplanes -

7.(a) Contact aeroplanes will fly over the Corps Front at the following times :- Zero plus 1 hour, Zero plus 3 hours, Zero plus 4 hours, Zero plus 5 hours, and subsequently as ordered.
Red flares, tin discs, and rifles placed 3 in a row with muzzles pointing towards the enemy will be employed to indicate the position of the troops to aircraft.

(b) A counter attack plane will be up continuously from daylight onwards with the sole mission of detecting enemy counter-attacks and signalling them by dropping a white parachute flare.

(c) The following light signals will be employed -

(i) S.O.S. No.32 grenade - RED over RED over RED.

(ii) Success Signal(i.e. "We have reached objective")
No. 32 grenade - WHITE over WHITE over WHITE.

8. Watches will be synchronised at 63rd Brigade R.F.A., H.Q., (W 29 d 9 9) at 7 p.m. on 28th September.

9. Brigade Headquarters are as follows -

35th Infantry Brigade	...	F 1 b 3 0
36th Infantry Brigade	...	W 29 d 9 0
37th Infantry Brigade	...	E 5 d 5 9

10. Brigades please ACKNOWLEDGE.

H W L Walker

Major,
Brigade Major R.A., 12th Division.

Distribution - Copy No. 1 to R.A., IIIrd Corps. ./.
2 to 12th Division "G". ∅
3 to 62nd Bde., R.F.A.(4 spare) ∅
4 to 63rd Bde.,R.F.A. (4 spare) ∅
5 to 12th D. T. M. O. ∅
6 to 12th D. A. Column.
7 to R.A. Signal Officer.
8 to S.C., 12th D. A.
9 to Liaison Officer H.A.
10 to 18th D. A. ∅
11 to 33rd D. A. ./.
12 to 4th Australian D.A. ./.
13-16 War Diary & File.

./. Tracing issued herewith.
∅ .. already issued.

S E C R E T & U R G E N T.

Amendment No. 1 to 12th D.A. Order No. 127 and Instructions.

---

1. Barrage "A" will not be fired.

2. Barrage "B" will be fired in accordance with 12th Division Barrage Map issued all concerned.
Times as follows:-

(a) The East and West Barrage will open on the Line A-A at Zero plus 25 and rest till Zero plus 40 - at Zero plus 40 it will creep at 100 yards every 4 minutes for 8 lifts. From then on it will creep 100 yards every 6 minutes till the 1st Protective Line is reached at Zero plus 110.
It will rest on the protective line till Zero plus 130 - at Zero plus 130 fire will cease.

(b) Barrage on line B-B will open at Zero plus 10 and will rest till Zero plus 26. At Zero plus 26 it will commence to creep 100 yards every 6 minutes as shown on Tracing till the line A-D is reached - when fire will jump to Protective Barrage Line C-C.
At Zero plus 130 they will cease.

3. D/62 - One 4.5" How. Battery 18th D.A. and all 6" Newton Trench Mortars will bombard area marked "K" from Zero plus 10 to Zero plus 80 - Fire will then cease.
No 106 Fuze to befired in this area after Zero plus 38.

4. D/63 - C/63 and One 4.5" How. Battery 18th D.A. will fire the Smoke Screen as ordered in Instructions No. 1 para.2.

5. At about Zero plus 5 hours patrols will be pushed forward to the canal. No Barrage will be put down East of the canal without special orders.

6. A C K N O W L E D G E.

H W h Walker
Major,
Brigade Major R.A., 12th Division.

20/9/18.

Copies to all recipients of 12th D.A. Order No. 127

S E C R E T.

12th Divisional Artillery Instruction No. 1 issued with 12th D. A. Order No. 127.

---

1. Two Barrages will be fired on "Z" Day -

(A) 18-pdr Barrage to be fired at Zero hour prolonging and conforming to the Left Flank of the 18th Divisional Barrage for 500 yards (Start Line X 29 c 9 6 to F 5 b 7 8).

This Barrage will be fired by Two 18-pdr. Batteries, 62nd Brigade R.F.A. on the lines, lifts, etc., shown on the 18th Division Barrage Tracing issued to all concerned.

At Zero plus 61 Barrage will jump back to the 18/21 Line, fire for 3 minutes then stop.

Rates of fire SLOW Throughout.

Ammunition 50% H.E. 50% Shrapnel.

(B) An 18-pdr Barrage as shown on Barrage tracing-issued to all concerned -

1. 2-18.pdr Batteries 62nd Brigade R.F.A. will fire Barrage marked "B-B". They will stop firing as they arrive on the Southern Boundary (Line A D) of the "A-A" Barrage.

2. 3-18.pdr. Batteries 63rd Brigade R.F.A., with one 18-pdr. Battery 62nd Brigade R.F.A., superimposed over the whole, will fire Barrage marked "A-A" They will halt on a Protective Line Marked "C-C".

3. Zero hour - Rate of Creep - Time of advance from 1st Protective Barrage - etc., will be notified later.

4. Rate of Fire -

During Creep	-	NORMAL.
On Protective	-	SLOW.

5. Ammunition -

(a) Batteries firing B-B and Southern Battery of A-A Barrage all Shrapnel while creeping - On protective 50% A 50% AX.

(b) Remaining Batteries 50% A 50% AX Throughout.

2. D/63 - D/62 and C/63 Batteries will fire a Smoke Screen from S 21 b 7 0 - S 21 a 6 0 - S 21 a 2 6 from Zero to Zero plus 3 hours.

O.C., 63rd Brigade R.F.A. will detail an officer who will be in charge of the screen. He will be stationed where he can observe the effect of the fire and will regulate the rate of fire.

He must be in communication with all three Batteries.

3. D/62, D/63, and all 6" Newton Trench Mortars will bombard the area marked "X" on the Barrage Tracing - from 2nd Zero hour till an hour which O.C., 62nd Brigade Group will arrange direct with G.O.C., 37th Infantry Brigade.

Troops have been warned not to approach within 200 yards of this area until these Batteries and Trench Mortars stop firing.

4. O.C., 63rd Bde.,

4. O.C., 63rd Brigade R.F.A., will detail one 18-pdr Battery to act in close support of the Infantry.

5. Brigades and D. T. M. O. please ACKNOWLEDGE.

H W L Waller.
Major,
Brigade Major R.A., 12th Division.

Copies to all recipients of 12th D.A. Order No. 126.

S E C R E T.   Copy No........

12th Divisional Artillery Instructions No. 2 issued
with 12th D.A. Order No. 127.

---

1. S.O.S.- In the case of an S.O.S. Call being received from the air or from the ground during the Barrage Programme all Artillery Brigades in the Divisional Area affected will at once switch one Battery per Brigade on to the threatened area for 5 minutes at the rate of 4 rounds per 18-pdr. per minute. Then for 5 minutes at the rate of 3 rounds per 18-pdr. per minute. After 10 minutes the fire will be slowed down and return to the Barrage Programme as the situation permits.

If the Call is near a Divisional Boundary the Flank Brigade will co-operate as detailed above.

2.(a) During the Barrage "LL" Calls only will be answered by Divisional Artillery as under -

One 18-pdr. Battery per Brigade.
Two 4.5" Howitzer Batteries per Division, if not detailed for Special Smoke Barrages.
These guns and Howitzers will be detailed beforehand.

LL CALLS.-
will be answered by three salvoes immediately on receipt of the call. If the call is repeated after a reasonable interval the bursts will be fired again.

ANTI-TANK GUNS.
If an enemy gun is observed from the air obviously firing on Tanks and within 1,200 yards from the Tanks it will be reported by the Call "LLNF" and answered as for other LL Calls.

(b) After the completion of the Barrage Programme.-

NF CALLS.
Will be answered by the Batteries allotted to Counter Battery Work.

GF CALLS.
Will be answered by a Section of all Field and Heavy Artillery Batteries that can bring fire to bear.

LL CALLS.
Will be answered by all Heavy Artillery Batteries in the Zone allotted to their Group and all Field Artillery Batteries that can bring fire to bear on the Target with the exception of one 18-pdr. Battery of each Brigade which will remain covering the Zone allotted to the Brigade.

GF and LL CALLS.
Three salvoes per Battery will be fired immediately on receipt of the Call.
If the Call is repeated after a reasonable interval those bursts will be fired again.

3. FLEETING TARGETS.
One 18-pdr. Battery per Brigade will be detailed to engage fleeting targets. They will be the same Batteries as those detailed to answer Calls from the air.

During the -

During the Barrage Programme the fire of these Batteries will be superimposed over that of the remainder of the Brigade so that in the event of their being taken off the Barrage no gaps will be left.

The Batteries will be in communication with suitable O.Ps.

4. ACKNOWLEDGE.

Hugh Walker

Major,

Brigade Major R.A., 12th Division.

Copies to – 62nd Brigade R.F.A.
63rd Brigade R.F.A.

S E C R E T .

12th Divisional Artillery Instructions No. 3

---

1. At Zero hour on "Z" day, the 18th and 74th Divisional Artillery will be transferred to command of 18th Division.
62nd and 63rd Brigades, R.F.A. remain with the 12th Division.

2. Lt.Col. H. WYNNE, D.S.O., O.C., 62nd Bde. R.F.A. will be in close Liaison with the G.O.C., 37th Infantry Bde. throughout the operation. He will have a call on and will transmit orders as required to 63rd Brigade, R.F.A.

H.W.L. Waller
Major,
Brigade Major R.A., 12th Division.

28th Sept. 1918.

Copy to all recipients of 12th D.A. Order No. 127.

"A" Form

Army Form C. 2121
(In pads of 100.)

MESSAGES AND SIGNALS.

No. of Message...........

Prefix.............Code..............m. | Words | Charge.

Office of Origin and Service Instructions

Priority

Sent
At ....m.
To ....
By ....

This message is on a/c of:
.............................*Service.*

(Signature of "Franking Officer")

Recd. at......m.
Date..............
From ....
By..................

TO: 62 Bde / 63 Bde / Wessex HA / 12 Div G

Sender's Number.	Day of Month.	In reply to Number.	AAA
BM 15	29 Sept		

Pending further orders
Protective Barrage will be formed
~~as follows~~ by Brigades 62
Bde from East and West Grid
through X 30 central to OSSUS
Wood Road (inclusive) aaa 63
Bde OSSUS Wood Road ~~also~~
inclusive to E + W Grid
through X 23 C 0 6 aaa Barrage
line to be reported to 12 DA HQ

From
Place 12 Div Arty
Time 5 40 pm

The above may be forwarded as now corrected. (Z)

....
Censor.

[illegible]

Signature of Addressor or person authorised to telegraph in his name

* This line should be erased if not required.

Order No. 1625. Wt. W3253/ P 511. 27/2. H. & K., Ltd. (E. 2634).

12th Div. Arty.

C. R. A.,

12th DIVISION,

O C T O B E R 1 9 1 8.

CONFIDENTIAL

14/281

W A R   D I A R Y

Headquarters, 12th Divisional Artillery,

October, 1918.

Vol. XLI .

Instructions regarding War Diaries and Intelligence Summaries are contained in F. S. Regs., Part II. and the Staff Manual respectively. Title pages will be prepared in manuscript.

Vol. XLI.
Oct 1918

WAR DIARY
or
~~INTELLIGENCE SUMMARY.~~
(Erase heading not required.)

Army Form C. 2118.

HQ 12th Div Arty. Sheet 1

Place	Date	Hour	Summary of Events and Information	Remarks and references to Appendices
D16C19	1 –		HQrs at D16C19 in rest.	
	5th		62nd & 63rd Bdes were withdrawn from the ~~[illegible]~~ line and went into rest in vicinity of LIERAMONT.	
	10th & 11th		62nd Bde, 63rd Bde & 12th DAC entrained at PERONNE & TINCOURT, detrained at ACQ & AUBIGNY and were billeted at ACQ (both Bdes) & FREVIN CAPELLE (D.A.C.) owing to delay in arrival of trains some batteries did not arrive until the morning of 12th inst.	
	12.	8am	Bde & Battery Commanders went forward in lorries to reconnoitre position to be occupied that night.	
	~~Night~~ 12/13.	noon	CRA 12th Div assumed responsibility of the front, taking over from CRA 50th Div.	
	Night 12/13.		62nd Bde RFA relieved 250th Bde RFA & 63rd Bde RFA relieved 242nd Army Bde RFA. 12th DAC relieved 50th DAC, all in accordance with 12 DA order No 128.	
	13		At 6 am command of 242nd Army Bde RFA passed to 58th Div on our left and Bdes were grouped as follows.	
			Right Group covering 35th Inf Bde. 293rd Army Bde RFA (Lt Col Mance DSO.) 277th " " "	
			Left Group " 36th " " 62nd Bde RFA (Lt Col Wynne DSO) 63rd " " "	
			Infantry continued to make progress towards HAUTE DEULE Canal but met with considerable resistance and fairly heavy artillery fire.	

(A7092). Wt. W12839/M1293. 750,000. 1/17. D. D. & L., Ltd. Forms/C.2118/14.

Army Form C. 2118.

Instructions regarding War Diaries and Intelligence Summaries are contained in F. S. Regs., Part II. and the Staff Manual respectively. Title pages will be prepared in manuscript.

VOL XLI

WAR DIARY
or
~~INTELLIGENCE SUMMARY~~.

(Erase heading not required.)

H.Q. 12th Div Arty — Sheet 2.

Place	Date	Hour	Summary of Events and Information (Oct. 1918.)	Remarks and references to Appendices
M35b06	13	-	Our artillery were active on hostile MGs and parties of enemy seen from time to time. Harassing fire carried out by batteries.	
	14	-	5.15 am Right group put down creeping barrage in support of an attack by 35th Inf Bde which was successful and 1 officer and 42 ORs were taken. Later however the Infantry were driven back by MG & TM fire. Batteries continued to fire on any fleeting targets which presented themselves. From 4pm - 7pm batteries of Right group bombarded the eastern half of AUBY preparatory to the Infantry retaking the village but attack did not materialise. During the night harassing fire on woods along side the canal bank and villages were harassed.	
	15.		Quiet day. During the evening some progress was made by our Infantry and batteries of Right group put forward sections. Harassing fire during the night.	
	16.		Fighting round AUBY continued. Arty Bdes kept in close touch with Inf. Bde and battalion commanders & engaged fleeting targets. In the course of the day 36th Inf Bde got 2 Coys over the HAUTE DEULE Canal at PONT A SAULT.	

(A7092). Wt. W12839/M1293. 75,000. 1/17. D. D. & L., Ltd. Forms/C.2118/14.

Army Form C. 2118.

WAR DIARY
or
~~INTELLIGENCE SUMMARY.~~
(Erase heading not required.)

Instructions regarding War Diaries and Intelligence Summaries are contained in F. S. Regs., Part II. and the Staff Manual respectively. Title pages will be prepared in manuscript.

VOL XLI

HQ 12th Div Arty

Place	Date	Hour	Summary of Events and Information	Remarks and references to Appendices
	17		Advance was continued and very little opposition was encountered; scarcely any shooting was carried out by batteries owing to the rapid advance. By the evening the general line N + S. through the Eastern outskirts of LE FOREST.	
	18	-	Advance continued by 35th Inf Bde supported by 63rd Bde RFA and 37th Inf Bde covered by 277th Army Bde RFA. Very little opposition was encountered, and practically no firing was done, the batteries being on wheels all day. 62nd + 293rd Bdes were in reserve. At nightfall 63rd Bde batteries were in action in R10 and 277 Bde batteries in R26	
RAIMBEAUCOURT	19		HQ 12th DA moved to RAIMBEAUCOURT. Advance continued by same Infantry Bdes covered by same artillery. No opposition was encountered and line was established east of ORCHIES + BEUVRY (H33). Batteries took up positions in M4 + 10. 293rd Army Bde RFA (still in reserve) moved forward to FLINES. Infantry line for night was ERMITAGE (N9) BEUVRY-LES-ORCHIES - LOMBERT FARM (H26) CARTONNERIE (H13C00) 293 Army Bde (in Div Reserve) moved to FLINES.	

D. D. & L., London, E.C. (A10266) Wt W5300/P713 750,000 2/18 Sch. 52 Forms/C2118/16.

WAR DIARY
or
~~INTELLIGENCE SUMMARY.~~
(Erase heading not required.)

Army Form C. 2118.

Instructions regarding War Diaries and Intelligence Summaries are contained in F. S. Regs., Part II. and the Staff Manual respectively. Title pages will be prepared in manuscript.

VOL XLI

H.Q. 12th Div Arty

Page (4)

Place	Date	Hour	Summary of Events and Information	Remarks and references to Appendices
RAIMBEAUCOURT	20	8 am.	advance continued objective being N & S. line between squares N + O & H + I (sheet 44). M G fire from a trench post W of SAMEON held up patrols for a short time and very little opposition was	
	17		62nd Bde RFA (in Div reserve) moved to MOLINEL area & No 2 section	
		9 am	DAC to FLINES. Resistance was quickly overcome and all objectives gained. The firing was the duty of batteries & their task as follows. North and South fire line between squares H & I & N + O.	
			advance was continued and line ran I 18 a 00 – I 21 c 00 –	
"	21	.	I 32 central – O 2 central.	
			Batteries of 63rd Bde moved to I 19.	
			277 " " " I 31 c & O 2 a.	
			orders were received that Infantry (37 Bde on Right & 36 Bde on left (after passing through 35 Bde) would advance to Canal & secure Bridgeheads	
			293 Bde moved to BEUVRY to reinforce 277 Bde & 62 Bde was ordered to pass through batteries of 63 Bde & cover 36 Infantry Bde.	
			No 2 section DAC moved to G 24 b.	
	22	1 am	Considerable progress was made by Infantry but bridges were found to be blown up, and tho' the river DECOURS was crossed it was found impossible to get across the SCARPE.	

D. D. & L., London, E.C.
(A10266) Wt W5300/P713 750,000 2/18 Sch. 52 Forms/C2118/16.

Instructions regarding War Diaries and Intelligence Summaries are contained in F. S. Regs., Part II. and the Staff Manual respectively. Title pages will be prepared in manuscript.

WAR DIARY
or
INTELLIGENCE SUMMARY.
(Erase heading not required.)

Army Form C. 2118.

VOL XLI

H.Q. 12th Div Arty

Page 5

Place	Date	Hour	Summary of Events and Information	Remarks and references to Appendices
			Oct 1918.	
ORCHIES	22	11am	H.Q. 12th Div Arty moved to ORCHIES. Batteries had a fair amount of shooting on small parties of the enemy and MGs. Hostile artillery was active on forward villages and battery areas. D/62 suffered many casualties in horses. Harassing fire by field and Heavy artillery during the night.	
	23.		Enemy were still holding FORT de MAULDE and this point was bombarded by heavy artillery from 8.30 am to 10 am. Progress was made by the Right 37th Inf Bde whereon 277 Bde RFA fell out and became divisional reserve. Hostile artillery was quiet during morning & afternoon but was active during the night with H.V. guns on LECELLES area. Our artillery carried out harassing fire.	
SAMEON.			HQ. 12th Div Arty moved to SAMEON	
	24	8am	Our artillery active on MONT de JUSTICE & MGs in houses at J15 d 97, and on BURIDON in J 30 c from 8 am to 8.40 am. Then infantry captured the village and advanced towards BRUILLE. 36th Inf Bde did not make so much progress, but artillery covering them were active shooting on targets they required. Later 37th I.B. captured BRUILLE & inflicted heavy casualties on the enemy. 63rd Bde & 277 Bde previously in reserve were ordered to uncommitted positions merely for S.O.S. purposes.	

D. D. & L., London, E.C.
(A10266) Wt W5300/P713 750,000 2/18 Sch. 52 Forms/C2118/16.

Instructions regarding War Diaries and Intelligence Summaries are contained in F. S. Regs., Part II. and the Staff Manual respectively. Title pages will be prepared in manuscript.

WAR DIARY
or
~~INTELLIGENCE SUMMARY.~~
(Erase heading not required.)

Army Form C. 2118.

VOL XLI — H Q 12th Div Arty — Page 6

Place	Date	Hour	Summary of Events and Information	Remarks and references to Appendices
			Oct 1918	
SAMEON.	24.		positions were chosen as follows, & occupied during the night 63rd Bde: HQ I14b83, batteries in I16d & I22 277 Bde. HQ P1c50 " " J26 & J33. Hostile arty was very active everywhere all day but especially so during the night when gas was used fairly freely. The villages of RUMEGIES & LECELLES received particular attention, also SAMEON.	
	25		3.30 am barrage was put down in support of attack on CHATEAU L' ABBAYE. Attack unsuccessful. This was repeated during the afternoon with no happier results. Hostile artillery again very active, probably emptying dumps as many explosions were observed during the afternoon, but at dusk MONT de la JUSTICE was still held by the enemy. Harassing fire was commenced early, roads leading from MORTAGNE and VERGNE being dealt with by 60 pdrs. Harassing fire was continued by field and heavy arty throughout the night. After 6 pm hostile artillery was quiet, being withdrawing probably.	
	26		Left Bde occupied MONT de JUSTICE and made good the line of the river DECOURS. CHATEAU L'ABBAYE in J24 were also held but enemy remained in rest of the village. The day passed much more quietly than preceding ones and harassing fire and SOS lines were the same as for 25th inst. 63rd Bde RFA moved forward to positions in J27 while 277 were ordered to reconnoitre position in J30, 35 & 36	
	27	2-	Batteries of 62nd + 63rd Bdes supported Infantry attack on CHATEAU L'ABBAYE which proved successful.	

D. D. & L., London, E.C.
(A10266) Wt W5300/P713 750,000 2/18 Sch. 52 Forms/C2118/16.

Instructions regarding War Diaries and Intelligence Summaries are contained in F. S. Regs., Part II. and the Staff Manual respectively. Title pages will be prepared in manuscript.

WAR DIARY
or
~~INTELLIGENCE SUMMARY~~.
(Erase heading not required.)

Army Form C. 2118.

VOL XLI — HQ 12th Div. Arty. — App 7

Place	Date	Hour	Summary of Events and Information	Remarks and references to Appendices
			Oct 1918.	
SAMEON	27		The rest of the day was quiet both on the part of our and hostile artillery. At 7 pm 63rd Bde RFA relieved 62nd Bde RFA & 277th Army Bde relieved 293rd Army Bde. Lt Col Thompson CMG. DSO. Commanding the group and covering 36th Inf Bde which took over the whole div front during the night.	
	28.	10pm	All 18pdr batteries swept roads in K15 in support of Infantry attack to form bridgehead over Canal du JARD in connection with 8th Div. This was unsuccessful. Harassing fire was carried out by field and heavy artillery.	
	28.		Much quieter day, movement was seen in K13 and engaged by B/63. Hostile artillery quiet during the day except for A.A. which was active. 12 Div (36 Inf Bde) was relieved by 52nd Div during the course of the night. 12 Div arty remained in the line. Harassing fire was carried out during night.	
	29	.	A quiet day on both sides. Nothing to report. Harassing fire by field and heavy arty during the night.	
	30		Bde and Bty Commanders visited 63rd & 277th Army Bde in view of prospective relief. Quiet day. Harassing fire carried out by field and heavy arty during the night.	

D. D. & L., London, E.C.
(A10266) Wt W5300/P713 750,000 2/18 Sch. 52 Forms/C2118/16.

Instructions regarding War Diaries and Intelligence Summaries are contained in F. S. Regs., Part II. and the Staff Manual respectively. Title pages will be prepared in manuscript.

WAR DIARY
or
~~INTELLIGENCE SUMMARY.~~
(Erase heading not required.)

Army Form C. 2118.

Vol: XLI

Page 8

Place	Date	Hour	Summary of Events and Information	Remarks and references to Appendices
SAMEON.	31	-	Command of 67th Bde RGA (which had been attached to 12 Div Arty) reverted to C.H.A. Balloons engaged movement and hostile mgs with good results. Hostile arty more active. C/277 was shelled from 10-00 to 12-00 and Major Fissage MC was wounded. Harassing fire carried out as usual.	

L H [illegible] Captain
[illegible] Brigade Div 12 D.A.

D. D. & L., London, E.C.
(A10266) Wt W5300/P713 750,000 2/18 Sch. 52 Forms/C2118/16.

S E C R E T.   Copy No.

12th Divisional Artillery Order No. 128.

11th October, 1918.

Reference Maps - 1/40,000 and 1/20,000.

1. On the 12th October, the 12th Divisional Artillery will relieve the 50th Divisional Artillery as shown in Table A. (attached).

2. Two lorries (one each for 62nd and 63rd Brigades) will be at the Church, ACQ at 8.00 on morning of 12th October to convey Brigade and Battery Commanders, one other officer per Battery and signalling personnel to the H.Q. of the Brigade they are relieving.
Brigades will arrange guides to meet these lorries and take them to their Headquarters in ACQ.

3. O.C. 62nd Brigade R.F.A. will take over command of the Centre Group covering 36th Infantry Brigade front from O.C. 250th Brigade R.F.A. as soon as the Group is in position and ready to cover the front.

4. Brigades will take over area stores, maps, telephone lines, etc.

5. A.R.P's. are established at -

(a) VIMY - S 24 d 3 3 (under charge of 293rd Army Bde. R.F.A.)
(b) COULOTTE - N 31 c 9 8
(c) LA TARGETTE - A 8 a. When present ammunition is expended this A.R.P. will close.

6. (a) The C.R.A., 12th Divisional Artillery will take over responsibility for the Artillery defence of the Line at 12 Noon on October 12th., when 12th D.A. H.Q. will open at M 35 b 0 6.
(b) At this hour following Army Brigades will come under C.R.A., 12th Divisional Artillery -
175th Army Brigade, R.F.A.
242nd " "
277th " "
293rd " "

7. On the night 12/13th October the Divisional front will be re-organised. Infantry Brigade boundaries and Artillery grouping on completion of the re-organisation are given in Table B.

8. Brigades, D.A. Column and D.T.M.O. to acknowledge.

J.H.W.H. Walker, Major,
Brigade Major, 12th D. A.

Copy No. 1. 12th Divn. (G).
2. 35th Inf. Bde.
3. 36th Inf. Bde.
4. 37th Inf. Bde.
5. 62nd Bde. RFA (4 spare)
6. 63rd Bde. RFA (4 spare)
7. D.T.M.O., 12th Divn.
8. 12th D.A.Column.
9. R.A. Signals.
10. Staff Capt. R.A.
11. VIII Corps R.A.
12. 50th D.A. (4 spare)
13. 30th Brigade R.G.A.
14-18. War Diary and File.

17.8.18

S E C R E T.

T A B L E A.

Issued with 12th Divisional Artillery Order No. 128.

Serial No.	Date	12th Divn. unit	Will relieve 50th Divn. unit	At	Remarks
1.	12th Oct.	62nd Bde. R.F.A.	250th Bde. R.F.A.	H.Q., - T 16 c 8 3	Batteries will occupy new positions forward to be reconnoitred on morning of Oct. 12th.
2.	12th Oct.	63rd Bde. R.F.A.	242nd Bde. R.F.A.	H.Q., - T 15 b 0 7	Batteries to either relieve batteries 242nd Bde., or move to new positions forward as necessary with view to range.
3.	12th Oct.	12th D.A.C.	50th D.A.C.	X 20 b (central)	Relief to be completed during daylight on the 12th Oct. All details to be arranged between Commanders concerned. O.C., 12th D.A.C. will arrange to take over A.R.P's at N 31 c 9 8 and LA TARGETTE (A 8 a).
4.	12th Oct.	12th T. M. Batteries	Will join the 12th D.A.C.	X 20 b (central)	12th D.T.M.O. will arrange to take over all area stores, maps, etc. from 50th D.T.M.O. now at S 27 a 8 0. 3 Lorries to transport Trench Mortars and personnel will be at the Mairie, AGNIERES at 8.00 on 12th Oct. They will make as many journeys as required.

S E C R E T.

T A B L E B.

Issued with 12th Divisional Artillery Order No. 128.

---

1. From completion of the re-organisation on 13th October, Boundaries will be -

35th Infantry Bde. Southern Divisional Boundary: As before to V 7 c 0 0 thence V 7 central - V 8 a 0 0 - V 4 central to HAUTE DEULE CANAL at Q 25 b 7 3.

Inter Brigade Boundary: As before to DRASTRIC TRENCH U 4 c thence c 4 5 - U 4 central (FOSSE I DE DROCOURT inclusive to Right Brigade) - O 35 c 0 0 - O 30 d 9 0 - P 25 c 0 0 - Railway at P 27 c 85 50 - P 23 central - thence to Canal at P 23 b 40 25.

36th Infantry Bde. Northern Divisional Boundary: As before to N 21 a 85 50 - thence to N 29 a 60 45 - O 26 b 0 5 - O 21 d 0 0 - O 23 c 0 6 - PONT-a-SAULT P 15 b 1 9.

2. Groups.

(a) Right Group. covering front of 35th Infantry Brigade.

O.C. Lt. Col. A.K. Main, D.S.O. 293rd Army Bde. RFA.

293rd Army Bde. R.F.A. 277th Army Bde. R.F.A.

(b) Left Group. covering front of 36th Infantry Brigade.

O.C. Lt. Col. H.E.S. Wynne, D.S.O. 62nd Brigade R.F.A.

62nd Brigade R.F.A. 63rd Brigade R.F.A.

12th Div. Arty.

C. R. A.,

12th DIVISION,

N O V E M B E R 1 9 1 8.

CONFIDENTIAL.

Vol 42

W A R   D I A R Y

Headquarters, 12th Divisional Artillery,

November, 1918.

Vol. XLII

11

Instructions regarding War Diaries and Intelligence Summaries are contained in F. S. Regs., Part II. and the Staff Manual respectively. Title pages will be prepared in manuscript.

XLII

WAR DIARY
or
~~INTELLIGENCE SUMMARY~~.
(Erase heading not required.)

Army Form C. 2118.

HQ 12th Div Arty

Sheet (1)

Place	Date	Hour	Summary of Events and Information Nov. 1918.	Remarks and references to Appendices
SAMEON.	1		62nd Bde RFA and No 1 Section DAC marched from wagon lines to WAZIERES + FRAIS MARAIS respectively on being relieved by units of 52nd Div. Arty. as laid down in 12 DA order no 130. The day passed quietly, also the night.	
	2	-	Quiet day and night. Prisoners captured by Canadians at VALENCIENNES said retreat was due to take place that night but enemy were much on alert and everything was reported normal on the morning of 4th inst.	
FRAIS MARAIS.	3	-	HQ DA moved to FRAIS MARAIS area to rest. 63rd Bde, No 2 Section + HQ 12 DAC marched to WAZIERES + FRAIS MARAIS area.	
		12 noon	CRA. 12th DA handed over to CRA 52nd DA.	
	11	8.30am	Wire received from VIII Corps with the information that hostilities would cease at 11 am that day.	
SAMEON.			12th Div. Arty marched to ROSULT area, HQrs forming the HQ 12th Div. at SAMEON.	
LEEWARDE	27	-	12th Div Arty marched to LEEWARDE 4 miles E. of DOUAI.	

[signature] Captain
for Brigade Major 12 DA

D. D. & L., London, E.C.
(A10266) Wt W5300/P713 750,000 2/18 Sch. 52 Forms/C2118/16.

C. R. A.,

12th DIVISION,

DECEMBER 1918.

CONFIDENTIAL.

W A R D I A R Y

Headquarters, 12th Divisional Artillery,

December, 1918.

Vol. XLIII

Instructions regarding War Diaries and Intelligence Summaries are contained in F. S. Regs., Part II. and the Staff Manual respectively. Title pages will be prepared in manuscript.

HQ RA 12th Division

WAR DIARY
or
INTELLIGENCE SUMMARY.

(Erase heading not required.)

Army Form C. 2118.

Vol XLIII

December 1918

Sheet 1.

Place	Date	Hour	Summary of Events and Information	Remarks and references to Appendices
LEWARDE	1	–	HQrs 12th Div arty at LEWARDE	
	17		Ceremonial parade and march past before Div. General.	
	31	–	HQrs 12th Div arty at LEWARDE.	

H.Q., R.A., 12TH DIVISION. 31.12.18

[signature] Captain
for Brigade Major 12th D.A.

D. D. & L., London, E.C.
(A10266) Wt W5300/P713 750,000 2/18 Sch. 52 Forms/C2118/16.

CONFIDENTIAL.

W A R   D I A R Y

Headquarters, 12th Divisional Artillery,

January, 1919.

Vol. XLIV.

Army Form C. 2118.

Instructions regarding War Diaries and Intelligence Summaries are contained in F. S. Regs., Part II. and the Staff Manual respectively. Title pages will be prepared in manuscript.

WAR DIARY
~~or~~
~~INTELLIGENCE~~ SUMMARY.

January 1919

HQ RA 12th Divn (Erase heading not required.)

Vol: XLIV

Place	Date	Hour	Summary of Events and Information	Remarks and references to Appendices
			Ref. Sheet 51 B 1/40,000	
	1st		HQ 12 DA at the Chateau, LEWARDE	
	31st		No change.	

[signature]
Captain
for Brigade Major 12th DA

31/1/19

D. D. & L., London, E.C.
(A10266) Wt W5300/P713 750,000 2/18 Sch. 52 Forms/C2118/16.

W A R   D I A R Y

-of the-

HEADQUARTERS 12TH DIVISIONAL ARTILLERY

F E B R U A R Y - 1919.

V O L U M E XLV.

9845

Army Form C. 2118.

WAR DIARY
or
~~INTELLIGENCE SUMMARY.~~
(Erase heading not required.)

Instructions regarding War Diaries and Intelligence Summaries are contained in F. S. Regs., Part II. and the Staff Manual respectively. Title pages will be prepared in manuscript.

VOL XLV. H.Q. 12th Div Arty. Sheet 1

Place	Date	Hour	Summary of Events and Information	Remarks and references to Appendices
			Feb 1919	
LEWARDE	1 – 28		Demobilization of men and horses continued normally	

L H Pow Capt
for
Br. General,
Commanding 12th Divisional Artillery

D. D. & L., London, E.C.
(A10266) Wt W5300/P713 750,000 2/18 Sch. 52 Forms/C2118/16.

WO 95/46

W A R -oOo- D I A R Y

of -o- the

Headquarters

12TH DIVISIONAL ARTILLERY.

FROM:- 1ST MARCH to 31ST MARCH.

1 9 1 9

V O L U M E - XLVI.

Army Form C. 2118.

WAR DIARY
or
INTELLIGENCE SUMMARY.
(Erase heading not required.)

Instructions regarding War Diaries and Intelligence Summaries are contained in F. S. Regs., Part II. and the Staff Manual respectively. Title pages will be prepared in manuscript.

VOL: XLVI

HEADQUARTERS, 12TH DIVISIONAL ARTILLERY.
Sheet (1).

Place	Date	Hour	Summary of Events and Information	Remarks and references to Appendices
			MARCH, 1919.	
			PERSONNEL.	
LEWARDE.	1/31.	-	Units within this Formation are now practically down to Cadre "A" Strength. Demobilization has continued normally.	
			HORSES.	
			The horses now in possession of this Formation comprise the "POOL" allowed to Divisional Artillery, all surplus animals having been disposed of.	
			CHANGES IN COMMAND.	
			Brigadier-General H.M. THOMAS, C.M.G., D.S.O., C.R.A. proceeded to ENGLAND on 28/3/1919. Lieut:Colonel H.E.S. WYNNE, C.M.G., D.S.O., assumed Command of the 12th Divisional Artillery with effect from 28/3/1919.	
			F J Taylor Captain, R.A. for Lt: Col: C. R A., 12TH DIVISION.	

D. D. & L., London, E.C.
(A10266) Wt W5300/P713 750,000 2/18 Sch. 52 Forms/C2118/16.

W A R   D I A R Y

-: of the :-

HEADQUARTERS, R.A. - 12TH DIVL: ARTILLERY.

for the

MONTH OF APRIL oOo 1 9 1 9..

V O L U M E   X L V I I

Army Form C. 2118.

Instructions regarding War Diaries and Intelligence Summaries are contained in F. S. Regs., Part II. and the Staff Manual respectively. Title pages will be prepared in manuscript.

WAR DIARY
or
INTELLIGENCE SUMMARY.

(Erase heading not required.) HEADQUARTERS, 12TH DIVISIONAL ARTILLERY.

VOL: XLVII

Sheet (1)

Place	Date	Hour	Summary of Events and Information	Remarks and references to Appendices
LEWARDE.	1/7.		LOCATION.	
			Stationed at LEWARDE from 1-7th April, 1919.	
AUBERCHICOURT.	7/30		The Headquarters, 12th Divisional Artillery moved to AUBERCHICOURT on morning of 7th April, 1919.	
			DEMOBILIZATION.	
			Almost completed. Units are now practically down to CADRE "A".	

[signature]
Captain, R.A.
for Lt: Colonel
Commanding 12th Divisional Artillery.

D. D. & L., London, E.C.
(A10266) Wt W5300/P715 750,000 2/18 Sch. 52 Forms/C2118/16.

WAR DIARY

of the

12th Divl Artillery Headquarters

for month of

MAY - 1919

VOLUME XLVIII

Army Form C. 2118.

Instructions regarding War Diaries and Intelligence Summaries are contained in F. S. Regs., Part II. and the Staff Manual respectively. Title pages will be prepared in manuscript.

WAR DIARY
or
INTELLIGENCE SUMMARY.

(Erase heading not required.) HEADQUARTERS, 12th Divisional Artillery.

VOL:XLVIII

Place	Date	Hour	Summary of Events and Information	Remarks and references to Appendices
AUBERCHICOURT.			CADRES - TRANSFER OF TO THE U.K.	
	1-31/5/19.		Cadres of 62nd Brigade, R.F.A. and 63rd Brigade, R.F.A. commenced entraining on 30th May, 1919 for the United Kingdom. Destination SUTTON-VENEY.	
			LOCATION.	
			Same as last month.	
			[signature] Captain, RFA. A/Staff Captain 12th Divl: Artillery Cadre.	

D. D. & L., London, E.C.
(A10266) Wt W5300/P713 750,000 2/18 Sch. 52 Forms/C2118/16.

www.ingramcontent.com/pod-product-compliance
Lightning Source LLC
Chambersburg PA
CBHW080804010526
44113CB00013B/2326